CRITICAL INSIGHTS

Tennessee Williams

CRITICAL INSIGHTS

Tennessee Williams

Editor
Brenda Murphy
University of Connecticut

Salem Press
Pasadena, California   Hackensack, New Jersey

Cover photo: Ann Rosener/Time & Life Pictures/Getty Images

Published by Salem Press

© 2011 by EBSCO Publishing
Editor's text © 2011 by Brenda Murphy
"The *Paris Review* Perspective" © 2011 by Sasha Weiss for *The Paris Review*

∞ The paper used in these volumes conforms to the American National Standard for Permanence of Paper for Printed Library Materials, Z39.48-1992 (R1997).

Library of Congress Cataloging-in-Publication Data
Tennessee Williams / editor, Brenda Murphy.
    p. cm. — (Critical insights)
Includes bibliographical references and index.
ISBN 978-1-58765-687-3 (alk. paper)
1. Williams, Tennessee, 1911-1983—Criticism and interpretation. I. Murphy, Brenda, 1950-
    PS3545.I5365Z8445 2010
    812'.54—dc22

                                                                    2010029142

PRINTED IN CANADA

Contents

Resources

About This Volume

Brenda Murphy

This collection of essays offers a diverse selection of criticism of one of the most significant American playwrights of the twentieth century. The volume is divided into two parts: The first is composed of essays that were commissioned specifically for this volume, and the second consists of reprinted essays that not only are interesting and revealing studies in themselves but reflect the history of Williams criticism as well.

As background for the individual critical studies, the editor's introduction presents a general critical context for thinking about Williams. Jennifer Banach then provides a comprehensive introduction to Williams's work and career as well as to the trajectory of Williams criticism, focusing on one of the pervasive critical clichés, that his work suffered a consistent decline after *The Night of the Iguana* (1961). Three new essays present Williams from different critical perspectives. Susan C. W. Abbotson provides a condensed, but remarkably comprehensive, overview of Williams's entire career and its interplay with American culture. Henry I. Schvey offers a detailed and nuanced study of what he argues is a unique integration of realism and expressionism in *A Streetcar Named Desire* (1947), informed by his extensive knowledge of European expressionism and the American theater. Kenneth Elliott provides an original take on the theme of mendacity in *Cat on a Hot Tin Roof* (1955) based on Williams's development of the play in collaboration with its first director, Elia Kazan, and the controversial changes Williams made, partly as a concession to the values and conventions of Broadway.

The reprinted essays in this volume include overviews of Williams's work, essays on specific plays, and essays on his prose. The two overviews include Nancy M. Tischler's influential archetypal analysis, which uses the archetypes discussed by Erich Neumann in *The Great Mother* to examine Williams's representations of women from Amanda

---

Wingfield to Flora Goforth, and Thomas P. Adler's expansive analysis of Williams's politics, both public and personal, as expressed throughout his playwriting career, and particularly in *The Night of the Iguana* and *The Red Devil Battery Sign* (1975).

The articles on the plays range from *The Glass Menagerie* (1944) to *Out Cry* (1971) and *The Two-Character Play* (1967). Jacqueline O'Connor makes use of George Pickering's concept of the "creative malady," that psychological illness may sometimes be an aid to artistic work, to analyze Williams's representation of Laura and Tom Wingfield in *The Glass Menagerie*. Lori Leathers Single's analysis of the screen device, which is often left out of *Menagerie* productions, makes a compelling case for its importance in the integrity of Williams's aesthetic design for the play. In his study of Lucretia Collins, Amanda Wingfield, and Blanche DuBois, George Hovis analyzes the cultural pressures that provoked the performance of the role of "southern belle" in Williams's plays and shows how the role has perpetuated the possibilities both for women's victimhood and for their survival. Philip C. Kolin traces the history of African American and multiracial productions of *A Streetcar Named Desire* to study what they reveal about the relationship between Williams's script and the prevailing ideologies of race and culture, pointing out a number of advantages to these productions, both practical and theoretical.

With his pioneering and controversial study of Williams's treatment of homosexuality, John M. Clum initiated what has become a major line of Williams criticism over the last two decades. In one of the best of these essays, John S. Bak analyzes Williams's most significant treatment of homosexuality, in *Cat on a Hot Tin Roof*, in the context of a Cold War Sartrean existentialism and the postwar conception of sexuality dominated by the Kinsey Report. In a rare ecocritical reading of a Williams play, Rod Phillips demonstrates the significance of the natural world within Williams's artistic vision in *The Night of the Iguana*. In his representation of *The Red Devil Battery Sign* as "mythopolitical" theater, James Schlatter shows how Williams radically refashioned his perennial characters, themes, and theatrical motifs to create a fundamentally new work. Nicholas O. Pagan examines the metadramatic nature of *Out Cry* and *The Two-Character Play*, arguing that these works are worthy of attention because they give us "one of the finest and most sustained meditations in all twentieth century drama on the difficulties facing *all* playwrights."

The final two essays provides analyses of Williams's prose, which has not received as much attention as it deserves. In his study of Williams's short fiction, George W. Crandell argues that the writer places the reader in the role of spectator and voyeur. D. Dean Shackelford shows that Williams's nonfiction is worthy of study for what it reveals about "Williams the individual, the artist, the intellectual, and the critic." A chronology of Williams's life, a list of his works, and a bibliography complete the volume.

CAREER, LIFE, AND INFLUENCE

On Tennessee Williams_____

Brenda Murphy

For a long time, the narrative of Tennessee Williams's career followed a generally accepted story line: the early disastrous failure of *Battle of Angels* (1940), which closed in Boston before it even had a chance to reach Broadway, was followed by the "discovery" of Williams as a major playwright by Chicago critic Claudia Cassidy, who recognized the power of *The Glass Menagerie* in 1944 before anyone else did, and the play's successful debut on Broadway in 1945. This was followed in turn by the triumph of *A Streetcar Named Desire* (1947), which ran for 855 performances and won Williams his first Pulitzer Prize, and his fifteen-year domination of the American stage with such plays as *Summer and Smoke* (1947), *The Rose Tattoo* (1950), *Cat on a Hot Tin Roof* (1955), *Orpheus Descending* (1957), *Suddenly Last Summer* (1958), *Sweet Bird of Youth* (1959), and *The Night of the Iguana* (1961). This high point was then followed by a steady decline, caused by Williams's dependency on alcohol and drugs, and a series of plays that were at best failed experiments and at worst embarrassing proof of his incapacity as a playwright.

This narrative has been altered significantly in recent years, owing largely to the archival work of Allean Hale and other Williams scholars on the early plays, the interest of New Directions in publishing Williams's previously unpublished plays from the 1930s, and the work of critics such as Linda Dorff, Philip C. Kolin, Robert Bray, and Annette J. Saddik in reevaluating the plays of the 1960s and 1970s. As the essays in this volume by Jennifer Banach and Susan C. W. Abbotson demonstrate, we now have a much more complete sense of Williams's writing career, of his evolution as a writer, and of the themes and ideas that pervade his work and that he developed through particular aesthetic strategies in different ways and at different times in his plays and fiction.

One thing that has only recently been given its due is Williams's engagement with politics. Allean Hale has shown that the early plays—written for the Mummers, a St. Louis theater group, and including *Candles to the Sun* (1937), a protest play about a miner's strike, and *Fugitive Kind* (1937), which is set in the lobby of a Depression-era flophouse—are imbued with the leftist politics of the 1930s. A more ambitious and significant play is *Not About Nightingales*, which he began in 1939 after reading about a horrific incident in a Pennsylvania prison in which twenty-five hunger-striking convicts were locked in a cell and blasted with steam until four of them died. Williams adapted the techniques of the Federal Theatre Project's Living Newspaper and of the European expressionism that he had been studying in his playwriting course at the University of Iowa to tell this story with a thematic slant that is now recognizable as deeply characteristic, emphasizing the themes of authoritarian oppression, entrapment and escape, human isolation, and the possibility for love as its answer. Traces of the 1930s playwright remain in Tom's poetic references to the hopelessness engendered by the Great Depression in *The Glass Menagerie*. I have suggested in another essay, "Tennessee Williams and Cold War Politics," that Williams's political thinking is central to several works throughout his career, especially in his responses to the oppression of McCarthyism and other Cold War trends in *Camino Real* (1953), *The Red Devil Battery Sign* (1975), and his novella *The Knightly Quest* (1966).

The theme of entrapment and escape is central to many well-known Williams plays, from Tom's family predicament in *The Glass Menagerie* to Blanche's terror of being "caught in a trap" in *Streetcar*, to the desperation of all the characters to escape from the Camino Real, to the frustration of Maggie the Cat on her hot tin roof, of the Reverend T. Lawrence Shannon tied in a hammock in *The Night of the Iguana*, and of Clare and Felice locked in their theater/house in *The Two-Character Play* (1967). Equally pervasive is Williams's notion of the "fugitive kind," used as a title both for the early play and for the film adaptation of *Orpheus Descending*. Most of the trapped characters in his plays are of this kind, people who live on the borders of society, always on the move, both searching for some indefinable fulfillment and fleeing persecution by the majority that is sometimes imagined and sometimes real. In recent years, particularly since John M. Clum's groundbreaking 1989 essay, reprinted in this volume, opened the issues of sexuality and gender identity as a major focus for the study of Williams, a great deal of critical attention has been given to gay characters, closeted or not, and those who struggle with their sexual and gender identities as examples of this group, notably Sebastian Venable (*Suddenly Last Summer*), Brick Pollitt and his friend Skipper (*Cat on a Hot Tin Roof*), and Blanche DuBois and her husband, Allan Grey. The implications of this perspective on Williams's work grow broader with each essay.

Perhaps the most significant implication of the concept of the fugitive kind is its application to the artist, which pervades Williams's career from beginning to end. One of his earliest plays, *Spring Storm* (1938), suggests the autobiographical implications of the theme, combining sexual frustration and sexual disgust with an artist and fugitive's flight from the entrapment of a small town. When he wrote *Battle of Angels*, a play he continued to revise for many years after its failure until it became *Orpheus Descending* and the 1960 movie *The Fugitive Kind*, Williams combined the artist and the fugitive with a powerful sexual potency and a martyr's destiny in the figure of Val Xavier, who is a writer in *Battle of Angels* and a musician in *Orpheus Descending*. Val has the artistic power and the desire to redeem the corrupted community in which he finds himself, but, like many of the artist figures who follow him in Williams's plays, he is persecuted by the community for his difference and is ultimately and horrifically destroyed. At the ends of their respective stories, Val is about to be tortured with a blowtorch, Sebastian Venable is literally eaten alive, Chance Wayne of *Sweet Bird of Youth* faces castration, and the titular *Gnädiges Fräulein* (1966), in Williams's most visceral treatment of the artist's suffering, has her eyes pecked out, her hair pulled out, and her clothes torn off by predatory birds, symbols of hostile critics, leaving her naked and bloody.

Throughout Williams's work, the artist is a misunderstood and persecuted figure, often regarded as insane by the "normal" community. In *In the Bar of a Tokyo Hotel* (1969), written just before Williams himself was committed to Barnes Hospital for detoxification and treatment, a painter who is on the verge of what he feels is a great artistic breakthrough is deserted by his wife, who thinks he is mad. In *Clothes for a Summer Hotel* (1980), an exploration of the conjunction of madness and creativity, Zelda Fitzgerald, who has had her artistic identity stolen from her by her husband, Scott, finally burns to death in a mental "asylum."

The play that Williams said was his most personally significant, the much-revised *Out Cry* or *The Two-Character Play* (1967-1971), concerns a brother who is a writer and a sister who is an actor. The play is deeply autobiographical, reflecting Williams's lifelong identification with his sister Rose, whom he called his anima and his other half, as well as his never-resolved feelings about his authoritarian, homophobic father and his dependent, emotionally manipulative mother. Williams felt a lifelong guilt that he was not able to save Rose from the lobotomy to which she was subjected in 1943, when she was in her thirties. Reduced to a placid but childlike state and unable to live on her own, Rose lived out the rest of her life mainly in institutions, supported by her brother. The play brings together most of Williams's pervasive themes, as brother and sister are trapped in a theater, abandoned by the rest of their theatrical troupe, and must put on the brother's play about the two of them. In his play, they are unable to leave the house where either their father shot their mother and then himself or vice versa. The brother raises a revolver to shoot his sister, but is unable to do it, and the play ends with their embrace.

Williams has Val say in *Orpheus Descending* that we are all "sentenced to solitary confinement inside our own skins, for life" (271). Val is preoccupied by a certain species of bird; these birds, he says, never land on earth, never come to rest until they die. Over and over in his work, however, Williams also suggests that there is a remedy for this solitary, fugitive condition in human communication and love. In *The Night of the Iguana*, the fugitive artist figure Hannah Jelkes travels the world ceaselessly, barely supporting herself and her grandfather with her quick-sketch skills. Nevertheless, she speaks of the "home" she has built with her grandfather through the love they have between them, a love they can "nest-rest-live in, emotionally speaking" (356-57).

Williams's work suggests that temporary homes are the best that can be hoped for, but that their lack of permanence does not mean they cannot be a source of comfort. When accompanied by sexual fulfillment, they can even be full of joy. *The Rose Tattoo*, a lusty comedy that Williams dedicated to his longtime partner Frank Merlo, ends in a hearty celebration of sexuality. *Period of Adjustment* (1959) is a marital comedy that ends with the reconciliation of two married couples, even if they are occupying a suburban bungalow built over a cavern into which the house is slowly sinking. Even *Cat on a Hot Tin Roof* ends on a note of reconciliation through sex as Brick surrenders to Maggie and they go to bed with the hope of creating new life. As dark as Williams's vision was at times, there was always an element of the self-described romantic in his work. He not only believed in the possibility of love and communication between people, he also dramatized it.

Works Cited

Murphy, Brenda. "Tennessee Williams and Cold War Politics." *Staging a Cultural Paradigm: The Political and the Personal in American Drama*. Ed. Barbara Ozieblo and Miriam López Rodriguez. New York: Peter Lang, 2002.

Williams, Tennessee. *The Night of the Iguana*. 1961. New York: New Directions, 1972.

_____. *Orpheus Descending*. 1957. New York: New Directions, 1971.

Biography of Tennessee Williams_____

Susan Rusinko

Thomas Lanier Williams, known as Tom during his boyhood and later as Tennessee, was born in his maternal grandparents' home, an Episcopalian rectory in Columbus, Mississippi, on March 26, 1911, to Edwina Dakin and Cornelius Coffin Williams. His mother came from a prominent old Mississippi family, and his father from an equally prominent old Tennessee family with a proud military and patriotic background. Williams was immediately thrust into a conflict between the genteel Puritanism of his mother and the cavalier lifestyle of his father.

From his father's origins, he was given his nickname, and he chose to use it for the rest of his life. Because of his father's continual absence from home during Williams's boyhood, Williams developed an unusual closeness to both his mother and his sister, Rose, and a distance from, and sometimes hostility toward, his father.

His boyhood experiences included many happy hours of reading in the library of his maternal grandfather, with whom Williams maintained a close relationship until his grandfather's death in 1955. Williams had strong support, as well, from his maternal grandmother, who would send him money from time to time.

Few dramatists write as autobiographically as Williams did in *The Glass Menagerie* (1944). Considered by many to be Williams's best play, *The Glass Menagerie* is one of the three most famous plays about the American family. The other two are Eugene O'Neill's *Long Day's Journey into Night* (1956) and Arthur Miller's *Death of a Salesman* (1949), the Catholic and Jewish versions, respectively, of Williams's Protestant family. Williams's other plays, although not so closely autobiographical, also draw on his experiences and, for all their theatricality, have the ring of authenticity.

Williams's nomadic life began during his university years. Having won literary prizes at the University of Missouri before being withdrawn from the university by his father for failing a Reserve Officers'

Critical Insights

Training Corps course, he worked as a shoe company stock clerk for three years. Finding the work intolerably boring, he returned to school, this time enrolling at Washington University in St. Louis, where he soon fell in with a theater group, the Mummers. In still another move, he transferred to the famous writers' school at the University of Iowa, from which he graduated in 1937.

After his first produced play (in Memphis, 1935), a farce titled *Cairo! Shanghai! Bombay!*, Williams had two plays produced by the Mummers in St. Louis in 1936. Soon, grant money began coming in from the Group Theatre, the Rockefeller Foundation, and the American Academy of Arts and Letters. Williams also received money from Hollywood in the form of a six-month contract with Metro-Goldwyn-Mayer (MGM). Among the many ironies of his life, one of the earliest is that MGM turned down his work, including *The Glass Menagerie*, in 1943. The studio continued, however, to pay Williams for the six months of his contract.

There was hardly a year after 1944 (when *The Glass Menagerie* opened in Chicago) in which Williams did not produce or publish a new play, a revised play, a play adapted from a short story, a film, or a collection of poems or short stories. In New York, *The Glass Menagerie*, *A Streetcar Named Desire* (1947), and *Cat on a Hot Tin Roof* (1955) won prizes such as the New York Drama Critics' Circle Award, the Pulitzer Prize, and the Sidney Howard Memorial Award.

With the influx of success and money, Williams embarked on a nomadic life that included trips to Paris and Italy and various residences in New York, Nantucket, Key West, and New Orleans. Like his boyhood, his adult life included bouts with illnesses, some of them nervous breakdowns. These were complicated by alcohol, barbiturates, and his bohemian lifestyle. Late in life, Williams converted to Roman Catholicism.

In his *Memoirs* (1975), Williams reveals in graphic detail his intimate personal and professional experiences. His most enduring and serious relationship was with Frank Merlo, whose death from cancer in 1963 devastated Williams. Among his long-standing friendships from the theater world were those with his New York agent, Audrey Wood, and actresses Maureen Stapleton and Anna Magnani. His plays and films attracted the major acting talents of his time, among them Margaret Leighton, Vivien Leigh, Vanessa Redgrave, Geraldine Page, Katharine Hepburn, Elizabeth Ashley, Paul Newman, and Jason Robards. On the stage, Laurette Taylor in *The Glass Menagerie* and the duo of Marlon Brando and Jessica Tandy in *A Streetcar Named Desire* became legends in their own time. An important part of those legends was the work of director Elia Kazan, a personal friend of Williams who was closely involved in the direction of a number of his plays.

Though awards were heaped on his three most successful dramas, reviewers heavily criticized many of Williams's other plays. Consequently, Williams's disappointment and bitterness with critics took their toll on him physically and psychologically. In *Small Craft Warnings* (1972), Williams even acted in a small role, hoping thereby to prolong the play's run.

Though he was surrounded by a wealth of admirers and actors, Williams remained a lonely man. On February 25, 1983, he was found dead in his New York apartment, after having choked on a plastic bottle cap. Despite his wandering lifestyle, Williams had a constant need for some permanent human attachment—provided early by his maternal grandparents, his mother, and sister, and later by Merlo. All but Rose were gone at the time of his death. His life and death are reminiscent of the loneliness of many of his characters.

Among the four generally acknowledged major American dramatists—Eugene O'Neill, Tennessee Williams, Arthur Miller, and Edward Albee—Williams holds the distinction of being a poet in the theater. In 1944, the same year that *The Glass Menagerie* opened in Chicago, some of his poems were published in *Five American Poets*. Selections from among these poems were revised and reappeared in a later volume, *In the Winter of Cities* (1956). Williams's poems contain many of the themes, images, and musical qualities that dominate the style of his plays.

Williams's most prominent and all-inclusive theme is the effect of an aggressively competitive society on sensitive characters such as Laura and Tom Wingfield (*The Glass Menagerie*), Blanche DuBois (*A Streetcar Named Desire*), Brick and Maggie Pollitt (*Cat on a Hot Tin Roof*), Alma Winemiller (*Summer and Smoke*, 1947), Catharine Holly and Sebastian Venable (*Suddenly Last Summer*, 1958), and the Reverend Shannon and Hannah Jelkes (*The Night of the Iguana*, 1961)—all of whom are social outcasts.

Williams's themes are dramatized in three major styles in *The Glass Menagerie*, *A Streetcar Named Desire*, and *Suddenly Last Summer*. These styles—poeticism, theatricality, and lush symbolism—are found at their strongest, respectively, in the realistic expressionism of *The Glass Menagerie*, the naturalistic theatricality of *A Streetcar Named Desire*, and the exotic surrealism of *Suddenly Last Summer*. It is the impact of Williams's poetic language and imagery on the American stage that remains his distinctive contribution to American drama.

Bibliography

Bloom, Harold, ed. *Tennessee Williams*. New York: Chelsea House, 1987. Collection of critical essays carries an introduction by Bloom that places Williams in the dramatic canon of American drama and within the psychological company of Hart Crane and Arthur Rimbaud. Contributors to the collection take traditional thematic and historical approaches, noting Williams's "grotesques," his morality and irony, his work in the "middle years," and the mythical qualities of his situations and characters.

Crandell, George W. *Tennessee Williams: A Descriptive Bibliography*. Pittsburgh: University of Pittsburgh Press, 1995. An important bibliographical resource.

Falk, Signi. *Tennessee Williams*. 2d ed. Boston: Twayne, 1978. Primarily discusses Williams's plays but also addresses many of the short stories, including "One Arm," "Desire and the Black Masseur," and "Portrait of a Girl in Glass."

Hayman, Ronald. *Tennessee Williams: Everyone Else Is an Audience*. New Haven:

Conn.: Yale University Press, 1993. Discusses Williams's work with a focus on the extent to which the playwright based his plays on events that took place in his own life.

Kolin, Philip C., ed. *The Tennessee Williams Encyclopedia*. Westport, Conn.: Greenwood Press, 2004. Provides a useful guide to Williams and his work. In 160 entries, Williams scholars offer a wealth of information.

Leverich, Lyle. *Tom: The Unknown Tennessee Williams*. New York: Crown, 1995. First volume of a planned two-volume biography traces Williams's life for the first thirty-three years, drawing on previously unpublished letters, journals, and notebooks. Discusses Williams's focus on how society has a destructive influence on sensitive people and his efforts to change drama into an unrealistic form.

Martin, Robert A., ed. *Critical Essays on Tennessee Williams*. New York: G. K. Hall, 1997. Excellent, accessible collection presents criticism of Williams's works.

Pagan, Nicholas O. *Rethinking Literary Biography: A Postmodern Approach to Tennessee Williams*. Rutherford, N.J.: Fairleigh Dickinson University Press, 1993. Discusses the symbolism of Williams's characters in relation to his life.

Rader, Dotson. *Tennessee: Cry of the Heart*. Garden City, N.Y.: Doubleday, 1985. Chatty biography has the appeal of a firsthand, fascinating account, filled with gossip and inside information, but lacks the virtue of notes or a scholarly bibliography.

Roudané, Matthew C., ed. *The Cambridge Companion to Tennessee Williams*. New York: Cambridge University Press, 1997. Collection comprises copious amounts of information on Williams and his works.

Spoto, Donald. *The Kindness of Strangers: The Life of Tennessee Williams*. Reprint. New York: DaCapo Press, 1998. Lively chronicle details Williams's encounters with such diverse influences as the Group Theatre, Frieda and D. H. Lawrence, Senator Joseph R. McCarthy, Fidel Castro, Hollywood stars, and the homosexual and drug subcultures of Key West. Forty-two pages of notes, bibliography, and index make this study a valuable resource for further scholarship.

Tharpe, Jac, ed. *Tennessee Williams: A Tribute*. Jackson: University Press of Mississippi, 1977. Collection presents fifty-three essays on various aspects of Williams's art.

Thompson, Judith. *Tennessee Williams' Plays: Memory, Myth, and Symbol*. New York: Peter Lang, 2002. Provides a Jungian analysis of Williams's plays, focusing on the manifestation of archetypes in his work.

Tischler, Nancy M. *Student Companion to Tennessee Williams*. Westport, Conn.: Greenwood Press, 2000. A well-known Williams scholar brings together the playwright's biography and critical assessments of his works to provide students with a thorough introduction to and appreciation of Williams's achievements.

Williams, Dakin, and Shepherd Mead. *Tennessee Williams: An Intimate Biography*. New York: Arbor House, 1983. One of the more bizarre duos in biographical writing, Williams (Tennessee's brother) and Mead (Tennessee's childhood friend) produce a credible biography in a highly readable, well-indexed work. Their account of the playwright also helps to capture his almost schizophrenic nature. A solid index and extensive research assist the serious scholar and the general reader.

Williams, Tennessee. *Five O'Clock Angel: Letters of Tennessee Williams to Maria St. Just, 1948-1982.* New York: Knopf, 1990. Collection of letters sheds light on Williams's personal life.

Windham, Donald. *As If. . . .* Verona, Italy: D. Windham, 1985. This reminiscence of Williams's onetime friend portrays the writer as a man of bizarre contradictions and reveals in telling vignettes the downward spiral of his self-destructive lifestyle.

Woodhouse, Reed. *Unlimited Embrace: A Canon of Gay Fiction, 1945-1995.* Amherst: University of Massachusetts Press, 1998. Includes a chapter on Williams's gay short stories. Argues that the most astonishing thing about the stories is their lack of special pleading, that while they are not graphic, they are not apologetic for their homosexuality. Provides an extended analysis of the story "Hard Candy."

The *Paris Review* Perspective_____
Sasha Weiss for *The Paris Review*

Tennessee Williams created what is now an archetypal figure in the American theater: the delusional southern woman. Her fantastic ideas about the charms of her youth cause her to behave, in middle age, with a manic, often absurd ebullience. Her personality is as frayed and brittle as the cheap imitation furs she wears, and her pretensions seem especially pathetic when juxtaposed against her shabby, poorly lit surroundings (the lighting in a Williams play is important: unnatural, dim, with shafts of brightness illuminating characters in moments of private reverie, creating a sense of stark memories pulled from the haze of passing time). She is diminished only further during the course of the play, as her circumstances abet, cruelly, the grandiosity of her dreams.

Who can forget Blanche DuBois, trembling and preening her way through the wreck of *A Streetcar Named Desire*, her affected, portentous speech and airs of correctitude yielding to panicked stuttering? Or the moment when Amanda Wingfield in *The Glass Menagerie*, giddy at the prospect of a "gentleman caller" for her crippled, socially maladroit daughter, Laura, emerges from her room in an outdated lace frock? The drama in a Tennessee Williams play emerges not from our creeping sense that the heroine's decline could have been avoided had her circumstances been different but from her inept attempts to brighten the pervasive atmosphere of gloom. As the critic Daniel Mendelsohn has written, Williams is "the dramatist of the beautiful failure, the poet of noble defeat."

Williams's plays drip with decay, and the effects he repeatedly uses to create this impression—tinkling, circuslike music, crescendos of emotion in every scene, the artificial lighting—appeal powerfully to sentiment. The critic Mary McCarthy famously denounced Williams's histrionics in an article in *The Partisan Review* soon after *Streetcar* was first performed in New York in December of 1947. She accused Williams of disguising what is essentially a comedic premise (a troublesome, loony in-law overstays her visit) as a meditation on the limitations of beauty: "Like Blanche DuBois in *A Streetcar Named Desire* and the mother in *The Glass Menagerie*, [Williams] is addicted to the embroidering lie. . . . His work creates in the end that very effect of painful falsity which is imparted to the Kowalski household by Blanche's pink lampshades and couch covers."

More than sixty years later, *Streetcar*'s popularity has grown and widened, and Blanche DuBois is now considered one of the most powerful, complex roles in all of American theater. In reading the text of the play, however, McCarthy's criticism does echo in the ear. Blanche *is* often loathsome and bathetic. Why, then, has she remained so essential?

Mendelsohn, writing in 2005 in the *New York Review of Books*, answers McCarthy convincingly. The very success of the play depends precisely on the audience's apprehension of what McCarthy calls "the thin, sleazy stuff of this character." "Precisely what makes this play so insinuating is the way in which it manages to hold Blanche's awfulness and her nobility in a kind of logic-defying suspension. There can be little doubt that the decision to endow her with both monstrousness and pathetic allure was a deliberate one on Williams's part." The presentation of the grandiose ego brought low, with the audience's attendant feelings of disgust and pity, is Williams's essential talent.

Williams himself was a man of exasperating contradictions. He was seductive and passionate, full of quips and compliments and charm, but also depressive, alcoholic, narcissistic, hypochondriacal, and a desperate courter of critics. Reading an interview he gave to *The Paris Review* two years before his death, one can easily see the campy cultivation of his persona, Tennessee Williams "doing" Tennessee Williams: "I'm restless. I like traveling. . . . I was once asked why I travel so much, and I said, 'because it's hard to hit a moving target!'"

A common observation in critical essays about Williams is that his dramatic preoccupations were excessively narrow. "He never picked up much information about the world during his half-century as an adult," wrote Gore Vidal, a friend of Williams as well as a penetrating critical adversary. "He also never tried, consciously at least, to make sense of the society into which he was born." Vidal also complained that Williams's emotional sensibility was constrained by the stuffy, puritanical mores of his youth, despite the playwright's numerous affairs with men. Williams was trapped in the early scenes of his childhood, obsessively reworking characters and impressions from his home in St. Louis, Missouri: his domineering mother, Edwina, who was probably insane, is thought to be the model for his vain self-deluding female characters; his beloved sister Rose, who underwent a lobotomy at Edwina's behest after she was hospitalized for schizophrenia, was a source of guilt and torment to Williams, and her apparition also appears in the plays; his father, gruff, cruel, and absent, is transposed into the virile, capricious male characters whom his women either worship or try to manipulate.

Williams's subject may be narrow, but his work comes from a place of intense self-investigation. Through his characters, whose aspirations for superior, beautiful lives are mocked by grim reality, he enacts versions of his own predicament. As Mendelsohn says, "He was, after all, a product of the deep South, where many families, like his, struggled to balance memories of a romanticized past with the realities of a less-than-exalted present; and he was, too, a homosexual living at a time when society still insisted on a certain furtiveness—a time when you couldn't openly acknowledge what it was you found to be beautiful."

One thinks of the reclusive Laura in *The Glass Menagerie*, compulsively polishing the delicate figurines that make up her entire universe. Laura is often thought to have derived from Williams's sister Rose, but she seems equally representative of his own, somewhat hermetic life; his characters are the figures of his own painful experiences, burnished to gleaming.

Bibliography

McCarthy, Mary. *A Bolt from the Blue and Other Essays*. Ed. A. O. Scott. New York: New York Review of Books, 2002.

Mendelsohn, Daniel. "Victims on Broadway." *New York Review of Books* 26 May 2005.

_____. "Victims on Broadway II." *New York Review of Books* 9 June 2005.

Vidal, Gore. "Immortal Bird." *New York Review of Books* 13 June 1985.

Williams, Tennessee. "The Art of Theater No. 5." Interview with Dotson Rader. *The Paris Review* 81 (Fall 1981).

_____. *The Theatre of Tennessee Williams*. Vol. 1. New York: New Directions, 1971.

CRITICAL
CONTEXTS

The Critical Reception of the Works of Tennessee Williams_____

Jennifer Banach

In 1944, a dramatic work written by a young playwright named Tennessee Williams debuted at Chicago's Civic Theatre and shortly thereafter opened on a Broadway stage. The play, titled *The Glass Menagerie*, told the story of the struggles of the Wingfield family through the eyes of the son, Tom, a young man hoping to escape his life in St. Louis and realize his dream of being a poet. It was hugely successful, winning over critics and audiences and catapulting the author to fame. Today, Tennessee Williams is recognized as one of the most important playwrights in the history of American drama, owing largely to the success of this play, which has come to be considered one of Williams's signature works and continues to be studied in classrooms and performed on stages all over the world.

When *The Glass Menagerie* premiered in 1944, critics were struck by the personal nature of the story, which bore an undeniable resemblance to the young playwright's own life. They praised Williams's ability to create dynamic characters of enormous depth, such as Laura, a fragile young woman modeled on Williams's own sister, Rose, and Amanda, a well-intentioned but suffocating mother who, abandoned by her husband, clings to her faded past as a southern belle. The breadth of thematic concerns treated in the work was also lauded. Williams was able to depict simultaneously the struggle of the American family within the urban life of a newly industrialized society and the contradictions inherent to the genteel way of life associated with the antebellum American South. The work also successfully treated more universal themes such as abandonment and the desire to escape, the intense moral conflict between responsibility and self-fulfillment, and the desire for love. In its revelation of a basic plot—the wait for a gentleman caller—and in its unexpected conclusions, *The Glass Menagerie* presented a simple story of enormous depth, a formula that won over popular audiences and critics alike.

Although prior to the composition of *The Glass Menagerie* Williams had written in a variety of forms, including poetry, short stories, and screenplays, following the success of this self-proclaimed memory play Williams exhibited a greater commitment to writing for the stage, presenting plays in a variety of styles until his death in 1983. *The Glass Menagerie* was recognized with a New York Drama Critics' Circle Award, and many of the works that followed it received similar commendations. In a relatively short span of time, Williams won two Pulitzer Prizes, three Tony Awards, and four New York Drama Critics' Circle Awards, among countless other accolades. With the success of subsequent works such as *A Streetcar Named Desire* (1947) and *Cat on a Hot Tin Roof* (1955), critics began to speculate about Williams's place within the history of American and world drama, and most concurred that he should be named among the most relevant American playwrights of all time. However, what seemed like a path of certain, uninterrupted success wandered off course during the second half of the playwright's career with the production of a long list of plays that were neither critically nor popularly successful.

While the criticism surrounding Williams's oeuvre covers an enormous range of topics and represents an equally broad variation of sentiments, which is to be expected in critical conversations on any work of literature, one concern seems to dominate critics' commentary and pervade analyses of Williams's work: namely, the notion that Williams's success was rooted only in his early works and that all his later works were failures springing from some type of personal and professional decline. In fact, while Williams's work has been examined from countless vantage points—ranging from traditional aesthetic readings to postmodernist, feminist, and sexual approaches—the overall understanding and perception of the author's oeuvre remains one of the most significant and intriguing areas associated with the critical study of his work. This broad issue holds its shape over time because it asks the fundamental questions that must be asked of all literature: Why is the work important? What value does it have for its audience? In light of the countless writings that are available on the subject of Williams and his work, a chronological consideration or general survey of Williams's plays and their reception helps to present a clearer picture of the trajectory of his works as a whole and also reveals the base from which these critical conversations originate as well as where critical readings of Williams's works begin to diverge, and why.

Tennessee Williams began writing at a young age, and while today he is best known as a playwright, he worked in a variety of forms as a young man and throughout his career. Although his work did not attract significant critical attention until the mid-1940s, his earliest works as a student were generally successful, and Williams received several awards at the start of his career, which no doubt motivated him to continue as a writer. In 1927, he won a prize for his essay "Can a Good Wife Be a Good Sport?," which was published in the American literary magazine *Smart Set*, as well as an award for a film review. One year later, Williams published a short story titled "The Vengeance of Nitocris," and in 1930, when he was a college freshman, his one-act play "Beauty Is the Word" won honorable mention in a contest sponsored by the school's Dramatic Arts Club.

Despite the success of this first dramatic work, Williams continued to write poetry and short stories, and in 1933 his short story "Stella for Star" won first prize in a St. Louis Writers' Guild contest. However, by 1935 Williams was showing a greater commitment to writing for the stage. His first staged play, a comedic work titled *Cairo! Shanghai! Bombay!* was performed by the Rose Arbor Players, a community theater group in Memphis, Tennessee. Although the play failed to generate any significant attention, Williams considered it a success, noting in his memoirs that "it was a great success for the group. . . . the laughter, genuine and loud, at the comedy I had written enchanted me. Then and there the theatre and I found each other for better and for worse" (41-42). During the next few years, Williams wrote additional plays, including *The Magic Tower* (1936), *Candles to the Sun* (1937), and *Fugitive Kind* (1937), for an amateur theater group called the Mummers. These plays also failed to achieve critical or popular success, although, as scholar and editor Allean Hale points out in her essay "Early Williams: The Making of a Playwright" (15-16), the experience had a profound impact on Williams, compelling the playwright to make intense emotional impact the goal of every work.

During the late 1930s and early 1940s, Williams continued to struggle with the negative reception of his works. In 1938, Williams presented a play called *Spring Storm* to his playwriting class at the University of Iowa. It was not well received, and his teacher dismissed it as an amateur work. The Mummers, who had produced several of Williams's other plays, did not wish to perform it either. The play was subsequently forgotten, resurrected only decades later when a scholar discovered a copy of the play while conducting research in the Tennessee Williams Collection at the Harry Ransom Humanities Research Center. Upon its rediscovery, critics did revisit the work, but not owing to the play's success; rather, they took an interest because the play showed evidence of the character types and concerns that would recur in Williams's later works. A 2004 *New York Magazine* review of a production of the play gave voice to this sentiment, with John Simon explaining, "Tennessee Williams's early and immature *Spring Storm* is best as a game for Williams fans: How many names, characters, situations, and devices of his later plays can you identify here?"

After moving to New Orleans in 1939, Williams submitted *Fugitive Kind* to the Federal Writers' Project and began work on a new play titled *Not About Nightingales*. *Fugitive Kind* was not a great success, and *Not About Nightingales* fared even worse, rejected by the Group Theatre and forgotten until actor Vanessa Redgrave uncovered references to the play years after Williams's death and coordinated its production and publication. Despite these setbacks, Williams received more accolades in 1939, including an award of one hundred dollars from the Group Theatre for a collection of one-act plays called *Ameri-*

---

can Blues (1948) and a one thousand dollar grant from the Rockefeller Foundation. It was also at this time that Audrey Wood, a well-known agent, began to represent Williams.

Battle of Angels, Williams's first major production, opened in Boston in 1940, despite being originally set to open in New Haven, Connecticut. The play was a failure, closing in less than two weeks. Presented with an invitation to revise the play and resubmit it, Williams set to work, but even his new version was rejected. He would continue to work on the play throughout his career, presenting an almost entirely reworked version titled *Orpheus Descending* (1957) many years later. Despite this additional rejection and his added failure as a screenwriter during this time, Williams continued to have some success with his dramatic works. His one-act play *Dos Ranchos, or The Purification*, was anthologized in 1942, and in 1944 the playwright received a one thousand dollar grant from the American Academy of Arts and Letters.

The following year marked a turning point in Williams's career. With his next work, *The Glass Menagerie*, he turned the heads of major critics and piqued the interest of popular audiences. A family drama inspired by the author's own life, it premiered at the Civic Theatre in Chicago in December of 1944, where it received rave reviews from critics, and later moved to Broadway. Although the Broadway production elicited a more mixed response than had the Chicago production, reviews of the work were still overwhelmingly favorable, and the play won a New York Drama Critics' Circle Award in 1945. The success of *The Glass Menagerie* also gave Williams financial stability, allowing him to devote more time to the creation of new plays.

While *A Streetcar Named Desire* is frequently misidentified as Williams's next work, before *Streetcar* he also wrote, with Donald Windham, *You Touched Me!* (first produced in Cleveland in 1943), a romantic comedy inspired by a short story of the same name by British author D. H. Lawrence, one of Williams's major influences. The play fell short of achieving the same success as *The Glass Menagerie*, shutting down its 1945 New York production after little more than one hundred performances. It was not until December 3, 1947, under the direction of Elia Kazan, a prominent director and producer who would maintain a long-standing work relationship with Williams, that *Streetcar* opened on Broadway at the Ethel Barrymore Theatre after a short debut run at the Shubert Theater in New Haven, Connecticut. The play did take some shots from a handful of reviewers who found the themes and plot appalling and considered the play to be little more than a creative demonstration of overt pessimism, but, like *The Glass Menagerie*, Williams's new play was hugely successful, again pleasing both audiences and critics. It received the Pulitzer Prize in 1948, and performances carried on for two years (the longest run of all of Williams's plays), further securing Williams's reputation as one of America's most significant playwrights.

Another Williams play also debuted on Broadway in 1948: *Summer and Smoke*, previously titled *Chart of Anatomy*, which took as its subject the clash between body and spirit. The play, first produced in Dallas, Texas, in 1947, opened at the Music Box Theatre in New York on October 6, 1948. Early productions of the play received mixed reviews and failed to achieve the success of either *The Glass Menagerie* or *Streetcar*. The 1952 Circle in the Square production starring Geraldine Page had greater success, playing a pivotal role in the genesis of the Off-Broadway movement. Still, Williams would continue to work on revisions of the play, presenting it to future audiences as *Eccentricities of a Nightingale* (1964). Williams's next play, *The Rose Tattoo*, did not open until 1950, and, unlike Williams's previous works, it presented a unique hybrid of Dionysian comedy and Greek tragedy that surprised critics and audiences. *The Rose Tattoo* fell short of the success of earlier works, but it was a box-office hit on Broadway, winning a Tony Award for Best Play and, more important, inspiring critics and audiences to take note of Williams's evolving style.

In 1952 Williams received further recognition when he was inducted as a lifetime member of the National Institute of Arts and Letters. The works that the playwright produced around this time were indicative of a conscious departure from his earliest works, and Williams seemed to feel more confident about openly experimenting with new styles and techniques. Unfortunately, critics and audiences in general failed to respond favorably to the changes in Williams's work. In 1953, audiences went to see Williams's most unexpected work to date, *Camino Real*, an expanded version of an earlier one-act called *Ten Blocks on the Camino Real*, which combined the absurd and the fantastical and abandoned most of the traditional elements associated with realist works and popular drama. Many audience members simply walked out of the theater long before the play concluded. Critics were no easier on the author. This was a failure that affected Williams deeply, one that some critics have suggested pushed him to return to his realist roots with the composition of *Cat on a Hot Tin Roof.*

Cat on a Hot Tin Roof premiered on Broadway after Williams made some revisions that director Elia Kazan requested, and the play attained critical and popular success. Williams was presented with a New York Drama Critics' Circle Award and another Pulitzer Prize. The next grouping of Williams's plays, however, met with mixed success. *Orpheus Descending*, the drastically revised version of *Battle of Angels*, opened in 1957, the same year that Williams's father died. The revisions on which Williams had spent so much time were not enough to please critics or theatergoers, and the play achieved only minimal success. A year later, the double bill *Garden District*, comprising *Something Unspoken* and *Suddenly Last Summer*, premiered Off-Broadway with some success, as did Williams's next work, *Sweet Bird of Youth* (1959), which received several Tony Award nominations. However, the remainder of Williams's plays presented at the end of the decade— such as the one-act play *I Rise in Flame, Cried the Phoenix* (1959); Williams's only verse play, *The Purification*; and *Period of Adjustment*, a play that Williams later confessed had been conceived under the influence of drugs and that attempted a more mainstream kind of comedy— failed to appease critics. Williams had one last burst of success with *The Night of the Iguana*, which tells the story of a defrocked minister who takes up employment as a half-rate tour guide. The play, which opened on Broadway in 1961, was nominated for a Tony Award for Best Play and won a Drama Critics' Circle Award for Best Play in 1962.

Although Williams's achievements were consistently acknowledged over the course of the next two decades—he was named a lifetime fellow of the American Academy of Arts and Sciences in 1962; received the National Institute of Arts and Letters' Gold Medal for Literature in 1969, the National Arts Club's Medal of Honor for Literature in 1975, and the Kennedy Center Honors in 1979; won the Common Wealth Award in 1981; and was awarded an honorary doctorate from Harvard University in 1982—the works that followed *The Night of the Iguana* were almost entirely critical disasters. *The Milk Train Doesn't Stop Here Anymore*, which opened in 1963, ran for only two months, and a subsequent revival ran for a tragic span of three days. Although a third revival of *Milk Train* in San Francisco had some limited critical success, the rest of Williams's plays throughout the 1960s also suffered short runs, leaving audiences and critics to speculate that Williams's career was, in essence, over. The double bill *Slapstick Tragedy* (1966) ran for less than a week in New York. *Kingdom of Earth*, which premiered in Philadelphia and was revised and performed in New York as *The Seven Descents of Myrtle* in 1968, ran for only one month; in a 1996 *New York Times* review of a later production, Ben Brantley noted that, when the work premiered, "critics recoiled in ways that spelled an early death for the play's run and Williams fell into a suicidal depression." *In the Bar of a Tokyo Hotel* (1969), which depicts an artist struggling to reignite his career by creating a new style (a subject that critics could not help but recognize as a reflection of Williams's own situation), also received terrible reviews, although some critics noted that it showed more glimmers of hope for future success than perhaps any other of Williams's other later works.

His plays that debuted in the 1970s failed to fare better. *Out Cry* (1971), a revision of *The Two-Character Play* (1967), was performed in Chicago and New York but closed after only a brief series of performances, and *The Red Devil Battery Sign* (1975), which ran in Boston, closed within two weeks, with international performances also receiving bitter criticism. Meanwhile, performances of Williams's earlier works, such as *The Glass Menagerie, Summer and Smoke,* and *Sweet Bird of Youth,* continued to be successful. Works from the latter half of the 1970s also failed, with *Vieux Carré* (1977) closing on Broadway after fewer than five performances; *Tiger Tail* (1978) and *A Lovely Sunday for Creve Coeur* (1979) also closed after limited runs. *Clothes for a Summer Hotel* (1980) was the last of Williams's plays to be performed on Broadway prior to his death; the work, which portrays the relationship between author F. Scott Fitzgerald and his wife, Zelda, also failed to impress critics. Finally, his last plays, *Something Cloudy, Something Clear* (1981) and the southern gothic *Some Problems for the Moose Lodge* (1980), which was also performed as *A House Not Meant to Stand* (1981), shared similar fates.

Overviews and surveys such as this one help to provide a global understanding of Williams's work and its critical reception; they also serve another purpose, alerting us to some of the challenges of literary criticism—especially those challenges associated with the criticism of dramatic works. Williams's plays exist not only in print form but also in a variety of incarnations as unique performances with different actors and directors, venues, and audiences—a complexity that creates some obstacles for those seeking a true understanding of the critical reception of dramatic works as a whole. Williams himself recognized the contradictions inherent to the critical reception of dramatic works:

> For me the production of a play is only an incident in the life of a play. I mean there's not only the continued work on the play but there are other productions of the play. Sometimes it's a failure on Broadway and it's a success off-Broadway. . . . Sometimes it's a failure in one country and in another country it's a great success. And consequently I feel that a play is dynamic and living far beyond the time of its Broadway opening and the press of the following morning. (*Conversations* 84)

To complicate matters further, Williams revised and reworked his plays throughout his career, keeping them in a state of flux. This habit often contributed to the dour criticism that Williams's work elicited in his later years, with many critics feeling that these works contained no more than recycled character portraits and rehashed themes, resulting in plays that lacked a fresh perspective and were merely disappointing examples of self-plagiarism. John Simon, for instance, wrote in 1977 that "a man who would steal and resteal from himself is the saddest of failures. Reprehensible as it may be to steal from others, it is at least enterprising: a sign of awareness that the outside world exists. . . . When he does write a play, it is perforce a rehash, or at the utmost a replay of youthful memories" ("Warmed-Over"). Critics such as Alan Rich and Harold Clurman concurred. Rich stated that "a playwright has every right to imitate himself, I suppose, but what is shocking is the ineptitude, the inexactitude of the imitation," and in a review of one of Williams's later works Clurman observed that "there is a certain wretched honesty and boldness in several of the scenes but they also seem tired: the tune has too often been replayed."

In light of such observations, other scholars have also seen contradictions in the criticism of Williams's work, arguing that those same traits that were praised in his earlier works—such as lyricism and symbolism—have also been the impetus for negative criticism of his later works. This theory has been explored by critics and scholars such as Annette J. Saddik and George W. Crandell, and in his book *The Late Plays of Tennessee Williams*, William Prossner uses this concept to argue against Simon, Rich, and Clurman, offering, "Perhaps critics, especially as consumer reporters, are too demanding of novelty, too hungry for this year's rage, too intolerant of yesterday's insights" (109).

In response to these issues, critics have initiated a reconsideration of the overall reception of Williams's oeuvre, including an examination of the earlier criticism of Williams's later works. Critics such as Linda Dorff and Annette Saddik have suggested that Williams's later works might have greater merit than past criticism would indicate, and they have done more than merely object to the overwhelming negative reception of these works—they have also presented for consideration the possibility that the negative reception of Williams's later works could be attributed, at least in part, to misunderstandings of the author, misreadings of his work, and earlier critics' inability to understand or accept works that strayed from prevailing trends in American theater. In 2002, a panel of critics and scholars that included Robert Bray, Allean Hale, Ruby Cohn, Philip C. Kolin, Brenda Murphy, Thomas Keith, and Annette Saddik convened at the Tennessee Williams Scholars' Conference to discuss these theories on Williams's later works; their conversation was published that same year in the *Tennessee Williams Annual Review* as a transcript titled "Looking at the Late Plays of Tennessee Williams."

As for misunderstandings of the author, many critics have noted that the beginning of Williams's career has often incorrectly been linked to production of *The Glass Menagerie*, thus creating a myth of the playwright's immediate success and propagating the incorrect notion that his early, uninterrupted success was cut short by an abrupt decline in his later years. Many critical writings and reviews have been littered with the false notion that Williams's success with *The Glass Menagerie* led seamlessly to the success of *A Streetcar Named Desire* and, subsequently, of *Cat on a Hot Tin Roof*, perpetuating the mistaken idea that Williams's success was linked only to the output of the first half of his career and relegating all works after *The Night of the Iguana* into a single group associated with mere decline. Prior critical considerations of Williams's work often neglected those works preceding *The Glass Menagerie* and *Streetcar*, such as *Spring Storm*, *Battle of Angels*, *Fugitive Kind*, and *Not About Nightingales*, as well as those works presented contemporaneously with *The Glass Menagerie* and *Streetcar*, such as *You Touched Me!* and *Summer and Smoke*, that could not be considered critically successful and, thus, would have shattered the myth of seamless success.

In addition to such problematic myths, critics have found evidence of the playwright being misunderstood in other ways. Williams created works in many different forms, including poetry, short stories, and screenplays, before committing to the composition of dramatic works, and later critics observed several problems that this variety created. First, there were those critics who recognized Williams's origins as poet and, therefore, saw a divide in his work. Second, there were those who overlooked Williams's background as poet altogether, refusing to see him as anything other than playwright, and misread his works because of their misconceptions about his lyricism and technique. Finally, there were those critics who not only seemed incapable of seeing Williams as something other than playwright but who also refused to accept him as anything other than *realist* playwright.

In his edited volume *The Critical Response to Tennessee Williams*, George W. Crandell gives voice to the first of these problems, suggesting that Williams's origins as poet created not only a divide in Williams's own work but also a divided critical response to his work. He explains:

> Williams's transformation from poet to dramatist . . . as reflected in the critical response to Tennessee Williams, was never wholly complete. Something of the poet always remained. . . . Just as Williams's "artistic personality" may be said to be divided, so too may be the critical response to his plays. (xxvi-xxvii)

Crandell makes note of Williams's deep concern with language and interest in forms that transcended a stage setting, presenting avenues for a reconsideration of these late works (xxvii). There is also proof that Williams himself was aware of how a failure to reconcile his roles as both poet and playwright could affect criticism of his work. In Williams's own words:

The tragedy of a poet writing drama is that when he writes well—from the . . . technical point of view, he is often writing badly. One must learn . . . to fuse lyricism and realism in a congruous unit. I guess my chief trouble is that I don't. (quoted in Leverich 334)

With Williams himself struggling to reconcile the two, it followed that many critics also have been unable to do so.

In her book *The Politics of Reputation*, Annette Saddik presents a parallel point of view: namely, that Williams was boxed in by critics, defined not only as playwright but also as *realist* playwright. Her work suggests that the critical acceptance of a Williams play waned in proportion to the degree of its departure from the realism that had come to be expected of Williams. Furthermore, Saddik encourages critics and readers to ask themselves if the poor reviews of Williams's later works could have stemmed from critics' failure to consider Williams within a vein of experimental and avant-garde theater that included Samuel Beckett, Harold Pinter, and Edward Albee (136-50). In fact, Saddik provides proof of Williams's interest in experimental drama and builds a case for arguing that the failure of his later work was the result of critics' and audiences' inability to accept work that departed from straight realism. She notes, too (as countless other critics have), that elements of experimental dramatic form and technique and a desire to create a new kind of theater were already evidenced in Williams's early works— even in *The Glass Menagerie* and *Streetcar*. Indeed, one cannot help but recall Williams's early declarations of his desire to create a new plastic theater or sculptural drama that would better serve modern audiences. Saddik also questions the general reception of avant-garde and experimental theater during Williams's lifetime, reaching the ultimate conclusion that the playwright's "later reputation . . . tells us more about the critical biases in the popular and academic press in this century than about Williams' work per se" (150).

Finally, contemporary criticism presents additional questions for consideration: Were critics correct that Williams's later works were somehow too personal? Reviews such as Clive Barnes's *New York Times* article on *In the Bar of a Tokyo Hotel* indicate that this was, in fact, a central problem. Other critics have asked whether the works were marred by the author's personal decline and addictions or if he, in essence, traded success for the right to experiment in the hope of creating a new dramatic form. New criticism also suggests that many previous critics have misunderstood Williams's characters, seeing Williams as sadistic, obsessed with desire and death. Critics today continue to revisit these questions.

Despite the pervasive opinion that his work suffered a steady decline, Williams remains at the forefront of the greatest American dramatists. Even those who fail to find success in his later works continue to praise Williams for his vivid characters, his intense portrayal of the human experience, and his courageous treatment of difficult themes. More than twenty-five years after his death, scholars and critics continue to acknowledge his contribution to American drama and to present new reflections on his work. The critical response to Williams's work might then best be characterized as an ongoing conversation, whereby participants continue not only to review past theories and criticism but also to pose new questions and present new responses to his work. These critical writings will, in turn, reveal new avenues for further research and yield a fresh understanding of Williams's work.

Works Cited

Barnes, Clive. Rev. of *In the Bar of a Tokyo Hotel*, by Tennessee Williams. *The New York Times*. 12 May 1969.

Brantley, Ben. "Redeeming a Williams Washout." Rev. of *Kingdom of Earth*, by Tennessee Williams. *The New York Times*. 26 June 1996.

Clurman, Harold. "Theatre." *The Nation*. 29 May 1977.

Crandell, George W., ed. *The Critical Response to Tennessee Williams*. Westport, CT: Greenwood Press, 1996.

Hale, Allean. "Early Williams: The Making of a Playwright." *The Cambridge Companion to Tennessee Williams*. Ed. Matthew C. Roudané. New York: Cambridge UP, 1997.

Leverich, Lyle. *Tom: The Unknown Tennessee Williams.* New York: Crown, 1995.

"Looking at the Late Plays of Tennessee Williams." *Tennessee Williams Annual Review* 5 (2002).

Prossner, William. *The Late Plays of Tennessee Williams.* Lanham, MD: Scarecrow Press, 2008.

Rich, Alan. "Morpheus Descending." *New York.* 30 May 1977.

Saddik, Annette J. *The Politics of Reputation: The Critical Reception of Tennessee Williams' Later Plays.* Madison, NJ: Fairleigh Dickinson UP, 1999.

Simon, John. "In Brief: Tennessee Williams's *Spring Storm.*" *New York Magazine.* 16 May 2004.

_____. "Warmed-Over Vice and Innocence." *The New Leader.* 20 June 1977.

Williams, Tennessee. *Conversations with Tennessee Williams.* Ed. Albert J. Devlin. Jackson: UP of Mississippi, 1985.

_____. *Memoirs.* 1975. New York: New Directions, 2006.

Suggested Reading

Adler, Thomas P. *American Drama, 1940-1960.* New York: Twayne, 1994.

Asibong, Emmanuel B. *Tennessee Williams: The Tragic Tension—A Study of the Plays of Tennessee Williams from "The Glass Menagerie" (1944) to "The Milk Train Doesn't Stop Here Anymore" (1966).* Ilfracombe, Devon, England: Stockwell, 1978.

Bigsby, C. W. E. *A Critical Introduction to Twentieth-Century American Drama.* 3 vols. New York: Cambridge UP, 1982-1985.

_____. *Modern American Drama, 1945-2000.* New York: Cambridge UP, 2000.

Bloom, Harold, ed. *Tennessee Williams.* Bloom's Biocritiques. Philadelphia: Chelsea House, 2003.

_____. *Tennessee Williams.* Bloom's Major Dramatists. Broomall, PA: Chelsea House, 2000.

_____. *Tennessee Williams.* Bloom's Modern Critical Views. New York: Chelsea House, 1987.

Booth, John E. *The Critic, Power, and the Performing Arts.* New York: Columbia UP, 1992.

Boxill, Roger. *Tennessee Williams.* 1987. London: Macmillan, 1996.

Crandell, George W. *Tennessee Williams: A Descriptive Bibliography.* Pittsburgh: U of Pittsburgh P, 1995.

Falk, Signi. *Tennessee Williams.* 2d ed. Boston: Twayne, 1978.

Gassner, John. *The Theatre in Our Times.* New York: Crown, 1954.

Griffin, Alice. *Understanding Tennessee Williams.* Columbia: U of South Carolina P, 1995.

Gross, Robert F., ed. *Tennessee Williams: A Casebook.* New York: Routledge, 2001.

Hayman, Ronald. *Tennessee Williams: Everyone Else Is an Audience.* New Haven, CT: Yale UP, 1993.

Holditch, Kenneth, and Richard Freeman Leavitt. *Tennessee Williams and the South.* Jackson: UP of Mississippi, 2002.

Jackson, Esther Merle. *The Broken World of Tennessee Williams.* Madison: U of Wisconsin P, 1965.

Kolin, Philip C., ed. *American Playwrights Since 1945: A Guide to Scholarship, Criticism, and Performance.* Westport, CT: Greenwood Press, 1989.

_____. *Tennessee Williams: A Guide to Research and Performance.* Westport, CT: Greenwood Press, 1998.

_____. *The Tennessee Williams Encyclopedia.* Westport, CT: Greenwood Press, 2004.

_____. *The Undiscovered Country: The Later Plays of Tennessee Williams.* New York: Peter Lang, 2002.

Leavitt, Richard F. *The World of Tennessee Williams.* New York: Putnam, 1978.

Londré, Felicia Hardison. *Tennessee Williams.* New York: Frederick Ungar, 1979.

McCann, John S. *The Critical Reputation of Tennessee Williams: A Reference Guide.* Boston: G. K. Hall, 1983.

Martin, Robert A., ed. *Critical Essays on Tennessee Williams.* New York: G. K. Hall, 1997.

Miller, Arthur. "The Shadows of the Gods: A Critical View of the American Theater." *Harper's* Aug. 1958: 35-43.

Murphy, Brenda. *Tennessee Williams and Elia Kazan: A Collaboration in the Theatre.* New York: Cambridge UP, 1992.

Pritner, Cal, and Scott E. Walters. *Introduction to Play Analysis.* New York: McGraw-Hill, 2004.

Rasky, Harry. *Tennessee Williams: A Portrait in Laughter and Lamentation.* New York: Dodd, Mead, 1986.

Roudané, Matthew C., ed. *The Cambridge Companion to Tennessee Williams.* New York: Cambridge UP, 1997.

Smith-Howard, Alycia, and Greta Heintzelman. *Critical Companion to Tennessee Williams.* New York: Facts On File, 2005.

Spoto, Donald. *The Kindness of Strangers: The Life of Tennessee Williams.* Boston: Little, Brown, 1985.

Stanton, Stephen S., ed. *Tennessee Williams: A Collection of Critical Essays.* Englewood Cliffs, NJ: Prentice-Hall, 1977.

Tharpe, Jac, ed. *Tennessee Williams: A Tribute.* Jackson: UP of Mississippi, 1977.

Tischler, Nancy M. *Student Companion to Tennessee Williams.* Westport, CT: Greenwood Press, 2000.

Voss, Ralph F., ed. *Magical Muse: Millennial Essays on Tennessee Williams.* Tuscaloosa: U of Alabama P, 2002.

Williams, Dakin. *Tennessee Williams: An Intimate Biography.* New York: Arbor House, 1983.

Williams, Tennessee. *The Collected Poems of Tennessee Williams.* Ed. Nicholas Moschovakis and David Roessel. New York: New Directions, 2007.

_____. *Collected Stories*. New York: New Directions, 1985.

_____. *Letters to Donald Windham, 1940-1965*. Ed. Donald Windham. New York: Holt, Rinehart and Winston, 1977.

_____. *Notebooks*. Ed. Margaret Bradham Thornton. New Haven, CT: Yale UP, 2006.

_____. *The Selected Letters of Tennessee Williams*. Ed. Albert J. Devlin and Nancy M. Tischler. New York: New Directions, 2000.

_____. *Where I Live: Selected Essays by Tennessee Williams*. Ed. Christine R. Day and Bob Woods. New York: New Directions, 1978.

Tennessee Williams on America_____

Susan C. W. Abbotson

> When I write I don't aim to shock people, and I'm surprised when I do. But
> I don't think that anything that occurs in life should be omitted from art,
> though the artist should present it in a fashion that is artistic and not ugly. I
> set out to tell the truth. And sometimes the truth is shocking.
>
> —Tennessee Williams (*Conversations* 321-22)

While reviewing a 1974 revival of *Cat on a Hot Tin Roof*, Clive Barnes declared, "People used to think that Tennessee Williams's plays were about sex and violence. How wrong they were—they are about love and survival" (25). While Barnes's assessment has the ring of truth, it may also be an oversimplification because it leaves out what Williams is ultimately saying about love and survival, a "truth" that is not pleasant. For Williams, while love and survival were definite goals for both himself and his more sympathetic characters, they were goals that he felt, in reality, were ultimately unattainable. While Williams may have begun to write as an escape from a reality he found uncomfortable, what he wrote was a re-creation of that reality. As Gerald Weales asserts, "From the beginning of his career, Williams has been trying to tell the real truth (his real truth, that is) about human beings and the way they live" (32-33). This reality is inescapable, as *The Glass Menagerie*'s Tom Wingfield understands when he exclaims "Oh, Laura, Laura, I tried to leave you behind me, but I am more faithful than I intended to be!" (*Plays* 465). In a 1939 letter to his agent, Audrey Wood, Williams wrote, "I have only one major theme for my work which is the destructive impact of society on the sensitive nonconformist individual." Though we can read Williams's work on a universal level, the society of which he speaks is particularly American, and this individual is himself, the sensitive American romanticist.

Nancy M. Tischler identifies the essentially romantic nature of the playwright's outlook and writing, explaining how "the Williams mythic

38   Critical Insights protagonist is a romanticized persona exploring and explaining facets of the artist himself" ("Romantic Textures" 156). Williams's life can be read as a romantic quest, with himself cast as the flawed and misunderstood hero featured in the works of Samuel Taylor Coleridge, Percy Bysshe Shelley, and Lord Byron. But whereas the British romantics quested within the pastoral and mountainous recesses of Europe, Williams, as an American artist whose persona is as much a reflection of American romanticism as of British, does so within the cities and small towns of an evolving American society.

As an American artist, Williams treads in the footsteps of transcendentalists such as Walt Whitman, Ralph Waldo Emerson, and Henry David Thoreau, who were particularly aware of nature, especially its wild aspects, and we see in their work a realization of the bitter truth that nature was being lost as quickly as they were finding new appreciation for it. The concept of "manifest destiny," which had bolstered the American pioneer, had reached the limits of its physical frontiers, leaving little wilderness remaining to explore or exploit. Like Whitman and Emerson before him, Williams sought new spiritual roots, personally involving and meaningful, but not traditional. However, where these earlier writers had turned to metaphysical and intellectual frontiers to recapture the ecstasy of exploration and discovery, Williams, coming later, cannot help but recognize the inescapable materialism of his society and the resultant narrowing down of any lasting options for escape. Although temporary respite is possible as lives briefly collide, any permanent bond appears impossible.

In a commentary on his 1966 novella *The Knightly Quest*, Williams asserts, "America, and particularly the Southern states, is the embodiment of an originally romantic gesture. It was discovered and established by the eternal Don Quixote in the human flux. Then, of course, the businessmen took over" (74). In the manner of Thoreau, Williams can be seen as committing an extended act of "civil disobedience" with his writing: his work refuses to condone or accept the status quo and encodes within its dynamics and symbolism a picture of a society long obsessed with segregation and othering, a society doomed by its own inability to cohere, fed by an adherence to aggressive capitalist values born from its founding patriarchy. As a writer whose life spanned much of the twentieth century, Williams offers in his drama his particular vision of America over the course of the century. The severities of the Great Depression; the horrors of war, the growth of capitalism, and the invasion of personal liberties in the 1940s and 1950s; and the civil wrongs, growing decadence, and absurdism of the 1960s and 1970s— all are contained within his plays.

Williams's formative years, like those of so many of his generation, were scarred by his experiences during the Great Depression, a key event in American history. During this period of intense economic hardship and massive unemployment, it became a struggle just to survive. The Depression's beginning is usually dated to the stock market crash on October 29, 1929, and it lasted until the late 1930s, when war production boosted the economy. As their livelihoods vanished, people lost their old certainties and securities, and although most eventually recovered financially, many were psychologically scarred by the experience. Writing to his grandfather in 1931 of his job at the shoe factory where his father was a manager, Williams admitted, "I believe I acquitted myself pretty well at the shoe company. . . . I was exceedingly lucky in getting the job, since I was practically the only fellow in the house who did work this summer. A good number have not been able to return to the University this Fall because they were not able to earn any money" (*Selected Letters* 56). The next year, Williams's father would force him to withdraw from college and work full-time at the factory. While he soon came to despise the monotony of the job his father obtained for him, Williams also knew he was lucky to have it, and his early work reflects his awareness of the widespread poverty surrounding him.

Williams's plays of the 1930s outwardly demand reform as they expose the brutalities of prison life (*Not About Nightingales*), mining (*Candles to the Sun*), and life on the streets (*Fugitive Kind*). In *Not*

About Nightingales, Williams details a corrupt prison system in which the inmates live under unbearable conditions that either drive them insane or lead to their deaths while the warden embezzles funds and makes lewd advances to his secretary. Although the warden falls to his death at the close, it is hard to see much hope in the one inmate who escapes, Canary Jim, whose plan is to swim to a luxury liner that has been circling the prison island throughout the play without any apparent interest in the prisoners' plight. *Candles to the Sun* paints a bleak portrait of the lives of Alabama mining families, who starve even while working and are decimated both by the brutality of their jobs and by the mine management's overtly repressive resistance to their attempts to unionize. Williams's directions for the dirty flophouse set of *Fugitive Kind*—which depicts people from the economic underclass enduring false arrest, imprisonment, work on chain gangs, and the harsh, inhospitable winter of St. Louis—call for a *"great window"* through which we see the *"skyline of the city whose towers are outlined at night by a faint electric glow, so that we are always conscious of the city as a great implacable force, pressing in upon the shabby room and crowding its fugitive inhabitants against their wall"* (3). The lives of these people, Williams underscores, are largely determined by the businessmen inhabiting those glowing towers of privilege and power.

Williams, according to Tischler, saw his own father in his managerial position at the International Shoe Company as "the very personification of capitalism," and Williams, from an early age, displayed a "visceral hatred of big business" (*Student Companion* 71). Whereas his father would have seen St. Louis as a city of opportunity, Williams's dislike of industrial city life can be summed up in his frequent references to St. Louis as "St. Pollution." *Battle of Angels* establishes an outlook that surfaces repeatedly in Williams's later works under a variety of guises: that money, or its lack, is a strong determinant of behavior. This is dramatically depicted through a central love triangle that assures that no one can attain satisfaction. In *Battle of Angels*, characters seek better lives in vain against the backdrop of a violent, alienating world. Local African Americans are hounded for vagrancy or lynched; an artist-hero and sexual rebel in a conservative South is compelled to steal and is killed by an angry mob; and a woman, abandoned by a man who chose to marry wealth, instead marries the self-righteous racist Jabe Torrance, who best represents the limitations of small-town life as he lurks in the dark underworld of his mercantile store. In one draft of the play, Robert Bray reminds us, this store was originally the church of a black socialist preacher who had been killed by the Ku Klux Klan (24). Jabe's cancer and his business dealings symbolize a corrupt, acquisitive core, and yet Jabe is allowed to rise transcendent as he shoots his wife in a vengeful act of victory—an act he happily repeats in *Orpheus Descending* and in the 1960 film *The Fugitive Kind*. For Williams, such is America, and most of his plays are protests against a puritanical and racist nation he saw as repressive and stultifying.

The encroachment of business on human lives repeats throughout Williams's oeuvre. In *Stairs to the Roof* a giant clock looms over the lives of the employees of Consolidated Shirtmakers, with Mr. Gum (evidently stuck in his ways) in charge. The play explores, as Annette J. Saddik observes, "the human costs of industrial capitalism" (68). Ben Murphy, suffocating in his office but trapped there by his responsibilities toward his pregnant wife, tries to escape by the titular stairs and finally meets the godlike Mr. E., who has been laughing at his exploits throughout the play. The fact that Ben, who dreams of a less bureaucratic and stifling existence, cannot achieve this on our earth but must be sent by Mr. E to start a new society, says it all: in this world, business reigns supreme and the clock cannot be stopped.

Even an apparently romantic comedy like *The Rose Tattoo* is structured around economics. The basic problem of the play—Serafina's devastating loss of her husband, Rosario—implicates the country's growing corruption: Rosario is killed while hauling illegal goods for the Mafia, a job he took so that he and his wife could "live with dignity in America" and have all the modern conveniences, such as an electric stove and deep-freeze (*Plays* 660-61). Business and narrow minds restrict the lives of these people: Serafina is forced to sew rather than attend her daughter's graduation, and Alvaro is blithely fired from his trucking job because he resists the racist remarks of a salesman.

"It is quite apparent," John Gassner states in a discussion of Williams's collection *American Blues*, "that Williams was nearly fully formed in these short plays as a painter of a segment of the American scene" (237). The segment in which Williams specialized had a distinctly southern flavor, but it covered America to all points of the compass. The collection's title points to Williams's understanding that the blues, America's indigenous music, born out of racial segregation and despair, colors the country's whole ethos. Nicholas O. Pagan envisions Williams as "living in a country of the blue, where he laments to the melancholy sound of the blues musicians" (126). The blues music we hear in *A Streetcar Named Desire* betokens more than a seamier side of life: it is a whole way of viewing the world. The plays of his *American Blues*—in the initial 1939 collection, *Moony's Kid Don't Cry*, *The Dark Room*, and *The Case of the Crushed Petunias*—offer a collective critique of the American Dream, exposing the dehumanizing conditions under which working-class Americans were living.

Moony's Kid Don't Cry takes place in a shabby apartment where a husband and wife tear each other apart in their fruitless quest for a better life. The fancy rocking horse placed center stage indicates that the lure of materialism reaches even those close to poverty, and Moony is condemned to continued work in the factory to provide for his family, despite his evident revulsion at such constraint. *The Case of the Crushed Petunias* conveys the repression of small-town life as Dorothy Simple seeks to escape the New England town of Primanproper, and *The Dark Room*, set in a dirty city tenement, tells a tale of immigrants badgered by an unsympathetic social service agent who breaks the family apart. This last play, Neal A. Lester observes, "attacks American capitalism and its power to reduce human lives to someone else's simplest terms" (15). Williams's work would continue to be filled with scenes of abandonment in which people are disdainfully and insensitively treated as less than human until they are worn out from such harsh lives and die alone or are blown away in the wind like Aunt Rose at the close of *The Long Stay Cut Short*, which Williams added to *American Blues* in 1948.

Although Williams despised the capitalist system, which he evoked early on through images of the mindless factory labor suffered through by characters such as Moony, Tom Wingfield, and Ben Murphy, he also admitted that one had to have money. Entering writing competitions as a teenager, Williams, too, was focused on personal success, even while understanding that this would make him part of the system he despised and that success itself would never be entirely satisfying. This conflict created an internal divide in him in which his desire for success as a writer was pitted against his artistic ideals. Williams's constant rewriting can be seen as a reflection of this tension, as he vacillated between wanting to please his audience (and thus maintain his cash flow) and wanting to be true to his art. The rewritten third act of *Cat on a Hot Tin Roof*, in which Maggie's character is softened, Big Daddy is given closure, and Brick chooses to be a husband, is a typical example of this desire to kowtow. Williams preferred his original, harsher, and less crowd-pleasing script, in which Big Daddy dies offstage in agony and Brick merely surrenders to a Maggie who is determined never to be poor.

Bigsby points us toward Williams's essay "The Catastrophe of Success," in which the playwright speaks disparagingly of the Cinderella rags-to-riches story as a "destructive American myth" in which all Cinderella achieves is a "suspect world of tainted wealth" ("Entering" 32). Almost as soon as he began to make money for himself, Williams could not help but berate Americans' obsession with wealth. Using *The Glass Menagerie* to make his point, Bigsby suggests that what the play's characters need more than anything is security, but this is something the Depression years have stripped away: "The pressure which threatens to break not only Laura but all the characters in this St. Louis apartment derive[s], at least in part, from the brutal urgencies of 1930s America, from the imperatives of a society dedicated in the words of Jim, the 'gentleman caller,' to 'Knowledge—Zzzzzp! Money—Zzzzzp!—Power! . . . the cycle democracy is built on!'" (34).

The Wingfields live with the proverbial wolf at the door, and poor Amanda suffers the indignity of modeling brassieres and selling magazine subscriptions over the phone to make ends meet. Finances here are crucial—Laura is clearly unable to support herself, and the loss of Tom's small wage can only bring suffering. Bigsby highlights the play's "sense of social oppression" and suggests that Williams is indicating "not merely that the animating myths of America have failed those who look for some structure to their lives, but that those myths are themselves the root of a destructive materialism or deceptive illusion" (35). In *The Glass Menagerie*, Williams depicts the beginning of an end from which America can never recover; it can only, like Tom, live on in remorse for what has been lost. As Tom tells us at the play's start, the 1930s was a time "when the huge middle class of America was matriculating in a school for the blind. Their eyes had failed them, or they had failed their eyes, and so they were having their fingers pressed forcibly down on the fiery Braille alphabet of a dissolving economy" (*Plays* 400). While war and revolution happened in Spain, America saw only "shouting and confusion" and "disturbances of labor" (400).

The avaricious world of *Cat on a Hot Tin Roof* and the machinations of the Pollitt family indicate Williams's opinion of the true state of American culture. Indeed, the leader of this rapacious group, Big Daddy, in his display of disgust with the mendacity with which the family lives and eventual disdain of his own accumulated fortune, indicates much. His rags-to-riches story makes him the epitome of an American hero, and he undercuts the authenticity of such aims by calling it all "crap," pointing out that "a man can't buy his life with it," and voicing his unhappiness with life despite his wealth (*Plays* 929). As Bigsby suggests, Williams intends these characters who deceive themselves and each other to reflect the world at large (*Critical Introduction* 82), and Big Daddy, despite his discontent, remains an intimidating emblem of acquisition and authority.

Big Daddy, like Jabe Torrance, is dying of cancer (signifying a rottenness at the core), and the evil of both these characters is combined in *Sweet Bird of Youth*'s Boss Finley, an even worse villain in a position of authority. Like Jabe, he is a sanctimonious and malevolent racist, and he is an even more vicious patriarch than Big Daddy. Finley's son bridles under his despotic control, and his daughter's hand in marriage is saved for the highest bidder as fuel for his political campaign, which is based on an insidious platform of racial purity. Money rules Finley's life—his answer to Heavenly's distress is to send her on a shopping spree, and his response to a dying wife is to buy her a big diamond (which is returned to the store as soon as she is dead). Finley's power grab displays the changing lines of power in the South during the 1950s, as businessmen invade the country-club terrain of the old aristocracy. Finley would never allow Heavenly to marry Chance, as Chance lacks the one thing this world reveres: money. Those who have money are secure and use those without it carelessly. The play's putative hero, Chance Wayne, a kept man of rich widows and bored wives who blackmails his current benefactress and is as dispassionately left by her to his fate, is clearly no match for Finley, if, indeed, he is any better. The play reveals a dysfunctional society and, as Thomas P. Adler concludes, a decisive portrayal of "pre-Civil Rights white South's peculiar blend of conservative Protestantism, capitalism, and racism" (658).

While evoking the golden age of an elegant and dignified southern past, encapsulated by the Sunday afternoons in Blue Mountain recalled by Amanda Wingfield, Williams recognized both its pastness and the probable inaccuracy of the depiction as he faced the growing rapacity of modern society. The aristocratic, agrarian economy of the plantation days, though built on the suffering of a slave population, had long been replaced by what seemed to Williams an even harsher industrialized society. Williams's plays are filled with references to creeping American materialism and greed, from Amanda Wingfield's blind insistence that money will solve all her and her children's problems through Stanley Kowalski's suspicion that he has been tricked out of an inheritance; the opulent and acquisitive lifestyles of the families and friends in *Cat on a Hot Tin Roof*, *Sweet Bird of Youth*, and *Suddenly Last Summer*; the well-appointed bungalow in *Period of Adjustment*; and even the lyncher in *Orpheus Descending*, who, Weales reminds us, pauses a moment to rob the till (25).

In *Period of Adjustment*, Williams asks us to envisage a house built over a cavern into which it is slowly sinking—an evident symbol for a society bent on self-destruction. It is a society dominated by cash. Dorothea, having been virtually sold to Ralph by her father as part of a business merger, and having left her husband at the play's start for quitting his job, is repurchased for the price of a beaver coat. Ralph tells her he bought the coat as a Christmas gift, but neglects to tell her he has already given the coat instead to visiting newlywed Isabel as a wedding present. Ralph and Dorothea's relationship is as precarious as their dwelling and the ownership of the coat. As Alycia Smith-Howard and Greta Heintzelman suggest, the play's surface shallowness, about which some critics have complained, "is a dramatic device that serves as a critical commentary on modern American society" (207). Its quintessentially American couples betoken Williams's belief that the suburban communities growing in this era were destined for failure, as they had no solid foundation and the relationships within them continued to be built on financial transactions. When Dorothea's parents arrive and begin berating Ralph, they are less concerned with their daughter's happiness than with her joint bank account and with their intended retrieval of a television set.

Suddenly Last Summer also depicts the soul-destroying dangers of American materialism. Robert Siegel observes that the sexual activity in *Suddenly Last Summer* "has the quality of imperialism, the rich Yankee flinging coins to the poor in exchange for favors" (21), and Steven Bruhm has written compellingly of Sebastian's commodity mentality

(530-31), describing the play's lurid scene of cannibalism as designed to collapse "the barrier between the city and the jungle. The city had tried to transform the primal need for consumption—into an orderly, regulated system of trade. But by collapsing back into its primal, repressed form, the jungle exposes the underside of consumption upon which the city is founded" (533). The real corruption of Sebastian is not his homosexuality but a careless wealth that leads him to use others as commodities. As Siegel points out, "the playwright's punishment for the devourer is to be devoured" (22), but in real life Williams knew that the devourers continued to rule the roost.

A romantic idealist who forced himself to acknowledge increasingly sordid realities, Williams became an apocalyptic playwright, heralding the inevitable decline of the American way of life. *The Demolition Downtown* (1971) depicts guerrilla warfare in a post-Cold War America, where the opulent suburbs are reduced to the survival of the fittest. It is as though the house in *Period of Adjustment* has plummeted headlong into that threatening cavern, and its inhabitants seem hardly to have noticed. The Lanes still boast of their Jaguar car even as their home literally crumbles around them, suggesting the blind materialism that may have led them to such an implosion.

From the Puritanical roots that guided the Founding Fathers, Williams sees America as having evolved into a masculine culture of strength and power based on capitalistic business principles; this culture prides itself on its competitiveness and aggression—values that are clearly at odds with Williams's preferred feminized culture of grace and gentility, which he encodes in his rose-tinted visions of the Old South and his sensitive romantic questers. Life, for Williams, becomes one long sellout as we all seek the money we need to be accepted and survive in what has become an unremittingly materialistic society. The Protestant work ethic is transmuted into a cult of success in which harsh Darwinian principles of survival dictate behavior, and people obey the urge to get rich quick using whatever means are available. Such behavior, antagonistic to community values, prevents rather than encourages connection and makes wariness of the outsider, or Other, endemic. In other words, it is American culture—rather than themselves—that prevents Williams's characters from finding spiritual fulfillment, and his plays can be read as illustrations of that evolving culture.

The Milk Train Doesn't Stop Here Anymore provides a vivid illustration of Williams's belief that the Edenic potential of America has been thwarted by the nation's wealth. In this play, the elderly Flora Goforth, having survived six husbands, finally succumbs to lung cancer, another victim of her own innate rottenness. The golden griffin banner she flies indicates a predatory nature, and the description of her 1924 costume of Lady Godiva, "All of me gilded, my whole body painted gold, except for—green velvet fig leaves" (*"Cat" and Other Plays* 159), evokes a materialized Eve. Goforth has led an intensely materialistic life, for which she will die unhappy and with little to show for it as Chris Flanders calmly removes the jewels from her fingers.

Traveling all over the United States throughout more than seven decades, Williams collected the images, phrases, ideas, and details that he would craft into plays, which can be read alongside those of Arthur Miller or August Wilson as chronicles of twentieth-century America—at least the century from Williams's perspective. Williams's identification as an American is quintessential to his art. He was proud of his relation to the nineteenth-century American poet Sidney Lanier, raised in a small southern town, and descended from pioneers and colonial settlers. Yet, as he once confessed to Kent Demaret, "I've always found life unsatisfactory" (34). As Tischler suggests, Williams was one of the "fugitive kind" about whom he so often wrote: "He lived his life as a peripatetic poet, one of the everlasting company of fugitives who discover their vocation in their art, transforming experience and giving shape to visions" ("Romantic Textures" 147). Williams was old-stock American, yet, ironically, he saw himself as a perennial outsider. This status was doubly conferred on him as both an artist and a homosexual. And we should see a connection here, as did Williams when he equated homosexuality to artistic genius: both force a person to live on the boundaries of mainstream society, and, in America, particularly, with its ingrained anti-intellectualism, both are viewed with deep suspicion and generally reviled. It is unsurprising that Williams felt the world was antagonistic toward him, as it was to everything he held dear.

While David Savran and John M. Clum are unhappy with what they see as Williams's critiques of homosexual experience, identifying an evident self-loathing, Tischler points out that "Williams was never an unambiguous advocate of homosexuality" (*Student Companion* 98). He never advocated for gay rights or described being homosexual as a happy condition, because for him, growing up in a country that predominantly viewed homosexuality as a perversion or pathological abnormality, it could not be. His anguished response was more a reflection of the contemporary attitude toward homosexuals, as throughout the twentieth century Americans continued to argue about whether homosexuality is inborn or a lifestyle choice. In such a climate, especially for a sensitive individual, how could any moment of sexual satisfaction not be followed by feelings of guilt and self-contempt?

Jack Fritscher suggests that Williams's plays reveal "the more difficult dichotomies of the interior American experience" (7), and, as Tischler continues, "Williams believed that the two conflicting strains in his own nature, the Puritan and the Cavalier, were also present in American thought. Neither Blanche nor Stanley, the spirit nor the flesh, is a proper expression of the fully developed human being" (*Student Companion* 50). We see this battle between culture and barbarism throughout his work, displayed as beauty versus truth, idealism versus reality, romanticism versus antiromanticism—contrary opposites, in Williams's view, that can never easily rest together.

These dualisms are conveyed by the struggles between spirit and flesh that are so frequently depicted in his work. In *Summer and Smoke*, for example, John and his flagrant sexuality are pitted against the more spiritual Alma, whose name means soul, in an irresolvable battle between flesh and spirit. The play ends, however, with John marrying the conventional Nellie and Alma seducing a salesman, suggesting that the ultimate winner in every contest is a conservative, business-minded America. Salesmen appear sporadically in Williams's work and seem to represent the destructive potential of business, which continues to win out over spiritual concerns.

As other critics have observed, there is a religious underpinning to Williams's work. Filled with references to saints, rituals, angels, and Christ figures, the plays display Williams's quest for meaning alongside his understanding that such meaning can never be attained. What lies behind this is his implicit understanding that, in America, the true religion is materialism. In *The Night of the Iguana*, the defrocked priest, Shannon, objects to the materialistic corruption of the world and the church he used to represent, reminding Hannah that religion was brought to the Americas by "gold-hungry Conquistadors that bore the flag of the Inquisition along with the cross of Christ" (*"Cat" and Other Plays* 270). Religion, wealth, and violence have long been integrated in American history. Delma Eugene Presley suggests that the "long delayed but always expected something" for which the Wingfields, especially Tom and Amanda, wait is really the Messiah, who will herald the end to their problems (277). Of course, it is Jim who arrives, less a messiah than an indication of future concerns with making money and fitting in as we learn all about Jim's plans to succeed in the business world he so admires. *Streetcar*'s Blanche DuBois's "hope" rests on the shadowy businessman Shep Huntleigh; Chance Wayne's in *Sweet Bird of Youth* relies on his Hollywood contacts; and Maggie the Cat, despite Robert Siegel's assertion that she "is no mercenary" (23), can be viewed as ultimately in it for the money. While Maggie may love Brick, she is also practical: "It takes money to take care of a drinker," she says, and, "You've got to be old *with* money because to be old without it is just too awful" (*Plays* 907-8). At the bottom line, money determines everyone's behavior. Everyone gets sucked into the materialistic world, just as Williams himself found as his desire for fame and comfort clashed with his artistic goals.

While Williams's plays contain few overt references to specific periods, an awareness of social trends exists in the background of each. *A Streetcar Named Desire*, for example, is keenly aware of the expanding postwar urban-industrialized society of the late 1940s, with Stanley as the brute, naturalistic force of the future of the city. Responding to a postnuclear, post-Freudian age of anxiety full of political and social upheaval, the edginess of the play, with its loose structure and moral ambivalence, was well suited to its era and spoke to it powerfully. The boldness of the play's sexuality excited the fantasies of a nation too long repressed. References to the recent war (Blanche's meetings with off-duty soldiers and the past military service of Stanley and his friends) give the play a realistic immediacy, and Stanley's victory over Blanche points to the direction in which Williams saw American society as heading. Stanley's rejection of the past and selfish concentration on what he needs out of life suggest a brutal future. The play's message, which, according to Williams, is "If we don't watch out, the apes will take over" (quoted in Tischler, *Rebellious Puritan* 137), indicates that the play was intended as a warning.

One of Williams's more openly political plays is *Camino Real*. With its images of a totalitarian regime—in which those with whom the despotic ringmaster, Gutman, is displeased get killed and thrown in the dustbin—the play betokens Williams's distrust of government power at a time when the House Un-American Activities Committee (HUAC) was investigating thousands of Americans, especially artists and entertainers, for supposed Communist ties, ruining many careers and lives in the process. Fearful of the mounting power of the Soviet Union, during the 1940s and 1950s America underwent a profound period of paranoia as HUAC as well as Senator Joseph McCarthy hounded anyone in any position of authority who was suspected of having Communist sympathies and pressured them to name others with similar sympathies to prove their own loyalty to the nation. While the program had begun with State Department officials, it soon targeted the more public sphere of entertainment.

The world of *Camino Real* suggests a kind of purgatory from which there is no real escape, a place in which Williams had seen many people he knew and respected become trapped as HUAC began to take an interest in their political opinions. Building on Esther Merle Jackson's observations in *The Broken World of Tennessee Williams*, Jan Balakian explains how "the play's division into sixteen stations represents missionary stations. In twentieth-century America, however, the old missionary way has become a street of commerce" (75). On this street, which Williams took pains to get people to pronounce as the Anglicanized "reel," money oils the wheels of social as well as business interaction and no one can be trusted, even those one tries to love. Kilroy, with his oversize heart and fighting spirit, represents an American Everyman caught in a social wasteland that clearly reflects the oppressive conservatism of the McCarthy era. While some, like Byron, Don Quixote, and even Kilroy, may seem to make an imaginative escape, the majority of the characters are left behind to Gutman and his intimidating Street Cleaners. As Michael Paller observes, "The Romantics want to live life honorably, but lack the bravery to face down Gutman and engage in what is now called 'regime change'" (108). The forbidden word *hermano* (brother) can remain only a whisper in the dark.

The idea that one can be restricted and ruined for speaking one's mind (a common result of that era's HUAC trials) is dramatized in *Suddenly Last Summer*'s Catherine, whose truths the family attempts to bury not only out of a squeamish conservatism but also out of financial greed. Sebastian's harsh Darwinian vision of predatory birds attacking defenseless turtles remains one of the most memorable images of the play. These birds return in 1966's *The Gnädiges Fräulein*, in which all the characters live under the constant threat of the swooping Cocaloony birds. One of Williams's favorite plays, *The Gnädiges Fräulein* depicts a group of destitute outsiders struggling to survive, with the title character losing her teeth and both eyes in the process. She is a victim of her own ambitions, unable to rest in life as she runs to the dock at the play's close in her never-ending battle with the birds. The continuation of a life like hers is hard to view as any kind of victory.

In a 1979 interview, Williams remarked: "I think the 1980s are going to be terrifying because we simply cannot feed all the people on the earth. When the middle class gets hungry, we could have Armageddon. I don't want to be around to see it" (Demaret 34). *The Red Devil Battery Sign*, which, Williams tells us, "deals with the progression of moral decay in today's society" ("New Williams Play" L40), depicts this sense of impending apocalypse. Williams's response to both the assassination of President John F. Kennedy and the Vietnam War, it is a play rife with conspiracy. As Smith-Howard and Heintzelman suggest, the theme of entrapment in the play "carries over as a metaphor for the entire nation, which after many political fallouts has become trapped in the 'new world order'" (219). Williams presents an America ruled by a sinister corporation that has engineered genocide to protect its investments and has dehumanized its workers and destroyed those it cannot control. The Woman Downtown, who appears in a gown of gold, a sign of the constricting wealth and privilege into which she was born, holds documents that could expose the corporation. Her passion for King Del Rey allows her to step out of her confining golden sheath and regain her humanity for a time, but his brain tumor ensures his eventual death and leads her to turn her back on society as she joins a wolflike pack of delinquents at the play's close. The consonance of Del Rey and Red Devil may hint that the two are connected, that money lies at the core of Del Rey's existence as much as it does the corporation's. Del Rey has, after all, always been driven by a desire to succeed, and he resents his wife's financial support, which eats away at him more than the tumor. As Colby H. Kullman suggests, *The Red Devil Battery Sign* presents "another broken world where money talks," in which "the redemptive powers of love prove fleeting and powerless" and "disorder and chaos turn into an ever-darkening landscape of cosmic evil" (195-96).

Williams's plays are filled with images of confinement and restriction. The majority of his characters are essentially trapped, be it in a shabby apartment, a rooming house, a prison, an asylum, or a workplace, and find only momentary glimpses of relief, most commonly through short-lived sexual liaisons. "Although considered by many an immoral, even a pornographic artist," Tischler asserts of Williams, "his most obscene gestures are often a groping for human community—not really for sexual experience" (*Student Companion* 24). Tischler suggests that *Out Cry/The Two-Character Play* is the "perfect work to sum up Williams because it reflects perfectly his vision of the world" (*Student Companion* 158). Its focus on a pair of siblings trapped in a love/hate relationship with their parents in a prisonlike setting with madness on the horizon can also be seen as a recursion of *The Glass Menagerie*. Williams's lifelong guilt over what he saw as his selfish abandonment of his sister, Rose, can be understood as emblematic for him of the American way, and these figures echo throughout his work. *Out Cry* presents a theatrical nightmare in which everything is uncertain—from audience to location—and we watch as two characters try to find their place within an uncertain script, attempt a fruitless escape, and end by creating a false reality to hold the past at bay, an agreed fiction that becomes their only sustenance. It is a bare-bones representation of the nightmare of Williams's own existence, his art being his means of survival in a harsh world.

Ruby Cohn points to the title of Williams's final play, *A House Not Meant to Stand*, as indicative of his continued view of America as a corrupt user culture: "The house is explicitly designated as a metaphor for the state of society" (233). Echoing earlier plots, the play depicts a redneck politician trying to institutionalize his wife to gain her wealth. With this last play, Williams remained consistent in his vision of America as colored by the racism, materialism, and entrapment that he had seen emerge during the harsh Depression years, only worsening as the century progressed. Williams set out to tell the truth, and he was right—it is shocking.

Works Cited

Adler, Thomas P. "Culture, Power, and the (En)gendering of Community: Tennessee Williams and Politics." *Mississippi Quarterly* 48.4 (1995): 649-65.

Balakian, Jan. "*Camino Real*: Williams's Allegory About the Fifties." *The Cambridge Companion to Tennessee Williams*. Ed. Matthew C. Roudané. New York: Cambridge UP, 1997. 67-94.

Barnes, Clive. "Williams's Eccentricities." *The New York Times* 24 Sept. 1974: sec. 2, 25.

Bigsby, C. W. E. *A Critical Introduction to Twentieth-Century American Drama*. Vol. 2. New York: Cambridge UP, 1984.

_____. "Entering *The Glass Menagerie*." *The Cambridge Companion to Tennessee Williams*. Ed. Matthew C. Roudané. New York: Cambridge UP, 1997. 29-44.

Bray, Robert. "*Battle of Angels* and *Orpheus Descending*." *Tennessee Williams: A Guide to Research and Performance*. Ed. Philip C. Kolin. Westport, CT: Greenwood Press, 1998. 22-33.

Bruhm, Steven. "Blackmailed by Sex: Tennessee Williams and the Economics of Desire." *Modern Drama* 34.4 (1991): 528-37.

Clum, John M. *Acting Gay: Male Homosexuality in American Drama*. New York: Columbia UP, 1992.

Cohn, Ruby. "Tennessee Williams: The Last Two Decades." *The Cambridge Companion to Tennessee Williams*. Ed. Matthew C. Roudané. New York: Cambridge UP, 1997. 232-43.

Demaret, Kent. "In His Beloved Key West, Tennessee Williams Is Center Stage in a Furor over Gays." *People* 7 May 1979: 32-35.

Fritscher, Jack. "Love and Death in Tennessee Williams." Ph.D. dissertation, Loyola University, 1967.

Gassner, John. "Tennessee Williams: Dramatist of Frustration." *Critical Essays on Tennessee Williams*. Ed. Robert A. Martin. New York: G. K. Hall, 1997. 234-42.

Jackson, Esther Merle. *The Broken World of Tennessee Williams*. Madison: U of Wisconsin P, 1965.

Kullman, Colby H. "*The Red Devil Battery Sign*." *Tennessee Williams: A Guide to Research and Performance*. Ed. Philip C. Kolin. Westport, CT: Greenwood Press, 1998. 194-203.

Lester, Neal A. "*American Blues*." *Tennessee Williams: A Guide to Research and Performance*. Ed. Philip C. Kolin. Westport, CT: Greenwood Press, 1998. 13-21.

"New Williams Play Set for August 12." *The New York Times* 12 May 1975: L40.

Pagan, Nicholas O. *Rethinking Literary Biography: A Postmodern Approach to Tennessee Williams*. Rutherford, NJ: Fairleigh Dickinson UP, 1993.

Paller, Michael. "A Playwright with a Social Conscience." *Tennessee Williams Annual Review* 10 (2009): 105-10.

Presley, Delma Eugene. "The Search for Hope in the Plays of Tennessee Williams." *Critical Essays on Tennessee Williams*. Ed. Robert A. Martin. New York: G. K. Hall, 1997. 276-85.

Saddik, Annette J. "'Blueprints for the Reconstruction': Postmodern Possibility in *Stairs to the Roof*." *Tennessee Williams Annual Review* 9 (2007): 67-75.

Savran, David. *Communists, Cowboys, and Queers: The Politics of Masculinity in the Works of Arthur Miller and Tennessee Williams*. Minneapolis: U of Minnesota P, 1992.

Siegel, Robert. "The Metaphysics of Tennessee Williams." *American Drama* 10.1 (2001): 11-37.

Smith-Howard, Alycia, and Greta Heintzelman. *Critical Companion to Tennessee Williams*. New York: Facts On File, 2005.

Tischler, Nancy M. "Romantic Textures in Williams's Plays and Short Stories." *The Cambridge Companion to Tennessee Williams*. Ed. Matthew C. Roudané. New York: Cambridge UP, 1997. 147-66.

_____. *Student Companion to Tennessee Williams*. Westport, CT: Greenwood Press, 2000.

_____. *Tennessee Williams: Rebellious Puritan*. New York: Citadel, 1961.

Weales, Gerald. *Tennessee Williams*. Minneapolis: U of Minnesota P, 1965.

Williams, Tennessee. *"Cat on a Hot Tin Roof" and Other Plays*. New York: Penguin, 1976.

_____. *Conversations with Tennessee Williams*. Ed. Albert J. Devlin. Jackson: UP of Mississippi, 1986.

_____. *Fugitive Kind*. 1937. New York: New Directions, 2001.

_____. *The Knightly Quest: A Novella and Twelve Short Stories*. London: Secker & Warburg, 1968.

_____. Letter to Audrey Wood. 1939. Tennessee Williams Collection, Harry Ransom Humanities Resource Center, University of Texas, Austin.

_____. *Plays 1937-1955*. New York: Library of America, 2000.

_____. *The Selected Letters of Tennessee Williams*. Vol. 1. Ed. Albert J. Devlin and Nancy M. Tischler. New York: New Directions, 2000.

"Getting the Colored Lights Going":
Expressionism in Tennessee Williams's
*A Streetcar Named Desire*_____

Henry I. Schvey

Long before he remade himself into "Tennessee Williams," young Thomas Lanier Williams submitted a one-act play to a college playwriting contest for Professor William G. B. Carson's English 16 class at Washington University in St. Louis. The year was 1937, and it seemed to Williams's classmates a foregone conclusion that the contribution by the twenty-five-year-old undergraduate, who had already had two plays produced (*Fugitive Kind* and *Candles to the Sun*, both in 1937) by The Mummers, a local avant-garde theater company, would be chosen as the winner of the contest and its fifty-dollar prize. They had already seen evidence of the young man's extraordinary talent in a series of short sketches based on his home life that he had produced for the class. Classmate A. E. Hotchner described them as "the most wonderful, little fragile vignettes about a mother and daughter and a son in St. Louis," leading him to conclude they were precursors to Willams's first great Broadway success, *The Glass Menagerie* (1944). "They were quite lyrical," he continued, "and we took it for granted that he would turn in a play based on these people" (quoted in Givens 30). But instead of a play based on these intimate domestic scenes, Williams submitted a bizarre little work, "Me, Vashya," about a megalomaniac arms manufacturer named Sir Vashya Shontine, who has locked his mentally unbalanced, aristocratic wife in their bedroom and "whose secret operations virtually control the affairs of all nations participating in the next world war" (1). As the play opens, Vashya is seated at his desk, smoking a cigar before the bust of some great dictator, "meditatively twirling a large globe of the world, which, throughout most of the play, he . . . twirls or strokes with his fingers" (1). At the end of the play, his neurasthenic, delusional wife, who bears a fascinating resemblance to Blanche DuBois, emerges from her bedroom wielding a gun and avenges her dead lover, whom Vashya has sent to the front, along with countless other young men whose deaths her husband has been responsible for. "Don't you see them, Vashya?" she says of the imaginary soldiers marching before her, "They're all coming into this room. They're standing around you now. They're waiting for you to go with them" (20).

The reaction from Williams's fellow students seems to have been one of amusement and contempt. Hotchner called the play "pretentious pap" (quoted in Givens 30), while another classmate, Martyl Schweig, observed that "my recollection of his droning voice and boring play [is that they] prompted me to do my next class' homework during the reading" (quoted in Leverich 216). Devastated by his "honorable mention," Williams refused to attend the ceremony honoring the winners at the university's Graham Chapel. His notebook entry for June 4, 1937, suggests the level of his anger and frustration: "Never a more ignominious failure! My play for English 16 rejected for presentation—given fourth place—Went to Carson's office this morning and he gave me the news—without any apparent compunction—But why should I expect sympathy from anyone—especially a Washington University Professor—the stronghold of the Reactionaries!" (*Notebooks* 89).

Shortly after the humiliation of "Me, Vashya," Williams failed his final examination in Greek and was obliged to leave Washington University. His state of mind at this time is reflected in the following entry: "Having no self-respect one doesn't have the pain of losing it. I am so used to being a worm that the condition seldom troubles me. Now I face the problem of the summer—What will I do? Heaven knows" (quoted in Leverich 214).

The point about this humiliation is that it was the first (though hardly the last) instance in which the playwright's artistic intentions were misunderstood by his public. Though the play was assumed to be a realistic (if highly pretentious) depiction of world affairs as Williams knew them, with the character of Vashya loosely based on self-made arms titan Sir Basil Zaharoff (who had, like Vashya, married into royalty), the playwright later observed that "Me, Vashya" was never supposed to be the realistic work his fellow students anticipated but instead was intended as "melodramatic fantasy" (quoted in Leverich 216).

Sixteen years later, a much more conspicuous and highly publicized failure, *Camino Real* (1953), fell victim to an audience similarly bewildered by the play's experimental structure and vision. As Williams observed caustically, "At each performance a number of people have stamped out of the auditorium, with little regard for those whom they have had to crawl over, almost as if the building had caught on fire, and there have been sibilant noises on the way out and demands for money back if the cashier was foolish enough to remain in his box" (*Where I Live* 65). Having grown used to the remarkable characters and lyricism of *The Glass Menagerie* and *A Streetcar Named Desire* (1947), audiences emphatically rejected Williams's desire to provide "my own sense of something wild and unrestricted that ran like water in the mountains, or clouds changing shape in a gale, of the continually dissolving and transforming images of a dream" (*Where I Live* 64).

In his foreword to *Camino Real,* the playwright persuasively argued that "this sort of freedom is not chaos or anarchy . . . it is the result of painstaking design, [and I paid] more conscious attention to form and construction than I have in any work before" (*Where I Live* 64). Nonetheless, hostile reviews indicate that audiences were unwilling to join with him on a journey heavily influenced by August Strindberg's *A Dream Play* (1902) and employing archetypal rather than three-dimensional characters and an episodic structure connected loosely by symbols instead of a linear plot. The critical failure of a work like *Camino Real* illustrates the profound division in audiences' reception of Williams's work when he strayed from the psychological realism and psychologically complex characterization for which he was (and is) rightly acclaimed in favor of a fluid, abstract dramaturgy with aims similar to those of the experimental poetry, drama, and visual arts associated with the later work of Strindberg and the German expressionists.

Although its chief impact was in the German-speaking countries during the so-called expressionist decade of 1910-1925, expressionist style had a significant impact on American drama of the 1920s and 1930s, and its influence can be found in the work of such figures as Eugene O'Neill (*The Emperor Jones*, 1920; *The Hairy Ape*, 1922; *The Great God Brown*, 1926), Sophie Treadwell (*Machinal*, 1928), Elmer Rice (*The Adding Machine*, 1923), and Thornton Wilder (*Our Town*, 1938).[1]

What was it that drove these and other American dramatists toward expressionism? According to O'Neill, it was the notion that theater ought not to reflect petty or mundane activity but rather should provide "refuge from the facts of life which . . . have nothing to do with the truth," bringing us "deep into the unknown within and behind ourselves" (Valgemae, "Expressionism" 196). Or, as Swiss artist Paul Klee noted in a maxim at the opening of his "Creative Confession," "Art does not seek to reproduce the visible, it makes visible the invisible" (quoted in Weisstein 23; translation mine). What expressionist art seeks to render, whether on canvas, in words, or in music, is the human being's inner life, the "extreme moods, such as numinous fear or ecstatic joy, externalized by means of projection and outwardly manifesting themselves as distortions of color, shape, syntax, vocabulary or tonal relationships" (Weisstein 23).

As noted above, Williams's greatest strength as a playwright was his indelible creation of character—especially the lonely, vulnerable outcasts who people his dramas: Amanda and Laura Wingfield in *The Glass Menagerie*, Blanche DuBois in *A Streetcar Named Desire*, Brick in *Cat on a Hot Tin Roof* (1955), Alma in *Summer and Smoke* (1947). As the playwright observed: "My characters make my play. I always start with them, they take spirit and body in my mind. Nothing they say or do is arbitrary or invented. They build the play about them like spiders weaving their webs, sea creatures making their shells. . . . I know them far better than I know myself, since I created them and not myself" (*Where I Live* 72).

However, in Williams's work there is, as suggested above, another tendency: the temptation to challenge audiences with unconventional, nonrealistic stage techniques. The production notes to his first great success, *The Glass Menagerie*, underscore this ambition to create a new kind of theater:

> Expressionism and all other unconventional techniques in drama have only one valid aim, and that is a closer approach to truth. When a play employs unconventional techniques, it is not, or certainly shouldn't be, trying to escape its responsibility of dealing with reality, or interpreting experience, but is actually or should be attempting to find a closer approach, a more penetrating and vivid expression of things as they are. The straight realistic play with its genuine Frigidaire and authentic ice-cubes, its characters who speak exactly as its audience speaks, corresponds to the academic landscape and has the same virtue of a photographic likeness. Everyone should know nowadays the unimportance of the photographic in art: that truth, life, or reality is an organic thing which the poetic imagination can represent or suggest, in essence, only through transformation, through changing into other art forms than those which were merely present in appearance. (*Glass Menagerie* xix)

What Williams argues for in *The Glass Menagerie* is nothing less than a new way of thinking about the theater that goes beyond conventional realism to pursue inner truth, or, as expressionist critic Kasimir Edschmid pithily observed, "The world is already here. It would be senseless to repeat it" (Weisstein 23; translation mine). Williams goes further to argue not only that this vision is present in *The Glass Menagerie*, the play that provided the occasion for his production notes, but also that it is part of an overall aspiration toward "a new, plastic theatre which must take the place of the exhausted theatre of realistic conventions if the theatre is to assume vitality as a part of our culture" (*Glass Menagerie* xix).

In order to illustrate how this new plastic theater might operate in practice, Williams proposed a number of specific design elements for *Menagerie,* including a musical leitmotif, a single recurring theme for Tom Wingfield's sister, Laura, that is "like circus music" and "weaves in and out of your pre-occupied consciousness" (xxi). He also advocated nonrealistic lighting in which "shafts of light are focused on selected areas or actors, sometimes in contradistinction to what is the apparent center," proposing that the light on Laura Wingfield be distinct from that on the other characters, "having a pristine clarity such as light used in early religious portraits of female saints or madonnas" (xxi-xxii). Finally, he encouraged the use of a "screen device" intended to project "magic-lantern slides bearing images or titles," which would "give accent to certain values in each scene" (xx). Unfortunately, the playwright's argument to employ this screen device (somewhat clumsily borrowed from Bertolt Brecht) was undercut by the fact that even in the original Broadway production it was omitted, although Williams tried to justify its omission by arguing that "the extraordinary power of Miss [Laurette] Taylor's performance made it suitable to have the utmost simplicity in the physical production" (xx). Not surprisingly, in later productions of *Menagerie* the screen device has seldom been employed. Despite the playwright's passionate exhortations for expressionist techniques to replace "the exhausted theatre of realistic conventions," this early play is often produced as realist drama bookended by the monologues of its narrator, Tom Wingfield, rather than as the expressionist drama it was conceived as. However, a purely realist production of *Menagerie* weakens the playwright's dramaturgical aims and allows an audience to forget that "the play is memory. Being a memory play, it is dimly lighted, it is sentimental, it is *not realistic*" (5; emphasis mine).

While in many of Williams's plays the marriage between character and symbol, between realist and expressionist production values, may seem uneasy or artificial, in one play in particular this union is absolutely seamless: *A Streetcar Named Desire.* In *Streetcar* as in no other American play (with the possible exception of Arthur Miller's *Death of a Salesman*, 1949), realistic characterization and expressionistic stagecraft are held in perfect equipoise, creating a tragedy that is completely satisfying as an aesthetic whole. Color, lighting, sound, and stage images consistently operate on two levels simultaneously, both enhancing the realistic journey of Blanche's arrival and eventual removal from the Kowalski home in the French Quarter and highlighting her internalized descent into madness.

As a playwright, Tennessee Williams was acutely aware of both the power and the limitations of the word. We know that he often tested out theatrical ideas in purely literary forms, such as poetry or short stories, including "Portrait of a Girl in Glass" (written 1942, published 1948), which contains the germ of *Menagerie*, and "Three Players of a Summer Game" (1952), which describes the arc of *Cat on a Hot Tin Roof*. But he was also cognizant that the theater is a visual art form, always more than mere *literature*. As he wrote to critic Brooks Atkinson:

> A book is only the shadow of a play and not even a clear shadow of it. . . . The printed script of a play is hardly more than an architect's blueprint of a house not yet built or built and destroyed. The color, the grace and levitation, the structural pattern in motion, the quick interplay of live beings, suspended like fitful lightning in a cloud, these things are the play, not words on paper. (quoted in Murphy 95)

For Williams, theater, then, is a highly visual art as well as a verbal one. In his *Memoirs*, he makes a trenchant observation about the power of painting to express emotion nonverbally:

> The work of a fine painter, committed only to vision, abstract and allusive as he pleases, is better able to create for you his moments of intensely perceptive being. Jackson Pollock could paint ecstasy as it could not be written. Van Gogh could capture for you moments of beauty, indescribably as descent into madness. (316)

In this context, it is significant that one of the original titles for *Street-car* was "The Poker Night," and that even after the title of the work as a whole was ultimately changed to *Streetcar*, he titled the play's third scene "The Poker Night," the only scene in the play that bears its own title. "The Poker Night" refers to a painting by Vincent van Gogh, *The Night Café* (1888), and the importance of this reference is indicated by the playwright's intricately detailed description of the *Streetcar* scene:

> There is a picture of Van Gogh's of a billiard-parlor at night. The kitchen now suggests that sort of lurid nocturnal brilliance, the raw colors of child-hood's spectrum. Over the yellow linoleum of the kitchen table hangs an electric bulb with a vivid green glass shade. The poker players—Stanley, Steve, Mitch and Pablo—wear colored shirts, solid blues, a purple, a red-and-white check, a light green, and they are men at the peak of their physi-cal manhood, as coarse and direct and powerful as the primary colors. There are vivid slices of watermelon on the table, whiskey bottles and glasses. For a moment, there is absorbed silence as a hand is dealt. (45)

It is obvious from this description that the playwright has taken consid-erable pains to "paint" this scene down to the most precise details of color and shape. The "absorbed silence" in the stage directions is a par-ticular clue that Williams wanted the action to pause for a beat to allow the audience to register the image as a *tableau vivant* before a word is spoken. However, Williams's choice to reference the van Gogh paint-ing would be little more than an interesting curiosity were it not that, like van Gogh, the dramatist is concerned not merely with the external but also with the internal depiction of emotion. *The Night Café*, which has been called van Gogh's "most expressionist painting" (Masina 29), is dominated by sharp color contrasts—the deep red walls and yellow floor contrast with the dark green of the coffin-shaped billiard table, which, set diagonally in the middle of the room, casts an ominous shadow. The eeriness of the scene is further conveyed by the figure of a landlord in a white coat, who faces the viewer from behind the table, and especially by the four lamps suspended from the ceiling and surrounded by circles of vibrating yellow light. In a letter to his brother, Theo, van Gogh describes the scene thus:

> In my picture of the Night Café, I have tried to express the idea that the café is a place where one can destroy oneself, go mad or commit a crime. In short, I have tried, by contrasting soft pink with blood-red and wine-red, soft Louis XV-green and Veronese green with yellow-greens and harsh blue-greens, all this in an atmosphere of an infernal furnace in pale sulphur, to express the powers of darkness in a common tavern. And yet under an outward show of Japanese gaiety and Tartarin's good nature. (van Gogh 399)

Just as Van Gogh attempted to create dynamic tension between the nature of this infernal world and the trappings of a simple café, so Williams uses color and shape—"the raw colors of childhood's spectrum"—to mask the harshness of a world "as coarse and direct as the primary colors" (*Streetcar* 45). Significantly, the scene begins with the line "Anything wild this deal?" and climaxes with Stanley violently hurling a radio out the window, striking Stella, and being forcibly restrained by the other poker players, who grapple with him and toss him into a cold shower to make him recover his senses. The scene concludes with a virtuoso stroke: the iconic reconciliation between Stanley and Stella in which he "throws back his head like a baying hound and bellows his wife's name" before the couple "come together with low animal moans" (59).

In this scene, Williams transforms the raffish French Quarter into a world of primordial, junglelike violence just as the protoexpressionist van Gogh transformed a simple café into an image of hell. It is a world in which Blanche DuBois is at first lost, then trapped, and finally destroyed. As she says to Stella the next morning, dazed and confused by the violence and her sister's submission to her husband's bestial sexuality:

Thousands and thousands of years have passed him right by, and there he is—Stanley Kowalski—survivor of the Stone Age! Bearing the raw meat home from the kill in the jungle! . . . Night falls and other apes gather! There in front of the cave, all grunting like him, swilling and gnawing and hulking! His poker night!—you call—this party of apes! (72)

Creating a savage, barbaric world underlying the ordinary domestic activity of a game of cards, the playwright employs harsh colors and violent distortion precisely as van Gogh and later expressionists such as Emil Nolde and Ernst Ludwig Kirchner did to suggest a subtle relationship between the surface veneer of the everyday and the howling dance of archetypal violence lurking underneath.

Were Williams simply alluding to this expressionist use of color in a single scene avowedly based on van Gogh's painting, it might not be terribly significant. However, the violent antagonism between Blanche and Stanley throughout the entire play is best understood through powerful contrasts in the uses of color, just as color contrasts are used to convey emotion in expressionist painting.

From the very beginning of the play, Williams makes it apparent that Blanche is to be identified with a moth: "Her delicate beauty must avoid a strong light. There is something about her uncertain manner, as well as her white clothes, that suggests a moth" (15).[2] By contrast, Stanley, her antagonist and ultimately her executioner, is associated with those primary colors to which she may be drawn like a moth to a flame, but which will finally destroy her. When we first see Stanley, he carries a "blood-stained package from a butcher's," which he tosses up to his wife, actions suggestive of both his primitive, animal nature and his sexual energy, recalling the playwright's stage directions in which we are informed that "he sizes women up at a glance, with sexual classifications, crude images flashing into his mind and determining the way he smiles at them" (29).

Throughout the play, Stanley is associated with harsh, primary colors in contrast to Blanche's pale, mothlike delicacy. His "gaudy pajamas" lie across the threshold of the bathroom in scene 4; in scene 5, he wears a green-and-scarlet bowling shirt (which he wears again at the beginning of the rape scene), and he waves a brilliantly colored pajama top as a flag just before his assault on Blanche. Even when not directly associated with the primary colors through costume, Stanley's speech reinforces a visual connection between his person and these bright, harsh colors. His pet name for sexual intercourse is to "get the colored lights going," and the evening of the rape he terms "a red-letter night" for both himself and Blanche. Moreover, in his stage directions the playwright refers to Stanley as a "richly feathered male bird" and "gaudy seed-bearer" (29).

Blanche, as her name suggests, is obviously most often associated with the color white, stressing her essential purity, even innocence, as she enters the jungle of the French Quarter seeking refuge.[3] DuBois, she tells Mitch, "means woods and Blanche means white, so the two together mean white woods. Like an orchard in spring! You can remember it by that" (54-55). The first words spoken to Blanche by Eunice are "What's the matter, honey? Are you lost?," suggesting her singular appearance in the Quarter as she arrives in her "white suit with fluffy bodice, necklace and earrings of pearl, white gloves and hat" (15). In view of the associations made between Blanche and whiteness, it is interesting to note that in the "Poker Night" scene Williams specifically identifies the object Stanley throws out the window in his rage as a "small white radio," thus prefiguring Blanche's demise by means of color symbolism.

However, Blanche's association with whiteness tells only a part of the story of her complex, contradictory nature, and it is a tribute to the playwright's subtle symbolism in *Streetcar* that she is not simply depicted as "white" against the backdrop of Stanley's "black-dyed villain."[4] In the "Poker Night" scene, for example, she dons the colors of desire with a "dark red satin wrapper" to make herself sexually desirable to Mitch, just as she deliberately stands in the light wearing only a "pink brassiere and white skirt" to attract the men's glances when it suits her purposes. Blanche's association with "whiteness," then, like her innocence, reveals only part of her character; her innocence is simultaneously both real and a pose that she uses as a defense and refuge in a dangerous world. In terms of the play's complex color symbolism, this may explain why Blanche's "whiteness" is often qualified by a more varied visual palette, including reds, pinks, and even "Della Robbia blue. The blue of the robe in the old Madonna pictures" (135) in the play's final moments, as we shall see.

In addition to his use of color in the play, Williams consistently makes symbolic use of lighting in *Streetcar*. Stanley, as noted above, associates sex with "getting the colored lights going." In juxtaposition to Blanche, who is at least consciously repulsed by Stanley's brutishness, her sister is sexually excited by it. Significantly, Stanley's predilection toward violent sexuality is conveyed through the image of smashing lightbulbs, ironically the very objects that Blanche must cloak with paper lanterns to conceal herself, reminding us of Williams's stage direction that "her delicate beauty must avoid a strong light" (15):

> Stella: Stanley's always smashed things. Why, on our wedding night—soon as we came in here—he snatched off one of my slippers and rushed about the place smashing light bulbs with it.
>
> Blanche: He did—what?
>
> Stella: He smashed all the light bulbs with the heel of my slipper! *She laughs.*
>
> Blanche: And you—you *let* him? Didn't *run*, didn't *scream*?
>
> Stella: I was—sort of—thrilled by it. (64)

To hide her age and remain physically alluring to men, Blanche covers the bare bulbs in Stanley and Stella's apartment, and alone with Mitch, she asserts that she is unable "to stand a naked light bulb, any more than I can a rude remark or a vulgar action" (55). After Blanche's promiscuous past has been illuminated to Mitch by Stanley, she attempts to parry his blunt comments about her fear of being seen in bold, unadorned lighting:

> *Mitch:* I've asked you to go out with me sometimes on Sundays but you always make an excuse. You never want to go out till after six and then it's always some place that's not lighted much.
>
> *Blanche:* There is some obscure meaning in this but I fail to catch it. (116)

Later, insisting on seeing her in bright light, Mitch tears the paper lantern off a bare bulb so that he is better able to see her, and she lets out a frightened gasp. To Mitch's insistence that he only wants to be "realistic," Blanche responds, "I don't want realism. I want magic!" (117). In contrast to the other characters in the play, including her sister, who has accommodated herself to the grossness of the world as it is by marrying Stanley, Blanche chooses either to hide from its glare or to transform it miraculously by trying to dwell in a world of fantasy and make-believe. This longing is underscored by the popular song she sings to herself while taking refuge, as she frequently does, in hot baths to calm her nerves:

> *Say, it's only a paper moon,*
> *Sailing over a cardboard sea*
> *—But it wouldn't be make-believe*
> *If you believed in me!* (99)

In describing her past to Mitch, she suggests her preference for the world of shadows was caused by her accidentally unmasking her young husband's homosexuality. Having subjected him to direct light ("I saw! I know!"), Blanche claims that "the searchlight which had been turned on the world was turned off again and never for one moment since has there been any light that's stronger than this—kitchen—candle" (96).

For roughly the first half of *Streetcar*'s eleven scenes, these elements—color, sound, and lighting—are used to develop character or to underscore the overall dramatic effect, just as they might in a realistic play. For example, in scenes 1 through 6, the ubiquitous "Blue Piano," screeching cats, and shouts of "Red Hots!" are employed chiefly to help enhance the charged and sensuous atmosphere of the French Quarter rather than as part of a nonrealistic dramaturgy. This half of the play concludes at the end of scene 6, when it appears that Blanche and Mitch might discover happiness together:

> Mitch (*drawing her slowly into his arms*):
> You need somebody. And I need somebody too. Could it be—you and me, Blanche?
> Blanche: Sometimes—there's God—so quickly! (96)

However, beginning with scene 7 the chronology of the play jumps from early May to mid-September, giving Stanley sufficient time to unearth Blanche's promiscuous past in Laurel and convey it to Mitch. It is only at this point that the play transitions from realist mode into an expressionist one as Blanche begins to lose her tenuous grasp on reality. As Blanche emerges from one of her frequent hot baths in the seventh scene, she becomes aware that something is desperately wrong; "Something has happened!—What is it?" At this moment, the Blue Piano, which is a constant feature of life in the Quarter, "goes into a hectic breakdown" (105), indicating through its soundscape the beginning of Blanche's own mental collapse.

As the play heads toward climax, the uses of both sound and light grow increasingly nonrealistic. Such sounds are present earlier in the play, as when the sound of the Varsouviana melody is heard playing inside Blanche's head as memory, capturing the moment in the past when she confronted her young husband about his homosexuality:

Polka music sounds, in a minor key faint with distance.

Blanche: We danced the Varsouviana! Suddenly in the middle of the dance the boy I had married broke away from me and ran out of the casino. A few moments later—a shot!

The polka stops abruptly. (96)

Once the gunshot sounds, the polka music fades out, and she is able to return to reality. As Blanche loses her grasp on the real, however, the music returns but the gunshot is withheld, delaying her (and the audience's) sense of resolution: "The 'Varsouviana'! The polka tune they were playing when Allan—Wait! *A distant revolver shot is heard. Blanche seems relieved*" (114). In the final scene only the Varsouviana music is heard without the return to normalcy provided by the gunshot. Like the alcoholic "click" in his head that Brick requires for calm in *Cat on a Hot Tin Roof*, through the gunshot Blanche seeks a kind of respite from the haunting memory of her past. But as she moves toward the abyss, there is only dissonance without an accompanying resolution.

By scene 9, the once clear-cut divisions between what is real and what is hallucination have eroded. For example, the Mexican woman's cry, "Flores para los muertos, flores—flores," may be interpreted as either actually occurring on the street or as a manifestation of Blanche's increasingly disordered consciousness (119). As Brenda Murphy notes, in the play's early drafts Blanche hears the woman's cries near the beginning of the play. In rehearsals, however, director Elia Kazan shifted the woman's appearance to scene 9, where she actually comes to the door and seems to speak directly to Blanche's innermost thoughts, provoking the scream, "No, no! Not now! Not now!" (*Streetcar* 119).[5]

Expressionistic use of lighting and sound are similarly developed as the play moves toward Blanche's mental breakdown. Scene 10 opens a few hours after she has chased Mitch from the house with cries of "Fire!" Her mask of purity having failed her, Mitch now only desires her for sex; "You're not pure enough to bring in the house with my mother," he tells her (121). Alone and bereft of any means of escape, she dons a costume befitting the mask of innocence and her bruised self-conception: "*a somewhat soiled and crumpled white satin evening gown, and a pair of scuffed silver slippers with brilliants set in their heels*" (122). While for Blanche the dress suggests an attempt to recapture a fading ideal, for Stanley it is merely a "worn-out Mardi Gras outfit, rented for fifty cents from some rag-picker!" (127). Now she is left alone with Stanley and retreats into her makeshift bedroom. As Stanley intrudes on her space, Williams metamorphoses Blanche's world into something altogether distorted and grotesque, manifesting her inner turmoil precisely as in expressionist drama and painting. As she attempts to flee her pursuer, she is cut off and unable to contact her imaginary suitor by telephone; when the operator presumably inquires about his address, she responds, "He's so well-known he doesn't require any address" (128). Abandoning the telephone as a means of escape, she is left alone with her antagonist, and as she crosses back into the kitchen in a frantic search for some oasis of safety, Williams remarkably creates the disturbed topography of Blanche's consciousness through sound and moving image: "*The night is filled with inhuman voices like cries in the jungle. . . . shadows and lurid reflections move sinuously as flames along the wall spaces*" (128). As Blanche plunges into madness, Williams raises the visual stakes even higher so that the division between interior and exterior space is also cracked open and becomes indistinct: "*Through the back wall of the rooms, which have become transparent, can be seen the sidewalk. A prostitute has rolled a drunkard. He pursues her along the walk, overtakes her and there is a struggle. A policeman's whistle breaks it up. The figures disappear*" (128). At this point, it is impossible for a theater audience to distinguish precisely what may be happening in objective reality from what is playing out in Blanche's mind, and this is consistent with Williams's expressionistic dramaturgy. As Stanley decides that "maybe you wouldn't be bad to—interfere with," not only do "*inhuman jungle voices rise up*" but Stanley himself also becomes a part of the primordial, savage eruption within her mind: "*He takes a step toward her, biting his tongue which protrudes between his lips*" (129).

The final scene, which occurs several weeks after Blanche's rape, appears at first glance to return us to the relative calm domestic realism of the first half of the play. Stella is packing Blanche's things, and the sound of water can be heard from the bathroom, where Blanche is bathing as she did earlier in the play. However, through visual cues, Williams maintains a bifurcated stage picture, suggesting that the world of savagery is not altogether absent; there is a poker game going on in the kitchen, and the stage directions remind us that the atmosphere is "*the same raw, lurid one of the disastrous poker night*" (131).

Despite the presence of the world of the poker night, much of the imagery associated with Blanche in this final scene is suggestive of divine innocence and purity, aligning her with the Virgin Mary. Her jacket, she insists, is "Della Robbia blue. The blue of the robe in the old Madonna pictures" (135), and she carries a silver-backed mirror in her hand, an image traditionally associated with the Virgin Mary in Renaissance iconography. Moments later, the cathedral chimes are heard ("the only clean thing in the Quarter," according to Blanche [136]). Even the grapes she is given to eat seem to allude to images of defiled innocence and self-willed martyrdom. She claims that "I shall die of eating an unwashed grape one day out on the ocean. . . . And I'll be buried at sea sewn up in a clean white sack and dropped overboard—at noon—in the blaze of summer—and into an ocean as blue as [*chimes again*] my first lover's eyes!" (136).

The play's conclusion is anything but simple or uncomplicated. Blanche's departure from the flat must take her through the kitchen and past her tormentor, Stanley. When she realizes that the doctor who has come for her is "not the gentleman I was expecting" (138), she attempts to rush back into her bedroom, but Stanley blocks her retreat. Once again, the playwright employs the language of visual and aural expressionism to suggest the primal threat she feels: "*She rushes past him into the bedroom. Lurid reflections appear on the walls in odd sin-*

uous shapes. The 'Varsouviana' is filtered into a weird distortion, accompanied by the cries and noises of the jungle. Blanche seizes the back of a chair to defend herself" (139).

The unity of expressionistic distortion and psychologically realistic characterization are perhaps most beautifully counterpointed as Blanche is about to retreat back into her bedroom. First the matron, *"a peculiarly sinister figure in her severe dress,"* advances on her, and her greeting, "Hello, Blanche," is *"echoed and re-echoed by other mysterious voices behind the walls, as if reverberated through a canyon of rock"* (139). Then, Stanley asks her if she has forgotten anything, adding, "You left nothing here but spilt talcum and old empty perfume bottles—unless it's the paper lantern you want to take with you. You want the lantern?" As Stanley tears the lantern off the lightbulb, Williams indicates that Blanche *"cries out as if the lantern was herself"* (140). Connecting the delicate paper lantern, which Blanche has bought as protection against the harsh light, with her inmost self, the playwright creates a seamless unity between literary symbol and stage metaphor.

The play's final moments are some of the most memorable in the canon of the American theater. After her renewed hysteria, Blanche has assumed a kind of calm dignity as the doctor utters her name, "Miss DuBois," and, supporting her with his arm, escorts her out the door. Interestingly, she allows herself to be led from the flat *"as if she were blind,"* (142), a stage direction that echoes the final moments of Strindberg's *Miss Julie* (1888), in which a doomed aristocratic woman is similarly drawn toward her virile, lowborn executioner. And just as Julie's final choice in Strindberg's play reestablishes her tragic dignity at the expense of Jean, an adversary who quivers at the sound of the Count's bell and the sight of his boots, so Blanche's last moments may be seen as a kind of tragic triumph as well as the culmination of her descent. As Blanche exits, her sister Stella accepts her newborn baby wrapped in a pale blue blanket, symbolic of renewed life after Blanche, the obstacle, has been removed from the Kowalski household. But of course, this final image of the play is more ironic, textured, and complex than that. In a sense the final moments of the play belong to neither of the play's larger-than-life antagonists but to Stella, the object of their mutual desire and mortal struggle. That Stanley has won the battle "for Stella's heart and mind" is clear, but the cost of his win is not (Londré 56).

In Kazan's celebrated 1951 film adaptation of the play (the ending of which was changed under pressure from the Legion of Decency and the film's producer, Warner Bros.), as Blanche is removed from the home, Stella races upstairs with her newborn baby to provide the wholesome impression that she may not return to Stanley. However, in the play, the imagery of rebirth is powerfully undercut when Stanley gropes at the opening of his wife's blouse, murmuring "*voluptuously, soothingly* Now, honey. Now, love. Now, now, love" (142). The implications of this ending are highly suggestive: by choosing to accept Stanley's "love" and the life with him in the Quarter, Stella may be sacrificing her integrity as well as her sister. The play ends with Stella's sobbing "*with inhuman abandon*" (142), suggesting the magnitude of the choice awaiting her. At the beginning of scene 11, she confides to her neighbor, "I couldn't believe her story and go on living with Stanley," to which Eunice replies, "Don't ever believe it. Life has got to go on. No matter what happens, you've got to keep on going" (133). But what if accommodation to life as it is, of "going on," involves living a perpetual lie? The play then ends not so much with an image of possible renewal as it does with Stella's choice of either motherhood and new life with Stanley or acceptance of the consequences of the fact that the father of her newborn has raped her sister. This choice will be the actual price of her remaining with Stanley and embracing his "colored lights" at all costs. It is in this context that the play's final line, "The game is seven-card stud" (142), is a brutally appropriate response to the question that opened the "Poker Night" scene: "Anything wild this deal?" (45). Unlike the compromised, "safe" answer provided to general audiences at the end of the film, Williams's play ends with an image of terrifying, open-ended uncertainty, on which the arrival of the child wrapped in his "pale blue blanket" (142) must be seen to comment ironically. Blanche has been forcibly removed from the Kowalski home in favor of a baby who not so much restores the threatened union between Stanley and Stella as conceals its inner corruption.

There are, of course, as many *Streetcar*s as there are directors. No single analysis of the script, no one production can ever be declared definitive, even its celebrated premiere. Some productions will make more or less use of Williams's incisive, poetic stage directions or his remarkably detailed suggestions with regard to costume, lighting, and sound design. Some productions will undoubtedly emphasize the play's expressionistic possibilities more than others. However, any director or student of the play must come to terms with the fact that *Streetcar* is a uniquely balanced concordance of two distinct impulses already present in Williams's dramaturgical arsenal at the beginning of his career: psychological realism and expressionism. In this one play, he is uniquely able to marry these two potentially conflicting tendencies in a way that is very close to perfection. Certainly no American play has done it better.

In a letter to Elia Kazan, the play's first director, Williams eloquently points out that the play's best quality is its "authenticity or its fidelity to life." This aspect is found in the principal antagonists' blindness to one another: "Nobody sees anybody truly but all through the flaws of their own egos. That is the way we all see each other in life." Thus Stanley sees Blanche as a "calculating bitch," not the desperate, driven creature she is. Blanche, in turn, is similarly blinded to Stanley's nature and Stella's needs. In traditional drama, however, Williams argues, people are never depicted as they really are: "We see from the *outside* what could not be seen *within*. It is not that one person was bad or good, one right or wrong but that all judged falsely concerning each other." Adding that he has written this out in case Kazan is unclear "over my intention" in the play, Williams points out the necessity of finding "a director . . . who can bring this play to life exactly as if it were happening in life." The qualities he seeks, however, are paradoxically not found in conventional realism, concluding that "sometimes a living quality is caught better by expressionism than what is supposed to be realistic treatment" (quoted in Kazan 330). Kazan notes in his autobiography that Williams's letter "became the key to the production to me" (330), and I think it might be argued that it should be essential reading for any director or student of the play.

Notes

1. See Mardi Valgemae's "Expressionism in the American Theater" and *Accelerated Grimace*. For more on Williams in the context of expressionism, see Esther Merle Jackson's *The Broken World of Tennessee Williams* (90-93) and Mary Ann Corrigan's "Realism and Theatricalism in *A Streetcar Named Desire*"; Corrigan avoids the term "expressionism" in favor of "theatricalism" in her essay.

2. In addition to "The Poker Night," "The Moth" was another one of Williams's working titles for *Streetcar.* The others included "The Primary Colors" and "Blanche's Chair in the Moon" (Williams, *Notebooks* 433).

3. In the original Broadway production, "[director Elia] Kazan, [scenic designer Jo] Mielziner, and [costume designer] Lucinda Ballard developed their own vestimentary code," and "Blanche did not wear white when she first appeared in Elysian Fields" (Murphy 32).

4. The phrase is used by Williams in a letter to director Elia Kazan to emphasize the fact that neither of the play's antagonists should be perceived as either entirely good or entirely evil, and that the tragedy depends on the fact that "nobody sees anybody truly but all through the flaws of their own egos." The ideal response to the play, Williams suggests, would be, "If only they all had known about each other" (quoted in Kazan 329-30).

5. For further discussion of how director Kazan was instrumental in "repositioning the significant figure of the flower vendor," see Murphy's *Tennessee Williams and Elia Kazan* (33).

Works Cited

Corrigan, Mary Ann. "Realism and Theatricalism in *A Streetcar Named Desire.*" *Tennessee Williams's "A Streetcar Named Desire."* Ed. Harold Bloom. New York: Chelsea House, 1988. 49-60.

Givens, Steve. "King of the Hill." *Washington University Magazine* Summer 1994: 30.

Jackson, Esther Merle. *The Broken World of Tennessee Williams*. Madison: U of Wisconsin P, 1965.

Kazan, Elia. *A Life*. New York: Alfred A. Knopf, 1988.

Leverich, Lyle. *Tom: The Unknown Tennessee Williams*. New York: Crown, 1995.

Londré, Felicia Hardison. "A Streetcar Running Fifty Years." *The Cambridge Companion to Tennessee Williams*. Ed. Matthew C. Roudané. New York: Cambridge UP, 1997. 45-66.

Masina, Lara Vinca. *Van Gogh: The Life and Work of the Artist*. Trans. Caroline Beamish. London: Thames and Hudson, 1967.

Murphy, Brenda. *Tennessee Williams and Elia Kazan: A Collaboration in the Theatre*. New York: Cambridge UP, 1992.

Valgemae, Mardi. *Accelerated Grimace: Expressionism in the American Drama of the 1920s*. Carbondale: Southern Illinois UP, 1972.

_____. "Expressionism in the American Theater." *Expressionism as an International Literary Phenomenon*. Ed. Ulrich Weisstein. Paris: Didier, 1973. 193-204.

van Gogh, Vincent. *The Letters of Vincent van Gogh*. Ed. Ronald de Leeuw. London: Penguin, 1977.

Weisstein, Ulrich. "Introduction." *Expressionism as an International Literary Phenomenon*. Ed. Ulrich Weisstein. Paris: Didier, 1973.

Williams, Tennessee. *The Glass Menagerie*. 1944. New York: New Directions, 1999.

_____. "Me, Vashya." William G. B. Carson Papers Collection, Washington University Libraries, Department of Special Collections, Washington University in St. Louis.

_____. *Memoirs*. Garden City, NY: Doubleday, 1975.

_____. *Notebooks*. Ed. Margaret Bradham Thornton. New Haven, CT: Yale UP, 2006.

_____. *A Streetcar Named Desire*. 1947. New York: Signet, 1974.

_____. *Where I Live: Selected Essays*. New York: New Directions, 1978.

Mendacity on the Stage:
"Lying and Liars" in *Cat on a Hot Tin Roof*_____

Kenneth Elliott

"Have you ever heard of the word 'mendacity'?" Brick asks his father at the height of their act 2 confrontation in *Cat on a Hot Tin Roof*. Typical of Tennessee Williams, the word has a lilting, elegant, poetic quality that belies its meaning, but Big Daddy knows precisely what his son is referring to: "lying and liars" (*Plays* 940). Lying, liars, and the shifting nature of truth are at the heart of all of Williams's major plays, but the playwright is not a crusading moralist. The lies of Williams's plays are often beautiful illusions, and some of his liars are his most compellingly sympathetic characters. It is "truth" (or "realism"), as it is defined in the plays, that is cold, ugly, and cruel, and it is his victimized protagonists' desperate avoidance of it against all odds that provides irresistible pathos. *Cat on a Hot Tin Roof* centers on a trio of memorable liars—Maggie, Brick, and Big Daddy—each of whom engages in a discourse on the nature of mendacity, both personal and societal, in the play's first two acts. Such discussions are bound to be open-ended and unresolved in any context, but they are particularly so in this play because Williams took the unusual step of publishing two versions of the play's third, concluding act, commenting on each within an accompanying and equivocal "Note of Explanation." In this "Note" he writes that while the first version (which he calls "*Cat* number one") conveys his original intent, the second version (known as the "Broadway Version") reflects the dramaturgical influence of his director, Elia Kazan. While Williams's preference for "*Cat* number one" is more than implied, he ends his "Note" with a challenge to the reader to "make up his own mind about it" (*Plays* 977-78). The divergent meaning of these iterations creates an additional discourse outside the play that illustrates the social and historical context that is essential to understanding its three central characters.

There is a bit of gracious mendacity at work in the "Note of Explanation" itself, as Williams extols the "deep mutual respect" that he and Kazan had for each other and praises the director as "keenly perceptive" before concluding with apparent (but not terribly genuine) equanimity regarding the two drafts. He was much less evenhanded about his preference for "*Cat* number one" years later, identifying it in his controversial *Memoirs* as "my favorite among the plays I have written."

> That play comes closest to being both a work of art and a work of craft. It is really very well put together, in my opinion, and all its characters are amusing and credible and touching. Also it adheres to the valuable edict of Aristotle that a tragedy must have a unity of time and place and magnitude of theme. (168)

He goes on to state that he "disagreed" with the adjustments made for the Broadway production, which he viewed as a "distortion" of his intention, and he asserts that, in making them, Kazan forced him to violate his intuition. To emphasize the gravity of the violation, he then indirectly blames Kazan's changes (along with a supposed snub from his agent, Audrey Wood) for the drug addiction and the "creative sterility" that overtook him soon after the play's opening (169). These charges are obviously over-the-top, but, given that *Memoirs* was written more than twenty years after *Cat on a Hot Tin Roof*, it is clear that time did not heal the festering resentment Williams obviously bore toward Kazan for what he considered an unfortunate compromise.

It might be difficult to imagine why Williams would have even considered making changes with which he disagreed. By the 1954-55 theater season, he was a playwright of enormous stature who had had major artistic and financial successes, including a Pulitzer Prize for *A Streetcar Named Desire*. But he had just suffered a devastating commercial failure with the 1953 Broadway production of his surrealist play *Camino Real* (also directed by Kazan), and his letters from this period suggest that he was not only insecure but also desperate for success. He was determined that he needed Kazan to direct *Cat*, writing to him, "There is certainly no use in my trying to disguise or dissimulate the fact that I passionately long for you to do this play" (*Selected Letters* 549). Kazan, who had started out as an actor with the Group Theatre before going on to direct many of the most important Broadway productions of the 1940s and 1950s, was the most sought-after theater director of the period, and Williams courted him assiduously. Kazan was in a position to play hard to get, and, up to a point, Williams was willing to make revisions in order to get him.

But Kazan had reservations about the play, mostly centering on the third act. Williams summarizes them in his "Note" as three main points: that Big Daddy must return in act 3 because he is "much too vivid and important a character" to become a mere offstage presence; that, as a result of his confrontation with Big Daddy in act 2, Brick must experience a recognition of some kind that effects a change in his character in act 3; and that Maggie must be "more clearly sympathetic to an audience" (*Plays* 977). The changes Williams made to address these points tidy up the dramatic structure by suggesting a sense of resolution for all three characters that did not exist in "*Cat* number one." The changes were not simply dramaturgical, however. As Brenda Murphy notes in her study of the collaboration of Williams and Kazan, "many critics have read the 'Note of Explanation' to suggest that Kazan had asked for changes in the script to assure the play's commercial success" (99). Williams's justification that "a failure reaches fewer people and touches fewer, than does a play that succeeds" certainly reinforces this interpretation (*Plays* 978). It is easy in retrospect to charge Williams (as some critics have done) with having made a Faustian bargain to surrender his artistic soul for financial gain, but this view romanticizes the playwright as an individual artist with a sacrosanct vision untouched by the vulgar forces of capitalism. In fact, most modern plays are revised to some degree during preproduction and the rehearsal process in collaboration with the director, designers, and actors. Furthermore, all Broadway plays of this period were inherently commercial because Broadway was (and is) a commercial venue.

As Williams had to concede, Kazan's production was a smashing success that earned the playwright his second Pulitzer Prize. The production was conceived in a boldly presentational style to accent the play's rhetorical language and staged on an abstract platform set designed by Jo Mielziner, who had collaborated with Kazan on *A Streetcar Named Desire* and Arthur Miller's *Death of a Salesman*, among other plays. During some of the longer speeches, actors were brought downstage to address the audience directly. Williams was surprised and not necessarily pleased by these choices, but as Kazan commented in his autobiography, "Dear Tennessee was stuck with my vision, like it or not" (543). However, Kazan's vision was not confined to the staging of the play. The substantive textual revisions made to the three major characters profoundly altered the meaning of the play by providing a more hopeful and upbeat ending that conformed, at least somewhat, to the prevalent mainstream values of 1950s America.

The mendacity that Brick cites to Big Daddy as the catalyst for his alcoholism is one of the keys to the play's meaning that was blurred in the Broadway version, although it was deliberately mysterious even in "*Cat* number one." Daniel Mendelsohn calls Williams "the great dramatist of the beautiful failure, the poet of the noble defeat" (30), and in this sense Brick is a prototypical Williams protagonist: a damaged victim whose cherished idealism has been shattered and who has consequently given up on life. Williams notes in his initial description of the character that he possesses the "charm of that cool air of detachment that people have who have given up the struggle" (*Plays* 885). His broken spirit is physically represented by the cast on his leg, the crutch he requires to walk, and, of course, the vast amount of liquor he consumes. There is no mistaking that Brick is a wounded creature, but what is the source of his deep disgust? He doesn't say much in act 1, which is largely given over to a series of lengthy monologues by his wife, Maggie, but she manages to provoke him into a nearly murderous rage by the end of the act because she cannot resist repeatedly returning to the subject of his late friend, Skipper. As she says, "I never could keep my fingers off a sore" (892). For Brick, this friendship was "the one great good true thing in his life," but Maggie identifies it as impossibly idealized, "one of those beautiful, ideal things they tell you about in the Greek legends" (909). Brick mourns Skipper with the bitter intensity of Achilles after the death of Patroclus. It was a friendship so noble that it could not last, which is why Maggie refers to it as "the *dream* of life" (910). In a lengthy speech of justification, she describes how she ended the dream by confronting Skipper about his homosexual love for Brick, "telling him the truth," which ultimately destroyed him (911). The very night of that confrontation, she claims, she and Skipper made love because it made both of them "feel a little bit closer" to Brick (909). It was also, she recalls, Skipper's "pitiful, ineffectual little attempt to prove that what I had said wasn't true" (911). Brick's response to this is violent. He twice attempts to strike his wife and finally "hurls his crutch at her" in an impotent rage and ends up sprawled on the floor (912). It is not Maggie's adulterous liaison with his friend that so enrages him—it is clear that he has always regarded her with indifference—it is rather that his "dream of life" has been sullied by the mere suggestion of homosexuality: "You are namin' it dirty!" (910). His indifference has transformed into contempt so profound that he cannot bear to hear her speak about Skipper.

Even after the room is cleared in act 2 for a father-son talk, Brick is singularly uncommunicative until Big Daddy cuts off his liquor to demand an explanation of why he drinks. Only then does Brick spin his own subjective interpretation of the events that Maggie described in act 1, the events that led to his current state. He claims that he had an "exceptional friendship, *real, real, deep, deep friendship!*" with Skipper, who was his college football teammate (*Plays* 948). This beautiful and true relationship was destroyed when Maggie, who was jealous of their closeness, planted in Skipper's mind the false notion that there was something unnatural about it. "Poor dumb Skipper," who was "less than an average student at Ole Miss," began to worry that Maggie's suggestion that he and Brick were frustrated homosexuals might in fact be true (950). It is an intriguing detail that Brick's ideal friendship was with a man he describes as "dumb." Clearly this was not an intellectual friendship, and Brick suggests that his friend's lack of intelligence allowed him to be taken in by Maggie's insinuation. In his ignorant desperation, Skipper sought to disprove it by pathetically attempting to seduce Maggie. When he was unable to perform sexually, he assumed that he indeed must be a homosexual. As a result he turned to liquor and quickly drank himself to death.

Big Daddy quite properly calls this a "half-ass story" because its central element, that a manipulative woman could trick an otherwise heterosexual man into believing that he was a homosexual, is not only outrageously misogynistic but also thoroughly illogical. When pressed by Big Daddy, Brick adds a crucial detail: Skipper telephoned him to make "a drunken confession" (presumably of his homosexual attraction to Brick), and Brick's response was to hang up on his friend and sever all communication with him. The cruelty of this action shocks Big Daddy, who zeroes in on his son:

> Anyhow now!—we have tracked down the lie with which you're disgusted and which you are drinking to kill your disgust with, Brick. You been passing the buck. This disgust with mendacity is disgust with yourself.
>
> *You!*—dug the grave of your friend and kicked him in it!—before you'd face the truth with him! (*Plays* 951)

Brick responds by passing the buck again ("*His* truth, not *mine!*") and then childishly changes the subject to cruelly reveal Big Daddy's cancer diagnosis (951).

Far from clearing up the mystery, this exchange raises more questions than it answers. But the answers never come: Brick does not mention his relationship with Skipper again in the remainder of either version of the play. The only opening-night critic to make note of this apparent lacuna was Walter F. Kerr, who, in his review for the *New York Herald Tribune*, called *Cat* "a play of evasion" (Rev. 342). Kerr observed "a tantalizing reluctance—beneath all the fire and all the apparent candor—to let the play blurt out its promised secret." The secret Kerr refers to, of course, is Brick's sexuality and his mendacity in coming to terms with it. In a later Sunday piece, Kerr was even more direct, asking, "Is he a homosexual?" ("Secret" 1). The virulent homophobic rage with which Brick responds to the slightest suggestion that there might have been a homosexual component to his relationship with his late friend has certainly implied to most recent critics that Brick is a tortured, closeted gay man who cannot come to terms with his sexuality. David Savran notes that Brick does not display so much as "an iota" of "heterosexual desire" (109). Dean Shackelford argues that there are "strong possibilities within the text" for reading Brick as a homosexual (109). Douglas Arrell sees signs of what Eve Sedgwick calls "homosexual panic" in his behavior (63). This implication is directly confirmed by Williams in a preproduction letter to Kazan:

> Here's the conclusion I've come to. Brick *did* love Skipper, "the one great good thing in his life which was true." He identified Skipper with sports, the romantic world of adolescence which he couldn't go past. Further: to reverse my original (somewhat tentative) premise, I now believe that, in the deeper sense, not the literal sense, Brick *is* homosexual with a heterosexual adjustment. (*Selected Letters* 555-56)

While "the deeper sense" is not a precise psychological term, it is evident that Williams is referring here to Brick's innate sexuality while maintaining that the character never engaged in homosexual acts in "the literal sense."

Williams's frankness in his letter to Kazan was for private consumption only. In fact, he felt compelled to respond to Kerr's charge of evasiveness by writing an evasive response that was published in the *New York Herald Tribune*: "Was Brick homosexual? He probably—no, I would even say even quite certainly—went no further in physical expression than clasping Skipper's hand across the space between their twin beds in hotel rooms—and yet his sexual nature was not innately 'normal'" (*Where I Live* 72). That Williams's peculiar syntax obfuscates the point *is* the point. The subject of homosexuality was verboten on the Broadway stage of the 1950s, and not simply because of the prevailing homophobia of the period. There was a New York State law (not repealed until 1967) that made the depiction of homosexuality on the stage illegal, so Williams skirted the issue. But while Brick's homosexuality is not confirmed in "*Cat* number one," it is not denied either. Williams defends this ambiguity in a controversial and lengthy stage direction for the published version of the play in which he claims that "the bird I hope to catch in the net of this play is not the solution of one man's psychological problems. . . . Some mystery should be left in the revelation of character in a play, just as a great deal of mystery is always left in the revelation of character in life" (*Plays* 945). As John M. Clum argues, this approach allows Williams "to proceed with a scene about homosexuality while denying that that is what he is doing" (161). And so the secret of Brick's sexuality (and the nature of his mendacity) intentionally remains a mystery to those who cannot read the code. The character says little in act 3 and is essentially a passive observer of his family's machinations who continues to anesthetize himself with bourbon while maintaining an air of detached cynicism to the final curtain. This extreme inertia enabled Williams to maintain the mystery surrounding the character, but it was theatrically problematic. His director preferred a more muscular plot structure.

Kazan wanted Brick to have a clear character arc, to undergo what is often called a "journey." And so Brick's behavior in act 3 of the "Broadway Version" differs markedly from the earlier draft, but, ironically, the mystery of his sexuality is even murkier. His first line after Big Daddy's exit is a confession to Maggie: "I didn't lie to Big Daddy. I've lied to nobody, nobody but myself" (*Plays* 980). This is a rather clumsy and perfunctory effort to create what Aristotle called an *anagnorisis*, or recognition, and it only gives the illusion of self-enlightenment, since it provides no details about the nature of the lie. The subject is promptly dropped. However, Brick's behavior changes as if he has had an epiphany. Gone is the utter detachment of "*Cat* number one," replaced by active disdain for the greedy manipulations of Mae and Gooper. In "*Cat* number one," Brick could not have cared less about their shameless money grubbing. In the "Broadway Version," he is so disturbed that he has to leave the room, saying, "I can't witness that thing in there!" (983). When he returns, it is not as an idle bystander. He throws himself into the fray by emphatically challenging his brother to award himself the estate, exclaiming, "Take it, Gooper!" (986). The most radical departure from the earlier draft is a new alliance with and sympathy for his wife, which is most evident when she claims to be pregnant. In "*Cat* number one" Brick remains silent from the time Maggie makes this false announcement until they are left alone in their room. In the "Broadway Version" he taunts Mae and Gooper for disbelieving Maggie's lie, defends his wife, implies that she actually is pregnant, orders Mae and Gooper out of the room, and asserts a newfound vitality. In the final moments of "*Cat* number one," when Maggie proposes to seduce him "to make the lie true," and asks him, "What do you say?" his reply could not be more noncommittal: "I don't say anything. I guess there's nothing to say" (976). His response to the same question in the "Broadway Version" is positive: "I admire you, Maggie" (1005). It is followed by a stage direction that calls for him to sit on the bed and glance first to the overhead light and then to Maggie—a "come hither" look. She understands precisely what he means and obediently turns off the light and kneels at his feet, possibly in gratitude for his sexual attention. The tables have turned, and Brick is in the power position, quietly seducing his wife.

This final change in Brick may be more than Williams had in mind by a "heterosexual adjustment," but there is no question that the third act of the "Broadway Version" ends with genuine hope for a marriage that had seemed doomed in the first two acts. A change has occurred in

Critical Insights

Brick; Skipper, "the dream of life," is forgotten. It is easy to see why Kazan would have preferred this ending. Not only does it almost eliminate the problematic issue of homosexuality, but it also provides the obligatory scene that the audience has been waiting for: the reconciliation of an attractive and intelligent couple. Unfortunately, there is only a *sense* of progression. There is no motivation for it beyond Brick's token admission at the top of the act that he had lied to himself. Brick's tortured denial of his homosexuality in the first two acts, which had been a central focus of the play, is simply replaced without explanation by an active heterosexual interest in his wife. His previous contempt for her is replaced by admiration. These adjustments also affect his alcoholism. In both versions, he continues to drink steadily throughout the third act, hoping to achieve the long-awaited "click" in his head. In "*Cat* number one," this makes sense because his situation is unchanged from act 2: he is drinking to forget his pain. In the "Broadway Version," when the "click" finally arrives it seems oddly unnecessary because the pain has apparently already ended and the character is no longer acting depressed or melancholy.

In order to complement the more assertive, more heterosexual Brick of the "Broadway Version," Kazan asked for adjustments to the role of Maggie to make her a more conventionally appealing wife. The Maggie of "*Cat* number one" is in the tradition of Williams's female characters who are adept at the beautiful lie known as performance—often with tragic consequences. Amanda Wingfield's rigorous stage management of the dinner party for the gentleman caller in *The Glass Menagerie* is intended to conceal the truth that her daughter is pathologically shy and physically disabled, but the evening ends in disaster. "I don't want realism," Blanche explains in *A Streetcar Named Desire*. "I'll tell you what I want. Magic!" (*Plays* 545). And so she performs the anachronistic role of the vivacious-but-chaste southern belle to conceal her unpalatable sexual history from Mitch, who ultimately confronts her with the merciless glare of a bare lightbulb. Maggie is also a performer with something to conceal, but unlike like Amanda and Blanche, her toughness and tenacity almost enable her to succeed in the end. From her first entrance, there is a sense that she is backstage preparing for her big scene, that she is powerfully aware of the visual impact she can create. She powders, carefully applies eye makeup, adjusts the lighting, and changes her costume—all in support of an utterly false performance that she will give for her in-laws, most particularly Big Daddy. She intends to create the fiction that her marriage is strong and that her alcoholic husband is fully functional and capable of inheriting Big Daddy's massive fortune and his plantation, "twenty-eight thousand acres of the richest land this side of the valley Nile" (*Plays* 929).

The strain of this performance is made clear by Williams in a stage direction. He describes Maggie as "a pretty young woman with anxious lines in her face" (*Plays* 883).These lines were not brought on simply by her disastrous marriage to Brick but by a condition she has suffered her entire life (and one that she shares with many of Williams's characters): impoverished gentility. Brick wryly comments to Big Daddy that he and Gooper "married into society," and Maggie is acutely aware of her social position (924). She dismisses Mae's family as mere "climbers," explaining that she knows "who rates an' who doesn't rate in Memphis society" (889). While she may have come from a family that "rates," her father was an alcoholic and her mother struggled to "keep appearances up, on an income of one hundred and fifty dollars a month on those old government bonds!" Her debut into Nashville society was marred by the humiliation that she owned only two evening dresses, one homemade by her mother and the other "a hand-me-down from a snotty rich cousin." She detested her rich relatives but had to "suck up" to them nevertheless. Poverty is the central defining fact of her life, as she tells her husband, "*I've been so God damn disgustingly poor all my life!*–That's the *truth,* Brick!" (907)

Maggie also uses her performative art to conceal her profound sexual frustration. Her intense physical attraction to her husband is and always has been unreciprocated. She pathetically flirts with Brick in a variety of ways, and even offers to give him an alcohol rub, to no avail. The ache of her longing is palpable as she describes to him how he had been "a wonderful lover. . . . Such a wonderful person to go to bed with because you were really indifferent to it" (*Plays* 892). Maggie, on the other hand, is far from indifferent to it. She is completely conscious of and pleased by her sexual allure. She has noticed that Big Daddy has a "lech" for her, and he is not the only one she has observed:

> Why, last week in Memphis everywhere that I went men's eyes burned holes in my clothes, at the country club and in restaurants and department stores, there wasn't a man I met or walked by that didn't just eat me up with his eyes and turn around when I passed him and look back at me. (904)

Of course Maggie would have had to turn back and look as well in order to know that these men she was passing were turning back to look at her. She was essentially engaging in sexual cruising. After describing an incident at a party when a man followed her to the powder room and tried to "force his way in," she admits that the reason she did not let him do so was that she did not want to be caught in the act (904). She performed propriety while she would have preferred a sexual encounter.

Poverty, rejection, and desire form the same lethal triad found in Blanche DuBois, but Maggie the Cat is not headed for the madhouse: "one thing I don't have is the charm of the defeated, my hat is still in the ring, and I am determined to win!" (*Plays* 892). A hot tin roof may be an uncomfortable, even painful, place to stay, but Maggie proclaims that "I can stay on it just as long as I have to." This determination is relentless, and it gives a desperate edge to her humor, reflected in a string of barbed zingers aimed primarily at Gooper, Mae, and their children, the "no-neck monsters," of whom she complains, "you can't wring their necks if they've got no necks to wring!" (883). Mae calls her "catty," and Brick echoes this epithet (896). Williams, who seems to feel the need to justify her behavior for the reader, explains in a stage direction that "it is constant rejection that makes her humor 'bitchy'" (888). She may be "bitchy," but her method of addressing her miserable situation with gallows humor is at least spirited. Williams described her in a letter to Kazan as "someone who's always crouched at the feet of the rich and lucky with the smile of a beggar and the claws of a cat" (*Notebooks* 658).

This is not the way Kazan saw the character, and he set out to declaw the cat. Another of Williams's letters suggested that Kazan intended to highlight "the good in Maggie" (*Selected Letters* 552). "Good" is a word that has been used to describe characters at least since Aristotle observed in his *Poetics* that "first and foremost, character should be good" (25). It is a vague word, and its meaning shifts over time. However, throughout centuries of Western drama the misogynist code of appropriate behavior for "good" female characters was strict and limiting: unmarried women had to be chaste and virginal, and married women had to be devoted to their husbands. Any female characters who did not conform to these roles would fall into the categories identified by Sue-Ellen Case as the Bitch, the Witch, and the Vamp (6). Amazingly, not much had changed in Broadway theater of the mid-1950s. Kazan persuaded Williams to soften the character to, as Murphy observes, "emphasize Maggie's difference from the others, the sense that her motivations were higher than the blind greed that characterized the Pollitts" (115). But Williams had already substantially differentiated Maggie from the Pollitts. She is genuinely witty whereas Mae and Gooper are merely mean and hypocritical. Many of Maggie's "catty" remarks, a few of which were excised for Broadway (including the line about wringing the necks of the no-neck monsters), are pointed commentaries on the greed of her in-laws. Kazan reinforced his view of the character by casting Barbara Bel Geddes as Maggie, an actress who was more prim and proper than sultry. This was done over the playwright's objections, and as Kazan bluntly recalled in his autobiography, "I'd forced her on him. She was not the kind of actress he liked; she was the kind of actress I liked" (540). But the most significant change forced by Kazan to reflect Maggie's higher motivations was a shift in her relationship with her husband. In the "Broadway Version" third act, Maggie is no longer going it alone; she and Brick become something of a team, and she is fighting for him. She even goes so far as to strike Gooper in defense of Brick. Whereas in the final moments of "*Cat* number one" she is in complete control when she confidently and assertively announces to Brick, "We're *going* to make the lie true" (*Plays* 975), in the "Broadway Version" she is much less aggressive. A slight change gives an utterly different nuance to her line: "We *can* make the lie true," she says instead (emphasis mine). The Broadway Maggie is softer, less assertive, and more deferential to her husband.

Kazan's justification for asking Williams to bring Big Daddy back for an encore in act 3—that he is too strong simply to disappear— seems benign enough. Once again, a character arc is provided where none previously existed. In "*Cat* number one," Big Daddy exits at the end of act 2 in a confused and horrified fury after learning that he is in-deed dying of cancer, and he does not return to the stage. His family has lied to him and he has lied to himself about the one thing he fears most: death. The realization that he has terminal cancer is devastating. De-spite his absence from act 3, his presence is felt as his "long drawn cry of agony and rage" twice punctuates the final moments of the play (*Plays* 973). This creates a gravity of tone suggestive of Greek tragedy, as it recalls Agamemnon's offstage screams in *The Oresteia*. It also serves as a grotesque counterpoint to Maggie's attempted seduction of Brick, vividly juxtaposing death and desire. Big Daddy's return in act 3 of the "Broadway Version" is more vaudeville than Greek tragedy. Williams found no compelling action for the character, so he originally decided to have him tell a long, off-color joke about elephants that was ultimately cut by the New York censors. Without the elephant joke, Big Daddy's reentrance (as published in the 1955 Dramatists' Play Service acting edition) is brief. He enters the room with a curious air of amused self-satisfaction and wryly comments to Brick about the "obnoxious odor of mendacity" in the room, obviously referring to the hapless

Gooper and Mae (77). This suggests a resolution to the utterly unresolved act 2 confrontation. What happened to the staggering rage with which Big Daddy made his dramatic exit? One can only assume that in the meantime he has somehow reconciled himself to death and has pulled himself together, but the audience has not seen this happen. He remains onstage for Maggie's lie about her pregnancy, and, after a rather lascivious laying on of hands, he pronounces "this girl has life in her body, that's no lie" (78). More dramaturgical housecleaning follows as he demands of Gooper, "I want my lawyer in the morning." The clear implication here is that the estate is going to Brick, the favored son, because he is finally providing the necessary heir. Gooper and Mae get their comeuppance, and Big Daddy can make a grand exit to the belvedere on the roof "to look over my kingdom before I give up my kingdom" (78). He may be dying, but he is going to die happy, satisfied, and at peace with himself.

Given Kazan's reputation as the most important and dynamic American theater director of his day and his decision to stage *Cat* in an unconventionally presentational style, it is ironic that the dramaturgical changes he requested of Williams are a throwback to the utterly conventional form of "the well-made play," developed in the nineteenth century by French playwright Eugène Scribe, with its careful plotting and obligatory scenes. But while such mechanics now seem false and dated, there is an absolute "odor of mendacity" to the thematic changes they support: homosexuality is erased, the cat is tamed, and the patriarchy is triumphant. All of this suited the Broadway audiences of 1955, as the show's robust box office attests. Williams had the hit he was looking for, but he was unsatisfied. He continued to revise *Cat on a Hot Tin Roof* throughout the rest of his career (including yet another version published in 1975). There was more mendacity on the stage than he had counted on.

Works Cited

Aristotle. *Aristotle's Poetics: A Translation and Commentary for Students of Literature.* Trans. Leon Golden. Tallahassee: Florida State UP, 1981.

Arrell, Douglas. "Homosexual Panic in *Cat on a Hot Tin Roof.*" *Modern Drama* 51.1 (Spring 2008): 60-72.

Case, Sue-Ellen. *Feminism and Theatre.* New York: Routledge, 1988.

Clum, John M. "'Something Cloudy, Something Clear': Homosexual Discourse in Tennessee Williams." *Displacing Homophobia: Gay Male Perspectives in Literature and Culture.* Ed. Ronald R. Butters, John M. Clum, and Michael Moon. Durham, NC: Duke UP, 1989. 149-67.

Kazan, Elia. *A Life.* New York: Alfred A. Knopf, 1988.

Kerr, Walter F. Rev. of *Cat on a Hot Tin Roof,* by Tennessee Williams. *New York Theatre Critics Reviews* 16 (1955): 342.

_____. "A Secret Is Half-Told in Fountains of Words." *New York Herald Tribune* 3 Apr. 1955: sec. 4, 1.

Mendelsohn, Daniel. *How Beautiful It Is and How Easily It Can Be Broken.* New York: Harper, 2008.

Murphy, Brenda. *Tennessee Williams and Elia Kazan: A Collaboration in the Theatre.* New York: Cambridge UP, 1992.

Savran, David. *Communists, Cowboys, and Queers: The Politics of Masculinity in the Work of Arthur Miller and Tennessee Williams.* Minneapolis: U of Minnesota P, 1992.

Shackelford, Dean. "The Truth That Must Be Told: Gay Subjectivity, Homophobia, and Social History in *Cat on a Hot Tin Roof.*" *Tennessee Williams Annual Review* 1 (1998): 103-18.

Williams, Tennessee. *Cat on a Hot Tin Roof.* New York: Dramatists Play Service, 1955.

_____. *Memoirs.* Garden City, NY: Doubleday, 1975.

_____. *Notebooks.* Ed. Margaret Bradham Thornton. New Haven, CT: Yale UP, 2006.

_____. *Plays 1937-1955.* New York: Library of America, 2000.

_____. *The Selected Letters of Tennessee Williams.* Vol. 2. Ed. Albert J. Devlin and Nancy M. Tischler. New York: New Directions, 2004.

_____. *Where I Live: Selected Essays.* Ed. Christine R. Day and Bob Woods. New York: New Directions, 1978.

CRITICAL
READINGS

A Gallery of Witches_____

Nancy M. Tischler

Amanda, Blanche, Big Mama, Myrtle, Mrs. Venable, Maggie, Mrs. Stone, Alexandra del Lago—some of the many remarkable women who dominate Tennessee Williams' world. Although Tom Wingfield is the admittedly autobiographical role in *The Glass Menagerie*, any actor or director would acknowledge that Amanda is the far more challenging role to play and the far more complex character to study. Blanche, not Stanley, dominates *Streetcar*; Maggie, not Big Daddy, controls the action of *Cat on a Hot Tin Roof*. Certain male characters do approach the complexity and power of Williams' female, but by and large—for a number of reasons, both biographical and psychological—the most memorable characters created by Tennessee Williams are women.

His heroines tend to fall into two or three categories. Signi Falk separates them into southern gentlewomen, southern wenches, and southern mothers, which she catalogues and discusses briefly as types (p. 169). In light of Williams' interest in myth, the recent scholarship on the archetype of the feminine, and the changing focus of Williams' later work, this decade-old perception requires reconsideration, correction, and expansion.

That Williams is interested in myth is obvious in such titles as *Orpheus Descending* or *I Rise in Flame, Cried the Phoenix*. Further, the cast of *Camino Real* provides a ready index to Williams' private and shared mythology: Mary the Mother of Christ and the perennial Virgin, the harlot Gypsy, and the superannuated Camille. The speeches of his plays are littered with symbols and images drawn from myth: for instance, Maggie compares her early days with Brick as Artemis and Apollo hunting in the woods; and her repeated cat symbolism combines with the repeated references to the Nile to associate her with ancient Egyptian myth. Even settings are usually symbolic of an archetypal human experience: *Summer and Smoke*, in its clearly bifurcated structure, mirrors the ancient perception of man's divided nature; *Orpheus Descending* and *Kingdom of Earth* both use the stairway as the archetypal ladder between the sterile and the fecund layers of his two-storied universe. Stanley emphasizes the stairs' Freudian implications by drawing Stella down them to his level of sensuality, as Maxine does Shannon as she leads him down to the sea-womb. Critics have consistently observed the symbolic structure undergirding Williams' plays, and directors have emphasized his archetypal contrasts for their inherent dramatic power.

Jungians have brought together a vast array of dream, myth, and story to outline the archetype of the Feminine. Neumann, for example, in *The Great Mother* describes four poles of development for the feminine character: the good Mother, the terrible Mother, the positive transformative character and the negative transformative character. The good mother would include the Mother aspect of Mary, of Demeter, of Isis-figures who bear and release. At the opposite pole lie the terrible Mother figures—Gorgon, Hecate, Kali—women who fix, ensnare, and even dismember their young. The other poles in his schema include the positive transformative characters—the Virgin Mary, Sophia, the Muse—sources of wisdom, vision, inspiration and ecstasy. Opposite these lie the young witches, Lilith, Circe, and Astarte, whose mysteries of drunkenness bring another pattern of ecstasy, leading to madness, impotence and stupor (p. 82).

At the conclusion of his study, Neumann insists that these universal forms he has described may be traced in modern woman as well as in ancient myth: "The stages of the self-revelation of the Feminine Self, objectivized in the world of archetypes, symbols, images, and rites, present us with a world that may be said to be both historical and eternal." He says that the realms of symbols in which the Feminine becomes visible (as Great Round, as Lady of the Plants and Animals, and finally as genetrix of the spirit, as nurturing Sophia) "correspond to stages in the self-unfolding of the feminine nature." This he calls "the Eternal Feminine, which infinitely transcends all its earthly incarnations—every woman and every individual symbol." And this "Archetypal Feminine" he insists manifests itself "in all times and all cultures," appearing "in the living reality of modern woman, in her dreams and visions, compulsions and fantasies, projections and relationships, fixations and transformations" (p. 336). Whether or not Neumann is correct in his assertions about the universal applicability of his findings, his observations appear relevant to the images in Tennessee Williams' work.

From the beginning, Williams rejected the beloved American stereotype: the good wife, good mother, loving sweetheart. One of his first plays described a woman inviting guests to dinner and then flooding the banquet hall (Tischler, *Tennessee Williams*, p. 31). Williams' mutilated people generally fall pathetically in love with the unloving or the unthinking brutes or icebergs who then ignore, abandon, or devour them. Children run from mothers or shrivel under their domination. Young men seek out old harpies who castrate them.

In a colorful article on this unAmerican, or all-too-American Williams world, Marion Magid wrote: "it is a tropical country whose vegetation is largely man-eating. . . . it has not yet been converted to Christianity, but continues to observe the myth of the annual death and resurrection of the sun-god, for which purposes it keeps on hand a constant supply of young men to sacrifice. Its young men are for the most part beautiful and fawnlike . . . ," and she continues, "The country does not observe the traditional Western sexual orientation which involves the pursuit of the female by the male; instead, its young men reluctantly allow themselves to be had on those occasions when there is no way of avoiding it. . . . They are right in general to be of two minds regarding the sexual embrace, for it is as often as not followed by the direct consequences: cannibalism, castration, burning alive, madness, surgery in various forms ranging from lobotomy to hysterectomy, depending on the nature of the offending organ" ("The Innocence of Tennessee Williams," p. 34).

Thus does Williams break the prevailing Western tradition, the standard American notions of male-female relationships, and the southern mystique of the woman. In *The Glass Menagerie*, Amanda broke the sentimental mother stereotype as well as the popular image of the southern belle. From his earliest plays he broke the southern tradition of polite evasion and chivalric gynolatry. Yet, in his very violation of American tradition, Williams has delved deeper than most of his contemporaries into the essential Feminine.

His variations in both plays and short stories of the Terrible Mother image testify to Williams' obsession with her. These variants also demonstrate the range of his talent and his method of characterization. Although some of the preliminary sketches for his fully developed character studies are cardboard and garish, he is clearly not simply an iconoclast, determined to shock and destroy. Those works in which this great hovering bird-woman is most primitive and fearful are his cartoons, not his masterpieces. A clear example of this variation on the theme would be Karen Stone, the hard-hearted harpy of Williams' solitary novel. Both Mrs. Stone and Meg Bishop, the lesbian friend, are tough older women, both career women, both verbally and psychologically aggressive. While Meg can find some satisfaction in her perversion, Karen is tragically heterosexual; she has deliberately avoided motherhood by spending her fecund years with a bunny rabbit of a husband, who has served as her surrogate baby, and whose death leaves the postmenopausal widow lusting after a lover who can also be a child. Turning to the gigolos of Rome in her furious search for the fountain of youth, the old actress finds that her hawkish manners frighten the Roman sparrows just as her predatory Juliet had overpowered her pallid Romeos.

Still cruder portrayal of the gorgon lady appears in *The Milk Train Doesn't Stop Here Anymore*. Flora Goforth has even less charm than Karen Stone, being older, more hawkish, less vulnerable. In the short story "Man Bring This Up Road," she is even more grotesque. Mistress of her sumptuous villa, she dispassionately examines her vulnerable young visitors, selecting those nubile boys most to her taste, and expelling the others from her kingdom.

A fourth appearance of this thespian witch was to become a fully developed character in Alexandra del Lago of *Sweet Bird of Youth*. Still drawing heavily on bird imagery for his aging predator, Williams again portrays the aging actress inviting the vulnerable and nubile young beach boy to her bed, where, in his fatuous egotism, he presumes to challenge the old pro to a game of King of the Mountain. Predictably, Chance Wayne, like Paolo and the poet, finds himself outmatched by the cynical old witch. He can play no Oedipus to her Sphinx, no Odysseus to her Circe. He is too gentle an antihero to take on the hazardous queen and master her. Thus, Williams encourages sympathy with her slightly balding gigolo while also creating a surprising magnificence in this great castrator.

The Princess is well past her prime, is even more dissipated by hashish and liquor than Karen Stone, but she exceeds Karen also in understanding and sympathy. Unwilling to let Chance blackmail or manipulate her to shore up the ruins of his own aborted life, she is nonetheless protective when the lynch mob threatens; she offers him the role of pet dog on a golden chain. She towers over the other characters in her rage and in her lust, sharing none of their pettiness or vengefulness. Recognizing that time is the ultimate enemy for both Chance and herself, she can acknowledge that they are both monsters, living in Beanstalk Country. She can pity Chance for being a minor monster, having neither talent nor character, and for having used up his scant store of good looks and good will so quickly and so foolishly. Although his touching faith in the Cinderella myth amuses the maternal old pro, her claws show when he tries to outwit her. Like Flora Goforth, the Princess restricts her kingdom to those who can and will pay her price. Chance insists this is the real castration, leaving him already mutilated before the lynch mob appears.

Thus does Williams pay tribute to the many heroic aging actresses he watched master his roles and their own lives—from Laurette Taylor and Helen Hayes to Tallulah Bankhead and Diana Barrymore. The Princess is no simple archetype; she incorporates the gestures and the complexity of individuals Williams came to know, respect, and admire in his long theatrical career.

The earlier older woman/mother image in Williams' work had followed more specifically autobiographical or regional paths. Williams admitted from its conception that *The Glass Menagerie* incorporated many details of the Williams/Wingfield family's painful experience in St. Louis (Tischler, *Tennessee Williams*, pp. 27 ff). Though Mrs. Williams would not admit to Laurette Taylor that she was Amanda, both tone and style of her book *Remember Me to Tom* justify the assumption that Amanda is based on the personality of Edwina Dakin Williams. Williams also stated explicitly that the play was about "mothers"—not just southern mothers. Amanda's characterization combines the antiquated southern belle with the image of the Terrible Mother to produce a gothic creation of enormous subtlety.

As Neumann says, the female archetype is most typically presented from the male point of view. The man sees the woman primarily in her elementary role as nourisher and protector. But in a pattern of negative development, parallel to Hansel's and Gretel's discovery that the inhabitant of the gingerbread house actually eats children, man's image of the Good Mother often is transformed by time and experience into the image of the Terrible Mother. This transformative development can drive the ego toward masculinization (the fight with the dragon) or toward castration (capitulation). Tom finally verbalizes this truth, screaming at Amanda, "You ugly . . . old—*witch*." Though he subsequently retreats, apologizes, and finally comes to a grudging admiration of his mother, he has nonetheless recognized that she is the dragon he must battle if he is to pass the threshold of manhood.

Neumann's explication of the image of the Terrible Mother reveals Amanda's universality: "it is typical for the matriarchal sphere that the son is dominated by the Great Mother who holds him fast even in his masculine movement and activity" (p. 48). Certainly every part of the Wingfield apartment testifies to the matriarchal dominance. Though Amanda also manipulates the pathetically crippled and withdrawn

Laura, it is Tom who provides her with a real challenge. She is determined to govern his work, his pleasures, his reading, and even his eating habits. Smothering attention is, according to Neumann, characteristic of the archetype: "in the clinging, ensnaring function of the woman we already discern a will to release nothing from her dominion, but in the function of diminution and devouring this will is still stronger and is seen to be aggressively negative" (p. 69). Certainly those moments in *Menagerie* when Amanda is triumphant after her tiny victories demonstrate her appetite for power. The wrestling of an apology from Tom and the redecoration of their dowdy, little tenement in preparation for the intended new victim should convince the audience that Tom is wise in electing the path to survival, to freedom, and to manhood.

Yet Amanda is no simple archetype any more than the Princess is. She may be frighteningly true on the mythic level, as a powerful universal image, but she also has her very human justifications for her nature. The absence of the father is perhaps symbolic—the praying mantis devours her mate when she lays her eggs, as Strindberg has so eloquently demonstrated in *The Father*. The Terrible Mother has no real need of a mate once her function has shifted from conception to nurture, for her nourishing milk flows without the male's involvement. But in *The Glass Menagerie*, the absence of the husband is no victory for Amanda. Rooted in a tradition of the genteel Southerner, she can have no social position, no financial security apart from her husband. The abandoned wife violates the code of chivalry and gynolatry; she casts suspicion on the immortality of romantic love and calls into doubt the validity of southern education of women. The woman who has no career plans outside of marriage must find her pride in her husband and her children. It is her husband who in his success adorns her with ornaments and surrounds her with comforts, and she serves as an advertisement of his power and his generosity. But Amanda, thrust unloved and unlovely into a lonely world, must construct her own symbols of comfort, hospitality and style. Thus Williams speaks of her world as "paranoia"—thereby accounting for the stridency in her voice, the faint vulgarity of her struggle for survival. She uses the D.A.R. to sell magazines, her daughter to run up grocery bills, and her son to rope in potential providers. Amanda retains her southern femininity in a grotesque ritual that has lost its meaning, a sad relic of her girlhood and her romantic marriage.

Her courage in the face of adversity makes her heroic on the human level, though threatening to her children and tiresome to her society. Williams has withdrawn from her the essentials that undergird her social being, thus forcing the audience to consider the travesty of the southern myth of woman. So much of the myth rests on the presuppositions of youth, beauty, and wealth, so little on wit, heroism, enduring love. Yet Amanda refuses to acknowledge that the myth has exploded in her face, preferring to escape into her memories of jonquil days filled with gentlemen callers. Sadly, she is more beautiful now in her strength than she could have been then in her innocence, but she ignores this new value and relishes the old, choosing the dream of voile to the reality of leather.

To this complex layering of myth and region, Williams adds yet another implication, which is often a part of both the myth and the southern treatment of it—a sexual possessiveness. Only in certain moments—the flirtation with the gentleman caller and the balcony scene with Tom—do we sense a repressed sexuality in the puritanical Amanda. It is, however, this very characteristic that Williams was to explore in Alma (of *Summer and Smoke*), Alma's mother and John's mother (in *Eccentricities of a Nightingale*), and finally and most completely in Blanche.

The heroine of *A Streetcar Named Desire* is even more complex and certainly more distraught than Amanda. Although Blanche like Amanda is an aging belle—sans youth, sans wealth, sans mate, she has less focus to her life than Amanda because she is also sans progeny. Her efforts to hover over her sister, Stella, clash with Stanley's need to dominate; her eagerness to substitute for Mitch's devouring mother crashes against his innocence and disillusionment. Blanche is at the end of a trail of such failures. Her life has become a parade of shadows that momentarily replace the lost boy of her life, her homosexual husband whom she blames herself for destroying. Each gesture of love and lust echoes her need for expiation for this guilt.

There is something of the White Goddess in Blanche. Under her white dresses—sometimes soiled white—she certainly brings sterility and destruction to the Kowalski household; she settles in as a school teacher-mother who plans to improve their minds and their manners while she peremptorily dismantles their sensual paradise. Stanley is shrewd enough to see the immediate changes in Stella and to sense the altered atmosphere of his cut-rate Elysium. Though Blanche is primarily victim in any confrontation with Stanley, she is also the "tiger"— the adversary, the threat. Elia Kazan speaks of Stanley's "spine" as being masculine pride and protection of his family. If so, then Blanche tries to break that "spine" and must at any price be cast out or destroyed.

Ironically, she has in her enough masochism that she seeks the violence he threatens. In her sick memory of her castrating attack on her young husband, she finds justification for her own rape. Enough of a Southerner to remain convinced of the propriety of clearly defined male-female roles, she seeks male dominance (e.g., Shep and Mitch, as she imagines their chivalric concern for her) so that she can relax and be truly feminine. The final poignant gesture of leaning on the doctor's arm confirms her longing to lean on a strong male.

In Blanche-Stanley, the older woman-younger man syndrome is in part a teacher-student relationship (emphasized by Blanche's profession and her attraction to young men). The teachers in *Night of the Iguana* are even more clearly harpies, attacking the exhausted Shannon, driving him out of their group. But in *Milk Train* and *Sweet Bird*, Williams abandons the pretense of the teacher role, creating instead witchlike guides into corruption. The older woman becomes the ogremother who initiates the perpetually virgin youth into the corruption of the human heart. In *Sweet Bird*, the Princess' education of Chance is done with combined sympathy and sternness, echoing her motherly function.

Perhaps the most extreme case of the possessive mother is Violet Venable of *Suddenly Last Summer*, whose tropical garden mirrors her sick mind. The play calls for a "jungle garden" with violent colors, a garden designed by Sebastian as an image of the world and preserved by his doting mother. "There are massive tree-flowers that suggest organs of a body, torn out, still glistening with undried blood; there are harsh cries and sibilant hissings and thrashing sounds in the garden as if it were inhabited by beasts, serpents and birds, all of a savage nature" (III, 349). The predatory female of the Williams world finds this a natural habitat: in "The Knightly Quest," the savage mother has her aviary and her castle; in *Night of the Iguana*, Maxine has her hilltop surrounded by tropical rain forest. The witch apparently requires such trappings to underscore the atavistic role she plays, which is further emphasized in *Suddenly Last Summer* by the grotesque image of the turtles. Mrs. Venable and her perverse son have come to equate this scene with God: "Over the narrow black beach of the Encantadas as the just-hatched sea turtles scrambled out of the sand pits and started their race to the sea. . . . To escape the flesh-eating birds that made the sky almost as black as the beach! . . . And the sand all alive, all alive, as the hatched sea turtles made their dash for the sea, while the birds hovered and swooped to attack. . . . They were diving down on the hatched sea turtles, turning them over to expose their soft undersides, tearing the undersides open and rending and eating their flesh . . ." (III, 356).

Mrs. Venable has made the classic mother's choice of son over husband, allowing her husband to die alone while she protects her child. Her hovering concern has a Freudian ring as she speaks of the poems the two of them took nine months to produce, poems which he could not write without her. She insists that at forty he was still celibate because she herself "was actually the only one in his life that satisfied the demands he made of people" (II, 362). And when he turns to another,

---

younger woman, even as an alternate decoy for his boy-victims, he dies, as if she willed it to punish him for cutting the umbilical cord. Catharine, in fact, replaces Violet as a mother-image to the man, though he is older than she; but neither Violet nor Catharine can save the perverse saint from his predetermined martyrdom. Violet now turns on Catharine, whom she must destroy to preserve the purity and the reputation of the departed Sebastian. Her willingness to lobotomize her niece is testimony to her veneration of her son and to her viciousness.

The fierce Mrs. Venable is an intensification of Mrs. Buchanan (*Eccentricities of a Nightingale*) and Serafina (*The Rose Tattoo*). But mothers in Williams' world show less violence toward daughters and a more jealous concern for themselves. The Gypsy with her daughter (*Camino Real*), Mrs. Winemiller with Alma (*Eccentricities* and *Summer and Smoke*), and Serafina with Rosa remind us in some way of Amanda with Laura. The daughter is a rival to the mother, challenging her role with men, reviving her own flirtatiousness along with a certain condescending and suspect solicitousness. But this relationship is quite different as a rule from mother-son confrontations.

Of all the Williams mothers, it is Big Mama who is wisest and gentlest and best. Again, the mother hangs lovingly onto the effeminate son, apparently contributing to his affliction. But in this case, Big Daddy causes more of Brick's weakness; such fierce masculinity almost demands a contrary response in the sensitive son. So long as Big Daddy dominates the scene, his wife seems like a loving doormat. But with the revelation of his sickness and his impending death, Big Mama is transformed into a strong figure, capable of managing her family, echoing the very language of her scatological husband: "I say CRAP too, like Big Daddy! . . . *Nobody's goin' to take nothin'!*—till Big Daddy lets go of it, and maybe, just possibly, not—not even then!" (III, 156). But she does hint that she would prefer to rely on her menfolks—preferably Brick. In fact, Big Mama is an almost completely sympathetic person—perhaps because Big Daddy is the monster in the family—except in her relationship with Gooper, her firstborn. The disowning of this Esau-figure appears to be both cause and result of his unappealing personality. Her need to lavish love on the unresponsive and undependable Brick testifies to her compulsion to love those men who can hurt her most. Masochism and perverse favoritism have been perennial mysteries of mother love, apparent throughout myth and history, but uncommon in the Williams woman; this doormat woman resembles Arthur Miller's characters. Big Mama displays the Good Mother image, with barely a hint of negativism.

The harpy in this play is not the ugly old witch, but the beautiful young one. Maggie the Cat is one of Williams' most interesting and unexpected heroines. Her earlier portrait in "Three Players of a Summer Game" delineates a sterile, castrating female, seeking to dominate the weak husband. The story ends with this impressive image: "Brick's driver's license had been revoked again for some misadventure on the highway due to insufficient control of the wheel, and it was his legal wife, Margaret, who sat in the driver's seat of the Pierce-Arrow touring car. Brick did not sit beside her. He was on the back seat of the car, pitching this way and that way with the car's jolting motion, like a loosely wrapped package being delivered somewhere. Margaret Pollitt handled the car with a wonderful male assurance, her bare arms brown and muscular as a Negro field hand's, and the car's canvas top had been lowered the better to expose on its back seat the sheepishly grinning and nodding figure of Brick Pollitt." The last sentence of the story captures the impression: "It was exactly the way that some ancient conqueror, such as Caesar or Alexander the Great or Hannibal, might have led in chains through a capital city the prince of a state newly conquered" (*Hard Candy*, pp. 43-4). The play blurs this simple image with more complex motivation. Maggie desires more than the domination of Brick; she has a lust for life, for love, for children, and for money. She is a scrappy little fighter, spitting at the enemy, purring for the master, clawing for survival. She combines the motherly attentions of Big Mama and the sexuality and aggressiveness of Big Daddy. Her youth and her determination will clearly make her the sexual victor, though it is unlikely that Brick will ever do much more than talk and drink. Her very strength will serve to replace Big Daddy's as an excuse for his diminishment. In her nurturing, protective role as mother to Brick, Maggie seeks to give Brick back his life. Her final, condescending, yet loving lines, emphasize this intent, while contrasting with the conclusion of the earlier story: "Oh, you weak, beautiful people who give up with such grace," she says to the vanquished Brick. "What you need is someone to take hold of you—gently, with love, and hand your life back to you, like something gold you let go of—and I can!" (III, 215).

The sexually aggressive female—an anathema to the Southerner—fascinates Williams. Usually her attack is on the younger male, though Maggie and Maxine are priestesses of Venus who are willing to consider males of any age. Maggie dominates Brick's friend Skip sexually and flirts with Big Daddy. Maxine (*Night of the Iguana*) moves easily from aging husband to beach boys to Shannon. She is a more highly developed and interesting version of the tough but motherly whore shown in Myrtle of the seven descents. The water imagery of *Night of the Iguana* echoes her role as womb and tomb. Her tropical retreat is the end of Shannon's world, where he can return to the earth mother, dance his final perverse, saintly dance, and die erotically in her motherly embrace. Maxine's wit makes her far more believable, colorful, and dramatic than Karen Stone as well as more motherly and warm, less hard and egocentric. Her symbols are natural ones of vegetation, water, and animal life—all indications of her archetypal function.

While Maxine, in her revealing shirt and slacks, demonstrates the amplitude of the mother, feeding her flock, offering them shelter for the night, she also demands her price. She flaunted her lusty "night-swimmers" before her dying husband, and she can tie up the iguana as she can tie up Shannon for future use. Her mothering of Shannon is both solicitous and salacious. The concluding scene, as they go down to the sea ("the cradle of life") for a night swim, is emphasized by Shannon's assertion that he can make it down the hill without her, but not back up. She insists that she can help him back up, but her comforts will not be the austere and spiritual ones that Shannon needs for renewal.

Hannah, on the other hand, the alternate mother figure in the play, is a New England spinster, who serves as a cool Oriental madonna, offering him poppy seed tea and sympathy as Shannon works through his voluptuous crucifixion. The pietà is a frequent Williams image, a combination of sexual purity, and that deep compassion that results from the blessedness of bearing and losing the child. La Madrecita de los Perdidos (*Camino Real*) is the image that haunts him, echoing the conclusion of *Glass Menagerie* (with Amanda hovering over the lost Laura), repeated in *Iguana* with Hannah cradling her dead grandfather. Ironically, this Mother Mary, who contrasts with the cruel mother of life, seems to be impotent, capable only of compassion. While Hannah would never tie up Shannon or the iguana, neither would she release them. We therefore should not expect her to travel with Shannon or to stay with him. She laughingly quips, "Spinster's loss, widow's gain," but Shannon recognizes the hovering irony of the comment.

The parallel female figures here summarize some of Williams' attitudes. Hannah-the-spinster and Maxine-the-widow are his most fully developed pair, though he uses parallel mothers in *Eccentricities of a Nightingale*, mothers and daughters in *Cat*, *Menagerie*, and *Rose Tattoo*, sisters in *Streetcar*. Hannah and Maxine are both characterized principally by their relationship to men—one having lived without sexuality, the other having reveled in it, and both now without mates. On the one hand, Hannah is proud of her virginity, wearing her purity with Athena's regality, neither ashamed nor puritanical, capable of love, of compassion, and of considerable wisdom. She has chosen her "nest" in the heart of her grandfather, with no hope of sexual satisfaction or propagation, content as Alma Winemiller could never have been.

On the other hand, Maxine has outlived one husband and proudly advertises her sexuality, planning to select a new king for her mountain, whom she will also outlive. She is no monster—any more than Maggie is a monster. She is a full-blooded woman who loved Fred, loves Shannon, and can love again when Shannon has gone. She did not kill Fred, but she does not mourn him deeply. Like Maggie, she is no willing participant in rituals of self-destruction. And also, like Maggie, her lust for life takes brutal forms that may appear excessive. Unlike the Strindberg nightmare of Omphale's ensnaring Heracles, the binding in *Iguana* is followed by a loosing. Maxine, a "bright widow spider" (IV, 317), can endure Shannon's pain with equanimity and even contribute to it. But the action of the play disproves Shannon's assertion that "All women, whether they face it or not, want to see a man in a tied-up situation. . . . Their lives are fulfilled, they're satisfied at last, when they get a man, or as many men as they can, in the tied-up situation" (IV, 345). The play itself moderates this harsh judgment: Maxine and Hannah both see the trussing as a means to curtail Shannon's self-destructive violence. He is not quite parallel to the iguana; since he is human, his ensnarement involves choice, not simply blind force. And Maxine's enjoyment of him will not be altogether unpleasant for him.

Williams characterizes both Maxine and Hannah in depth, yet balances them as types and further exploits them as elements of Shannon's nature—his flesh and spirit, bad and good angels, id and superego. They are remarkably rich portraits of classic Williams women. Alma, Blanche, Amanda, Laura all share traits with the Yankee lady Buddha; Stella, Rosa, Maggie, Big Mama all foreshadow the earth mother of the rain forest. But they are both different from their predecessors, less tormented, more understanding of themselves and others, more content to accept their own limitations. Both are visually and verbally contrasted; both range from tragedy to comedy, but in very different modes. They share the resilience of Williams' beloved phoenix and appear to be his tribute to woman's appetite for life and capacity for survival.

If there is such a thing as development in an author, the critic must note that the movement from Amanda to Blanche to Maggie to Alexandra del Lago to Maxine/Hannah demonstrates an increasing acknowledgment of the corruption of the male victim and an expanding acceptance of therapeutic cruelty. Certainly, Amanda/Tom is modified in Maggie/Brick, which is again expanded in Alexandra/Chance, and finally almost balanced in Maxine/Shannon. The mother-figure appears less cruel as the child grows older and more corrupt, blinder, more self-mutilating, more demonstrably wrongheaded.

It is by no means strange that Tennessee Williams should have meditated so long and with such baroque results on this mother-son syndrome. Mom and Venus are the dominant female images for America. The grotesque marriages of Venus with the spider, and the mother with the monster, appeal more to Williams—perhaps the artist's reaction against the simplistic assertions of advertisers, perhaps the Southerner's need to destroy the cloying rhetoric of gynolatry, perhaps the homosexual's observations of actual women, certainly the man's observation and confrontations in his life. Whatever the reason, his images are testimony to his versatility and his artistry. That he can play so many compelling variations on these themes demonstrates his rich sensitivity; that he must trace his redundant arabesques in so narrow a sphere suggests his compulsive and romantic mode of creativity.

The literary critic enjoys the recurrent pattern as an exciting vehicle for isolating levels of characterization: On the most universal level, he can trace the image of the Great Mother in her most terrible aspect—as primitive and frightening as the Gorgon or the dreaded Sphinx, as furious with her mate and destructive of her children as Medea, or as temptingly vicious as Circe. At this level, she is frighteningly presented as a trial to be faced by the hero—often to be fought by indirection, necessarily to be escaped if he is to survive with his manhood intact.

On the more cultural, historical level, he can trace the lineaments of the American South: the veneration of the woman, the matriarchal culture, the possessive and charming mother/belle. Under her drawl and her wit, behind her charm and vivacity is a frenzy, a desperation, a possessiveness, a clue to the more vicious archetype.

But the focus on the predatory female bird and the ensnared male iguana/turtle victim takes on an individual stress with Tennessee Williams. His signature is in the jungle imagery, the cats and birds. No other contemporary playwright has such a gallery of handsome male victims in so many stages of mutilation. The violence of Williams exceeds primitive violence because it is wrapped in the decadently lavish style of southern rhetoric. And his combinations are more subtle and more haunting than most, perhaps because they are so visual, so grotesque, so dramatic. His characters seldom live on the level of moral absolutes, though they pretend to hold to certain private ideals; victims tend to deserve their crucifixions, brutes have justification and grandeur and moments of gentleness. Witches need not be old, and youths need not be innocent. Both the hero and the Gorgon may have their recognition scene, admitting their own monstrosity, determining to accept their grim fate.

Thus, in his evaluation, the critic is bound to admit that Williams does indeed create timeless beauty and dredge haunting insights out of the hideous chaos of his memories, observations, and imagination. Although no one would select Karen Stone or Flora Goforth as memorable characters, no one should deny the brilliance of Amanda, Blanche, Maggie, Maxine, or Alexandra. Somehow, Tennessee Williams has domesticated his monsters by providing them a history, a motivation, individualism, and charm. When the Gorgon reveals that she is a former belle, now destructive, aging, and confused, when she frets about her snaky hair, and when she speaks with sardonic wit in a southern accent, we no longer fear her or approach her with mirrors. She has become one of us.

From *Tennessee Williams: A Tribute* (Jackson: University Press of Mississippi, 1977): 494-509. Copyright © 1977 by University Press of Mississippi. Reprinted with permission of University Press of Mississippi.

Works Cited

Falk, Signi. *Tennessee Williams*. New Haven: College and University Press, 1961.

Magid, Marion. "The Innocence of Tennessee Williams." *Commentary* 25 (January 1963), 34-43.

Neumann, Erich. *The Great Mother*. New York: Pantheon Books, 1955.

Strindberg, August. *Eight Expressionistic Plays*. Trans. Arvid Paulson. New York: New York University Press.

Tischler, Nancy M. *Tennessee Williams: Rebellious Puritan*. New York: Citadel Press, 1961.

Williams, Tennessee. *Hard Candy: A Book of Stories*. New York: New Directions paperbook, 1967.

_____. *I Rise in Flame, Cried the Phoenix*. Norfolk, Conn.: [New Directions], 1951.

_____. *Kingdom of Earth*. New York: New Directions, 1967.

_____. *The Knightly Quest: A Novella and Four Short Stories*. New York: New Directions, 1966.

_____. *The Milk Train Doesn't Stop Here Anymore*. Norfolk, Conn.: New Directions, 1964.

_____. *One Arm and Other Stories*. New York: New Directions paperbook, 1967.

_____. *The Theatre of Tennessee Williams*. Five volumes. New York: New Directions, 1971-1976.

Culture, Power, and the (En)gendering of Community:
Tennessee Williams and Politics

Thomas P. Adler

I think it is only in the case of Brecht that a man's politics, if the man is an artist, are of particular importance in his work; his degrees of talent and of humanity are what count.

—Tennessee Williams, *Memoirs* (1975)

I

Not long into Act One of *The Night of the Iguana* (1961), otherwise seemingly an apolitical play, Tennessee Williams rather jarringly brings onto the scene of the remote Costa Verde Hotel in Mexico a family of German tourists—and effectively "stages" for contemporary theatre audiences the reality of the blitzkriegs and firebombings and concentration camps of World War II. Herr Fahrenkopf, a tank manufacturer, his wife, and his honeymooning daughter and son-in-law "suddenly make a startling, dreamlike entrance . . . dressed in the minimal concession to decency . . . pink and gold like baroque cupids in various sizes—Rubenesque, splendidly physical."[1] After hearing a short-wave radio broadcast of the Battle of Britain, they break into a rousing "Nazi marching song." They reappear similarly described near the beginning of Act Two—though now "The women have decked themselves with garlands of pale green seaweed"—with Fahrenkopf exclaiming "[ecstatically]: London is burning, the heart of London's on fire!" (p. 293). Later on, hearing Hitler address the Reichstag over the short-wave radio, his "voice like a mad dog's bark," transforms Fahrenkopf, who is obsessed with the erotics of power, into a grotesque circus clown, "the light catch[ing] his polished glasses so that he appears for a moment to have electric light bulbs in his forehead" (p. 295). In Act Three, after the Germans have taunted the aged Nonno over his faltering memory as he tries to recite one of his poems, Shannon passes the playwright's own unassailable judgment upon them: "Fiends out of hell with the . . . voices of . . . angels" (p. 351).

This coexistence of culture with evil, the fact that highly civilized societies not only countenance but actually become complicitous in inhuman acts, is an observation that Williams shares with other twentieth-century writers who explore the fate of culture and art as it is threatened by commerce and power: with novelists such as Henry James and E. M. Forster; with his fellow Southern dramatist Lillian Hellman in *Watch on the Rhine* (1941) and *The Searching Wind* (1944); or with G. B. Shaw in *Major Barbara* (1903), which proposes a marriage of culture and power, and *Heartbreak House* (1919), which mourns its failure. In fact, the apocalypticism with which the later Shaw play closes (where the ontologically bored English express an almost religious sense of deliverance from their inadequate world by welcoming the aerial bombing as "a glorious experience! . . . like Beethoven"[2]) will find echoes in the apocalyptic endings of several Williams works from *Battle of Angels* (1940) through *The Red Devil Battery Sign* (1977) and *Clothes for a Summer Hotel* (1980).

Moreover, as his treatment of Herr Fahrenkopf and family makes abundantly evident, Williams seems to have associated, as did Virginia Woolf, patriarchy in its many manifestations with racism in all its forms. In *Three Guineas* (1938), Woolf, after claiming that education has failed by teaching the "use" of force rather than abhorrence of it and by espousing "possessiveness" rather than "magnanimity"—in short, by fostering the "arts of dominating . . . of ruling, of killing, of acquiring"—argues that the monstrous "tyranny of the Fascist state" in Germany, Italy, and Spain is akin or analogous to "the tyranny of the patriarchal state": both "dictate how" one will live; both exclude on the basis of sexual, ethnic, and religious difference, creating the outsider and then ostracizing her/him for being Other.[3] From his early years, when his father taunted him as a sissified "Miss Nancy," Williams must have gradually come to see himself as excluded by the patriarchy, until later because of sexual difference he chose to live free from and in rebellion against that patriarchy's repressive and exclusionary mores, rejecting the flawed patriarchy—as Woolf herself did—in favor of what might be seen as a more androgynous political and moral order.

To what extent these concerns render Williams a "political playwright" remains open to debate. Much depends, of course, on how one understands the term. Recently, Gerald Berkowitz has claimed that "Williams is an almost completely non-political writer," while Marc Robinson has proposed that the "private world is Williams's only true purview": "While his plays are inseparable from what we have come to understand as Southern literature, he finds it almost impossible to imagine 'societies.'"[4] On the other hand, C. W. E. Bigsby, in discussing Williams's "radicalism" in his earliest efforts as a writer "creating a series of protest plays for a political theatre group in St. Louis," has cautioned us to temper such unequivocal suggestions: "If, after the 1930s, Williams rarely chose to formulate his sense of political oppression in overtly political ways, his portraits of individuals pressed to the margins of social concern, trapped in a diminishing social and psychological space, are not without ideological significance, for, as Michel Foucault has reminded us, there is a link between space and power."[5] In his own essays and interviews spanning several decades, Williams comments extensively on his private politics and on larger sociocultural issues from a personal perspective. Essentially, he attaches to himself the designations Humanitarian and Revolutionary. In "Facts About Me" (1952), Williams, although asserting "I don't think any writer has much purpose back of him unless he feels bitterly the inequities of the society he lives in," goes on to say that he has "no acquaintance with political and social dialectics. If you ask what my politics are, I am a Humanitarian."[6] And yet, when he cast his only ballot ever in a presidential election in 1932, he voted for the Socialist candidate, Norman Thomas, evidencing his "interest in the discovery of a new social system . . . , an enlightened form of socialism, I would suppose."[7]

By the early 1970s, Williams had become openly vocal in criticizing

America's expansionist, imperialist mission as "the beginning of our moral collapse," decrying as "incomprehensibly evil" the whole Vietnam morass; as a counter to the "atrocity of American involvement" and "Nixon's total lack of honesty and of a moral sense," he cited his own "devotion . . . to the cause of Senator McGovern" (*Memoirs*, p. 95). Indeed, already in an insert accompanying the theater program for *Slapstick Tragedy* (1966), Williams had "denounced [Vietnam] as 'incredibly cruel': 'believe me, nothing that will be won out of this war will be worth the life of a single man who died in it.'"[8] The year 1971 actually found him publicly addressing an antiwar rally in New York's Cathedral of St. John the Divine, which would later honor him with its first arts medal. In what could undoubtedly be challenged as too simplistic and naive a layman's analysis, he eventually came to see Vietnam as the culmination of a pattern reaching back beyond recent events to include even the bombing of Hiroshima and Nagasaki and the McCarthy witch hunts of the '50s: "It's the moral decay of America, which really began with the Korean War, way before the Kennedy assassination. The main reason we were involved in Vietnam was so two hundred billion dollars worth of equipment could be destroyed and would have to be bought again. We're the death merchants of the world, this once great and beautiful democracy. People think I'm a communist, but I hate all bureaucracy, all isms. I'm a revolutionary only in the sense that I want to see us escape from this sort of trap."[9] And so the title of his late play, *A House Not Meant to Stand* (1982), becomes—like Shaw's title *Heartbreak House*—"a metaphor for society in our times" (*Conversations*, p. 336).

In Williams's nomenclature, the concepts "artist" and "revolutionary" are virtually synonymous and, by implication, activist; as he says in "The Misunderstandings and Fears of an Artist's Revolt" (1978), the designation "Artist . . . must always remain a word most compatible with the word Revolutionary, and so be more than a word" (*Essays*, p. 171). As an artist, he particularly rebelled against the thought-police mentality of a government enforcing "prescribed ideas," forbidding any "very explicit criticism from within," and sanctioning "the all but complete suppression of any dissident voices," a condition that left him "trembling before the specter of investigating committees and even with Buchenwald in the back of our minds" (*Essays*, pp. 13, 35). All such repression runs counter to the agenda that Williams in a 1960 essay claimed for the art form in which he most often worked: "I dare to suggest, from my POV [Point of View], that the theater has made in our time its greatest artistic advance through the unlocking and lighting up and ventilation of the closets, attics, and basements of human behavior and experience" (*Essays*, pp. 116-117). Immensely effective in forwarding such an expansive personal aesthetic agenda, Williams expressed as well a deterministic view of progress as possessing an "inexorable . . . flow . . . towards some form of social upheaval." Nevertheless, he finally remained skeptical "that any play, any playwright, or any work of art is going to make any difference in the course of history" (*Conversations*, p. 292).

A few examples may be sufficient to convey some sense of the variety of ways in which recent critics have pointed to specific traces of national "social upheaval" in plays throughout Williams's career. Bigsby's Marxist reading, for example, finds in the apprentice works from the 1930s protest against "a political and economic system that encouraged corruption and broke the individual on the rack of private profit" (Bigsby, pp. 36-37). Writing about *Kingdom of Earth* (1968), Philip Kolin inventively rereads the play as Williams's exploration of "racial inequities and the ravages of colonization" and his effort to "demoralize [the] mythologies upon which racial stereotypes are grounded"; in order to accomplish this end, the playwright presents the dominant white culture—in the person of Lot—as the "colonizing white man" who attempts to deny his racially mixed half-brother Chicken's "right to signify" through dispossessing him of the land.[10] More directly pertinent to the line of argument pursued here are Robert Bray's and Lionel Kelly's analyses of *A Streetcar Named Desire* (1947). In his essay on "The Political and Historical Subtext," Bray examines *Streetcar* for its commentary on the passing of property—and therefore of power—from an old, stratified agrarian order that took ownership as a sanction for oppression of workers to a new, expanding industrial/ factory society for whom economic advantage ensures progress; in short, "the proletariat become the ruling class."[11] In "The White Goddess, Ethnicity, and the Politics of Desire," Kelly proposes that the socially and racially pluralistic New Orleans of *Streetcar*, rather than being a melting pot, is actually marked by an "ethnic divisiveness" that the presence of Stanley Kowalski, the "extraneous . . . intruder" and "exploiter" with "immigrant *arriviste* ambitions," only exacerbates. Stanley's "claims on American identity come with a brutal disregard for competing claims," so that "the myth of national union is questioned."[12] (Interestingly enough, a "Victory Liberty Loan" poster designed by Howard Chandler Christy and dating from 1919 coincidentally lists in its honor roll, under the heading of "Americans All!," the family names DuBois, Kowalski, and Gonzáles, along with the more predictable Smith, O'Brien, and Levy;[13] the existence of such cultural artifacts might help provide a context for Williams's perhaps overly idealistic assurance of an "easy intermingling of races" amongst inhabitants of the Quarter—though, as Kelly points out, the playwright, however unintentionally, still marginalizes the Negro Woman by leaving her unnamed.)

Even as avowedly "personal" a work as the autobiographical *The Glass Menagerie* (1944) is not without its social dimension. In the narrative passages that frame and otherwise punctuate the acted-out scenes from the past, the authorial character Tom Wingfield "turn[s] back time . . . to that quaint period, the thirties, when the huge middle class of America was matriculating in a school for the blind," mired in "a dissolving economy" and beset by "disturbances of labor, sometimes pretty violent."[14] Moreover, the floridly rhetorical description of the building that houses the Wingfield apartment ("one of those vast hive-like conglomerations of cellular living-units that flower as warty growths in overcrowded urban centers of lower middle-class population and are symptomatic of the impulse of this largest and fundamentally enslaved section of American society to avoid fluidity and differentiation and to exist and function as one interfused mass of automatism" [p. 143]) is cast in terms of socioeconomic analysis. The demands of late-Depression-era day-to-day existence had caused Americans to turn inward and seek escape in "hot swing music and liquor, dance halls, bars, and music, and sex that hung in the gloom like a chandelier and flooded the world with brief, deceptive rainbows" (p. 179), rendering them barely aware of Guernica and revolution in Spain, or of Chamberlain at Berchtesgaden, which would lead imminently to Western civilization being "lit by lightning!"

This national mood of isolationism (a policy that other dramatists such as Hellman and Robert Sherwood also were questioning by the early 1940s) finds its analogue in the insularity of the Wingfield nuclear family that is coming apart at the seams: already deserted by carefree husband and father, Amanda and Laura now face abandonment by a conflicted son and brother as Tom breaks away to become a merchant seaman. To answer, on one level, the call of the larger world community (and, granted, pursue his own vocation as artist), he must, ironically, make the family foreign to him—with the resultant guilt that propels this memory play. As I have suggested elsewhere, the memory structure itself that Williams adopts in *Menagerie* may not be without its own implicit "sexual" politics or agenda: Because it depends on and is even tied not only to a more imagistically evocative language but also to certain poetic and nonrealistic theatrical devices (as described in Williams's Production Notes on what he calls the "new, plastic theatre"), memory might be construed as a feminine mode of discourse that partially subverts more patriarchically embedded literary texts that comprise linear narrative history.[15]

Though not, like *Menagerie*, literally autobiographical, *Camino Real* (1953) retains some claim to being considered spiritual autobiography; in fact, Elia Kazan, who directed its initial Broadway production, regards it as the dramatist's most personal work, "as private as a nightmare that penetrates the soul of the artist."[16] In any case, Donald Spoto (apparently either forgetting or categorizing differently both *Orpheus Descending* [1957] and *Sweet Bird of Youth* [1959]) has termed it Williams's only "frankly political play to open in New York."[17] If *Menagerie* is expressionistic insofar as it attempts to objectify Tom Wingfield's inner reality, *Camino Real* is expressionistic in that it stages the subjectivity of Tennessee Williams himself, casting it as a dream vision—part social nightmare—in the mind of a literary figure, Cervantes's Don Quixote, who arrives in the town square of the mythical Tierra Caliente in some unspecified Latin American "collectivist state." (Other literary figures from the past, such as Baron Charlus, Jacques Casanova, Marguerite Gauthier/Camille, Lord Byron, and the mythical American and archetypal outsider Kilroy, help people the canvas of romantics wandering through space and time.) On opposite sides of the square, Williams juxtaposes the Siete Mares Hotel, a watering hole for the well-to-do run by the sinister Gutman, with the Ritz Men Only, a lowlife flophouse overseen by the unsavory A. Ratt. This setting throws society's haves into sharp contrast with its have-nots.

Periodically traversing the desolate plaza, which at one point resembles a city devastated by bombardment, are the street cleaners, actually collectors of the dead. Ruling over this banana republic by force of "military police" is an unseen Generalissimo evidently supported by imperialist guns and money. The text contains explicit references to thought patrol, to intolerance of the revolutionary spirit, and to a squelching of the anarchic impulse—enough for this McCarthy-era play to be openly "attacked" by columnists Walter Winchell and Ed Sullivan "as anti-American" (Spoto, pp. 187, 189). Certain words are forbidden as "wanton incitement[s] to riot"; the cry "brother," for instance, which should be the most harmless of words and the most beautiful in its fostering of solidarity, when uttered by an idealist to inspire open rebellion, becomes "the most dangerous word in any human tongue."[18] Yet the play seems finally, Spoto's assertion notwithstanding, less blatantly political in its import than richly metaphysical, as is strongly hinted at by the presence of the Terra Incognita, the "waste-land" or "void" that lies in wait beyond the city for all life's powerless and permanent fugitives who would dare to venture forth.

II

If politics can be understood very broadly as the relations of power that govern individuals, then, from what has already been said, Williams would seem to qualify as a political playwright. What makes his perspective perhaps somewhat unique is that, in Williams, power—and the abuse of power—are gendered concepts. The same holds true for his notion of community, as will become clear if, first, we explore more fully the dynamics of power in *Battle of Angels/Orpheus Descending* (conflated here into one text for purposes of discussion), and *Sweet Bird of Youth*; and then examine the construction of community in *Cat on a Hot Tin Roof*, *Angels/Orpheus*, and *Red Devil Battery Sign*, with a brief return to *Iguana* at the end.

With the exception of *Sweet Bird of Youth*'s middle act, *Battle of Angels* and its revision, *Orpheus Descending*, constitute Williams's most explicit foray into sociopolitical drama until near the end of his career with *Red Devil Battery Sign*. In them, he explores the prejudice of the old propertied Southern aristocracy against the new mercantile class as well as middle-class exploitation of poor whites. Furthermore, he exposes how societal mores and economic dependency constrict individual freedom, victimizing the Other, along with considering the mandate for civilization to be feminized and humanized as a counter to masculine strength and power. Most forcefully, he dramatizes the bigotry against racial and ethnic groups that often eventuates in physical violence: Italian immigrants are regularly denigrated as "Dagos" and "Wops"; those with liberal political and social leanings face ostracism; Bessie Smith, we are reminded, was "killed" by Jim Crow; attack dogs tear apart chain-gang escapees; blacks are literally run out of town. The masculine (mis)use of power comes into sharpest focus through exposition of action that occurred long before the play opens, when the "Prince of Darkness" Jabe Torrance—in what may be a not-too-veiled reference to the forces of darkness being unleashed by the Nazis during World War II—led the Mystic Crew, a Klan-like mob of vigilantes, who burned down the orchard-taverna and killed its proprietor, Papa Romano, because he was serving blacks. Jabe then "bought" the Italian's daughter, Myra, for his wife and ensconced her in the mercantile store that he owns, symbolic of the way he commodifies all relationships, buying and using and abusing others.

In the present action, as Jabe lies dying of cancer upstairs, the childless Lady Myra conceives a love child by Val Xavier, a fugitive guitar player. Together, as Val says, they break free from humankind's "lifelong sentence to solitary confinement inside our own lonely skins for as long as we live on this earth!"[19] On Good Friday in *Angels*, on the Saturday before Easter in *Orpheus*, Jabe rises from his bed, shoots and kills Myra and the unborn baby, thus ending generativity, and sets fire to the orchard-like confectionery that Myra and Val have built. As his punishment, Val—like the black man accused of rape—is lynched from the cottonwood tree and blowtorched by Jabe's henchmen. In Williams's version of the American myth, faith in a recoverable Edenic innocence has been rooted out by an ethic of material success and cultural domination constructed upon a rejection of difference and an exploitation of the weaker. Violence has invaded the garden.

Similar violence at the hands of the patriarchy pervades Act Two and the ending of *Sweet Bird of Youth*, where Williams most decisively portrays the pre-Civil Rights white South's peculiar blend of conservative Protestantism, capitalism, and racism through the speech and actions of a political demagogue. Boss Finley casts himself as the anointed prophet of the Old Testament God of vengeance, claiming to have heard the call at age fifteen and "come down barefoot out of red clay hills" on a "sacred mission" to protect "from pollution" Southern womanhood.[20] To accomplish this, he has ordered a black castrated at random to serve as an example to those who would "adulterate pure white blood." Furthermore, he fetishizes his white-clad daughter Heavenly, using her to manipulate the crowd's reaction at the political rally projected onto a huge TV screen on the back wall of the set. His media-transmitted "Voice of God" speech co-opts the rhetoric of traditional theology (as Foucault would argue, power has become imbricated with discourse) just as his applying the word "crucified" to the effigy of himself that was burned two days earlier on Good Friday reinscribes the notion of savior onto a sadistic racist. Earlier, after her teenage romance with Chance Wayne, Boss forced his daughter to undergo an abortion that has left her sterile; at the end of the play, continuing the same imagistic pattern, he will have his son and assorted henchmen close in on Chance to castrate him and thereby confirm an equivalency between Chance and the racially and politically marginalized Other.

Yet a further symbolic castration occurs in Act Two when the Heckler with a "face [like] El Greco gave to [his] saints" (p. 75)—although a minor character still given privileged status as the audience's representative on stage—is beaten by Boss's thugs, silenced and denied a voice. Power can be misused to prevent the word from becoming flesh so that, as the Heckler remarks, God is rendered "absolutely speechless." Through Williams's metatheatrical devices such as the screen in *Sweet Bird*, the audience in the theatre is repositioned as part of the crowd at the political gathering, and thereby faced with the moral challenge, verbalized by the Heckler, to reject all that Boss Finley embodies. In Brechtian fashion, they are challenged intellectually to distrust the steamroller tactics of media magnification and to read the rhetorical and symbolic text correctly, as the Heckler does. If the pervasive castration imagery (which extends as well to include the effects of time upon youth and beauty and artistic talent) signifies the fate of all black men unjustly accused of violating white women, Williams inserts into Act Two a fleeting, transcendent image of a black protecting a white woman, as the Bellboy bodies forth "the kindness of strangers" by escorting back to the protection of her room the fading movie star, Alexandra del Lago, herself victim of Hollywood's absolute power to construct personality and then commodify it. So the outsider who has been defiled by racist categories becomes (like Chance and the Princess herself momentarily are when they can move beyond solipsistic obsession with self) the purveyor of a little act of grace in a corrupt social order constructed on the original sin of slavery.

Since, on the surface anyway, *Cat on a Hot Tin Roof* (1955) is a play about which of Big Daddy Pollitt's two sons, Gooper or Brick, will inherit the earth—in this instance, "twenty-eight thousand acres of the richest land this side of the valley Nile"[21]—one might expect that it would reassert the culture and power traditionally associated with the patriarchy. Yet Williams asserts instead the values of a homosocial economy as normative. As Williams's contemporary, Arthur Miller, astutely proposes, Brick in his friendship with Skipper might be seen as "flaunt[ing] . . . the decree of nature to reproduce himself, to become in turn the father, the master of the earth, the administrator of the tainted and impure world [of] money-lust, power-lust";[22] to challenge that imperative is to overturn the male hegemony. Much of the recent criticism of *Cat* has focused on whether Williams was evasive or even dishonest in refusing to come to terms unambiguously with the issue of Brick's homosexuality; John Clum goes so far, in fact, as to find Williams heterosexist and homophobic.[23] The pained subtext of the play, however, may indeed very well be that of the latent homosexual forced by societal pressures and family expectations to remain securely in the closet and "cure" his natural sexual orientation (and thereby secure the inheritance) through a heterosexual union.

But equally as important as any final determination of Brick's homosexuality or the precise nature of his relationship with Skipper— whom he failed by denying his cry for authenticity just before the latter's suicide—is Williams's courageous choice of the homosexual space as the site for the play's action. Despite the repressive atmosphere of the early 1950s during which homosexuality remained something unspoken and the gay character largely absent or severely disguised when present (HUAC impugned both gays and Communists almost equally as security risks to be ferreted out), Williams in *Cat* does open the door on the closet and stage the homosexual bedroom. The bed-sitting room of the plantation house, dominated by an ornate double bed, had once been occupied by two bachelors, Jack Straw and Peter Ochello. This room, shared by the two lovers for thirty years, "is gently and poetically haunted by a relationship that must have involved a tenderness which was uncommon" (p. 15). Big Daddy, who was once a field hand and so knows firsthand the taint of being owned, and who has sufficient social conscience to abhor the poverty he saw on his European travels, had been taken in by Straw and Ochello and had inherited the land from them; so their patrimony, the power they pass on, is both financial as well as sexual in nature. As Kolin reminds us in another context, "Land traditionally confers power, and those who own the land control the power" (p. 152). Significantly, though, blood was not the determiner of Big Daddy's property rights; having himself "knocked around in [his] time" (p. 115), he developed an unusual "tolerance" for the relationship between his adoptive fathers, and it was that sympathy for a way of life—indeed, for a way of loving—that proved decisive in securing the inheritance. Williams consistently subverts audience expectations in the way that he presents established institutions: the religious, medical, and legal systems are treated satirically through the characterizations, respectively, of Reverend Tooker, Doctor Baugh, and Gooper. And Straw and Ochello's homosexual "marriage," discussed fairly extensively and openly during the confrontation between Brick and Big Daddy in Act Two, is presented in terms of a mutuality and unselfishness that none of the heterosexual unions—Big Daddy and Big Mama's; Gooper and Mae's; Brick and Maggie's—share. Culture and the exercise of power need not, therefore, be bigoted and exclusionary.

The creation of a gendered alternative space had been presaged as far back in Williams's writing for the stage as *Battle of Angels*, where Myra's Papa had built and fostered an inclusive community that rejected ostracizing others on the basis of ethnic and racial difference; he ignored the color line. For his daughter, the orchard-taverna was symbolically the garden place of innocence from which she was expelled. By constructing a confectionery decorated in imitation of her father's wine garden in the back room behind the "harsh and drab" store, she now attempts to recreate a substitute feminine space where people can freely mingle together, and which is linked with her womb that is "alive once more." Myra, like the no-longer barren fig tree in the parable she tells, decorates herself with tinsel and Christmas ornaments in a kind of fertility ritual. On one level, the room, "shadowy and poetic as some inner dimension of the play" (p. 227), becomes a place of illusion, of art—a precursor to and echo of Blanche's room transformed by "magic" in *Streetcar.* And in its destruction in flames, it becomes as much an image of Myra herself as the dead child is. A badly needed second coming for this corrupt society is thus foreshortened.

The Red Devil Battery Sign, which closed in Boston before ever reaching New York (though it later played in London), might be called Williams's "Apocalypse Now," pervaded as it is with further imagery of destruction by fire, a recurrent motif in the playwright's work almost since the very beginning. From one perspective, the work exists as a prophetic jeremiad about the potential inherent danger that cultural pluralism and diversity will perpetuate a destructive divisiveness and ghettoization rather than promote cohesiveness. Yet even more importantly within the context of any consideration of Williams as political dramatist, *Red Devil* stands as a culmination of the three strains being followed here: the question of the ethnic Other within American society, the patriarchy's abuse of power, and the engendering of a matriarchal community. The play dramatizes two relationships in which physical sexuality once again proves humanizing and restorative—one between King Del Rey, the lead singer with a mariachi band, and The Woman Downtown; and the other simultaneous yet hardly subsidiary one between the pregnant Nina, daughter of King and also a performer, and McCabe—set against a background of urban disintegration, for King and his wife Perla inhabit a bungalow in a suburban plot now known as Crest-View by the Dump Heap. *Red Devil* is an unabashedly bilingual play, with many of the lines spoken in Spanish and not translated. The relationships are also ethnically mixed. King is a Texan with Spanish-Indian blood, who has been able to cross class lines through his artistry; yet, in angry moments, he calls Perla a "Spick chambermaid." Woman Downtown's father was a state senator whose Apache mistress raised her, and so she has a half-sister named Running Spring. And Nina's lover Terrence McCabe is an Irish-American, whom the possessive King slightingly refers to as a "prick of a mick."

In *Red Devil*, Williams indicates the paradoxical coexistence of culture with brutal power—more accurately, in fact, the aestheticizing of pain, the fetishizing of the infliction of hurt similar to what occurs in some of Harold Pinter's recent political plays—through Woman Downtown's "elegant" sheath dress, gift from an Asian General's wife who could only bear the feel of silk next to her "delicate" skin: "She was utterly barbaric in her instincts, loved watching decapitations through binoculars from a mound of silk cushions in the cupola on the roof of the palace."[24] Tyranny and "moral corruption" are no barriers to "exquisite taste." At her husband's walled-in hacienda, so heavily guarded by murderous thugs and electronic devices that it seemed a "prison," Woman Downtown was forced to play "hostess to—monsters!" who engineer foreign wars. The Woman Downtown's entire life from early childhood on has, indeed, been a succession of confinements (à la Tennessee's sister, Rose), most recently at the Paradise Meadows Nursing Home, where, before escaping to the Yellow Rose Hotel, she was subjected to electric shock therapy because of her familiarity with payola and decoded documents belonging to the Red Devil Battery Group, whose henchmen control all walks of life.

They permeate even the entertainment business, as is seen in the character of the Drummer, the perverted "artist" who infiltrates the mariachi band to undermine their allegiance to King and who later physically assaults Woman Downtown. Power glories in the demeaning of culture. Without necessarily subscribing to his social analysis, it is still possible, however, to find applicable here Christopher Lasch's recent categorization and castigation of a postmodern elite that "control[s] the international flow of money and information"; part of "an international culture . . . of business, entertainment . . . and information retrieval, this favored few monopolize the advantages of money, education, and power."[25] For the secret Red Devil organization is a worldwide military-industrial complex that would protect its "huge, secret investments" by replacing Asian democracies with "sympathetically corrupt regimes" that "rule by power conspiracy." Williams finds an innate racism (all too apparent in the Drunk's denigration of the "gooks in 'Nam") embedded in an imperialist hegemony that would perpetuate civil strife among "Barefoot little rice-paddie and canefield people, innocent-eyed, simple-hearted as water oxen, asking just rice in a hand or a bowl out of a day's or a night's work-set to war with each other in spite of their blood connection, religious and culture connection" (p. 53). The complex's dedication to "genocide for profits undeclared" will lead to ever-increasing involvement in an ever-widening armed conflict that Williams carefully contextualizes. By direct reference, he situates it within the historic framework of such other colonizing agendas as Napoleon's installing Maximilian (who would later be shot) as King of Mexico, as well as England's presence in Northern Ireland.

King Del Rey and Woman Downtown's relationship plays itself out against a nightmarish background of unrest and chaos, expressionistically suggested in this at times hallucinatory, stream-of-consciousness play through ominous Wasteland sounds of wolf calls, warning trumpets, and quadraphonically distorted music, and through lights from flares and explosions of "soft drink bottles with nitro" as draft resisters blow up police squad cars and the National Guard is called out. Dominating the city skyline (downtown Dallas where President John F. Kennedy was assassinated in 1963) is the neon Red Devil Battery sign "puls[ing] like blood." Had Nina, now pregnant by McCabe, remained a singer and flamenco dancer, the sign advertising her act "could have stood higher than the new sign on the new skyscraper" (p. 79), indicating the way that art can potentially counteract tyranny and oppression. And yet, the very fact that she is with child, a child whose blood further dilutes, and thereby perhaps harmonizes, the ethnic strains, becomes a powerful image of generativity in this matrifocal play. In a fantastic, almost futuristic, ending after King's death from a brain tumor, "the play stylistically makes its final break with realism" as the adolescent gang of "wild young denizens of the Hollow," led by Wolf, protect and embrace The Woman Downtown as "Mother of all." Uttering the "awesome . . . defiant outcry of the she-wolf," she joins the band of rebels—the only viable, if unlikely, "community" left to fight the Battery group and the authorities who countenance them—as they advance to the front of the stage and, in a Brechtian moment of both castigation and challenge, confront the audience "who have failed or betrayed them" (p. 94). Whereas previously the appellation "she-wolf" came only in the context of lovemaking that proved personally salvific in an inhuman world, now it signals Woman Downtown's transformation into an agent of community nurturance and cohesiveness. Williams implies that the system has become so corrupted by the drive for power enough "to obliterate all life on earth: generals, rulers, presidents" and for money that "talks, not heads, not hearts, not tongues of prophets or angels" (pp. 62-63)—that it can be restored only by beginning a painful, new evolution up from savagery, with a matriarchy overthrowing and replacing the values of the patriarchy (an idea with seeds as far back in Williams as Blanche's warning to Stella about culture's demise and the need for a feminization of culture in *A Streetcar Named Desire*).

In such apocalyptic times—the "greater, whiter flare, exposing more desolation" (p. 94) at the close of *Red Devil* carries an almost nuclear-blast aura—the use of force may, sadly, be a *sine qua non* on the slow march back upward toward a renewed civilization. But elsewhere, Williams points a better way. In *Night of the Iguana*, it is the relinquishing of power and dominion that, ironically, engenders and empowers community. And here the political begins in and with the personal, human response. Late in the play, the androgynous-looking portraitist Hannah Jelkes pleads with the defrocked priest Shannon to release the iguana that has been tethered beneath the veranda, for the animal is, after all, "one of God's creatures." Only when Shannon cuts the rope can the aged poet Nonno complete and recite his long-gestating epithanaton about finding courage to go on in the face of despair. Hannah helps Shannon to rediscover within himself a degree of the goodness and self-worth whose existence he had come to doubt; he, in turn, frees the iguana—and the result is art. And the creator of the poem sees that it is "good." The names themselves of this trinity of characters underscore Williams's point about interconnectedness and human community, for "Shannon" contains all the letters necessary to spell the other two. The patristic theologians averred long ago that even the godhead required a community of persons in order to flourish and be efficacious. As Garry Wills explains: "By reflecting on the Trinity, Saint Augustine developed a whole new view of human personality—that we are selves, not a self; that even God must exist in dialogue; that he is not only a unit (as Plato thought), but a community."[26] It is within just such a notion of a community of persons that Williams situates his "politics," and it is from this notion that any discussion of that "politics" must begin.

Notes

1. Tennessee Williams, *The Night of the Iguana*, in *The Theatre of Tennessee Williams* (New York: New Directions, 1972), IV, 260-261.

2. G. B. Shaw, *Heartbreak House* (New York: Penguin Books, 1964), p. 158.

3. Virginia Woolf, *Three Guineas* (San Diego, California: Harcourt, Brace, 1966), pp. 29-30, 34.

4. Gerald Berkowitz, *American Drama in the Twentieth Century* (London: Longmans, 1992), p. 86; Marc Robinson, *The Other American Drama* (Cambridge: Cambridge University Press, 1994), p. 52.

5. C. W. E. Bigsby, *Modern American Drama, 1945-1990* (Cambridge: Cambridge University Press, 1992), p. 37.

6. Tennessee Williams, *Where I Live: Selected Essays*, ed. Christine R. Day and Bob Woods (New York: New Directions, 1978), p. 60.

7. Tennessee Williams, *Memoirs* (Garden City, New York: Doubleday, 1975), p. 94.

8. Ronald Hayman, *Tennessee Williams: Everyone Else Is an Audience* (New Haven, Connecticut: Yale University Press, 1993), p. 202.

9. Tennessee Williams, *Conversations with Tennessee Williams*, ed. Albert J. Devlin (Jackson: University Press of Mississippi, 1986), pp. 128, 292.

10. Philip C. Kolin, "Sleeping with Caliban: The Politics of Race in Tennessee Williams's *Kingdom of Earth*," *Studies in American Drama, 1945-Present*, 8, no. 2 (1993), 143-144.

11. Robert Bray, "*A Streetcar Named Desire*: The Political and Historical Subtext," in *Confronting Tennessee Williams's "A Streetcar Named Desire," Essays in Cultural Pluralism*, ed. Philip C. Kolin (Westport, Connecticut: Greenwood Press, 1993), p. 191.

12. Lionel Kelly, "The White Goddess, Ethnicity, and the Politics of Desire," in *Confronting Tennessee Williams's "A Streetcar Named Desire," Essays in Cultural Pluralism*, ed. Philip C. Kolin (Westport, Connecticut: Greenwood Press, 1993), pp. 127, 136.

13. Collection of the Tippecanoe County Historical Association, Lafayette, Indiana.

14. Tennessee Williams, *The Glass Menagerie*, in *The Theatre of Tennessee Williams* (New York: New Directions, 1971), I, 145.

15. Thomas P. Adler, *American Drama, 1940-1960: A Critical History* (New York & Toronto: Twayne and Macmillan, 1994), p. 134.

16. Elia Kazan, *A Life* (New York: Knopf, 1988), p. 494.

17. Donald Spoto, *The Kindness of Strangers: A Life of Tennessee Williams* (New York: Little, Brown, 1985), p. 185.

18. Tennessee Williams, *Camino Real*, in *The Theatre of Tennessee Williams* (New York: New Directions, 1971), II, 451.

19. Tennessee Williams, *Orpheus Descending*, in *The Theatre of Tennessee Williams* (New York: New Directions, 1971), III, 271.

20. Tennessee Williams, *Sweet Bird of Youth*, in *The Theatre of Tennessee Williams* (New York: New Directions, 1972), IV, 73.

21. Tennessee Williams, *Cat on a Hot Tin Roof*, in *The Theatre of Tennessee Williams* (New York: New Directions, 1971), III, 126.

22. Arthur Miller, "The Shadow of the Gods," in *Theater Essays*, ed. Robert A. Martin (New York: Penguin, 1978), pp. 190-191.

23. John Clum, *Acting Gay: Male Homosexuality in Modern Drama* (New York: Columbia University Press, 1992), p. 157. For a less judgmental reading, see David Savran, *Cowboys, Communists, and Queers: The Politics of Masculinity in the Works of Arthur Miller and Tennessee Williams* (Minneapolis: University of Minnesota Press, 1992), p. 109.

24. Tennessee Williams, *The Red Devil Battery Sign* (New York: New Directions, 1988), p. 23.

25. Christopher Lasch, *The Revolt of the Elites and the Betrayal of Democracy* (New York: W.W. Norton, 1995), pp. 25-26, 29, 45.

26. Garry Wills, "The Tragic Pope?" *New York Review of Books*, December 22, 1994, p. 6.

Deranged Artists:
Creativity and Madness_____

Jacqueline O'Connor

My discussion begins with one of Williams's most enduring and popular plays, which introduces the playwright's alter ego, the poet Tom Wingfield. *The Glass Menagerie* was Williams's first successful play, opening in New York in 1945; *Menagerie* is considered a thinly disguised version of Williams's own family life in St. Louis. One of the complications that arises immediately in discussing the autobiographical origins of the play comes with determining how much Laura resembles Williams's sister Rose. Laura is physically crippled, shy, and withdrawn; she hides in the St. Louis apartment, content to play with her glass figures and listen to the victrola. Williams's sister, although not physically disabled, was emotionally unstable. The question is whether we can assume Rose's problems to be Laura's problems—is Laura mentally ill? If so, does Tom's escape from the family contribute to Laura's final collapse; furthermore, does Tom's own sanity make this escape necessary?

Some critics conclude that Laura is mentally ill. Thomas L. King, for example, sets up the connection between the artist and the disturbed relative in his essay on *The Glass Menagerie*. King argues that scene three of the play "begins with Tom writing, Tom the artist, and in it we see how the artistic sensibility turns a painful situation into 'art' by using distance" (87). King continues by contrasting Tom and Laura, calling her a "severely disturbed woman," whereas Tom is not similarly disturbed because he makes art (87).

King elaborates on the differences between Tom and Laura by comparing them to real-life relatives James Joyce and his daughter, Lucia, who was treated by Jung for severe mental problems. Jung wrote about the situation, comparing the father and daughter, maintaining that Joyce had a schizophrenic style, but he willed it and developed it consciously, which gave him control over his psychosis; Lucia, meanwhile, "'was not a genius like her father, but merely a victim of her disease'" (87). In comparing these couples, King argues: "Jung's theory is a psychoanalyst's perception of the problem of artist and non-artist which is much the same as the problem of Tom and Laura" (87). His suggestion is, then, that the brother and sister in the play are both susceptible to mental illness, by virtue of heredity and family experience, but Tom escapes psychosis because he finds an outlet for his anxieties.

King's argument suggests a number of issues that are central to the study of the artist in Williams's plays, but before I consider the validity of the contrast King draws between the artist and the mad person who does not write, I need to consider further the critics' position on Laura's sanity. C. W. E. Bigsby also connects Laura with Rose, but he does not make explicit what he thinks Laura's fate might be. He admits that Laura and Amanda suffer from Tom's need to escape, stating that "the world closes in on Amanda and Laura as Tom offers them up as sacrifices to his art and his freedom" (Bigsby 2: 40). Bigsby goes on to claim:

> Laura is a loving portrait of Williams' own sister locked up in her own inner world, her lobotomy trapping her in a permanent adolescence. It is a withdrawal from sociality for which Williams offers a gentler image, in terms of Laura's limp, an imperfection less intrusive, less totally disabling, but the play is a homage to her. (48)

Bigsby's comments are typical of the critics' logic that if *Menagerie* is autobiographical, and Laura is Rose, then Laura is disturbed mentally to the extent of withdrawing completely from life. Joseph K. Davis, in an essay about the play, says Laura "withdraws into the world of her glass animals, and so flees into a no-time of approaching mental collapse" (194). Rather than similarly claiming that Laura and Rose are alike in their mental conditions, I would argue that we cannot know exactly what will happen to Laura when Tom leaves the family at the end of the play, but that the play provides enough clues to indicate that

Laura's mental stability is as fragile as her glass figures, and that her inability to provide for herself makes her a likely candidate for an institution.

Laura's fear of others and inability to pursue either a career or a suitable marriage partner indicate that she may indeed fulfill the prophecy her mother predicts for her after the "fiasco" at Rubicam's Business College. Amanda suggests that Laura's insistence on staying home might well result in a life of dependence, and claims to have seen evidence of this kind of life, the life of "barely tolerated spinsters . . . stuck away in some little mousetrap of a room . . . little birdlike women without any nest" (I, 156).

As we saw in both *Streetcar* and *Portrait of a Madonna*, Williams believes that a woman without economic means may end up at the state asylum. Laura's nearly pathological shyness and inability to cope with life's pressures predispose her to such a fate. Near the end of the play, right after Jim tells Laura that he cannot call on her because of his tie to Betty, the scenic directions explain that the "holy candles in the altar of Laura's face have been snuffed out" (I, 230). The next screen legend to appear, just as Amanda enters the room, explains, "Things have a way of turning out so badly," and Amanda inadvertently underscores this with her lemonade song: "Good enough for any old maid" (I, 231). Thus, when Tom instructs Laura to blow out her candles at the close of the play, Jim's rejection, things turning out so badly, and Amanda's song about an old maid all conspire to suggest what Laura's future holds for her. Once Jim leaves, Amanda's first words reiterate the outcome, both of the evening with Jim, and probably, life, by repeating the words of the legend: "Things have a way of turning out so badly" (I, 234).

Amanda's speech in scene two follows Laura's description of the days that she spent while pretending to be attending the business school; these days were filled with trips to the zoo, and to the Jewel Box, "that big glass house where they raise the tropical flowers" (I, 155). Laura is associated with these locations and thus with enclosed spaces, the zoo complete with bars, and the Jewel Box, a place for observation of rare objects. Throughout the play, Laura is linked with her glass menagerie, so the zoo becomes a pertinent symbol for her possible fate.[1] These images cannot prove that Laura ends up in an asylum, but they do compare her to the confined animals, and Amanda's speech about the trapped life of a spinster confirms that comparison. However, at this point in the play, Laura's fate is not yet determined, and Amanda's desperate attempts to provide security for her daughter shift focus from pursuing a career to obtaining a husband, Laura's only other option.

This consideration of Laura's impossible future without a career or a marriage connects Laura to the women discussed in chapter 3, for without an income or the protection of family members, she becomes vulnerable to institutionalization, and thus her encounter with Jim becomes all the more poignant. We cannot speculate whether Jim might have saved Laura from the loneliness of her life in the apartment if he were not already engaged, but we are sure that this is the only chance Laura has for escape. Once Tom leaves, no more gentleman callers will appear, for Laura is too withdrawn and isolated to attract them herself.

When Amanda helps Laura to dress before Jim's arrival, and the stage directions indicate that a "fragile, unearthly prettiness has come out in Laura" (I, 191), Amanda undercuts the hope in this transformation by exclaiming to her daughter that this is "the prettiest you will ever be!" (I, 192). This remark differs from Amanda's other assessments of Laura, for she is more inclined to overrate her daughter. In the opening scene: "I want you to stay fresh and pretty—for gentleman callers!" even though none are expected (I, 147). When Tom calls her "different," Amanda replies: "I think the difference is all to her advantage" (I, 187). In the moments before Laura's touching encounter with her one and only gentleman caller, however, Amanda indicates that Laura's attractiveness is momentary.

We might use Amanda as an example of what happens to Laura, for although readers of the play do not question Amanda's sanity, and Williams characterizes her as someone with "endurance," he also claims that "having failed to establish contact with reality," Amanda "continues to live vitally in her illusions" (I, 129). Amanda's focus on her past as a young debutante in Mississippi closely allies her with such madwomen as Blanche and Lucretia, and her appearance in her cotillion dress when Jim arrives provides evidence that she lacks sense and acts inappropriately. In her strength and ability to endure, however, she resembles Williams's later characters, who despite their eccentricities and illusions, do not succumb to madness but continue to struggle in the world. Laura lacks Amanda's determination, however, and her endurance is questionable.

Although Amanda concerns herself with economic realities, and is careful to make "plans and provisions," she depends on Tom for economic survival as much as Laura does, and shows scant evidence that she could support herself. She did have a job demonstrating brassieres when Laura first started business college, but she no longer has that job, and we don't know why. In a letter to Audrey Wood, written on Metro-Goldwyn stationery, Williams outlines the scenes of the play for her. In this version, still entitled *The Gentleman Caller*, Williams notes in the outline of scene two that when Amanda comes home and confronts Laura about business college, "Amanda has been working as a model for matron's dresses at down-town dept. store and has just lost the job because of faded appearance."[2] She attempts to sell magazine subscriptions by phone, but with little apparent success. We hear two separate calls: the first woman hangs up on her, and the second pitch ends before we know what response she will get. From her nonstop chatter on both calls, we surmise that she is a nuisance to these women, and that her sales career would not sustain her in the absence of Tom's salary. Comparing Amanda with Laura, then, it seems safe to assume that Laura would be even less effective at supporting herself.

When Tom directs Laura to blow out her candles at the close of the play, it is more than a stage direction to secure lights out; the blackout occurs in Laura's briefly lit life as well. Since she cannot escape the apartment and her limited life there, by either a career or a husband, and since Tom, the breadwinner, has left the family, Laura's existence is tenuous. Her emotional stability is questionable, and she loses her brother's financial and emotional support. What is left to be considered is whether Laura's emotional instability and Tom's artistic talents stem from a single source, and whether Tom sacrifices her future to ensure his as an artist.

In *Creative Malady*, George Pickering speculates whether or not "illness, and particularly psychological illness, may sometimes be an aid to creative work" (17). Looking at the lives of a selection of creative and influential people, including Darwin and Freud, Pickering concludes that passion is the "chief characteristic . . . which relates the psychoneuroses of the characters here described and the creative work which brought them fame. In brief, a psychoneurosis represents passion thwarted, a great creative work, passion fulfilled" (309). Do Tom and Laura prove Pickering's theory?

Scene one is the only scene in the play in which Amanda, Laura, and Tom interact as a family. After Tom's opening monologue as narrator, he joins his sister and his mother at the dinner table. Although the togetherness of the meal is soon cut short by Tom's abrupt departure from the table, and he finishes out the scene standing by the portieres, the stage directions inform us that Amanda continues to address him "as though he were seated in the vacant chair at the table though he remains by the portieres" (I, 148). More importantly, though, the characters have their only three-way conversation of the play, on a well-rehearsed subject, Amanda's life in Blue Mountain. In this scene, then, Tom and Laura are brother and sister, participating in a familiar family ritual, the narrative of their mother's past.

The opening scene thus prepares for the eventual divergence of their paths, by briefly dramatizing apartment life before this divergence. Though Tom chooses escape, and Laura cannot, they share their family history, and our awareness of this bond at the opening of the play leads us to consider that they share the same family experiences. We do not yet know that Tom works, and Laura does not; the only reference to occupations is to Laura's typing and shorthand, and we have received no indication that Laura's business career is only wishful thinking on Amanda's part. Scene two exposes Laura's inability to pursue a career, and scene three explains Tom's frustration with his job and his life, but the play opens with the brother and sister equally engaged in tolerating their mother's dominating personality.

Scenes two and three feature dialogues between Amanda and Laura, and Amanda and Tom, respectively; Tom is not present as either narrator or character in scene two, and although Laura is present for scene three, she is almost totally silent until the end of the scene, when Tom knocks against her glass menagerie, and she cries out. Although in these two scenes we begin to see the differences between Tom and Laura, both scenes revolve around Amanda's complaints about their career choices. What does become apparent, however, is the distinction between the brother and sister that will ultimately send them to different futures, despite their shared past. In scene two, Amanda returns home and interrupts Laura washing and polishing her glass collection. When she hears Amanda ascending the fire escape, "Laura catches her breath, thrusts the bowl of ornaments away, and seats herself stiffly before the diagram of the typewriter keyboard as though it held her spellbound" (I, 151). Laura pretends to have an interest in a career, even to the point of pretending to attend business school, but she has no ambitions, no plans, no goals.

By contrast, Tom thinks of little except his plans. The typewriter that represents Laura's career failure provides Tom an escape from his warehouse job. In scene three, Amanda and Tom argue, and the stage directions tell us: "The upright typewriter now stands on the drop-leaf table, along with a wild disarray of manuscripts. The quarrel was probably precipitated by Amanda's interruption of Tom's creative labor" (I, 162). Tom dreams of a career as a writer; the lack of Laura's ambition is strongly contrasted with the artistic ambitions of Tom. Amanda berates Laura for her refusal to have a career, and interrogates Tom about the career he plans. She interrupts Laura's play, and interrupts Tom's artistic work. In Amanda's eyes, therefore, Tom's desire to find satisfying work is as dangerous to the family security as Laura's resistance to any kind of career. Being an artist is as unreliable as being a recluse.

Tom's nightly flights from the apartment stand in strong contrast to Laura's status as a "home girl." She leaves the apartment once during the play, and then it is reluctantly: she dreads an encounter with the grocer, and goes only at her mother's insistence. As she rushes out, she slips on the landing, emphasizing her lameness; her fall also signifies her inability to negotiate the world outside the apartment. Tom, on the other hand, wants adventure; while he is tied to his job at the warehouse, his only opportunity for adventure is vicarious, through the movies he attends. Although he sees his nightly wanderings as biding time, and is impatient for real adventure, we see them differently: his narrative about the movies and the magic show demonstrates his storytelling abilities, and contrasts his life with Laura's isolated one.

As a means of escape, however, Laura's withdrawal and Tom's writing are similar, and they use them in similar ways to cope with their present situation. Laura is temporarily safe from her mother's demands and from the world in general when she attends to her glass menagerie; she even uses her glass figures to explain to Jim what she has been doing since high school. Jim's interrogation of her career goals constitutes the only inquiry Laura receives since her mother gave up on that course in scene two; just making conversation, Jim inquires twice during scene seven about Laura's interests and plans. Both times Laura mentions her glass collection, explaining to Jim that it "takes up a good deal of time" (I, 220). In fact, for Laura it is a full-time job, and although Jim does not understand this, she does manage to divert his attention away from his questioning of her. As Bigsby points out:

Laura's powerlessness is symbolized by the fact that she cannot master the typewriter. Her hesitant speeches are in fact a series of withdrawals. The only language which is wholly uninfected by commerce, bitterness and

---

Deranged Artists

disillusionment is that which she employs when describing her glass menagerie, the private language in which she addresses her own inventions. (44)

Tom uses his own form of escape, his writing, to make his life bearable. Ironically, he uses the same typewriter for his escape that represents Laura's defeat. When first describing Jim to the audience, he informs us that he was on friendly terms with Jim at work, and Jim "knew of my secret practice of retiring to a cabinet of the washroom to work on poems when business was slack in the warehouse" (I, 190). With this commentary, Tom explains his friendship with Jim, but also relates his writing practices. He is able to tolerate his life in the warehouse by fleeing to his writing whenever possible. However, his mother interrupts him when he tries to write at home, and eventually his boss ends his writing at work, for Tom tells us at the end of the play, "I was fired for writing a poem on the lid of a shoe-box" (I, 236). Losing his job proves to be the impetus for Tom's escape, and he leaves home after this, descending "the steps of this fire escape for a last time" (I, 236).

Tom's need to write, then, is stronger than his desire to protect Laura, or, for that matter, Amanda. As the opening description of Tom's character explains, he is a "poet with a job in a warehouse. His nature is not remorseless, but to escape from a trap he must act without pity" (I, 129). Not only does Tom use the experience of his family life to create art, but in order to create that art he must abandon the family. Laura's emotional and economic precariousness does not prevent Tom from taking the escape that losing his job provides, and he leaves his mother and sister to whatever fate holds for them. Tom's decision to leave is a necessary act of self-preservation, for he cannot tolerate his "two-by-four" situation; this escape is limited, however, for his closing monologue indicates that he is trapped by the memories of Laura.

From the action of this play, then, we can surmise that if the artist is not the mad person, he may contribute to the breakdown of someone he

---

loves. While Niesen claims that in Williams's early plays the artist figure is the one who dies, and his sensitivity leads to that death, in *The Glass Menagerie* we see the pattern that Niesen identifies as that of his later plays: Tom is an "angel of death" for Laura. In this case the death is more likely a descent into madness, or at least poverty, but when Laura blows out her candles, we sense the end of her fragile existence. Williams creates a play that dramatizes that sad existence, and as the narrator of that play he distances himself from the action in order to comment on it, and provide a way in for the audience. As a character he distances himself when he descends the fire escape for the last time.

The question also becomes one of arguing whether Laura's safety or sanity is sacrificed for Tom's escape. If Williams does attempt to exorcise his personal demons by turning his family into the characters in his plays, especially in *The Glass Menagerie*, and we recognize what he is doing by its similarity to what Tom is doing, that may help us to understand the playwright. We must also consider that the statement this play makes is much more significant than a study of how one playwright deals with his sister's insanity and confinement. In an interview, Williams identified himself as an "incomplete person," claiming interest in "people that have to fight for their reason, people for whom the impact of life and experience from day to day, night to night, is difficult, people who come close to cracking" (Devlin 82). But he goes on to claim that his is not a unique perspective: "I don't think you will find many artists who aren't more or less in the same situation. Give a person an acute sensibility and you're bound to find a person who is under a good deal of torment, especially in this particular time" (82).

Tom and Laura are both sensitive people, and both suffer from the abandonment by their father, their mother's unrealistic expectations, and from the lack of opportunity offered by life in a St. Louis tenement during the Depression. The play establishes that although the brother and sister have the same background, and both seem to be the incomplete persons that Williams identifies with, they deal with their torments differently. Tom finds a creative outlet for his painful memories, and his very abandonment of Laura becomes the subject matter of the play he narrates. In the case of the characters in *The Glass Menagerie*, Pickering's theory of the "creative malady" seems to hold true, for while Tom can create, Laura is emotionally crippled by her anxieties.

Notes

1. Also see Tennessee Williams, *The Two-Character Play* (New York: New Directions, 1969) 57. In this, the first published version of a play that also focuses on a brother and sister, and specifically mentions insanity, the brother Felice warns his sister: "Don't you know your behavior, if it goes on like this, will get the two of us hauled by force out of the house and put like two wild animals in separate, locked, barred cages in what's called a zoo or a zoological garden—publicly naked for the grinning to stare at?" This description of an asylum as a zoo indicates that Williams may have had something similar in mind when he associates Laura with the zoo and the glass house. Both images signal confinement and observation, the two main components of an asylum.
2. Letter from Williams to Audrey Wood, undated, Humanities Research Center, U of Texas, Austin.

Works Cited

Bigsby, C. W. E. *A Critical Introduction to Twentieth-Century American Drama*, volume 2: *Williams, Miller, Albee*. Cambridge: Cambridge UP, 1984.
_____. *Modern American Drama, 1945-1990*. Cambridge: Cambridge UP, 1992.
Davis, Joseph K. "Landscapes of the Dislocated Mind in Williams' *The Glass Menagerie*." *Tennessee Williams: A Tribute*. Ed. Jac Tharpe. Jackson: UP of Mississippi, 1977. 192-206.
Devlin, Albert J. *Conversations with Tennessee Williams*. Jackson: UP of Mississippi, 1986.
King, Thomas L. "Irony and Distance in *The Glass Menagerie*." Rpt. in *Tennessee Williams*. Ed. Harold Bloom. New York: Chelsea, 1987. 85-94.
Niesen, George. "The Artist Against the Reality in the Plays of Tennessee Wil-

liams." *Tennessee Williams: A Tribute*. Ed. Jac Tharpe. Jackson: UP of Mississippi, 1977. 463-93.

Pickering, George. *Creative Malady*. London: Allen & Unwin, 1974.

Williams, Tennessee. *A Streetcar Named Desire*. New York: New Directions, 1947.

_____. *The Theatre of Tennessee Williams*. 8 volumes. New York: New Directions, 1971-1992.

_____. *27 Wagons Full of Cotton and Other One-Act Plays*. Norfolk: New Directions, 1945; London: Grey Walls, 1947. Contains *27 Wagons Full of Cotton*, *The Purification: The Lady of Larkspur Lotion*, *The Last of My Solid Gold Watches*, *Portrait of a Madonna*, *Auto-Da-Fe*, *Lord Byron's Love Letters*, *The Strangest Kind of Romance*, *The Long Goodbye*, *Hello from Bertha*, *This Property Is Condemned*, *Talk to Me Like the Rain and Let Me Listen . . .* , and *Something Unspoken*.

_____. *The Two-Character Play*. New York: New Directions, 1969.

Flying the Jolly Roger:
Images of Escape and Selfhood in
Tennessee Williams's *The Glass Menagerie*_____

Lori Leathers Single

One of the more interesting aspects in Williams's concept of a new "plastic theatre" is a metatheatrical technique known as the screen device. According to Esther Merle Jackson, and, more recently, Thomas P. Adler, Tennessee Williams's 1945 preface to *The Glass Menagerie* merits our attention as an important "manifesto" in the history of modern American drama (Jackson 90, Adler 137). In these "Production Notes," Williams called for a "new, plastic theatre 'to replace' the exhausted theatre of realistic conventions" (131).[1] To this end, Williams proposed the use of such non-realistic elements as theme music, unusual lighting, and "a screen on which were projected magic-lantern slides bearing images or titles" (132-134). Although these projections that Williams collectively called "The Screen Device" (132) have been for the most part critically neglected, a closer study of them as they operate in Williams's play supports a new psychological interpretation of *The Glass Menagerie*.

Included in the original script, this device calls for forty-three separate "legends" and images to be projected onto the wall between the dining room and the front room of the set during the performance (132). Although Williams's use of projected images is generally assumed to have been influenced by the German director Erwin Piscator, founder and director of The Dramatic Workshop of the New School for Social Research in New York, where Williams studied as a young man, actually he first encountered this innovation while a student at the State University of Iowa. In fact, Williams had experimented with the use of projected images as early as 1938 in *Not About Nightingales*. Nevertheless, any discussion of Williams's screen device needs to be contextualized in light of Piscator's work. As John Willett notes "no other director used film so extensively or thought about it so systematically as

Piscator, who came to employ front projection, back projection, and simultaneous or overlapping projection from more than one source" (Willett 113). In one Berlin production, Piscator used four projection screens, which makes Williams's proposed use of a single screen, "indistinguishable from the rest when not in use" (132), seem conservative by comparison.

In addition, Williams's use of the projected legends and images in *The Glass Menagerie* differs from that of the two great German practitioners Piscator and Brecht, whose interests in the development of nonrealist or "epic theatre" were primarily political (Esslin 23). Instead, Williams was more interested in private issues than public ones. In focusing on the social and political backdrop of the play, C. W. E. Bigsby has convincingly argued that "*The Glass Menagerie* is no more a play of purely private emotions and concerns than Chekhov's *The Cherry Orchard*" (36). Certainly, the harsh economic and political realities of 1930's America are a driving force in the action of the play. However, private emotions were the driving force within the playwright himself. In a 1981 interview with Dotson Rader, Williams recalled that "*Menagerie* grew out of the intense emotions I felt seeing my sister's mind begin to go" (qtd. in Devlin 331). Not only is *The Glass Menagerie* his most autobiographical work, but it is also a public form of personal expiation. Just as Tom's memory play may be interpreted as his way of exorcising his guilt, Adler believes that Williams wrote the play in order to come to terms with his own sense of culpability over his failure "to do anything to prevent the prefrontal lobotomy performed on his schizophrenic sister, Rose" (Adler 139). Williams suffered guilt for having survived the familial tensions that ultimately destroyed Rose. Like Tom in the play, remorse was the price he paid for his escape. So, where Piscator used projected images to create a public language for addressing political issues, Williams used projected images to create a private language for coping with personal tensions.

Williams was striving toward a style he called "personal lyricism" (qtd. in Jackson 29), a poetic dramatic form that Adler suggests is capable of "delineating and probing character psychology" (126). In his "Production Notes," Williams wrote:

> Expressionism and all other unconventional techniques in drama have only one valid aim, and that is a closer approach to truth . . . a more penetrating and vivid expression of things as they are . . . which the poetic imagination can represent or suggest, in essence, only through transformation, through changing into other forms than those which were merely present in appearance. (131)

In other words, he wanted to create a poetic dramatic language capable of revealing the reality beyond what on the surface appears to be real.

This was his original artistic vision; however, because of the collaborative nature of theatrical production, many of the unconventional techniques were cut from Eddie Dowling's original production (1944 Chicago, 1945 New York), resulting in two different published versions of the play. The Acting Edition caters to the American preference for realistic theatre "that asks its audience to make believe they are not making believe by accepting the illusion for the real thing" (Adler 136-7), or theatre in which illusion "has the appearance of truth" (144). In contrast, the Reading Edition with the original didascalia calls for the use of the metatheatrical screen device to break the illusion of reality which is so popular in the realistic tradition of American theatre. These projections are part of Williams's strategy to reveal the truth behind the mere "appearance" of reality (131).

The Dowling production and the Acting Edition have set the standard for performances of this play, while the more widely published Reading Edition is used as a literary text by students, teachers, and scholars. Although some controversy regarding reading theatrical texts as literature remains, Mary Ann Frese Witt and others have presented convincing arguments for reading the "voice in the didascaliae" (Witt 105).[2] In fact, Williams invites such practice by including in the Reading Edition a wealth of paratextual information. In addition to the stage directions concerning the screen device, he provides an epigraph from E. E. Cummings, a brief production background, an abbreviated outline of the play, character descriptions, "The Production Notes," and an essay called "The Catastrophe of Success" (123-41). In fact, he claims to have included the screen device in this edition because it might "be of some interest to some readers to see how this device was conceived" (132). No doubt the most compelling reason for studying the screen device as a written text is that performances using this technique are rare. In brief, Williams's screen device survives almost exclusively as a written rather than a performed text.

In this written text, the Reading Edition, Williams describes the two-fold function of the screen device as having both a "structural" and an "emotional" value (132). It serves "to give accent to certain values in each scene," thereby clarifying the narrative line and providing "a definite emotional appeal, less definable but just as important" (132). Actually, the screen device is more complex than Williams's notes would indicate. According to Pfister's dramatic theory, both the non-verbal "images" and the verbal "legends," which make up the screen device, are "epic communication structures" and as such function in the following way:

> As far as the aesthetics of reception is concerned, these epic elements have an anti-illusionist function which is intended to counter any identification or empathy on the part of the audience with the figures and situations within the internal communication system, thereby encouraging a posture of critical distance. (71)

In other words, in addition to the structural and emotional values that Williams cites, the screen device by its very nature also functions as a Brechtian distancing technique. It disturbs the illusion of reality and keeps the audience from readily identifying with the characters in the play. As Borny suggests, this critical distance is important because it keeps the audience from reading the play as a "soap-opera" or melodrama (112). Because the play is about familial dysfunction, there are no heroes or villains in *The Glass Menagerie*. In order to understand the truth beneath the surface, the audience needs to maintain its objectivity. Tom's escape must be viewed as a necessary evil. Williams positions his audience for this perception in the character description; Tom's "nature is not remorseless, but to escape from a trap he has to act without pity" (129).

In addition to creating a critical distance between the audience and the play, metatheatrical techniques have other characteristics that make them particularly suitable to this play. In his assessment of metatheatrical reception aesthetics, Lionel Abel suggests a number of qualities that underline the appropriateness of Williams's use of these techniques. According to Abel, metatheatre "glorifies the unwillingness of the imagination to regard any image of the world as ultimate" (113). Given the fact that Williams believes reality to be an "organic thing" (131), mutable and illusive, something that only the poetic imagination can come close to representing, it is fitting that he makes metatheatrical techniques part of his poetic vocabulary. Abel also claims that metatheatre creates the "sense that the world is a projection of human consciousness" (113). In the case of *The Glass Menagerie*, the world is a projection of Tom's consciousness. Rather than standing as a record of what has actually happened, the play represents what happened as Tom remembers it. And memory, as Williams tells us, "takes a lot of poetic license. It omits some details; others are exaggerated" (143); it is subjective and "not realistic" (145). In other words, Williams warns his audience from the beginning that Tom may be an unreliable narrator. As George W. Crandell notes, the "imperfections" of Tom's memory are highlighted by the fact that Tom "remembers scenes he could not possibly have witnessed" (5). For example, Crandell cites Tom's description of the beginning of scene 6, a scene that occurs while Tom is still at work. Once again, Abel's assessment of metatheatre seems to fit nicely with what Williams says he wants to accomplish in this play. Moreover, the subjective nature of Tom's world is all the more reason for the audience to be objective, to maintain a critical distance.

In short, the screen device and other metatheatrical elements that Williams proposed in his original script were suited to the kind of play he wished to present. Nevertheless, the screen device has been controversial from the beginning. Although the use of projected images had been used in opera houses since before World War I, mainstream audiences of the mid-1940s seemed unready for this particular metatheatrical technique. As Brian Parker suggests, "American audiences were familiar with realism and theatricalism separately," but not when used in conjunction as Williams proposed to do in *The Glass Menagerie* (417). At any rate, Eddie Dowling, the original Broadway producer, "considered this device superfluous" (qtd. in Tischler 38), and the success of his production (561 performances) certainly helped to justify his opinion of the screen device.

Jo Mielziner, the set designer, thought that the screen device would be both distracting and redundant. Ironically, these are two of the screen device's intended functions. It distracts the audience's sense of reality within the play by calling their attention to its own theatricality; in so doing, it creates critical distance. The verbal legends are often redundant in that many of them either foreshadow or repeat lines from the dialogue of the play, thereby accentuating specific aspects of each scene. Despite the fact that Mielziner, like Williams, was interested in the renunciation of realism, apparently, he did not like the screen device as Williams conceived it.[3]

Even more surprising is John Gassner's negative critique of the screen device. Because he taught playwriting at The Dramatic Workshop (1940-1941) while it was under the direction of Piscator, the champion of projection devices, one would expect him to have been more receptive to the screen device. Instead, Gassner, Williams's former teacher, said "*The Glass Menagerie* was marred only by some preciosity [sic], mainly in the form of stage directions, most of which were eliminated in Eddie Dowling's memorable Broadway production" (qtd. in Borny 103). Nancy M. Tischler reports that Gassner "considered the screen device 'redundant and rather precious.' Williams is 'straining for effect not knowing that his simple tale, so hauntingly self-sufficient, needs no adornments'" (39). Perhaps he felt that the use of epic communication structures was inappropriate in a play that is more concerned with private tensions than public issues.

Since this initial negative reception, critics have voiced a variety of complaints about the screen device. These generally fall into one of three categories: 1) the screen device reflects the playwright's distrust of the performance aspect of the play; 2) it reflects the playwright's distrust of the reception aspect of the play; and 3) it is distracting. Roger B. Stein's comments invoke the first type of complaint when he writes that the "awkwardness" of the screen device is one case "where Williams has failed to develop and then rely upon the dramatic situation" (11). The second and third complaints are voiced by Lester A. Beaurline, who claims the "weakness of the device lies in the author's anxiousness and small confidence in his audience. . . . I suspect that if the screen device has ever been tried, it distracted the audience from the actors" (29). John Styan, author of *Modern Drama in Theory and Practice*, said that "the screen device got in the way of the direct impact of the play's action, and was wisely abandoned" (119).

There is, of course, validity in all three complaints. Williams did intend for the legends and images to "strengthen the effect" of both the written and the spoken lines in order to augment the dramatic situation (132). He also sought to guide the audience's attention by accenting "certain values in each scene" (132). The only aspect that he did not mention in regard to the screen device was the distancing effect. Significantly, all three complaints are directed at standard uses for meta-theatrical techniques, which suggests a general privileging of realistic over non-realistic techniques. As Borny discovered in his brief survey of the play's critical reception, "critics who prefer the Acting Edition usually do so because that version is more realistic" (106).

However, some critics who take their cue from the "Production

Notes" in the Reading Edition argue for the importance of this device on the basis of its non-realistic or metatheatrical functions. As a Brechtian distancing device, it has been championed by Borny and R. B. Parker. According to these two critics, the ironic commentary provided by the screen device creates an important critical distance. Borny says that the device effectively prevents the audience "from empathising too readily with the characters from Tom's past" (113) and that this distance positions the audience to receive the "symbolic truth" of the play (108). Without this irony, he says, "all we have is soap-opera" (112). Parker, in his psychological reading, says the "device achieves more than reducing the sentimental 'nostalgia'" of the play (529); it also sheds light on Tom's "ironic, self-defensive distancing" from the grief and guilt he feels (529). Moreover, it adds to the sense of ambiguity that, according to Parker, is the key to understanding this play (531). Thomas P. Adler has suggested that the screen device "might also function to replicate how memory works by association as well as to diminish any excessively sentimental response in the manner of a Brechtian distanciatian device" (138). Delma E. Presley echoes Adler's observation, saying that the screen device recaptures "the im-pressionistic qualities of the human memory—Tom's and ours" (80). Others, like Jackson and Frank Durham, value the device for its sym-bolic qualities. Durham makes the interesting claim that "the motion picture serves as the symbol determining the overall form of the play" while the screen device operates as subtitles in a silent movie (63). Jackson, an early advocate of the screen device, is mostly concerned with the device's poetic aspects as part of Williams's symbolic lan-guage for the plastic theatre (90-94).

Although each of these critics has a different interpretation of *The Glass Menagerie*, they all agree that the screen device adds richness and complexity to the play. Borny is "convinced" that rejection of the non-realistic elements "results in a trivialization of the play" (102). Parker says that to "insist, as most critics do, that the projection device is jejune or pretentious is to do Williams and his play a grave injustice" (416). Williams himself claims to have proposed the use of non-realistic techniques, including the screen device, in order to "find a closer approach, a more penetrating and vivid expression of things as they are" (131), and what he achieved was a realistic psychological portrait of a dysfunctional family. Interestingly, only in the last thirty years has the psychiatric community developed the theory and terminology that allows us to discuss Williams's play in terms of the dynamics of familial dysfunction.

If Tennessee Williams intended *The Glass Menagerie* to hold "its audience through the revelation of quiet and ordinary truths," as he said in an interview with R. C. Lewis in 1947 (qtd. in Devlin 28), then any interpretation of this work must first begin by asking, "What are the quiet and ordinary truths that *The Glass Menagerie* reveals?" As the play opens, Tom, a narrator who has tricks in his pocket, promises to give us "truth in the pleasant disguise of illusion" (144), and part of the illusion he weaves are the forty-three legends and images known as the screen device. As mentioned above, this device as metatheatrical technique may function in a number of ways; however, of particular interest is the way it functions as part of Tom's subjective memory. From a more objective perspective, the non-verbal projection images associated with Amanda, Laura, and Tom function symbolically to reveal the psychological underpinnings of the dysfunctional Wingfield family. In doing so, these projections help Williams position his audience to receive the difficult, but unavoidable truths about such family situations.

Before examining these particular screen images, it is important to establish the familial context that makes them so meaningful. According to Irene and Herbert Goldenberg, co-authors of *Family Therapy: An Overview*, in "families that produce dysfunctional behavior—one or both adults and any of the children may be assigned roles inappropriately or be treated as if they have only a single personality characteristic . . . instead of a wide range of human feelings and attitudes" (73). Within the dynamics of the Wingfield household, Tom, Amanda, and Laura have assumed certain roles; each character's role is "a rigid and constricted set of solutions to the problem of whom to be and how to act" (Gurman II 450). As in all dysfunctional families, a kind of stasis exists that appears to work as long as everyone stays within their prescribed roles. The roles in this Wingfield family drama/memory play consist of the "rejected parent," the "identified-patient," and the "parentified-child" (Goldenberg 74, 330, 333).

Amanda is the "rejected parent," whose husband abandoned her sixteen years before and who, consequently, "seeks gratification" through her children (Goldenberg 74) and her idealized past. The physically and emotionally crippled Laura assumes the role of "scapegoat . . . the identified-patient who is carrying the pathology for the entire family" (Goldenberg 76). As the one who most clearly has a problem, Laura is the "symptom bearer . . . expressing a family's 'disequilibrium'" (Goldenberg 7). Finally, just as one might expect in a single parent dysfunctional family, the void left by the absent parent is filled by the "parentified-child" (Gurman II 449). In the Wingfield family, the parentified-child is Tom. Although parentification of a child may occur in a number of situations, the Goldenbergs report that more and more frequently they "see the phenomenon when a parent deserts the family . . . [and] the child is expected to fill the parent role, physically as well as psychologically" (Goldenberg 73n2). When the father left, Tom apparently became "the little man of the house." Typical of the conflictual nature of child parentification, Tom is forced to assume the responsibilities that his father abandoned sixteen years ago while never being granted the autonomy that normally accompanies these adult responsibilities.

Ironically, within this stasis of rigidly assigned roles, there is typically a perpetual dance of mask swapping, with each character taking turns at playing the persecutor, the victim, and the rescuer.[4] In a dysfunctional family system, things appear to happen through the action of the dance, but nothing ever really changes, as illustrated in the discussion of scene 3 below. Amanda will continue reciting the story of the seventeen gentlemen callers:

Tom:	I know what's coming!
Laura:	Yes. But let her tell it.
Tom:	Again?
Laura:	She loves to tell it. (147)

Laura will continue to polish her glass collection, lost in whatever secret solace it affords her. As she says, "My glass collection takes up a
good deal of time. Glass is something you have to take good care of"
(220). And Tom will continue going to the movies and writing poems;
"Nobody in their right minds goes to the movies as often as you pretend to" (163); "Shakespeare probably wrote a poem on that light bill,
Mrs. Wingfield" (209). There will be small rebellions, accusations, re-
criminations, and acts of contrition, but nothing will ever change. The
Wingfield family system is a sort of dance of death, "a nailed-up coffin" (167). In order for Tom to escape from this trap, Williams tells us
that he will have "to act without pity" (129).

Given the dysfunctional context I have briefly outlined, Tom, author
and narrator of his memory play, is also the "parentified-child" trying
to make a clean break from his assigned familial role. At the beginning
of the play, he has managed to escape from this role physically, but he
remains bound to it by the guilt he feels over rejected parental responsibilities that should have never been his in the first place. His need to lay
his past to rest, to exorcise his guilt, affects his choice of the non-verbal
screen images linked to Amanda, Laura, and himself. Assuming the
play is Tom's public form of personal expiation and by extension Williams's as well, it becomes important to look at how these images function symbolically to reveal the psychological truths about the Wingfield family—truths that might at last set Tom free.

As the single parent in the Wingfield household, Tom's mother represents the cornerstone of this family's dysfunction. Therefore, it is fitting to begin this discussion with Amanda. After Mr. Wingfield deserts
her, she becomes the rejected parent. In order to compensate for the
damage her ego sustains by this rejection, she has been, as Williams

tells us, "clinging frantically to another time and place," one that is significantly populated by her younger self and her seventeen gentlemen callers (129). When she is not working at Famous-Barr demonstrating brassieres, she is busy selling subscriptions to a magazine that caters to female visions of romance. Consequently, the images Tom chooses to associate with his mother have to do with Amanda's idealized past, two slightly different images of her as a young girl (148, 203), and the romantic fantasies, two images of a glamour magazine cover (159, 179), that he correctly senses to be at the core of the family's dysfunction. In her failed adjustment to her new position as a single parent, she has victimized both of her children in different ways.

She victimizes Tom by assigning to him the inappropriate role of parent/partner. In the parentification of a child, "the child comes to feel responsible for the well-being of the parent(s)," while the parent shows a lack of empathy for the parentified-child (Gurman II 450-51). The larger-than-life photograph of the absent Mr. Wingfield and Amanda's frequent allusions to "your father" are constant reminders of the role Tom is expected to fill. When Tom apologizes after their big fight, Amanda takes advantage of his remorse to focus immediate attention on her role as the rejected parent.

> *Amanda:* I've had to put up a solitary battle all these years. But you're my right-hand bower! Don't fall down, don't fail!
>
> *Tom* [gently]: I try, Mother. (171)

More than just a simple bid for his sympathy; this is an effort to reposition Tom into his role as the parentified-child, the role he temporarily escapes when he defies her parental authority the previous night. To pull him back into his role, she repeats the theme of us against the world, telling him, "all we have to cling to is—each other" (171). Once back in his role of parent/child, she quickly heaps parental responsibility on his shoulders. Although he is two years younger than his sister,

Amanda tries to make Tom feel responsible for Laura's future while his own needs and dreams remain on hold (174-76).

In addition, the implicit incestuous aspect to this parent/child relationship need not be actual for it to work its damage on the child (Goldenberg 74). Without having actually replaced his father in Amanda's bed, he has been forced to be her partner in other equally inappropriate ways. That Amanda, in her accepted role as the rejected parent, has come to depend on Tom to shore up her image of herself as young and desirable is evidenced by the fact that in his anger he knows exactly what button to push. He ends their fight by delivering the *coup de grâce*, "You ugly—babbling old—witch . . ." (164). Williams's stage directions emphasize her self-absorption by pointing out that she is so "*stunned and stupefied by the 'ugly witch'*" that she hardly notices the damage to Laura's glass collection (165). From Tom's perspective as the parentified-child, the screen image of Amanda as a young girl reflects the seductive nature of their parent/child relationship. He is more than her child. As her confidante, her husband substitute, Tom assumes the role of her "right-hand bower" in every area but her bower.

The screen images associated with Amanda also relate to her victimization of Laura. In her role as the rejected parent, Amanda persistently needs to have her own desirability affirmed. One of the ways she reinforces her own self-image is to accentuate Laura's difference. Despite the fact that Laura's handicap "need not be more than suggested on the stage" (129), Amanda has exaggerated its ugliness by making it an unmentionable in their house: "Nonsense! Laura, I've told you never, never to use that word" (157). Typically in dysfunctional families, "some chance characteristic that distinguishes the child from other family members . . . is singled out and focused on by the others" in a process called "scapegoating" (Goldenberg 74-75). Once the role of the identified-patient becomes fixed, "the basis for chronic behavioral disturbance is established" (Goldenberg 75). By the time of the memory play, Laura's difference has developed into a serious problem, as evidenced by her emotional breakdown at the Rubicam Business

College. She has become so withdrawn from the real world that Williams says, "she is like a piece of her own glass collection, too exquisitely fragile to move from the shelf" (129).

Years of listening to her mother's story of the seventeen gentlemen callers has slowly eroded her self-confidence. Amanda tells her laconic daughter that it is not enough to have a "pretty face and a graceful figure—although I wasn't slighted in either respect." One must also understand the "art of conversation" (148). If her mother, who had all the qualities of a "pretty trap" (192), could not hold her man, how is Laura supposed to have any hope of trapping and holding a man? Convinced that she cannot hope to compete in the romantic arena, she concedes her failure: "I'm just not popular like you" (150). While Amanda speaks of "our gentlemen callers," and "flounces girlishly," Tom groans twice and Laura, with a catch in her voice, pronounces the dreaded truth: "Mother's afraid I'm going to be an old maid" (150).

In fact, the mother has to some extent set Laura up to be an "old maid" by providing a competitive rather than nurturing environment. Even on the night of Laura's gentleman caller, Amanda jealously tries to upstage her daughter. Just before she enters wearing the same "*girlish frock*" that she has worn for her own gentlemen callers, she announces, "I'm going to make a spectacular appearance!" (193). Significantly, the stage directions state that "*the legend of her youth is nearly revived*" (193). Tom is naturally "*embarrassed*" by his mother's inappropriate dress and demeanor, but Jim "*is altogether won over*" (203). Immediately, the screen image of Amanda as a girl appears; although the seventeen gentlemen callers are missing this time, the image still recalls the seductive powers of his mother in her youth.

Like the images associated with Amanda, Laura's non-verbal screen images also highlight her own failure to adjust to the adult role expected of a person her age, but they do so from a more sympathetic perspective. The depth and complexity of Tom's feelings for Laura are reflected in the fact that most of the non-verbal screen images are associated with her. Although he feels a tremendous amount of love for his sister, he also feels some justifiable resentment. Ultimately, she becomes the one who haunts his memory, the one he cannot completely leave behind. Consequently, the images associated with Laura point out her dysfunction, but they do so more gently and with more forgiveness than the images associated with Amanda.

All three non-verbal screen images associated with Laura are introduced in scene 2, in which Amanda uncovers Laura's "deception" (151), the situation that Tom refers to as "the fiasco at Rubicam's Business College" (159). This stands out as the turning point in the play, because in this scene Amanda begins to realize that Laura cannot cope with the world outside. The screen image of a bee-like "swarm of typewriters" precedes Amanda's revelation of the truth: "you had dropped out of school" (153). Tom's choice of a threatening mechanical screen image is an attempt to see things from Laura's perspective. At the same time, the surrealism of the image highlights her mental instability.

The second image associated with Laura is a "Winter scene in a park" (155). Her crippling shyness caused her to drop out of school, so she has spent the time alone "mostly in the park" (154) visiting the penguins and "the Jewel Box, that big glass house where they raise the tropical flowers" (155). This screen image and the solitary activities associated with it suggest a coldness about Laura. Like the image, Laura is lovely but cold and frozen in time. As Tom says, "She lives in a world of her own—a world of—little glass ornaments" (188). Even the glass of her menagerie and the big glass house seem to suggest ice. Like the penguins in the park and the tropical flowers in the big glass house, she is as "peculiar" as a flightless bird and incapable of surviving in the world outside as a hot-house plant (188).

Similarly, the screen image of blue roses symbolizes Laura's peculiarity and is the most important of the three non-verbal screen images associated with Laura. In addition to Laura and Amanda's dialogue concerning this nickname and Jim and Laura's dialogue concerning the same, this image gets projected three times in the course of Tom's memory play (151, 157, 227). Just as red is a hot color, blue is a cold color. If red roses are the traditional symbol for romantic love, then blue roses must symbolize Laura's lack of passion or, as Bert Cardullo has suggested, her desire to transcend this world (82). Although blue is the wrong color for roses, it is the right color for Laura (228). She has no passion for life. She has dropped out of high school, out of business school, and out of life. In order for Tom to exorcise his guilt, he must reject the role of parentified-child and acknowledge the fact that he cannot be responsible for Laura's future. The coldness of the images associated with her correctly places some of the blame for her condition on Laura. Her withdrawal from life, to a large extent, remains her own choice. As George W. Crandell observes, "Laura actively resists both the role that society prescribes for women as well as Amanda's insistence that she conform to it" (9). Although the nickname was originally linked to a physical illness, the screen image becomes linked to a psychological illness.

Whereas Laura's screen images reflect the complexity of Tom's feelings for the sister he has abandoned, the one image he associates with his escape reflects the ambiguity he feels for having made that choice. On one hand, the sailing vessel represents the freedom and movement of the open sea and the Union of Merchant Seamen. On the other hand, the vessel is a pirate ship whose Jolly Roger, the skull and cross bones, symbolizes criminality and death. As Cardullo notes, Merchant Marine ships became primary targets when World War II broke out (91), and may be represented as the lightning that Tom refers to at the end of the play. Since the memory play is Tom's attempt to lay the past to rest, the most telling of screen images is the one he chooses for himself. "A sailing vessel with the Jolly Roger" (173, 200).[5]

On one level, the ship image represents Tom's desire to move from the claustrophobic confines of the Wingfield's tiny apartment to the vast open spaces of the ocean. Indeed, Williams establishes the motif of claustrophobia from the very first sentence of the opening stage directions: "The Wingfield apartment is in the rear of the building, one of those vast hive-like conglomerations of cellular living-units that flower as warty growths in overcrowded urban centers" (143). Significantly, it "is entered by a fire escape, a structure whose name is a touch of accidental poetic truth" (143).

For Tom, the claustrophobia is both physical and psychological. There are not enough bedrooms; Laura has to sleep in the living room. In addition to the absence of personal space, the real sense of claustrophobia comes from the way their lives are enmeshed, another common symptom of dysfunctional families (Gurman 449).[6] This problem is both voiced and demonstrated in the course of Tom's fight with Amanda.

> *Amanda:* What is the matter with you, you—big—big—IDIOT!
> *Tom:* Look!—I've got no thing, no single thing—
> *Amanda:* Lower your voice!
> *Tom:* —in my life here that I can call my OWN! (161)

They both interrupt each other throughout the argument so that even their voices become enmeshed. Only when Tom becomes physically threatening does she back off (164).

Typical of their dance of death, they switch masks at this point. Tom becomes the persecutor, and Amanda becomes the victim of his rage. However, when he is "pinioned" by his coat, he rips it off and throws it across the room, accidentally breaking part of Laura's glass collection (164). "Laura cries out as if wounded" (164); Tom gets down on his knees and begins his act of contrition (165). So the scene ends with Tom back in his prescribed role as care-giver to Laura, the identified-patient, as he begins to collect the fallen glass. Given the fact that this family system allows Tom no space to take care of himself, to have a life of his own, it is no wonder that he dreams of wide open spaces and oceans of freedom.

In contrast to this stifling world of female domination, the manly world of the Union of Merchant Seamen represented by the image of a sailing ship seems like a breath of fresh air. Just before Tom confides in

Jim about his plans to leave home via the merchant marines, the screen image of a sailing vessel with the Jolly Roger appears for the second time (200), and the stage directions tell us that Tom "looks like a voyager" (201). One can almost imagine the breeze in his hair.

In addition, Tom's decision to escape into an exclusively masculine world highlights an important gender issue in the play. In the Wingfield household, Tom's sexuality must be held in check. Amanda will not allow Tom even vicarious access into the world of adult sexuality. She will not allow the "filth" of that "insane Mr. Lawrence" in her house (161). Her outrage over Lawrence masks the genuine fear that Tom's sexual interests could result in his growing up and leaving home to create his own family. In short, her prudish outrage is not really about sex, but about Tom's independence.

Lawrence may be banned; however, when it comes down to trapping a man for Laura, Amanda openly peddles *The Homemaker's Companion*, with its female sexuality couched in terms such as "delicate cuplike breasts," "creamy thighs," and "bodies as powerful as Etruscan sculpture" (159). Appropriately, in this way Amanda earns the extra money "needed to properly feather the nest and plume the bird" (159). When the long awaited night of the gentleman caller arrives, Amanda transforms her daughter into a "pretty trap" (192) with a new dress (191) and a bra stuffed with "'Gay Deceivers'" (192). "All pretty girls are a trap, a pretty trap, and men expect them to be" (192). Ironically, the "tragic mistake" in Amanda's personal life was falling for a pretty trap in the form of the now absent Mr. Wingfield (186): "No girl can do worse than put herself at the mercy of a handsome appearance! I hope that Mr. O'Connor is not too good-looking" (186). As the rejected parent and victim of her own sexuality, Amanda views sex as a dangerous force that must be either suppressed or properly manipulated toward the goal of marriage. Tom's sexuality, having no place in Amanda's plans for Laura, must be suppressed, while Jim's sexuality, having everything to do with Amanda's plans, must be manipulated. Understandably, Tom associates escape with a masculine world.

Significantly, the sailing vessel that symbolizes Tom's escape is a pirate ship, a symbol rich in ambiguity. It represents a special species of ruthless thieves and murderers who are as often knighted as hung for their actions. Our culture's love/hate relationship with the pirate parallels Tom's love/hate relationship with himself and with the sister he has tried unsuccessfully to leave behind. The brutality and criminality generally associated with pirates represent Tom's uneasy conscience, the motivating force behind this memory play. Tom in the present is trying to lay his past to rest, to break the bond of guilt that still hampers his development as an adult.

The boyish naiveté implicit in the pirate ship image is also indicative of Tom's arrested growth. It links him to Jim, the high school star of *The Pirates of Penzance*, an operetta in which a group of unsuccessful pirates fall in love. It also links him to the romanticized pirates and adventures he experiences in the movies. He thinks he longs for adventure, but he really longs for the childhood he was never allowed to have. As the parentified-child, he has been unfairly forced into being a father to his sister by a mother who assumed that Laura was their shared responsibility. As if she were their child, Amanda tells Tom, "We have to be making some plans and provisions for her" (174). Ironically, the parentified-child can never grow up until he/she gives up the responsibilities unjustly placed upon him/her as a child. Tom has to renounce his adult responsibilities toward his family in order to become an adult in his own right.

Consequently, Tom, the narrator, sees himself as both hero and villain for having left home. Although leaving home is the natural step into adulthood from a normal childhood, Tom's experience as the parentified-child, as a stand-in for the husband of his mother and father of himself and his sister, has made this move toward selfhood almost impossible. It has taken him a long time to muster the pirate-like sense of villainy and daring necessary for him to make his move. As he prepares himself to follow in his father's footsteps, Tom tells Jim, "I'm like my father. The bastard son of a bastard! Did you notice how he's grinning in his picture in there? And he's been absent going on sixteen years!" (202). This simultaneous announcement/denouncement of self occurs in scene 6 some time after the morning his father's photograph lights up in response to Tom's question about the nailed-up coffin: "You know it don't take much intelligence to get yourself into a nailed-up coffin, Laura. But who in hell ever got himself out of one without removing one nail? [As if in answer, the father's grinning photograph lights up. The scene dims out]" (167-68).

It takes Tom a great deal of time to work up his anger about his victimization. His explosive speech in scene 3 is the culmination of years of frustration: "You think I'm in love with the Continental Shoe-makers? Look! I'd rather somebody picked up a crowbar and battered out my brains—than go back there mornings! . . . If self is what I thought of, Mother, I'd be where he is—GONE!" (163). What finally pushes Tom over the edge is Amanda's failure to acknowledge the extent of his sacrifice. Amanda cannot face this truth without also acknowledging the injustice of Tom's prescribed role as parentified-child. Her accusations of selfishness are more than he can bear: "The more you shout about my selfishness to me the quicker I'll go, and I won't go to the movies!" (236).

The power and poignancy of *The Glass Menagerie* lie in the revelation of two difficult truths about the Wingfield family. First, Laura is not going to awaken suddenly and begin to participate in the real world. Jim's kiss was just a human kiss and not the magic kiss of a fairy-tale prince. The dynamics of this dysfunctional family inhibit self-development and discourage autonomy. Sometimes, as in Laura's case, individual growth is forever arrested; as with the delicate creatures in her glass collection, she remains frozen in time. In the end she lifts her head and smiles at her mother, completely resigned to her role as identified-patient: "Amanda's gestures are slow and graceful, almost dancelike, as she comforts her daughter" (236). Laura has renounced all responsibility for making a life for herself.

Secondly, Tom's decision to leave becomes a matter of self-preservation, a necessary evil. If he stays, he will have to sacrifice his identity in favor of a role imposed on him by the familial dynamics. Tom realizes that his identity and dreams are unimportant to Amanda, the rejected parent, and incomprehensible to Laura, the identified-patient. As the parentified-child, he must sacrifice his self for the financial security of the family. "For sixty-five dollars a month I give up all that I dream of doing and being *ever*!" (64). Tom repeatedly associates his role as bread winner with a living death, a nailed-up coffin, because for him to remain is to commit psychic suicide. As he tells Amanda, "Every time you come in yelling that God damn *'Rise and Shine*!' *'Rise and Shine*!' I say to myself, 'How *lucky dead* people are!' But I get up. I *go*!" (164).

So in the Wingfield family, as with many dysfunctional families, the natural process of leaving the nest, which should be a life-affirming celebration of a person's independence, has been perverted into a sort of exorcism of all family ties. Tom wants a total disassociation with his past, not because he does not love his mother and sister, but because of the pain that love causes him. He wants more than forgiveness; he wants forgetfulness; he wants to wish it all away. This, of course, is no more possible for Tom than it was for Williams himself.

Perhaps the most one can hope for is to make peace with oneself by recognizing the necessity of one's actions. As Adler has suggested, it is possible to view Tom's remembering as a therapeutic process, a way of working through the pain and guilt he feels for having escaped the nailed coffin, for having abandoned his mother and sister (139). In Tom's memory play, as in real life, the process of recovery involves recognizing the dysfunctional familial roles, accepting responsibility for one's own life, and learning to lay the past to rest. If one imagines that through the ritual of this process, Tom will be able to get on with his life, then Laura's final gesture of blowing out the candles can be interpreted as a release. This play is very much about what Williams called "the fragile, delicate ties that must be broken, that you inevitably break, when you try to fulfill yourself" (qtd. in Devlin 10).

Notes

1. All future references to *The Glass Menagerie* will be noted by page number only.

2. For more on the current discourse concerning didascalia, see Michael Issacharoff and Robin F. Jones, ed., *Performing Texts* (Philadelphia: U of Pennsylvania P, 1988).

3. This does not mean that Mielziner was completely opposed to the use of projected images as is evidenced by his use of projections to leaf out the house and surrounding area in *Death of a Salesman* (1949).

4. In transactional analysis, this configuration is called the Karpman Triangle. It is discussed in *Born to Win: Transactional Analysis with Gestalt Experiments* by Muriel James and Dorothy Jongeward in the unit called "The Drama of Life Scripts" as being "illegitimate" when used for the purpose of manipulation (Reading, MA: Addison-Wesley, 1973. 84-89).

5. In Cardullo's romanticized reading of the play, the pirate ship both mocks "Tom's fantasy of high adventure" and "augurs his own demise" (91).

6. The Goldenbergs define enmeshment as "an extreme form of proximity and intensity in family interactions in which members are overconnected and overinvolved in each others lives" (329).

Works Cited

Abel, Lionel. *Metatheatre: A View of Dramatic Form*. New York: Hill and Wang, 1963.

Adler, Thomas P. *American Drama, 1940-1960: A Critical History*. New York: Twayne, 1994.

Bigsby, C. W. E. "Entering *The Glass Menagerie*." *The Cambridge Companion to Tennessee Williams*. Ed. Matthew C. Roudané. Boston: Cambridge UP, 1997. 29-44.

Borny, Geoffrey. "The Two *Glass Menagerie*s: Reading Edition and Acting Edition." *Modern Critical Interpretations: Tennessee Williams's The Glass Menagerie*. Ed. Harold Bloom. New York: Chelsea House, 1988.

Cardullo, Bert. "The Blue Rose of St. Louis: Laura, Romanticism, and *The Glass Menagerie*." *The Tennessee Williams Annual Review* (1998): 81-92.

Crandell, George W. "The Cinematic Eye in Tennessee Williams's *The Glass Menagerie*." *The Tennessee Williams Annual Review* (1998): 1-11.

Devlin, Albert, ed. *Conversations with Tennessee Williams*. Jackson: UP of Mississippi, 1986.

Durham, Frank. "Tennessee Williams, Theatre Poet in Prose." *Modern Critical Interpretations: Tennessee Williams's The Glass Menagerie*. Ed. Harold Bloom. New York: Chelsea House, 1988. 59-73.

Esslin, Martin. *Brecht: A Choice of Evils: A Critical Study of the Man, His Work and His Opinions*. 4th ed. London: Methuen, 1984.

Goldenberg, Irene, and Herbert Goldenberg. *Family Therapy: An Overview*. 2nd ed. Pacific Grove, CA: Brooks/Cole, 1985.

Gurman, Alan S., and David P. Kniskem, eds. *Handbook of Family Therapy*. Vol. 1. New York: Brunner/Mazel, 1991.

Jackson, Esther Merle. *The Broken World of Tennessee Williams*. Madison: U of Wisconsin P, 1965.

Parker, Brian (R. B. Parker). "The Composition of *The Glass Menagerie*: An Argument for Complexity." *Modern Drama* 25 (1982): 409-422.

Pfister, Manfred. *The Theory and Analysis of Drama*. Trans. John Halliday. Cambridge: Cambridge UP, 1988.

Presley, Delma E. *The Glass Menagerie: An American Memory*. Boston: Twayne, 1990.

Styan, J. L. *Modern Drama in Theory and Practice*. Vol. 3. Cambridge: Cambridge UP, 1981. 3 vols.

Tischler, Nancy M. "The Glass Menagerie: The Revelation of Quiet Truth." *Modern Critical Interpretations: Tennessee Williams's The Glass Menagerie*. Ed. Harold Bloom. New York: Chelsea House, 1988. 31-41.

Willett, John. *The Theatre of Erwin Piscator: Half a Century of Politics in the Theatre*. London: Methuen, 1978.

Williams, Tennessee. *The Glass Menagerie*. 1945. *The Theatre of Tennessee Williams*. Vol. 1. New York: Peter Lang, 1989.

Witt, Mary Ann Frese. "Reading Modern Drama: Voice in the Didascaliae." *Studies in the Literary Imagination*. 25.1 (1992): 103-112.

"Fifty Percent Illusion":
The Mask of the Southern Belle in Tennessee Williams's *A Streetcar Named Desire, The Glass Menagerie,* and "Portrait of a Madonna"

George Hovis

> After all, a woman's charm is fifty percent illusion.
> —Blanche DuBois, *A Streetcar Named Desire*

> For conjure is a power of transformation that causes definitions of "form" as a fixed and comprehensible "thing" to dissolve.
> —Houston Baker, Jr., *Modernism and the Harlem Renaissance*

Tennessee Williams achieved his early success largely on the strength of his unforgettable female leads, the southern belles of *The Glass Menagerie* and *A Streetcar Named Desire*. They are strong, articulate, assertive—and yet often tender and vulnerable. They are women who are acutely aware of being watched and heard because they have been reared in a culture with a strict decorum for the accepted behavior of its women. Because the belle can only be understood by considering her in a specific historical context, it is necessary to examine the cultural pressures that have provoked her performances. A comparative examination of Lucretia Collins of "Portrait of a Madonna," Amanda Wingfield of *The Glass Menagerie*, and Blanche DuBois of *A Streetcar Named Desire* shows how the role of the belle has perpetuated the possibilities both for victimhood and for survival. Amanda and Blanche adopt the role of the belle in an effort to survive within a social milieu in which they are disempowered. Unlike Lucretia, they both adopt the role as a means of literal survival by securing economic and social stability. More importantly, in the case of Blanche, she performs subtle transformations in the role of the belle and thereby effects a revolution within the gender consciousness of Williams's audience.

Ironically, a striking comparison can be made between the dilemma faced by these socially privileged belles and the situation of black men and women in much of this century's black American literature. During the long decades before feminism and civil rights, both blacks and white women found themselves in discursive situations at a marked disadvantage, speaking and behaving according to rules that were forced upon them. In *Modernism and the Harlem Renaissance*, Houston Baker examines the crisis of voice in interracial discourse during the Jim Crow era and the problem of black speakers, who were politically disempowered and who therefore necessarily had to develop methods of subterfuge, of illusion and deception, in order to speak and be heard. Baker identifies the minstrel mask as the form taken by black speakers seeking some measure of freedom, safety, and leverage in interracial discourse. Like the guise of the belle, however, the minstrel mask is not the creation of the wearer so much as the creation of the interlocutor with whom the wearer is engaged. White speakers misappropriated elements from black vernacular and black culture and then exaggerated and arranged them "into a comic array, a mask of *selective memory* [. . .] designed to remind white consciousness that black men and women are *mis-speakers* bereft of humanity—carefree devils strumming and humming all day" (21). The occurrence of masking is more prevalent in the literature of twentieth century black male writers than in the work of black women. In *Moorings and Metaphors: Figures of Culture and Gender in Black Women's Literature*, Karla Holloway finds that the writings of black men and women fundamentally differ in that the men concentrate on individual ways of acting, while the women focus on shared ways of speaking. Holloway argues that this distinction is based not simply on sociological factors but on the fact that black male writers have adopted white male modernist assumptions about the self in relation to a community. In portraying his southern belles as alienated performers, Tennessee Williams similarly views them from perhaps a distinctly male point of view. Like his contemporaries Richard Wright and Ralph Ellison, Williams inherits from the male tradition of Anglo-American modernism a preoccupation with isolation, a factor which was, of course, heightened by his sexual orientation.

In the Jim Crow era, black male speakers consistently needed to reassure white men of black powerlessness before proceeding to negotiate for a position of relative power. Baker promotes Booker T. Washington as the foremost black American leader during Reconstruction and attributes Washington's success—in both oral address and in his autobiography, *Up From Slavery*—to Washington's ability to "master the form" of minstrelsy (25-36), his ability to convince his white benefactors that blacks posed no threat to the ascendancy of the white male ego. Likewise, belles recognized the necessity of pacifying their men with recognizably subservient, sexually passive behaviors. In the unreconstructed South, both white women and black men were often recognized not as fully complex individuals but as representatives of a type; both the servant and the belle were reified as platonic ideals with a kind of static purity of form that would allow them reliably to serve as objects to white male subjects. In his *The Mind of the South*, W. J. Cash observes the Southern white man's obsessiveness over the utter purity of his women: "'Woman!!! The center and circumference, diameter and periphery, sine, tangent and secant of all our affections!' Such was the toast which brought twenty great cheers from the audience at the celebration of Georgia's one-hundredth anniversary in the 1830's" (87). While the white "massa" was down in the slave quarters regularly indulging his own sexual appetite, his wife was securely ensconced in the big house upholding the virtues of the Old South. In compensation for denying her own libidinal needs, she was made the emblem of moral virtue. Cash remarks: "There was hardly a sermon that did not begin and end with tributes in her honor, hardly a brave speech that did not open and close with the clashing of shields and the flourishing of swords for her glory. At the last, I verily believe, the ranks of the Confederacy went rolling into battle in the misty conviction that it was wholly for her that they fought" (86-87). Of course, the world of Williams's dramas is not the Old South but his contemporary America, an ethnically and culturally heterogeneous urban world, a setting in which Williams's belles appear comically out of place. As a remnant of the antebellum South, their presence serves to reenact the dynamics of that earlier culture within a contemporary context and thereby critiques both the earlier culture and its continuing presence in the contemporary world. In particular, Williams targets the unjust sexual mores of Southern society, mores which he shows to be virtually identical to those he finds throughout his contemporary America.

As Faulkner had, Tennessee Williams recognized the psychic damage done to Southern women by this stereotype of the belle and its attendant demand of sexual purity. As with Faulkner's Miss Emily and Rosa Coldfield, Miss Lucretia Collins of "Portrait of a Madonna" is a "middle-aged spinster" (109), who remains fixated upon her frustrated sexuality well past her prime. The daughter of an Episcopal minister, Lucretia is a woman who has long borne the brunt of her culture's puritanism. Since the death of her mother fifteen years earlier, she has remained isolated in a run-down "moderate-priced" apartment in a northern city, and she has evidently given up the weekly meetings at the church, so that now her only society is her limited contact with the building's landlord and elderly porter. As the play opens, we see an alarmed Lucretia telephoning her landlord to report that she has lately been the recurrent victim of a man who has been forcing his way into her bedroom for the purpose of "indulging his senses!" (109). Lucretia is wearing the negligee she has been saving since girlhood in her hope chest, and the stage directions consistently confront us with the comically grotesque image of a faded belle performing the actions of a young woman: "*Self-consciously she touches her ridiculous corkscrew curls with the faded pink ribbon tied through them. Her manner becomes that of a slightly coquettish but prim little Southern belle*" (114). Her manner is both "coquettish" and "prim," demonstrating the war raging inside her between libidinal energies and puritan repressions. The coquettish manner is designed to assure the prospective suitor that she is capable of sexuality, and the primness assures him that she is nevertheless virginal, waiting for the appropriate suitor. This position of waiting, of utter passivity, is the target of Williams's satire. In her middle age, with time running out, Lucretia grows desperate of waiting and so conjures for herself the fantasy of the man whom she loved in her youth. Night after night, she has imagined that he has forced himself upon her, and now she believes herself pregnant with his child. In a series of digressions, she relives her youthful attachment to Richard and her loss of him to a rival belle, a woman who was likely less sexually repressed than she. Appropriately, Lucretia lost her beau on a Sunday school faculty picnic.

Indeed, her sexual nature is repeatedly considered in relation to the church. In the opening scene when Lucretia phones her landlord to report that she has been raped, she says, "I've refrained from making any complaint because of my connections with the church. I used to be assistant to the Sunday school superintendent and I once had the primary class. I helped them put on the Christmas pageant. I made the dress for the Virgin and Mother, made robes for the Wise Men. Yes, and now this has happened, I'm not responsible for it, but night after night after night this man has been coming into my apartment and—indulging his senses!" (109). At the end of the play when the doctor and nurse from the state asylum come to take her away, she exclaims, "I know! [*Excitedly*] You're come from the Holy Communion to place me under arrest! On moral charges!" (125). Ironically, her words contain the truth that, at least on a figurative level, she is being institutionalized because of a sexual crime. She has been allowed to carry on in her delusions without disturbance for fifteen years; it is only when she affronts her limited society with the possibility of sexuality, even if it is imagined, that she is denied her freedom. The porter serves as the voice of this society and restores social order at the end of the play by denying any actual sexual transgression, when he says, "She was always a lady, Doctor, such a perfect lady" (125).

As in Faulkner's "A Rose for Emily," Williams shocks us with the disparity between the facade of the belle and her psychological reality. Unlike Emily, however, Lucretia is an impotent belle, the victim of her society's sexual mores. We are likely to agree with the porter, who tries to convince the elevator boy that Lucretia is more "pitiful" than "disgusting" (113-14). She is pitiful because she is unable to gain the necessary critical distance from her culture that would allow her to reject the imposition of its moral judgments. For a moment at least, she is capable of this rejection, and, as she is being carried away to the asylum, she shouts out that her child will receive a secular education so that "it won't come under the evil influence of the Christian church!" (123). This denouncement comes only in a moment of passion and derives from an emotional core that periodically eclipses her rational self. On a deep libidinal level she is autonomous, but on a rational level Lucretia is dominated by her culture. This lack of rational autonomy, of self-awareness, dooms her to victimhood.

Lucretia Collins's behaviors bear a striking resemblance to those of Amanda Wingfield and Blanche DuBois. All three women are constantly and acutely aware of how they are being perceived by men. Each is aware that she is beyond what her culture considers to be her "prime" and therefore engages in an elaborate scheme of denial, which involves a repetition of some critical moment from the past that marks a missed opportunity. Both Lucretia and Amanda seem to be reliving their debuts, reenacting the ritual that is designed to ensure their sexual and economic gratification. Like Lucretia in her hope-chest negligee, Amanda dons the party dress she wore while being courted as a girl at Blue Mountain, and Blanche puts on the gown and rhinestone tiara that she likely wore to the Moon Lake Casino the night her husband killed himself. Each costume is comically grotesque and out of place and thus serves as a theatrical device to remind us how each woman is trapped in a moment that passed her by years before. Perhaps the most important comparison among these women is that each feels she has been cheated, that her society has not lived up to its end of the bargain. Each has played the role of the belle without receiving the promised economic and psychosexual compensation; instead of standing amid her family surveying acres of cotton from a porch lined with columns, each woman is alone and destitute, relying upon "the kindness of strangers" and alienated family members for her bare existence.

In contrast to Lucretia, however, one feels a power, a sense of control—and a sexuality—in Blanche and Amanda that is absent from the more religiously orthodox Lucretia. Considering Lucretia's narrative of the Sunday school picnic when Richard briefly "put his arm around her," it is difficult to imagine that, even in her "prime," she ever managed to overcome the sexual repressions of her minister father. More importantly, she has never sufficiently questioned the forms of behavior expected of her as a woman. She may be emotionally outraged, but she never rationally distances herself from the role of the belle she unconsciously adopts. By contrast, with Amanda and even more so with Blanche, we see a character who may be trapped in the role of the belle but one that recognizes the entrapment. Rather than naïvely and passively expecting the deference and protection of the men around them, Blanche and Amanda relentlessly extract the expected behaviors by constantly reminding the men of the social contract of chivalry in the South and demanding the appropriate ritualized behaviors.

This problem of self-consciousness is central to both the belle and the minstrel. Richard Wright feared the adoption of masking behaviors as simply a capitulation to the expectations of white America. Throughout his autobiography, *Black Boy*, Wright explains that he survived and managed to find a writing voice precisely because he was relatively successful in avoiding situations that required him to ape the subservient behaviors of the "dumb nigger" universally expected by whites in the Jim Crow South where he grew up. For Wright, to engage in masking was to give up the struggle for equal rights. Conversely, Houston Baker argues that, during the early decades of this century, masking behaviors were the most viable form of resistance available to blacks. He sees the mastery of the forms of minstrelsy as the mode of disguising revolutionary content in the pacifying sounds of nonsense: "The mas-

---

tery of form conceals, disguises, floats like a trickster butterfly in order to sting like a bee" (50). Williams's feelings about masking appear to fall somewhere between those of Wright and Baker. While he dramatizes masking as a possible mode of revolution (especially with Blanche), his maskers tend to martyr themselves for their cause. Like Wright, Williams recognizes the chief danger of masking to be the performer's loss of the ability to distinguish the difference between the performance and reality. *Streetcar* ends with a deluded Blanche, who seems to retreat to fantasy as irrevocably as the prematurely senile Lucretia in "Portrait." Throughout most of the play, however, Blanche demonstrates a much more controlled performance in which she calculates the effect of her performance on her various audiences (principally Mitch, Stanley, and Stella).

By contrast, Stella dispenses with the role of the belle and speaks candidly to her husband, trusting him to respect her openness with commensurate tenderness and honesty. Stella fled Belle Reve and the example of her older sister perhaps because she recognized the dangers of performance. Unfortunately, Stella fails to recognize the dangers of *not* performing. Unlike Blanche's, Stella's passivity is real, and Stanley takes advantage of it by intermittently bullying her and by virtually denying her a voice in the affairs of their home. He invites his drinking buddies over for poker nights and ignores her objections. He physically and emotionally abuses her, even when she is pregnant—and afterward, to the chagrin of Blanche, Stella returns home to forgive and make love to her husband. When Stanley ultimately betrays Stella's trust by raping her sister while Stella is in labor at the hospital, Stella passively accepts Stanley's denial of Blanche's report and even acquiesces to his demand that her sister be institutionalized for her delusions. Williams seems to be acknowledging that, even in the postwar melting pot of regional and ethnic traditions, America is no less chauvinistic than the Old South and that for women to deny the uneven gender dynamics is naively to accept a position of powerlessness.

The contrast between Blanche and Stella is mirrored by the relationship between Amanda Wingfield and her daughter Laura in *The Glass Menagerie*. Like Stella, Laura is incapable of adopting the role of the belle. Her intense sexual frustration combined with her father's abandonment and her mother's tyranny have produced such a fragile sense of self that she is utterly incapable of the kind of projection required in the coquettish behaviors Amanda prescribes. It would be easy to succumb to a simple and sentimentalized reading of *Menagerie* in which Laura is seen as her mother's victim and Amanda as selfishly wishing only to relive her youth through her daughter's courtship. However, if Amanda is less capable than her son, Tom, of appreciating Laura's "true self," it is because Amanda recognizes her daughter's inability to survive in the world outside their apartment. There is a strong naturalistic element in all of Williams's drama, and the world of *Menagerie* is perhaps his most Darwinian. We should hear less malice than desperation in Amanda's voice when she warns her daughter of the possibilities awaiting her:

> So what are we going to do the rest of our lives? Stay home and watch the parades go by? [. . .] What is there left but dependency all our lives? I know so well what becomes of unmarried women who aren't prepared to occupy a position. I've seen such pitiful cases in the South—barely tolerated spinsters living upon the grudging patronage of sister's husband or brother's wife!—stuck away in some little mousetrap of a room—encouraged by one in-law to visit another—little birdlike women without any nest—eating the crust of humility all their life! (852)

Amanda understands the social and economic realities of their world, and, by modeling the role of the belle, she attempts to teach her daughter an important survival technique.

Like Laura, Blanche was vulnerable as a girl. Stella explains to Stanley, "You didn't know Blanche as a girl. Nobody, nobody, was tender and trusting as she was. But people like you abused her, and forced her to change" (136). Blanche changed by developing an outer self that served to protect her inner self from scrutiny and judgment. She tells Stella, "I never was hard or self-sufficient enough. When people are soft—soft people have got to shimmer and glow—they've got to put on soft colors, the colors of butterfly wings, and put a—paper lantern over the light. [. . .] It isn't enough to be soft. You've got to be soft *and attractive*" (92). One might also remark that Blanche is not only attractive but manipulative, aggressive, and domineering. In her article "Destructive Power Games: A Study of Blanche DuBois and Amanda Wingfield," Nancy O. Wilhelmi criticizes Blanche's obsessions with surfaces as well as her relationships based "on dominance rather than intimacy, on one person's victory rather than the success of both individuals" (33). Wilhelmi appreciates how such power dynamics inevitably lead to exploitation and how Blanche perpetuates her own victimization by engaging in such a "game of deception" (33). However, Wilhelmi stops short of exploring the complexities of victimization at work in *Streetcar*. She denies Blanche an awareness of her interior life or an understanding of the history that has shaped her behaviors. Wilhelmi calls attention to Blanche's duplicity with Mitch and says that "Even the game that Blanche has been playing is a lie: she wants to marry Mitch not because she loves him but because she wants to secure her future. She betrays herself by not recognizing her own worth, as an intelligent and sensitive woman" (34-35). It is perhaps a serious misreading of the play to suggest that Blanche is actually interested in marrying Mitch at all. Someone as complex and perceptive as Blanche would likely not be interested in someone as dull and simple as Mitch, at least not for long. Blanche remarks to Mitch that no one can be sensitive without having suffered, and certainly one of the few commonalities between them is an acquaintance with suffering and death. Yet Mitch's suffering for his mother and the girl who died is simple and pitifully conventional by comparison to the complex and imaginative articulation of suffering that Blanche has managed.

As with all her other "intimacies with strangers," including her recent string of escapades in Laurel, there is a doubleness about Blanche's involvement with Mitch. In each case, she seems less interested in the affair for its own sake than in the ritual of romance in its relation to her first love, the defining relationship of her life. In easily the most tender moment between them, Blanche divulges to Mitch the history of her early marriage: "When I was sixteen, I made the discovery—love. All at once and much, much too completely. It was like you suddenly turned a blinding light on something that had always been half in shadow, that's how it struck the world for me" (114). She explains how she came to learn of her husband's homosexuality and how she reacted to it by pronouncing the judgment that precipitated his suicide: "It was because—on the dance floor—I'd suddenly said—'I saw! I know! You disgust me . . .' And then the searchlight which had been turned on the world was turned off again and never for one moment since has there been any light that's stronger than this—kitchen—candle" (115). If Blanche's neurotic avoidance of sunlight is considered in relation to this passage, then her obsession with colored lights reveals more than a paranoia about the marks of age. The sun, like a searchlight, too easily penetrates her facade of self-control and discloses the naked truth of guilt and loss that she spends her life alternately obsessing about and trying to avoid. The artificial colored lights that Blanche habitually manipulates in order to create an atmosphere conducive to the awakening of libidinal desire serve as a reminder that any love she experiences will only be a pale counterfeit of her young marriage. In reenacting the ritual of romance, however halfheartedly, Blanche is resurrecting the spirit of her first love. After apologizing for her lack of interest during their date to the amusement park, she invites Mitch into her flat, lights a candle, pours each of them a shot of liquor, and declares, "We're going to be very Bohemian. We are going to pretend that we are sitting in a little artists' cafe on the Left Bank in Paris!" (102). Blanche's involvement with Mitch here is essentially autoerotic; she is interested in the moment only for the possibility of projecting fantasies that stem from her first introduction to Bohemia with her poet husband. Similarly, she recognizes the possibilities for imaginatively evoking the past when she flirts with the newspaper boy and asks him, "Don't you just love these long rainy afternoons in New Orleans when an hour isn't just an hour—but a little piece of eternity dropped into your hands—and who knows what to do with it?" (97-98). Desire is the key to eternity; by kissing the young newspaper boy, she reenacts her passion for her late husband, who died when both he and Blanche were very young.

True to her Southern gothic nature, Blanche is a character overwhelmed by the past, both her own past and a familial and cultural past. Just as her present involvement with Mitch must be considered in relation to her first romantic attachment, all of her sexual experience must be considered in relation to the sexual history of Belle Reve and of the plantation South. In giving herself to the young soldiers who come drunken to the front lawn of Belle Reve, Blanche is reenacting the sexual attraction she felt for her young husband, but she is simultaneously revenging herself upon the self-indulgent sex lives of her "improvident grandfathers and father and uncles and brothers," who "exchanged the land for their epic fornications" (44). In explaining to Stella the loss of Belle Reve, Blanche says, "The four-letter word deprived us of our plantation" (44). One is left to guess at the degree to which Blanche's own extravagances helped precipitate that loss. In mimicking the sexual indulgence of her male forebears, she aggressively dismantles the gender roles that subject women to passive victimhood. The loss of Belle Reve, the "beautiful dream," becomes an objective correlative for the collapse of a hypocritical tradition that depends upon the belle's sexual purity, a tradition designed to perpetuate the exclusive sexual freedom of aristocratic men. As a consummate belle, Blanche has to realize the psychic and economic damage that such a collapse will deal her, and so her participation in the demise of Belle Reve must be seen at least in part as masochistic, perhaps as a sort of penance for her acquiescence to that same conservative and exclusionary tradition of sexual mores that led to her homosexual husband's suicide.

Two historical sources serve as sufficient context for Blanche's rebellion. In her *Incidents in the Life of a Slave Girl*, Harriet Jacobs candidly describes the sexual abuses of slave masters, which were silenced even in the quarters during slavery: "The secrets of slavery are concealed like those of the Inquisition. My master was, to my knowledge, the father of eleven slaves. But did the mothers dare to tell who was the father of their children? Did the other slaves dare to allude to it, except in whispers among themselves? No, indeed! They knew too well the terrible consequences" (367). Armed with reports of slavery's atrocities such as those described in *Incidents*, detractors of the Confederacy launched an assault on the notions of honor and chivalry so highly prized by Southern aristocracy. The South reacted with a collective denial that only intensified after the loss of the Civil War. W. J. Cash recognized the central role of the belle in this cultural denial. The Yankee, Cash says, had to "be answered by proclaiming from the housetops that southern Virtue, so far from being inferior, was superior, not alone to the North's but to any on earth, and adducing southern Womanhood in proof" (86). Cash explains that the history of inhumanity and rape practiced by plantation owners was categorically denied, a denial that was "enforced under penalty of being shot"; furthermore, the "fiction" of sexually pure Southern women developed to help shore up this denial (86). The moral superiority of the South, then, depended upon the sexual purity of its women.

It is this cultural fiction that Blanche attacks. She delights in transgressing Southern decorum and mocking the chauvinistic gender dynamics of her culture that deny women sexual initiative and forgive men their excesses. After being informed by Stanley about Blanche's sordid past at the seedy Flamingo Hotel in Laurel, Mitch confronts Blanche with the charges, and, after initially defending herself, she sadistically delights in her refusal to be judged by him:

| *Blanche:* | Flamingo? No! Tarantula was the name of it! I stayed at a hotel called The Tarantula Arms! |
| *Mitch* [*stupidly*]: | Tarantula? |

| *Blanche:* | Yes, a big spider! That's where I brought my victims. [*She pours herself another drink*] Yes, I had many intimacies with strangers. After the death of Allan [. . .] here and there in the most— unlikely places—even, at last, in a seventeen-year-old boy but—somebody wrote the superintendent about it—"This woman is morally unfit for her position!" |

[*She throws back her head with convulsive, sobbing laughter. Then she repeats the statement, gasps, and drinks.*]

True? Yes, I suppose—unfit somehow—anyway. (146-47)

Not surprisingly, Mitch is unprepared for such an unreserved affront to his sense of decorum, but he is not the only male threatened by Blanche's assertive sexuality. For all that might be remarked about Stanley's animal sexuality, he is actually quite conventional in his attitudes toward women. He relishes the sexual jokes and innuendo at the table with his poker buddies, and he is unfazed by the rumor of his friend Steve's infidelity with a prostitute at the Four Deuces, but he would not even consider the possibility of infidelity among their wives. Clearly he expects Stella's undivided attention and her utter fidelity. He is even shocked by Blanche's coquettish flirtations with him. After she playfully sprays him with her perfume, he says, "If I didn't know that you was my wife's sister I'd get ideas about you!" (41). Though he openly proclaims his right to relax around his home in any stage of undress that suits him, he shows intolerance for Blanche's exhibitionism. In the third scene when Stanley leaves the poker game and violently intrudes into the bedroom to turn off the radio Blanche is playing, he finds her sitting in the chair wearing only a pink silk brassiere and a white skirt, and he ambivalently responds with a mixture of desire and uneasiness: "*Stanley jumps up and, crossing to the radio, turns it off. He stops short at the sight of Blanche in the chair. She re-*

turns his look without flinching. Then he sits again at the poker table" (55). There is the vaguest sense of a confrontation in this scene, one that foreshadows the more violent confrontations to come.

If Blanche were recognizably and openly a prostitute, then she would be much less threatening to Stanley. Because she is both "whore" and belle, she occupies a liminal space in which labels are less easily affixed. Blanche wears the mask of the belle both to appease and to shock; it is the fluidity of the form that allows her to exploit conventional ideas about feminine sexuality. Of the transformative powers of masking, Houston Baker writes, "Conjure's spirit work moves behind—within, and through—the mask of minstrelsy to ensure survival, to operate changes, to acquire necessary resources for continuance, and to cure a sick world" (47). In both the literature of black America and in Williams's dramas, masking subverts the notion of culturally fixed identities. In creating a situation where two antithetical identities coexist in one person, masking creates the possibility for a range of multiple identities. For both black Americans in the Jim Crow South and for women before the advent of feminism, masking provided a liberating sense of freedom to people who had been objectified and categorized and thereby denied the basic right of self-determination.

Of course, one cannot overlook the subtext of homosexual guilt and the problem of passing for "straight" that underlies the main drama. Like Blanche, Williams was intimately familiar with the sexual prohibitions and the obsession for labels that accompanied Southern society. Like Blanche, he lived a life divided between the world of accepted society and that of Bohemia. In his *Memoirs* he records the shock of certain society friends in New Orleans when he came out to them about his homosexuality. He describes a party he and his lover-roommate threw in their apartment located in the Vieux Carré, an area where, he says, their debutante guests had probably never been before, an area seen as dissolute by "the Garden District mothers." Upon discovering that Williams and his roommate shared a bed that "was somewhere between single and double," the debutantes "began to whisper to their escorts, there were little secretive colloquies among them and presently they began to thank us for an unusual and delightful evening and to take their leave as though a storm were impending" (100). Significantly, the debutantes—not their male escorts—take the initiative to preserve social decorum. Like their Garden District mothers, these young women bear the responsibility of perpetuating their society's sexual norms. In Blanche DuBois, Williams creates a belle who comes to recognize—at least subconsciously—the damage caused by such a preservation of the status quo: the death of her husband, the loss of Belle Reve, and the loss of her own liberty. If Blanche does not explicitly serve as a surrogate for Williams, then she certainly represents his interests as a gay male who is ostracized and judged by mainstream America.

Like Belle Reve, Blanche has outwardly progressed toward a state of increasing dissolution, but inwardly she moves toward a more definite sense of self, one determined by her identification with the homosexual husband whom she unfairly judged and pushed toward suicide. The dearest possessions among the souvenirs she carries in her trunk as all the tangible proof of her existence are the love letters she received from her poet husband, and she protects these letters from her intrusive brother-in-law with as much (or more) determination than she demonstrates when protecting her own body:

> *Blanche:* Now that you've touched them I'll burn them!
>
> *Stanley:* What do you mean by saying you'll have to burn them?
>
> *Blanche:* Poems a dead boy wrote. I hurt him the way that you would like to hurt me, but you can't! I'm not young and vulnerable any more. But my young husband was and I— never mind about that! Just give them back to me!
>
> *Stanley:* What do you mean by saying you'll have to burn them?
>
> *Blanche:* I'm sorry, I must have lost my head for a moment. Everyone has something he won't let others touch because of their—intimate nature [. . .]. (42-43)

This scene reveals both the earliest demonstration of her intense identification with her husband and the hint that she anticipates the rape that marks the climax of the play. Later she tells Mitch that Stanley "hates me. Or why would he insult me? The first time I laid eyes on him I thought to myself, that man is my executioner! That man will destroy me, unless—" (111). The fact that she recognizes the threat Stanley poses complicates her flirtation with him. Indeed, the question of their relationship has generated a vast diversity of readings. Perhaps she believes that as long as she maintains his sexual interest, if not his respect, then he will not "destroy" her or put her out onto the street. Perhaps, on the other hand, by provoking in Stanley an inappropriate sexual interest, Blanche expects to expose the degree of his crudeness and thereby gain control over him—in the same way that he wishes to unmask and dominate her. Their ongoing battle is largely one of name-calling and labeling. He calls her "loco," "nuts" (121), and she calls him a "Polack" (22), "primitive" (39), an "animal" and "ape-like" (83). Before he rapes her, Stanley pursues a campaign of slander in an effort to ostracize her from the allegiance she enjoys from Stella and Mitch. Upon learning of her behaviors at the Flamingo and the subsequent scandal at the high school where she taught, Stanley exults, "Yep, it was practickly [sic] a town ordinance passed against her!" (101). Before he can rape her, he must penetrate her mask of the belle and confidently label her a whore. As much as the actual rape, it is this unmasking that Blanche fears and perhaps, to some degree, guiltily expects; in being judged and then raped by Stanley, she becomes a martyr to the same mainstream chauvinism in which she participated when judging her young husband's homosexuality.

It is easy to yield to the temptation to read the conclusion of the play as somehow inevitable and necessary. On a superficial level, Blanche's increasing delusion seems to legitimize her interment in the state asylum. However, one must not forget the trauma of being raped, nor should we overlook Stanley's desperation to eliminate her from the household, as well as Stella's betrayal. Not only is her ejection necessary to preserve his honor, but it is facilitated by the full disclosure of her recent illicit sexual behavior in Laurel. The play ends with Blanche serving as the scapegoat for Stanley's sexual offense, thus preserving the social order that has not changed since the height of Victorianism in America and especially in the patrician South. As with Lucretia Collins in "Portrait of a Madonna," it is Blanche's sexuality rather than her insanity that cannot be tolerated.

Streetcar ends, however, without the social order's being fully restored. With the loss of her sister, Stella is left alone in the world with no remnant of her family and its culture. The breach of trust between her and Stanley will likely not be healed, at least not fully. Stella's clandestine letters to Belle Reve are a thing of the past; now she is fully immersed in the rough and heterogeneous lower culture of New Orleans. Recognizing her loss, she collapses not in the arms of her husband but in the arms of the neighbor woman, Eunice, to whom she had felt herself superior earlier in the play. We see the beginning of an alliance forming between the two women, as Stella confesses to Eunice, "I couldn't believe her story and go on living with Stanley" (165), after which Eunice instructs Stella in the sort of day-to-day denial necessary for survival on the streets: "Don't ever believe it. Life has got to go on. No matter what happens, you've got to keep on going" (166). While the doctor and nurse from the asylum lead Blanche away, Stella recognizes her own complicity in destroying Blanche and says, "What have I done to my sister? Oh, God, what have I done to my sister?" (176). Just as Blanche spends her life reliving and coming to terms with her guilt for precipitating the suicide of her husband, Stella is likely to spend the rest of her life reliving this moment, forgoing Eunice's advice and obsessing over the possibility of Stanley's guilt, internalizing it as her own, and idealizing Blanche as a pure martyr, worthy of worship and emulation. Stella learns her own survival skills the hard way, just as Blanche and Eunice have, and the role of the innocent is no longer available to her without further moral compromise. Whether or not she dons the mask of the belle, it is certain that, like the belle and the minstrel, Stella will have to develop a double consciousness that will make her depend, not upon her husband, but upon herself for empowerment.

Works Cited

Baker, Houston A., Jr. *Modernism and the Harlem Renaissance*. 1987. Chicago: U of Chicago P, 1989.

Cash, W. J. *The Mind of the South*. 1941. New York: Vintage, 1991.

Holloway, Karla F. C. *Moorings & Metaphors: Figures of Culture and Gender in Black Women's Literature*. New Brunswick, NJ: Rutgers UP, 1992.

Jacobs, Harriet. *Incidents in the Life of a Slave Girl*. 1861. Rpt. in *The Classic Slave Narratives*. Ed. Henry Louis Gates, Jr. New York: Mentor, 1987.

Wilhelmi, Nancy O. "Destructive Power Games: A Study of Blanche DuBois and Amanda Wingfield." *Tennessee Williams Literary Journal* 2.2 (1991): 33-40.

Williams, Tennessee. *The Glass Menagerie*. 1944. Rpt. in *The Harcourt Brace Anthology of Drama*. 2nd ed. Ed. W. B. Worthen. New York: Harcourt, 1996. 849-871.

_____. *Memoirs*. New York: Doubleday, 1975.

_____. "Portrait of a Madonna." *27 Wagons Full of Cotton and Other One-Act Plays*. 1953. Rpt. in *The Theatre of Tennessee Williams*. Vol. 45. New York: New Directions, 1981.

_____. *A Streetcar Named Desire*. New York: New Directions, 1947.

Wright, Richard. *Black Boy: A Record of Childhood and Youth*. New York: Harper, 1945.

Williams in Ebony:
Black and Multi-racial Productions
of *A Streetcar Named Desire*

Philip C. Kolin

Arthur Gelb reported in the *New York Times* for July 14, 1958, that a "desegregated 'Streetcar Named Desire' w[ould] begin an off-Broadway" run at the Carnegie Hall Playhouse on September 17 with black actress Hilda Simms as Blanche. Simms was looking forward to playing Blanche, she said, since "most of the plays with roles for Negro actresses are inferior vehicles," and it is "altogether plausible to play Blanche as a Creole, or mixed French, Spanish and Negro ancestry." Black actors and actresses were to audition for the roles of Stella and Stanley, though the "smaller parts . . . [were to have been] played by white actors." Williams gave his blessing to this "desegregated" *Streetcar* since, according to his agent Audrey Wood, "he has always been an avid admirer of Negro actors." Moreover, Williams permitted some of the dialogue to be changed "to fit the Negro characters."

But a week after the projected September 17th premiere of the "desegregated" *Streetcar*, Louis Calta announced that, at Williams's request, this *Streetcar* was to be "shelved" until the following fall because he was concerned about its "proximity in time to a new play," *Sweet Bird of Youth*, which opened on March 10, 1959. We may never unearth all the reasons why this multi-racial off-Broadway *Streetcar* never opened—financial, technical, Williams's possible apprehension. Speaking again for her client, Wood explained that Williams still considered *Streetcar* with black cast members in the central roles "an advance in relations and I look forward eagerly to it" (Calta).

A strong black presence has always inhabited *Streetcar*. Pulitzer Prize-winning black playwright Charles Gordone clearly sensed it when he remarked of Williams, "in most of his plays I have always detected the black existential lurking in between the lines" (qtd. in Kolin

182). The opening stage direction in *Streetcar* reads: "*New Orleans is a cosmopolitan city where there is a relatively warm and easy intermingling of races in the old part of town*" (13). To prove the point, the first two characters Williams brings on stage are Eunice and a "colored woman" who are "*taking the air on the steps of the building.*" Some famous black actresses have played the "colored woman"—Gee Gee James in the original Broadway production, Eulabelle Moore in the road company production in Chicago with Uta Hagen as Blanche and Anthony Quinn as Stanley, and Vinette Carroll in Tallulah Bankhead's unforgettable 1955 *Streetcar.* From the opening scene onward, blacks frequently appear in the famed 1951 film version of *Streetcar.* Over the years, directors of white productions of *Streetcar* have incorporated black actors into other minor roles to convey Williams's strong sense of the "easy intermingling of races." In a 1960 production at Detroit's Northwood Playhouse, for example, Walton Mason played the Doctor; and in the *Streetcar* done at Jackson, Mississippi's New Stage Theatre in 1984, W. C. McMullin was Steve.

Streetcar is saturated with a black synesthesia. Evoking the pleasures of sight, sound, and smell, Williams asks us to inhale "*the warm breath of the brown river beyond the river warehouses*" if the Mississippi were transformed into a fragrant brown god of fertility. He further points out that "*a corresponding air is evoked by the music of Negro entertainers at a room around the corner*" where "*a tinny piano [is] being played with the infatuated fluency of brown fingers*" (13). The honky-tonk music in *Streetcar* brings to mind the blues, jazz, and other black musical forms. Jean Cocteau deeply felt the brown infatuation in his 1949 adaptation of *Streetcar, Un tramway nommé Désir,* where he took the liberty of adding a black woman dancer, naked from the waist up, whose pulsating, gyrating movements served as an appropriate accompaniment to the intoxicating music of sexuality in Williams's lyrical script.

I

In this essay I will trace the history, in part, of black and multi-racial *Streetcar*s to explore what these productions tell us about the relationship of the script of Williams's classic to prevailing ideologies of race and culture, white as well as black. Staging *Streetcar* with an all-black or multi-racial cast offers directors, actors and actresses, audiences, and critics a number of advantages, both practical and theoretical.

Throughout its forty-four-year production history *Streetcar* has been acclaimed as a classic, a work which expresses universal truths and has universal application. Countless foreign productions of the play in other languages amplify the claim that *Streetcar* speaks eternal truths (of the heart). Yet, since an overwhelming majority of these productions—at home and abroad—have been staged with all-white casts, blacks have been excluded from participating in the script-life of the play. Black or multi-racial *Streetcar*s affirm the universality of the play. By emphasizing that its truths are as applicable to blacks as to whites and by representing the black experience through the play, *Streetcar* becomes an inclusive rather than exclusive script.

Second, black or multi-racial *Streetcar*s can enlarge Williams's script, thus opening up the play to racial and social messages not privileged in all-white productions. Releasing such messages in productions with people of color substantially increases *Streetcar*'s electrifying power, and *Streetcar* criticism itself can profit from moving away from seeing the play in terms established by exclusively white casts. Of course, the text may have to be destabilized in the process. For example, actors and actresses of color doing *Streetcar* necessitate changes in the script, as Williams himself recognized by giving permission to Hilda Simms and others for the production that was to have been staged in New York in 1958. Such changes reveal that the script can deconstruct racial/social views encrusted on it through the traditions of stage history.

Third, a production of *Streetcar* with a black or multi-racial cast releases Williams's characters from the stereotypes imposed by dominant, prototypical white productions. On the most superficial level, a Blanche or Stanley of color challenges the received and restrictive notion that all Blanches should look and act like Jessica Tandy or Vivien Leigh and that all Stanleys must imitate Marlon Brando with his Group Theatre acting style. The ideal production of *Streetcar* for playwright Joan Schenkar takes place in her mind, for that production "resists the temptation to focus on Stanley's bare chest (Marlon Brando's chest, actually, since the role of Stanley has long since dissolved into Mr. Brando's representation of it) or on Blanche's fluttering and frangible culpability" (qtd. in Kolin 195).

On a deeper level, a black or multi-racial cast effectively disrupts what Sue-Ellen Case refers to as "cultural encoding":

> . . . casting blonde women in the roles of ingenues, and dark women in secondary and vamp roles is not based on the demands of the text, but betrays cultural attitudes about the relative innocence, purity[,] and desirability of certain racial features. . . . For feminists, these discoveries help to illuminate how the image of a woman on stage participates directly in the dominant ideology of gender. (117)

Casting Blanche as a white, Southern belle, in the tradition of a debauched Scarlett O'Hara via Vivien Leigh, perpetuates such cultural encoding and reveals the prejudices of the dominant white culture. Seeing Blanche as a Creole, for example, is entirely consistent with Williams's text and can be easily accommodated in production. And Stanley certainly does not have to be Polish to be Blanche's ravaging executioner and Stella's sometimes-tender loving husband.

Fourth, seeing *Streetcar* with a black or racially mixed cast forces audiences, white and black, to come to terms with their own subconscious racism. A production in which Blanche is cast as a woman of color—of one in which, as a white woman, she is attracted to a Stanley of color—effectively challenges or may even alter racial feelings which might lurk in the heart of a theatregoer.

Finally, black and multi-racial productions of *Streetcar* further the cause of non-traditional casting, which offers numerous benefits both for actors and actresses and for the theatre as a whole. Clinton Turner Davis and Harry Newman have identified a number of types of non-traditional casting relevant to productions of *Streetcar*. The first is *blind casting*, in which "all actors are cast without regard to their race, ethnicity, gender, or physical capability" (10). The practical implications of such a policy are many for black actors and actresses who for years have been denied parts in the white repertoire because they were not the right color. Much has been written about the differences in style and presentation among the Blanches of Jessica Tandy, Uta Hagen, and Vivien Leigh. Given the opportunity to portray Blanche, actresses of color could provide different interpretations of the role from a black perspective, enlarging both an acting tradition and the critical interpretations based upon that tradition. Multi-racial productions of *Streetcar* can also exemplify *conceptual casting*, whereby "an ethnic, female[,] or disabled actor is cast in a role to give a play greater resonance" (10). In those multi-racial *Streetcar*s, for example, where Stanley is black and Blanche and Stella are white, the issue of Stanley's race, totally absent in all-white productions, becomes a leading critical and performative concept. The following discussion of black and multi-racial *Streetcar*s illustrates these advantages. Included are major productions that represent different black approaches to *Streetcar* over the more than four decades the play has created a sensation in the theatre world.

II

Perhaps the first all-black *Streetcar* was done by the Summer Theatre Company at Lincoln University in Jefferson City, Missouri, on August 3-4, 1953. An offering in Lincoln University's Second Annual Summer Theatre program, this *Streetcar* was directed by noted teacher and playwright Thomas D. Pawley, a former classmate of Williams's at Iowa.[1] The cast included professionals and students alike. Blanche was played by Carolyn Hill Stewart of Washington, D.C., who had toured in the U.S. and abroad with her own repertoire, "Fool's Motley," and had been active in summer theatre at Harvard, Iowa, and Howard (where she played Ophelia). Stella was played by Shauneille Perry, an acting instructor from North Carolina A&T and a member of the Howard Players. A veteran of little theatre, Perry earned her MA at the Goodman School while working for WGN television in Chicago. Another teacher, Bertram Martin from Alabama, was Mitch. Students filled out the rest of the cast. Ray Parks, a twenty-two-year-old business administration major at Lincoln, played Stanley. Director Pawley recalls that Parks "was physically perfect but had little or no acting experience" (Letter, 16 Aug. 1990). Winona Fletcher, who like Pawley went on to a distinguished teaching career, designed the costumes for the play.

Unfortunately, there were no reviews of this *Streetcar*; the Lincoln student newspaper was not published during the summer, and the Jefferson City press chose to ignore the production. In a letter of June 7, 1990, Professor Pawley informed me that he "made no particular attempt to make the play relevant to our predominantly black audiences. We focused on Williams's presentation of human fallibilities." For Pawley, doing *Streetcar* with an all-black cast was no more risky than doing the play at all in conservative Central Missouri in 1953, where Williams was persona non grata because of the earthy subject matter of his plays. Pawley elaborated about his production of *Streetcar* in a subsequent letter:

Staging *A Streetcar Named Desire* in the 1950s on a college campus was both a challenge and a risky venture. Colleagues at two neighboring colleges in Columbia, Missouri, wondered at my gall in doing the play since they dared not attempt it for fear of reprisals by their administrations. In fact, one told me that when it was rumored that he was considering a production of the play, a group of Southern ladies advised the president of the college that they would withdraw their daughters from the institution if he were permitted to do so. They felt that Williams's plays disparaged Southern womanhood.

The Lincoln University administration offered no such objection to our production, although I understand that some members of our predominantly African-American audience were somewhat stunned by the language and subject matter. But Lincoln University audiences had become accustomed to our doing the risqué. In fact, a member of the English faculty, who was on campus being interviewed for a professorship at the time, told me later that seeing this production and the audience's sophisticated reaction to it were factors in his decision to come to Lincoln.

Although Lincoln was racially segregated by law at the time, the audience was integrated. I recall that Mrs. Canada Lee was present and made an appeal for funds for a memorial to her late actor-husband.

The success of *Streetcar* prompted us to include Williams's *Summer and Smoke* with Shauneille Perry and Bertram Martin in the principal roles the following summer, and it was a factor in our later doing *Suddenly Last Summer* and *The Night of the Iguana* as part of our regular season. (16 Aug. 1990)

Given the place and time, Pawley's *Streetcar* was both daring and imaginative. Bringing a controversial play to Lincoln University was far more liberal than what could have been done at neighboring white schools that would have never consented to do *Streetcar* in the early 1950s. Pawley did not need to politicize or change the script to establish its timeless relevance for his audience.

The first professional production of *Streetcar* with an all-black cast was done at Ebony Showcase Theatre in Los Angeles. In fact, Ebony did two productions of the play, one from February 19, 1955, to March 10, 1955, and another in November and December of 1956. Ebony was and still is owned by Edna and Nick Stewart, who produced *Streetcar*. Nick Stewart is a legendary black actor who has worked in vaudeville, played at the Apollo and Cotton Club, and appeared (under the name of Nick O'Demus) as Lightnin' in the *Amos 'n' Andy* television show.

Edna Stewart has had an equally prominent career on the stage. The Stewarts founded Ebony Showcase Theatre in 1949 to stage both Broadway and original plays with black casts. Their 1956 *Streetcar*, for example, was the first of six plays of the winter season, which also included *Tea and Sympathy*. The fact that Williams's agent Audrey Wood was also Nick Stewart's helped make *Streetcar*'s performance at the Ebony possible. Wood was in total sympathy with the Stewarts' attempts to showcase black talent in important, serious theatre. In an interview on August 24, 1990, Mr. Stewart recalled:

> Audrey Wood saw what I was doing at the Ebony to uplift the image in our community, to do humanitarian things, and she helped me in this respect. You see, I have been in several Broadway shows, and I saw how blacks were, in most cases, presented in the negative, and I thought that we would just do people plays, showing us as people, too. At that time there were no positive roles for black actors. Blacks were cast as buffoons and clowns, distorting images which were damaging to the black community. Theatre can be used to change such attitudes.

The Stewarts did more than change attitudes; they made theatre history with their *Streetcar*. When the Stewarts brought *Streetcar* to the Ebony, they did not make any changes for their actors or the audiences. In fact, Nick Stewart was strongly opposed to changing the script for racial reasons:

> On that particular play [*Streetcar*] we're people, and it's unfortunate that we think we have to, what you might say, make it black. . . . the play is not black: it is humanitarian. Some plays I have had to bring around, trying to correct attitudes and concepts, but not *Streetcar*. That was a good play. (Interview)

The Stewarts' pioneering *Streetcar*s did not escape notice by those who read them in light of contemporary racial issues. Writing of the 1956 production, Leo Guild of the *Hollywood Reporter* observed that "Nick and Edna Stewart have gathered a fine all-Negro cast to portray the dramatic story of a decadent white South, an ironic twist in these days of problems over segregation. . . . the crowd was sparse . . . but it is the public's loss."

The *Streetcar* the Stewarts mounted in February of 1955 was directed by Paul Rodgers and starred Camille Canady as Blanche, Vilmore Schexnayder as Stanley, Shirley Higgenbotham as Stella, and Sylvester Bell as Mitch. The production received strong reviews from both white and black critics. According to Harold Hildebrand of the *Los Angeles Examiner*, "This all-Negro troupe offer[ed] a vivid and moving portrayal . . . ," and after summarizing the plot of *Streetcar*, he acknowledged that "the story, of course, is old hat to most theatre and moviegoers. It is repeated only to point up the arresting performances necessary to carry it across the footlights" ("Vivid Acting"). Hazel L. Lamarre, Theatrical Editor for the *Los Angeles Sentinel*, the city's widely read black newspaper, enthusiastically urged readers: "If you like real, stark heavy drama, be sure to see this one" (3 Mar. 1955). Surprisingly, Lamarre did not comment on why and how a professional black troupe did *Streetcar* for the first time. There is no mention of the historic, or aesthetic, triumph of the Stewarts.

Clearly, Camille Canady stole the show and the reviewers' hearts. Katherine Von Blon applauded her "beautifully keyed performance which rose to moving heights in her last scene" ("'Streetcar' Offered"). Lamarre remarked that "Camille Canady's portrayal of the bewildered school-teacher will long be remembered by all who see her. Miss Canady's voice, expression[,] and every gesture [are] in character with the psychopathetic heroine" (3 Mar. 1955). Hildebrand was similarly effusive: "As Blanche, the talky, coquettish trollop, Camille Canady achieves an acting tour de force. On stage practically from the opening to the closing curtain with extremely long speeches, Miss Canady delivers an exacting portrayal with proper shading and seasoned skill" ("Vivid Acting"). The fair-skinned, fine-featured Canady played an elegant-looking Blanche, which no doubt contributed to the character's tragedy, for Blanche is notoriously smug about her aristocratic lineage. Edna Stewart reports that Canady was an excellent actress who, because of her race, was denied many parts in Hollywood (Interview). We can only wonder how many more roles—on stage and on screen—Canady would have had were she not struggling for a career in the age of segregation.

Canady's co-star Vilmore Schexnayder did not receive the same unqualified praise. As Hildebrand warned his readers, Canady "lets it be known that the role of Stanley Kowalski is not the most important" ("Vivid Acting"). While Hildebrand did concede that Schexnayder's Stanley was "properly frank, loud, and carnal," others, including the *Los Angeles Times*'s Von Blon, found him overbearing, perhaps imitating Marlon Brando's style too zealously. Hazel Lamarre concurred: "Vilmore Schexnayder's interpretation of the rough and rugged Stanley is, in our opinion, a little too rough and might be toned down a bit for the good of the whole production" (3 Mar. 1955). Easily deceived by Blanche's wiles and haughty airs, Sylvester Bell's Mitch seems to have been her victim.

The second Ebony *Streetcar*, which opened almost two years after the first, on November 28, 1956, was staged because of the popular demand generated by the 1955 production. It offered a new director, John Blankenship, and an all new cast, with one major exception—Camille Canady returned as Blanche. The critics raved about this repeat of *Streetcar*. "Another excellent staging," claimed Harold Hildebrand ("'Streetcar' on Stage"). "The drama has never been done more effectively," announced Hazel Lamarre (6 Dec. 1956). One of the most impressive compliments came from Wylie Williams at the *Los Angeles Times*, who informed readers that this black cast could represent Williams's characters just as well as a white one could: "The play . . . is distinctive for its excruciating delineation of character—so much so that Stanley Kowalski is a household word for brute and Blanche DuBois is the epitome of a Southern aristocrat. . . . Portrayal of these people is all the more exacting. James Edwards and Camille Canady do a highly creditable job of impersonating the hunter and his adversary." The implication is that white actors and actresses do not have exclusive claim to Williams's characters. Kap of *Variety* was the only critic to fault the production—"Somewhere between the central staging little theatre where it was first presented and the group's new proscenium house, this *Streetcar* got off the track"—, although the reviewer did applaud the "valiant efforts of some of the cast." The size of the new and larger Ebony theatre, Kap felt, made the acoustics poor and intimacy impossible.

Hailed as "Hollywood's most popular Negro actor" ("James Edwards Stars"), James Edwards brought a host of credits to the part of Stanley. Critics differed, though, in their opinions of his performance. Lamarre found Edwards "thoroughly convincing as the bestial husband of Blanche's sister" (6 Dec. 1956), and David Bongard at the *Los Angeles Herald & Express* stated that Edwards was "ideally suited" to play the "brooding hulk" Stanley. While acknowledging that what Edwards "lacks in physical requirements he is able to make up in acting prowess," Guild accused him of not being "quite tough or rough enough for the part of Stanley." For Katherine Von Blon Edwards's acting prowess was uneven, and the actor a bit reticent to get into the role. "The dynamic James Edwards did not come into his full stride until the last act when the full sweep of his power was felt." ("'A Streetcar' Begins"). Whatever limitations Von Blon saw in Edwards, when he and Blanche faced each other "the pair really set sparks in their key scenes," according to Bongard. Unquestionably, Edwards created a different, more subtle Stanley than that portrayed by Schexnayder. Kap's passing remark that Edwards was "stereotyped as Stanley" seems odd in light of the opinions of other critics, who suggest that Edwards departed rather creatively from the stereotypical Stanley epitomized by Brando.

As she had done in the earlier Ebony production of *Streetcar*, Camille Canady won the critics' hearts. White critics were more effusive in their praise than the reviewer for the *Los Angeles Sentinel*, who perfunctorily honored Canady for her "complete understanding" ("James Edwards Stars"). Guild at the *Hollywood Reporter* exclaimed that Canady's Blanche was "as good as you will ever see portrayed." Despite the size of the theatre in which she had to work, Canady for Kap provided a "sensitive and understanding delineation." Bongard praised her experience in the part and the sophistication she brought to it: Her "successive playing of [Blanche] has brought into sharp focus the pathetic lights and shadows of the role."

Also winning the critics' respect was Isabelle Cooley, who played Stella. A veteran actress who had recently done *Anna Lucasta* on the New York and London stages, Cooley was praised for her warmth, sincerity, and rich voice. Hildebrand singled her out for special merit: "Isabelle Cooley seems to be the only normal, well adjusted person on stage. She has good stage movements and is thoroughly believable as she tries to balance the personalities of the other two" ("'Streetcar' on Stage").

The Stewarts' *Streetcar*s showed that black actors and actresses could portray Williams's characters with as much strength and sincerity as could white actors and actresses. *Streetcar* had crossed the color line. But the Stewarts' work showed something more. Their *Streetcar*s doubtless lifted the spirits of black audiences, who took justified pride in seeing members of their own race enact a play that had captured the (white) theatre world. Nick Stewart's dream of having his theatre change attitudes surely must have been realized when *Streetcar* first was staged, then restaged, at the Ebony.

Howard University's Drama Department presented a multi-racial *Streetcar* on February 20, 25-27, 1965, at the Ira Aldridge Theatre. Sally Crowell, a white student at Howard, was Blanche, while Renato Coutinho, a professional actor from Brazil, played Stanley. The other roles were performed by black students. Despite its racially mixed cast, the production departed little from traditional, white interpretations of *Streetcar.* Judging from his eloquent "Director's Comments," included in the program, Whitney J. LeBlanc interpreted the major themes of *Streetcar* as those of illusion, self-deception, and the troubles of the human heart.

> Blanche DuBois . . . understands what some of us spend a lifetime trying to conceal from ourselves—truth. Yet she prefers to see by the flickering candle of illusion. Her weapons of survival in a world of practical expediency fall as drops of water on a hot stove, and vanish as quickly. She is, however, not without consequence for she sees[,] with frightening clarity, the human soul. She becomes a victim of her own desire for beauty of the mind and richness of the spirit. She will continue to be a victim over and over again because she is out of step with the society in which she lives. . . . She relies on the kindness of strangers because it is more secure than the understanding of friends. She is a victim because she dares to cast her pearls among swine.
>
> To know truth and live it is one thing. To know truth and pretend that it is illusion is another. There is a bit of Blanche in us all, but we survive; we dare allow ourselves to say: . . . It was like you suddenly turned a blinding light on something that had always been half in shadow.

If the idea of race surfaced at all for LeBlanc's audience, he did not encourage them to pursue it. As his comment about Blanche suggests, he wanted them to forget racial differences: "There is a bit of Blanche in us all. . . ."

LeBlanc's *Streetcar* had the strengths and limitations of an amateur production. It "misses a professional sheen," confessed Emerson Beauchamp. Yet for all its lapses in diction and timing, Beauchamp regarded it as an exciting production "thanks to the two leading roles." Coutinho's Stanley, said Beauchamp, was "slouchy, scratchy, sweaty[,] and boisterous"—not a stylish Brando imitation. And Coutinho's "accented English [proved], if anything, an asset; it seem[ed] appropriate for Stanley, even though he specifies that he was born in America, not Poland." For a *Washington Post* reviewer, Coutinho "fully stated Kowalski's hard case," while Sally Crowell's Blanche was done most "affectingly" (R. L. C.). Though Beauchamp judged Crowell's acting "something of a triumph," getting more laughs than would be expected, he conceded that Crowell may have robbed Blanche "of the pity and terror that are her birthright by overemphasizing her wit."

Perhaps the most insightful and, for our purposes, relevant observation about this 1965 production comes from Beauchamp who, though he dismissed the talents of the rest of the cast, commended Loretta Greene for the "essential gusto" of her Stella and concluded: "It is . . . a measure of the production's effectiveness that she and Miss Crowell—one Negro and one white—come to seem not such unlikely sisters after all." Traditional casting, clearly, is less important than sincerity in presenting the affection of sisters. A universalizing force was at work in this *Streetcar* that director LeBlanc doubtless intended. There is a bit of Blanche in all of us, and perhaps a bit of Stella, too.

A 1974 German production of *Streetcar* with a black Stanley (Gunther Kaufmann) deserves more credit for what it shows as a failure than for what it contributed to the achievements of a black theatre aesthetic. Staged by the Free People's Theatre (Freie Volksbuhne) in West Berlin in July 1974, and directed by Charles Lang, this production sparked both a professional and legal controversy. The premiere of this Berlin *Streetcar*, planned for June 26, was prevented by the Sixth Chamber Court of Berlin, which slapped a restraining order on the Free People's Theatre, stating that "performance was forbidden by request of the author." A story in the *Frankfurter Rundschau* stated that Williams as well as his publisher Kiepenheuer objected to Kaufmann's playing Stanley and to Lang's cuts and changes to the ending of the play ("Williams—Aufführung verboten"). In Lang's version, Blanche supposedly took great pleasure in the rape (Holloway).

After considerable wrangling, Lang proposed a compromise with Williams's publisher on July 11, 1974, by which Kaufmann would be allowed to play Stanley Kowalski provided he put on make-up that would give the impression he was white and wear a wig which made his dark, curly hair appear straight (Wiegenstein). Lang's proposal deserves comparison with Bottom's view of theatrical illusion in *A Midsummer Night's Dream*. Although Maria Sommer, the representative for Williams's publisher, "rejected this Lang idea as a farce and a mockery of copyright" (Holloway), the court allowed the Free People's Theatre to stage *Streetcar*, provided Lang reinstate the cut scenes and restore Williams's ending. Happily, Kaufmann never appeared in white face. Further, Lang had to pay a fine of 2000 marks and a fee of 650 marks per performance ("Freie Volksbuhne"). The total sum turned out not to be terribly oppressive: Lang's *Streetcar* ran for only five closed performances for subscribers to the Free People's Theatre and then four public ones.

German objections to a black Stanley Kowalski may have been motivated less by considerations of race than concern over the sanctity of Williams's script. In general, a black actor would not signal anything extraordinary to a German audience. In fact, Roland Wiegenstein remarked that Kaufmann was a good choice for his looks, if not his "speech techniques." What may have disturbed Germans the most about Lang's casting Kaufmann as Stanley was that such casting required changes in the original script of *Streetcar*, a play which Germans know extremely well. Ultimately, perhaps, German audiences may have regarded a black actor as another unjustifiable "experiment" by director Lang to draw attention to his work. This seems to be the reasoning behind Wiegenstein's assessment that

> . . . no one really understands why the Free People's Theatre picked *Streetcar*. Evidently Lang had intended a restructuring of a rather private conflict into a racial conflict. Even so it meant doing an injustice to the play. He might have given the piece some new and more timely focus. What the Free People's Theatre actually did show was an indecisive performance which only approximates *Streetcar*.

In sum, German resistance to an interpretation of *Streetcar* based on racial conflict appears to have been rooted in a narrow, traditional view of the script of the play.

An important all-black ballet adaptation of *Streetcar* was done by the Dance Theatre of Harlem at the City Center in New York in January of 1982. Shortly before her death, Valerie Bettis, who originally prepared the ballet version of *Streetcar* for the Slavenska-Franklin Ballet Company in 1952, reset it for the DTH. Dedicated to Tennessee Williams in honor of his seventieth birthday, Bettis's *Streetcar* freely adapted Williams's play by introducing symbolic characters, including Blanche's young husband Allan Grey, and by using flashbacks. Virginia Johnson was Blanche; Lowell Smith was Stanley; Carol Crawford played Stella; and Ronald Perry was Mitch. The Dance Theatre of Harlem redid their *Streetcar* for PBS in February 1986 in a co-production sponsored by WNET-TV in New York and Dansmark Radio. Filmed in Denmark, this ballet *Streetcar* ran for forty minutes and again starred Johnson and Smith, with Julie Felix as Stella and Donald Williams as Mitch.

A number of reviewers in 1986 asked why the Harlem troupe decided to do *Streetcar* when so many of its works came from black composers. For example, they had recently done a Creole *Giselle* as well as works by Geoffrey Holder. Arthur Mitchell, the Dance Theatre's artistic director, addressed this question directly by affirming that "DTH is not a black ballet company. It is a ballet company that just happens to be black" (qtd. in Ulrich). Allan Ulrich took Mitchell at his word and observed that Bettis's *Streetcar*, as performed by the DTH, "reinforces that universality" claimed by Williams's own play. Yet Nancy Goldner, a syndicated columnist for Knight-Ridder newspapers, called attention to the troupe's historic identity: "Mitchell's statement, however noble, is not totally true. As a ballet troupe, the Dance Theatre of Harlem has always been unique for having a chunk of repertory whose sources spring from black culture." Goldner did conclude, however, that the Bettis interpretation of *Streetcar* put on by the DTH "captures the company in its currently strongest profile."

This black troupe brought a renewed vitality, a true grit, to the ballet—and hence the play. Lewis Segal summed up the reaction of many critics when he said that "Johnson and Smith dance the roles to blazes." In place of the impetuously frightened Blanche of Vivien Leigh, Johnson offered a "less ravaged, more willful Blanche" (Segal). Goldner described Johnson's Blanche as "provocative . . . a troublemaker who's out to get Stanley." Unlike Brando's interpretation of the role, Lowell Smith's Stanley was, in Goldner's estimation, in a state of "befuddlement and horror with himself"; he was the "victim" in the DTH's *Streetcar*. Segal concurred: Smith played "an unusually confused Stanley who is partly victimized by events." On the other hand, while the ballet obviously did not allow Smith to yell Stella's name or shout anything, it would be misleading to dismiss Smith's Stanley as a pansy. Reviewing the 1982 production, Anna Kisselgoff noted that Stanley grabs Blanche's hanky and wipes the sweat from his body. Like Brando, Smith first wore an undershirt, but it was yellow, and later he put on a "bright red windbreaker with a yellow lining." In a jazzy chase sequence, a feverish Stanley, dressed in his red pajamas, pursues Blanche "through all the portals" in Peter Larkin's set of "movable shutters," to suggest different rooms of the Kowalski household (Kisselgoff).

Clearly, in Mitchell's production, the company's own charm and personality contributed a novel interpretation of a black *Streetcar*. Mitchell said that he discovered Bettis's dance-drama while he was searching for a vehicle for the DTH: "I felt it was just the sort of ballet our company needed. . . . And it's in keeping with our title—'dance theatre'" (qtd. in "Dance Theater"). The DTH's *Streetcar* was effective because of the strength of its prima ballerina, jazzy choreography, and mute acting. But it was successful, too, because of Mitchell's direction and the innovative interpretation given Williams's characters by black dancers who challenged traditional expectations associated with those roles.

Race also played an important part in director-playwright Charles

Gordone's 1983 revival of *Streetcar* at the American Stage Company in Berkeley, California. The first black playwright to win the Pulitzer Prize (for his 1970 *No Place to Be Somebody*), Gordone had directed productions of *Night of the Iguana* and *Iceman Cometh*. His future wife, Susan Kouyomjian, was the artistic director of American Stage Company at the time. The first *Streetcar* to be produced in the Bay area in over twenty years, Gordone's production ran from May 12 through June 12. Consistent with the American Stage Company's goal of developing "a uniquely American idiom for the classics that reflects today's changing social realities" (Está), Gordone cast black actor Paul Santiago as Stanley but chose white actresses for Blanche (Peggy Linz) and Stella (Kate Black) and a white actor for Mitch (Robert Pierson). While Gordone was firmly dedicated to an "American Theatre" in which there is "full participation for all of our performing artists" (Letter, 12 June 1990), he did not want an all-black cast for his *Streetcar*:

> It is my belief that Tennessee wouldn't have approved of such a production at all! Furthermore, it is my opinion that the play would suffer the loss of its socio-economic framework from which the work makes its most important statement. To force "a black existential" would result in the play['s] being frightfully pretentious and strained, to say the least. Perhaps some value could be ascertained in using an "all-black cast" on an experimental or teaching level. . . . I don't know. (Letter, 29 May 1990)

Gordone felt that interracial casting with "a Stanley of color seemed more logical and historically correct to most audiences, not to mention the dramatic impact" (Letter, 29 May 1990).

A number of reviewers had incorrectly inferred that Tennessee Williams himself may have told Gordone that a Stanley of color was the best choice for the part. Gordone explains his reasoning for casting a Creole Stanley:

I never heard Tennessee Williams say that he had originally intended Stanley to be a black character. Nor have I ever heard Elia Kazan mention it. But I did hear it mumbled and rumored about in black theatre circles. Actually, the first time I heard it voiced was by the late Frank Silvera, the well-known black stage (*Hat Full of Rain*) and film (*Viva Zapata*) actor in the forties and fifties. Since both of them are deceased, we may never really know for sure. With the great success of Marlon Brando in the part, one could hardly mourn the loss of a black actor in the role!

Blanche's warning to Stella "not to hang back with the apes" and other derogatory remarks fit very well with the fact that Stanley in her institutionally bigoted mind came from "a lower order."

There were those who thought casting Stanley as a black man reinforced the stereotype. Certainly if you wanted to stretch it, a black Stanley raping Blanche, a white woman, could be construed that way. However, the subtle use of a socially and historically correct mix-blooded Creole gives some defense to the contrary. In most cases of rape it is "a power thing" more than the sexual which gave the act a deeper meaning socially and psychologically. (Letter, 12 June 1990)

To accommodate a Stanley of color, Gordone deleted all references to Stanley's being Polish and dropped the name of Kowalski from the program. A Creole Stanley, after all, would be a far more likely resident of New Orleans in the 1940s (Williams's time frame) than a white Pole named Kowalski.

Generally speaking, the critics approved of Gordone's decision and applauded his work. Steve Jensen auspiciously began his review with this assessment: "Charles Gordone's production . . . doesn't suffer too badly by comparison to a legendary Broadway production and a famous film version universally regarded as a four-star classic." Casting Paul Santiago as Stanley was an encouraging sign to A. J. Está, who felt that Santiago's presence allowed "the play [to] take on an even more tangled dimension and opens up some unexplored aspects of this marvelous work."

Most reviewers endorsed Santiago's playing Stanley. The reviewer for the *California Voice* exclaimed, "Santiago superbly portrays Stanley, creating a character filled with animal passion and human warmth," and went on: "Together Santiago and Kate Black sizzle, creating an undercurrent of sexual tension" ("A Hot *Streetcar*"). This is exactly the effect Gordone wanted. "Stanley is a good-looking Creole with working class drive and brute sensuality," claimed Linda Aube (25). While Está found Santiago "physically perfect for the role," he objected to the actor's mumbling, leading one to wonder if Santiago was aping Brando playing Stanley. The only strong objection to Santiago came from Steven Winn, who complained that Stanley is "played by a type-defying Creole, Paul Santiago, who suggests neither the brutish silences nor menacing sexual calculations that backlight and precipitate Blanche's quivery undoing."

For most reviewers, though, Santiago's Stanley and Peggy Linz's Blanche penetratingly enacted Gordone's racial/social/sexual message in this *Streetcar*, without distorting Williams's original intention. Under Gordone's direction, Peggy Linz gave an unusually strong performance as Blanche. She "makes the character less a victim and more a catalyst than in previous productions," asserted Está. In keeping with her symbolic role as Southern belle, Blanche is both butterfly and bigot. As Aube so beautifully stated, Blanche as portrayed by Linz was, "at the same time, a charming bigot, an erudite patrician, a scholar, and a sexually starved individual treading a tightrope toward insanity." The black Santiago significantly highlighted and drew out Blanche's multiple roles in ways no white actor could have. Imagine the "absolute horror that Blanche (an aging Southern Belle who represents the passing of the Old South) feels when she discovers her brother-in-law" is a Creole, observed Está. Aube described Blanche's horror similarly and gave a related reason for Stanley's motivation: "Stella's marriage to a non-white, lower-class, poor 'animal' is almost more than Blanche can bear, and Blanche's uppity attitude makes Stanley act even uglier and increases his desire to hurt her, which is inevitable." In keeping with the "socioeconomic framework" of this production, Blanche, as a representative of the Old South, carries with her "a value system grounded in oppression," as Gordone has explained elsewhere (qtd. in Kolin 183).

Blanche's sexual attraction for a Creole Stanley, the outsider in Blanche's view, shows how deeply the subtext of *Streetcar* deals with gender and race. As Gordone has pointed out, "Blanche's 'hang back with the apes' speech expresses a frighteningly literal prejudice" (Letter, 12 June 1990). Gordone's *Streetcar* thereby counteracts the critical views of this speech that place it along side of Hamlet's "What is man" speech as a paean to civilization. Gordone's multi-racial cast allowed him to inject new meanings into this classic of American theatre. As Steve Jensen aptly pointed out, "The discipline of the American Stage's careful production wipes away the encrustations of familiarity and allows Williams' great gifts for metaphor, humor, and strikingly original observation to shine anew."

One of the most significant productions of *Streetcar* with an all-black cast was done by the Dashiki Project Theatre at the Contemporary Arts Center in New Orleans from November 1 through 18, 1984. While Dashiki could not lay claim to having staged the first all-black production of the play, there is no doubt that it was a major achievement. Celebrating its sixteenth anniversary, Dashiki assembled an excellent cast, including the celebrated Hollywood actor (and New Orleans native) Harold Sylvester to play Stanley. Barbara Tasker, one of Dashiki's founding members, was Blanche; Gwendolyn Fox was Stella; and Harold Evans played Mitch. The production was directed by Theodore E. Gilliam, another of Dashiki's founding members, and a drama teacher at Southern and Loyola Universities.

Gilliam got the idea of doing an all-black *Streetcar* from a conversation he had with friends in 1982 in New York at a National Endowment for the Arts conference. One of the panel participants was Woody King, Jr., director of New York's New Federal Theatre. Gilliam recalls that it was at this time that O'Neill's *A Long Day's Journey into Night* was being done successfully with a black cast off-Broadway: "Woody mentioned that many black theaters wanted to do *Streetcar* but that Williams had disapproved. Woody thought it might be better if a smaller theater tried to do it rather than expose it in a professional production, and he thought of Dashiki because of Williams's connection to New Orleans" (qtd. in Dodds, "Minimal Rewriting"). Why Williams had earlier objected to a black *Streetcar* is open to speculation. Perhaps he feared unapproved, unacceptable changes in the sacrosanct script. However, it turned out that Williams was amenable to Dashiki's doing *Streetcar.* But before Gilliam could convince Williams to work with him on the production of the play, Williams died (Gilliam interview).

Gilliam did not stage *Streetcar* primarily to make a statement about race, though racial considerations did play a significant role in the production. For Gilliam, "The conflict in *Streetcar* between Blanche and Stanley is universal" (Interview). As Richard Dodds has affirmed, "That Blanche could be black is reasonable; no race has a monopoly on shattered dreams" ("Black 'Streetcar'"). Gilliam did not see *Streetcar* as "a white play. I see it more simply as an American work. We don't give enough attention to the fact that Americans, regardless of their backgrounds or complexions, are Americans with common experiences that cross all barriers" ("Dashiki Theatre"). In his note about the production included in the Dashiki playbill, Gilliam observes that "great art transcends all barriers when it addresses the human spirit. In this production of *Streetcar* we have tried to remain faithful to the spirit of Tennessee Williams's play. It is not intended to be *A Streetcar Named Desire* in blackface, but a rendering of the play from a black perspective."

Staging *Streetcar* from a black perspective, though, necessitated some changes in the script. The Dashiki production altered a few phrases that seemed particularly white, especially of local place names, to make them more consistent with the all-black cast playing before a New Orleans audience. Stella and Blanche go to Mule's, not Galatoire's, for dinner at the end of Scene Two; and Stanley talks about the Dryades

YMCA, a traditionally black Y in the city (Orr). Moreover, "reference to the number of an army unit [was] changed to an actual black unit, and Stanley's bowling alley [was] given the name of an alley that catered to blacks during the 1940s" (Dodds, "Minimal Rewriting").

Leaving Blanche as the owner of a plantation in Mississippi, though, strained the critics' credulity, and perhaps the audience's, too. Gilliam maintained that there were some slight changes in referring to the plantation, even though "there were several actual instances where a black person or family would inherit a plantation. Although a black plantation is rare, it is not implausible" (Interview). Marian Orr kindly pointed out that Gilliam's *Streetcar* works "with one basic suspension of disbelief (that the DuBois family owned a big plantation house in Laurel, Mississippi)." Fran Lawless, too, found the plantation to be the only "flaw in this production," and even though Blanche tried to "minimize the image" by explaining that it was just one house with columns and a few acres of land, the possibility is "highly unlikely." Lawless added: "The director could very well have expanded on the plausibility of that notion had he added the pressure of such a predicament, that of a black female plantation owner, to Blanche's other problems when the property began to slip through her hands." Edward Real was more troubled by the plantation's being in Mississippi, a state which "hardly had the tradition of free people of color that Louisiana did. Perhaps more work could have been done to adapt the script in this regard." It seems that the reference to the plantation was as troublesome for critics of this black production of *Streetcar* as the allusions to Blanche's young husband's homosexuality were to the censors in the late 1940s and early 1950s.

A black *Streetcar* for many New Orleans reviewers seemed "radical" or "surprising," yet they thought it succeeded. The transition from an all-white to an all-black cast was not frustrated by Williams's script but actually aided by it, according to Dodds: "There are moments when the concept of a black 'Streetcar Named Desire' just doesn't work, but most of the time, the Kowalski household at 632 Elysian Fields is right at home in a black environment . . . almost stereotypically so" ("Black 'Streetcar'"). Agreeing with such an assessment, Real asserted that "there is much here that reflects the black experience, or at least popular notions of that experience," including "Stanley's self-consciously macho bearing, the domestic passions and violence of the Kowalski's [sic] and their neighbors, [and] the strong matriarchal influence in Mitch's family." (Real wisely observes that such characteristics would apply to whites as well.) Although Gilliam conceded that Stanley and Stella's relationship may "resemble the stereotypical one of a black family," he himself "did not agree wholeheartedly" with such a view (Interview).

Harold Sylvester's reputation so dominated the production that the Dashiki *Streetcar* became Stanley's play. "Harold Sylvester in *A Streetcar Named Desire*," the playbill proclaimed. A New Orleans native, a graduate of Tulane, and a veteran of the Free Southern Theatre, Sylvester received much publicity in the local press about playing Stanley. A long interview appeared in the *Spectator News Journal* of November 3, 1984, which pictured Sylvester's Stanley on the cover and carried the headline "Hollywood Star Returns Home."

Sylvester created a Stanley far different from that portrayed by other actors, including Brando's Stanley memorialized in the 1951 film. In an interview, Sylvester acknowledged that "It's a real challenge to develop the character and bring a person alive on stage that is a lot different from yourself. . . . I'm not as mean and hateful as Kowalski is" ("Vibrations"). And in a profile on him in the New Orleans *Times-Picayune*, Sylvester remarked: "Stanley is very raw, very different from my own personality, so I was intrigued. . . . There's a vicarious pleasure in doing something very far from yourself. . . . I never [before] played a bad guy" ("Lagniappe"). In that same profile, Gilliam is quoted as saying of Sylvester, "I'm doing as much as possible to steer him away from that all-American image."

Sylvester's Stanley was no mere brute, no ape to hang back with. His Stanley was applauded for being more subtle, more sullen. As

N. R. Davidson noted, "You are aware of an animal cunning at work—alongside the spiteful child his character is." Fran Lawless pointed out that Sylvester departed "from the traditional seethingly sensual brother-in-law" Brando exemplified. Unlike Brando, Sylvester did not swagger or mumble; he was praised for including tenderness and wit in the role. A number of critics even commented on his being less muscular than Brando! As Marian Orr observed, Sylvester is "not the menacing, seductive, Marlon Brando type . . . just a straightforward guy who gets sweaty and likes his poker night. . . ." It is no wonder that Lawless labeled Sylvester's Stanley a "blue collar Everyman." Although Sylvester still projected a menacing presence against which Blanche is ultimately powerless to repel Stanley's spine-chilling pronouncement, "We've had this date with each other from the beginning," his assault seemed "less the brutal act that it is, and more an act of destiny" for Lawless. Commenting on both the warmer and darker sides of Sylvester's Stanley, Davidson warned, "You understand that he can do harm, that there is a malevolence lurking behind his humor."

Critics judged Barbara Tasker's Blanche to be less effective than Sylvester's Stanley. Though she may have begun as a wronged, Southern lady, according to Marian Orr, Tasker changed from that role "fairly abruptly" into a "real manipulator." Similarly, Edward Real found that, in Tasker's interpretation, "Blanche's airs are more the result of deliberate pretense and fantasy than of an actual declining aristocracy." Lawless faulted Tasker's Blanche for not being amorous enough: "She carries off the image of the prima donna but fails to move the audience as the femme fatale." Tasker's voice and gestures contributed significantly to a tougher Blanche. Davidson, for example, concluded that Tasker's "hoarse/husky voice seems to take her away from Blanche at times" and that Tasker was "not always up to the challenge" the role demanded.

When asked how his Blanche compared with Tallulah Bankhead's portrayal of Blanche, Gilliam laughed and said, "No, not that aggressive" (Interview). While Tasker may have been a more forceful and assertive Blanche than other actresses who have played the part, there is nothing in Williams's script that forbids such an interpretation. In fact, Tasker's portrayal of Blanche was consistent with Gilliam's projection of black womanhood. A black Blanche brings a different, albeit valid, response to the role. Consequently, critics—like many audiences—may need to rid themselves of expectations of the prototypical Blanche based on the mannerisms of a few leading (white) actresses.

A more radical production of *Streetcar* with an all-black cast was presented by the Black Ensemble at the Leo Lerner Theater in Chicago from February 21 through March 29, 1987. Directed by Marianne Zuccaro, it starred Jackie Taylor as Blanche, Darryl Manuel as Stanley, Bellary Darden as Stella, and David Barr III as Mitch. Taylor, who founded the Black Ensemble in 1976 and was its artistic director, was the driving force behind the Black Ensemble's *Streetcar.*

Sid Smith summed up many critics' reactions: "The all-black casting proves no problem" ("'Streetcar' Risky"). As Dashiki had done, the Black Ensemble perceptively interpreted Williams's *Streetcar* from a black perspective. Before the stage action began, audiences heard Billie Holiday music. During the production "occasional uses of a smoky blues score help[ed] set the right mood," observed Smith, whose other comments are worth quoting, too. Stanley and Stella "represent the real, seamy side of life, as well as the prototypes of the ordinary lower class household. As a black family melodrama, *Streetcar* falls right into place." The critics thought that more humor went into this production than in corresponding white ones. Darryl Manuel's Stanley was praised for being unbelievably funny, and the neighbors' "indulging in a bit of funk br[ought] new life to their short atmospheric bits." As in other black productions, references to Stanley's Polish ancestry were dropped; in addition, the Black Ensemble cut the reference to "colored maids" ("'Streetcar' Risky").

Jackie Taylor's "standout performance" (Nuccio) as Blanche represented the company's most significant statement about the play from a black vantage point. A Chicago native. Taylor grew up in the Cabrini

Green housing projects on the near south side of the city and became a celebrated actress. She told Sid Smith:

> I've wanted to do this ever since I read "*Streetcar.*" . . . I don't look at this in just black and white terms. But when I read the play I see a lot of it from the black perspective. It's a tragic story, but it's one that in some ways we're still living today, especially from the viewpoint of the black woman. ("Black Ensemble")

Similarly, she explained to Christina January Adachi that "I never thought of Blanche as being black or white, just tragic. It's such a statement about how women's lives have been shaped, a historical view that needs to be pressed in time."

Taylor's feminist view of contemporary history erased the kinds of (white) historical clashes that have dominated *Streetcar* since it opened in 1947. Taylor played Blanche not as a faded belle but as a "ghostly figure of fantasy and lost hope," the victim of a terrifying past and horrifying present. Taylor concentrated on Blanche's mental deterioration, abandoning "the drippy belle mannerisms" that have undone many Blanches (Smith, "'Streetcar' Risky"). The "coquettishness, the sparkling flashes of wit, and the undiminished vanity [we]re kept quite low key," reported Hedy Weiss. As if filtering Williams's play through the works of Adrienne Kennedy, Taylor created a Blanche who "c[a]me off fresh, her madness rooted in deeper psychological imbalance and horror" (Smith, "'Streetcar' Risky"). A true tragic woman, she nonetheless possessed a repertoire of nuances drawn from her black heritage. According to Smith, Taylor showed herself to be a "kind of jazz actress who brings a truckload of styles and feelings to her many scenes" ("'Streetcar' Risky").

Unlike Smith, Hedy Weiss found Taylor too "severe" and "unyielding," adding, "This is a Blanche with a considerably tougher surface than one has come to expect: more brittle and belligerent than sexually provocative, more overtly bruised and angry." While this portrayal made Blanche more vulnerable, it also "prevent[ed] Blanche's relationship with Stanley from ever reaching the sizzling danger point it should and ma[d]e her romance with Mitch . . . less potent as well."

While actresses such as Jessica Tandy, Vivien Leigh, and Blythe Danner may have limited the aggressive side of Blanche's nature, Williams's text allows black actresses such as Jackie Taylor and Barbara Tasker the freedom to emphasize the feisty part of Blanche's character as a woman much wronged. Such an interpretation certainly has sociological roots in poor black communities where women have to be strong to survive and keep families alive. On aesthetic grounds, too, a more forceful Blanche deepens our appreciation of *Streetcar* as a feminist tragedy.

If Weiss was disappointed by Taylor's low levels of sexual energy, Darryl Manuel's Stanley was hardly perceived as a sex symbol. Weiss herself acknowledged that the "lack of sexual tension in this production [wa]s partly the result of Manuel's portrayal of Stanley." Though Manuel was cocky, had a "rich, vibrant voice," and was a good man for Stella, "he was no match for Blanche," reported Fred Nuccio. "He's too boyish and direct." Manuel's portrayal lacked "the brutishness and sexual magnetism the part requires" (Nuccio). Obviously, the actor was not following the Brando tradition.

Thanks to Taylor's magnificent Blanche, the Black Ensemble *Streetcar* comes closest to being a black feminist tragedy that does not need to oppose the heavy historicism of Blanche's Southern aristocracy against Stanley's Polish heritage to make the play work. The Black Ensemble's interpretation may have struck a "rather strange historical chord" for Hedy Weiss, making *Streetcar* "narrower and more personal in its focus—and somewhat difficult to place." Yet a *Streetcar* which exhibits a clear feminist emphasis seems to me easily placed, since the Black Ensemble situated the tragedy at the point originally intended by Williams—the human heart as represented by the deeply hurt Blanche.

As we saw, in 1965 Howard University's Drama Department did a multi-racial production of *Streetcar* which offered a traditional interpretation of Williams's play. A second *Streetcar* done at Howard in 1988 provided one of the most insightful and deeply political readings of *Streetcar* by a black theatre company. Presented from March 10 through 19, in the university's small (sixty-seat) Experimental Theatre, this production featured an original rhythm-and-blues score composed by Thomas A. Korth. Because the play ran so many nights, it had a double cast of student actors. Blanche was alternately played by Andrea Hart and Robin McClamb, Stanley by Omar C. Coubourne and Mason Carmichael, and Mitch by Mason Carmichael and Ernest R. Mercer. It is interesting but not surprising that Carmichael doubled as Stanley and Mitch; many actors have played opposing roles, such as Iago and Othello, on successive nights. Wendy D. Davis had the role of Stella all to herself. There were two student directors as well— Courtney Long and Danielle Peake. The faculty director was Vera Katz, who taught Phylicia Rashad, Lynda Gravatt, Charles Brown, and other students at Howard who went on to highly successful acting careers.

Katz was determined to stage a *Streetcar* with a highly charged set of conflicts for her mostly black audience. Her hope was to make *Streetcar* "relevant to the university audience and to show how great classics have relevance to all people" (Bethel, "Drama Department"). In her "Director's Notes," included in the program, Katz informed her audience that she was departing from the conventional reading of *Streetcar* which polarized the aristocratic Old South and the aggressive North:

> We are attempting to bring you a new message in this production of *A Streetcar Named Desire*. . . . Our production focuses on the clash of class (education and background; French Creole versus Gullah) and the clash of color (light-skinned versus dark). "People have to learn to tolerate each other's differences," says Stella, and we have an urgent call in today's world that is being ripped apart by an over-emphasis on our differences. Traditions of Black people may vary; gradations of color may bring forth different hues, but the commonality of race is an everbinding factor that cannot be destroyed.

Katz was not the first director to see Blanche as a Creole. Some thirty years earlier, Hilda Simms was to have starred as a Creole Blanche in the aborted production of *Streetcar* in New York. But Katz's production was unique in using *Streetcar* as a vehicle to depict and declaim "intraracial racism."

Elaborating on the ways in which Katz's production developed the theme of color prejudice, Renée Simmons, the acting coach for this *Streetcar* and a professor in the Drama Department at Howard, supplied this assessment in her "Notes on Creole & Gullah," also included in the playbill:

> Colorism can be defined as discrimination or polarization within a race of people based on color differences. Within the Black community colorism takes its shape in the struggles between light-skinned and dark-skinned Blacks.
>
> For this particular production of *Streetcar*, Blanche is not only a Southern belle but also a descendant of the "coloured" French Creoles. . . . Many had large plantations, like Belle Reve, and some even owned slaves. They took pride in their ability to emulate the habits and social graces of their white counterparts. Many considered themselves "superior" to other Blacks because of their French heritage.
>
> Stanley, on the other hand, is no longer a Polish American, but is from the Sea Islands off the coast of South Carolina where they speak Gullah . . . a creolized form of English revealing survivals from many African languages spoken by the slaves who were brought to South Carolina and Georgia during the 18th century. These islands and their distinctive dialect are significant to Black history because the early inhabitants of these islands were runaway slaves who refused to succumb to the white slave owners. These proud and independent slaves isolated themselves and were able to maintain much of their African heritage.
>
> Thus, we add yet another dimension to the conflict between Blanche and Stanley—colorism. . . . as novelist Alice Walker has put it, ". . . colorism, like colonialism, sexism, and racism, impedes us."

To accomplish her goal of making the classic *Streetcar* relevant for her audience, Katz changed the characters' ethnic backgrounds and overall motivation. She daringly dislodged the traditional sympathy audiences have for Blanche and their animosity for Stanley. In her production, these two characters seem to have reversed symbolic places. Blanche is no longer the weak victim whose refinement and tastes are seen as charming and whose mournful nostalgia is pitiable. Instead, she becomes the arrogant Creole, guilty of double racism. She has acquired the prejudices of a bigoted white woman toward blacks while she herself is guilty of the prejudice of colorism. In the political subtext of Katz's *Streetcar*, Stanley becomes Blanche's victim and the underdog for the audience. No longer Polish, he's now Stanley Williams. With his Jamaican accent approximating the Gullah, Stanley becomes a ready target for Blanche's racist snubs.

The way in which Robin McClamb played Blanche deepened this tragedy of color. "She captures the audience into her web of lust, disillusionment, snobbery, and somehow subtle gentleness" (Bethel, "McClamb"). To this student reviewer as well as to other members of the audience no doubt, Blanche was like the Spider Lady, enticing yet intimidating—arrogant, insulting, and self-righteous, as when she tries to seduce the paper boy. In white productions of *Streetcar*, Blanche's high-handed airs, flighty gestures, and self-consciously placed bon mots can be charming, comic, supercilious. But in this production with an all-black cast before a black audience, Blanche's airs become subversive, fraught with the sinister implications of color prejudice. In a recent letter to me, Katz recalled:

> The audience found Blanche to represent racism within the African-American culture which favors those of lighter color than the darker. This is a sensitive topic within the Black community as witnessed in Spike Lee's film *School Daze*, which opened six months after my production of *Streetcar*. Blanche's airs and her visual hostility to Stanley made the audience respond with jeers and titters of awareness of the problem. My

Blanche with her airs and superiority did not amend the traditional view of Blanche, for within the African-American culture there are those who profess superiority because of their lightness and straight hair and because of their lineage. Creoles, as Blanche was in my production, have considered themselves to possess a more respected background than the Gullah peoples which Stanley represented. The Creoles, given their Spanish, French, and Indian mix, have traditionally looked down on the Gullahs. Thus the existing mores lent [them]sel[ves] nicely to my production concept.

But Blanche's prejudice extended to more than just color. Katz mentions differences in education between Blanche and Stanley in her "Director's Notes," and her production clearly "represented the gap that exists between educated and uneducated blacks" (Bethel, "Drama Department"). Unquestionably, Katz's audience of students and others of the Howard University community were extremely sensitive to this issue. In a city such as Washington, D.C., with its large black population, educational advantages signal economic and political ones as well. Blanche is arrogant because of her educational background (she is an English teacher—a role more playfully interpreted by Vivien Leigh or Ann-Margret). Yet her educational advantages in Katz's production are the grounds for Blanche's exploitation of and alienation from the black community.

A careful and moving production, Katz's *Streetcar* offered the audience a clear explanation for Blanche's tragedy, founded on color, and an even clearer call to avoid this prejudice in the black community. Katz persuasively pointed out in her "Director's Notes" that "Blanche and Stella have allowed this to happen through their mistrust, fear, need for power[,] and ignorance of each other's heritage and ways. We must not follow their paths." The commonality of race binding the DuBois sisters together has been destroyed in this production of *Streetcar*, but the bonds of unity need not be broken by a black audience aware of this divisive canker.

III

Tennessee Williams will continue to be pluralized by succeeding generations. It seems as if each year witnesses a remake, for film or television, of one of his plays. *Cat on a Hot Tin Roof*, *Sweet Bird of Youth*, and *Orpheus Descending* are three of Williams's plays that have received major reinterpretations for film or television in 1989-1990. Given Williams's marvelous imaginative resiliency and protean scripts, the black and multi-racial productions of *Streetcar* that I have surveyed really should not be surprising, though it is disconcerting that they have not received more critical attention. These black and multi-racial productions validate *Streetcar*'s universality by extending the boundaries of Williams's script. Black directors have accomplished this in a variety of ways. Though Thomas Pawley and the Stewarts were strongly opposed to changing the script for black audiences or actors, the very fact that black theatres performed *Streetcar* in the mid-1950s is a significant comment on and tribute to black culture. Later productions of *Streetcar*, as we have seen, discovered social and political messages in the (sub)text of Williams's play that white productions ignored or were incapable of representing. *Streetcar* can never remain the exclusive right of any specific cultural repertoire. As Nick Stewart said of *Streetcar* when he referred to plays that uplifted rather than denigrated the image of blacks, "That was a good play" (Interview).[2]

From *Black American Literature Forum* 25, no. 1 (1991): 147-181. Copyright © 1991 by *African American Review*. Reprinted with permission of *African American Review*.

Notes

1. In fact, Williams played the role of a black preacher in Pawley's play *Ku Klux*, staged at an Iowa drama workshop in 1938 (Pawley, "Experimental" 67).
2. I am deeply grateful to the following individuals, without whose help I could never have gathered the information upon which this article is based: Thomas D. Pawley; Nick and Edna Stewart, and their daughter Valerie Stewart Knight; Christine Bocek at the Los Angeles Public Library; Jürgen Wolter at the Universität Wuppertal;

Charles Gordone and Susan Kouyomjian; Theodore E. Gilliam; Jackie Taylor; and Vera Katz. My thanks also go to my colleagues Steven Barthelme and Irmgard Wolfe as well as LaNelle Daniel and Anne Stascavage, two of my doctoral students, for their assistance.

Works Cited

Adachi, Christina January. "Taylor at Black Ensemble." *Today's Chicago Woman* Mar. 1987: 12.

Aube, Linda. "'Streetcar' on Right Track." *Argus* 18 May 1983: 25.

Beauchamp, Emerson. "Tennessee Williams Hero at Howard U." *Washington Evening Star* 22 Feb. 1965: A8.

Bethel, Alison. "Drama Department Performs *Streetcar* Deviation." *Hilltop* [Howard U] 8 Mar. 1988.

_____. "McClamb, Cast Are a 'Must See' In *Streetcar*." *Hilltop* [Howard U] 18 Mar. 1988.

Bongard, David. "'Streetcar' Revived at Ebony Showcase Theatre." *Los Angeles Herald & Express* 1 Dec. 1956: B7.

C., R. L. "Howard U.'s 'Streetcar' Set on the Right Track." *Washington Post* 20 Feb. 1965: E44.

Calta, Louis. "Opening of Play." *New York Times* 25 Sept. 1958: 30.

Case, Sue-Ellen. *Feminism and Theatre*. New York: Methuen, 1988.

"Dance Theater of Harlem Will Present *A Streetcar Named Desire* on Public Television." *Twin Cities Courier* [Minneapolis] 20 Feb. 1986.

"Dashiki Theatre Producing Tennessee Williams Classic." *Louisiana Weekly* [New Orleans] 3 Nov. 1984, sec. 1:14.

Davidson, N. R. "This *Streetcar*'s Flawed But Not Easily Forgotten." *Louisiana Weekly* [New Orleans] 10 Nov. 1984, sec. 1:6.

Davis, Clinton Turner, and Harry Newman. *Beyond Tradition: Transcripts of the First National Symposium on Non-Traditional Casting*. New York: Non-Traditional Casting Protect, 1988.

Dodds, Richard. "Black 'Streetcar' Travels Well." *Times-Picayune* [New Orleans] 8 Nov. 1984: E3.

_____. "Minimal Rewriting Needed to Create a Black 'Streetcar.'" *Times-Picayune* [New Orleans] 1 Nov. 1984: E3.

Está, A. J. "Gordone Directs New 'Streetcar.'" *Drama-Logue* 23 June 1983: 22.

"Freie Volksbuhne darf nun doch . . . 'Endstation Sehnsucht' spielen." *Frankfurter Rundschau* 11 July 1974: 6.

Gelb, Arthur. "Negroes Slated for 'Streetcar.'" *New York Times* 14 July 1958: L16.

Gilliam, Theodore E. Telephone interview. 29 June 1989.

Goldner, Nancy. "Cameras Enhance Performance of Dance Theater of Harlem." *Youngstown Vindicator* 21 Feb. 1986: 23.

Gordone, Charles. Letter to the author. 29 May 1990.

_____. Letter to the author. 12 June 1990.

Guild, Leo. "Play Review: 'A Streetcar Named Desire' (Ebony Showcase Theatre)." *Hollywood Reporter* 3 Dec. 1956: 3.

Hildebrand, Harold. "'Streetcar' on Stage at Ebony." *Los Angeles Examiner* 30 Nov. 1956.

_____. "Vivid Acting in 'Streetcar.'" *Los Angeles Examiner* 19 Feb. 1955.

Holloway, Ronald. "Stop That 'Streetcar' Named Lang: Berlin Failed to Tell Dramatist of Slight Switch, a Black Lead." *Variety* 17 July 1974: 103.

"Hollywood Star Returns Home." *Spectator News Journal* [New Orleans] 3 Nov. 1984.

"A Hot *Streetcar*." *California Voice* 3 June 1983: 20.

"James Edwards Stars in Ebony's 'Streetcar.'" *Los Angeles Sentinel* 22 Nov. 1956.

Jensen, Steve. "Impressive Revival of 'Streetcar.'" *Berkeley Gazette: Berkeley's Weekly Entertainment Magazine* 20 May 1983: P1.

Kap. "Legit Review: *Streetcar Named Desire* (Ebony Showcase)." *Variety* 30 Nov. 1956.

Katz, Vera. Letter to the author. 1 Oct. 1990.

Kisselgoff, Anna. "Dance: Harlem Troupe Performs 'Streetcar.'" *New York Times* 16 Jan. 1982: L11.

Kolin, Philip C. "*A Streetcar Named Desire*: A Playwrights' Forum." *Michigan Quarterly Review* 19 (Spring 1990): 173-203.

"Lagniappe." *Times-Picayune* [New Orleans] 2 Nov. 1984: 3.

Lamarre, Hazel L. "Applause! In the Theatre." *Los Angeles Sentinel* 3 Mar. 1955: A10.

_____. "Applause! In the Theatre." *Los Angeles Sentinel* 6 Dec. 1956: B10.

Lawless, Fran. "Critique: 'Streetcar': A Triumph." *Spectator News Journal* [New Orleans] 14 Nov. 1984.

Nuccio, Fred. "Taylor a Standout in 'Streetcar' Role." *Skyline* [Chicago] 10-11 Mar. 1987, sec. 2:1.

Orr, Marian. "A Line of *Streetcar*s." *Gambit* [New Orleans] 10 Nov. 1984.

Pawley, Thomas D. "Experimental Theatre Seminar; or the Basic Training of Tennessee Williams: A Memoir." *Iowa Review* 19 (Winter 1989): 65-76.

_____. Letter to the author. 7 June 1990.

_____. Letter to the author. 16 Aug. 1990.

Real, Edward. "Life upon the Wicked Stage." *Impact* [New Orleans] 9 (16 Nov. 1984): 17.

Segal, Lewis. "PBS on the Right Track with 'Streetcar' Ballet." *Los Angeles Times* 21 Feb. 1986, sec. 6:26.

Smith, Sid. "Black Ensemble Boards 'Streetcar.'" *Chicago Tribune* 29 Jan. 1987, sec. 5:9.

_____. "'Streetcar' Risky But Refreshing." *Chicago Tribune* 23 Feb. 1987, Tempo, sec. 4.

Stewart, Edna. Telephone interview. 25 Sept. 1990.

Stewart, Nick. Telephone interview. 24 Aug. 1990.

Ulrich, Allan. "Harlem Dancers Return to TV." *San Francisco Examiner* 21 Feb. 1986: E1.

"Vibrations: New Orleans Actor Wants to Build Film Industry Here." *Data Newsweekly* [New Orleans] 20 Nov. 1984: 6.

Von Blon, Katherine. "'Streetcar' Begins Run at Ebony Showcase." *Los Angeles Times* 1 Dec. 1956, sec. 3:2.

_____. "'Streetcar' Offered at Ebony Showcase." *Los Angeles Times* 25 Feb. 1955, sec. 1:22.

Weiss, Hedy. "Ensemble Takes 'Streetcar' for Bumpy, Interesting Ride." *Chicago Sun-Times* 3 Mar. 1987: 46.

Wiegenstein, Roland H. "Hubners beste Talente Liegen brach . . . Nach dem Williams-Skandal." *Frankfurter Rundschau* 16 July 1974: 9.

Williams, Tennessee. *A Streetcar Named Desire*. New York: NAL, 1947.

Williams, Wylie. "All-Negro Cast Scores with 'Streetcar Named Desire.'" *Citizen News* [Hollywood, CA] 29 Nov. 1956: 21.

"Williams—Aufführung verboten." *Frankfurter Rundschau* 28 June 1974.

Winn, Steven. "A Vivid Blanche DuBois in a Murky 'Streetcar.'" *San Francisco Chronicle* 26 May 1983: 70.

"Something Cloudy, Something Clear":
Homophobic Discourse in Tennessee Williams_____
John M. Clum

Throughout his career, Tennessee Williams was attacked from all sides for his treatment or nontreatment of homosexuality in his work. During the early years of gay liberation, gay critics complained that Williams was not "out" enough in his work and demanded that he stop writing around his homosexuality. One gay playwright went so far as to assert: "He has yet to contribute any work of understanding to gay theater."[1] Williams's response to such attacks was a series of candid personal disclosures culminating in the unfortunate volume of memoirs, and more explicit treatment of homosexuality in his later, often autobiographical works. This new candor led to attacks by heterosexual critics, one of whom even referred to one play of the seventies as "faggotty fantasizing."[2]

The first critic to deal intelligently with this aspect of Williams's work was Edward A. Sklepowitch, whose formulation was too simplistic, though typical of early work in gay studies:

> Williams' so-called "decadent" vision and his preoccupation with loneliness, evasion, role-playing, wastage, sexual reluctance and sexual excess are in many instances functions of a homosexual sensibility which has been evolving steadily in the more than quarter century since the publication of *One Arm and Other Stories*. In this period, Williams' treatment of homosexuality has undergone significant changes, moving from a mystical to a more social perspective, a personal, if fictional microcosm of the wider cultural demystification of homosexuality.[3]

I do not see such a steady evolution in Williams's "homosexual sensibility": rather, there seems to be a constant attitude toward homosexual acts, though Williams's presentation of homosexual persons changed when public tolerance allowed a candidness in drama which Williams had previously restricted to his stories and poems. That change in presentation, alas, was also a function of his decreased ability to convert memory or self-judgment into a controlled work of art. But the constant in Williams's career is the dual vision that shaped his presentation of the homosexuality he was always impelled to write about.

Some relatively late statements issued by Williams demonstrate his sense of a split personality which separated the homosexual artist from his work, and they provide a crucial starting point for any discussion of the relation of Williams's sexual orientation to his work, particularly his plays. This one is from an interview with Dotson Rader:

> I never found it necessary to deal with it [homosexuality] in my work. It was never a preoccupation of mine, except in my intimate, private life.[4]

Quibbling with this statement becomes a matter of semantics. Williams may not have found it "necessary" to "deal with" homosexuality in his work, but the fact is he did. His poetry is filled with homoerotic visions and encounters with "gentlemen callers." Indeed, no poet has so vividly and poignantly captured the tension, excitement, and loneliness of the anonymous sexual encounter as Williams, from the wry humor of "Life Story" to the poignancy of "Young Men Waking at Daybreak." The focus of these poems is not so much homo*sexuality* as it is the peculiar alienation of the brief sexual encounter. Williams's best stories also feature homosexuals as central characters. The semicanonization of the boxer/hustler/murderer in "One Arm," who dies with love letters from the men with whom he has tricked jammed between his legs, is typical in its combination of religion, mortality, and impersonal gay sex which pervades many of Williams's best stories. The plays, too, are filled with homosexual characters: from the offstage martyrs of the plays of the major period, to the happy, ideal "marriage" of Jack Straw and Peter Ochello in *Cat on a Hot Tin Roof*, to the writers, artists, and hustlers of the later plays for whom sex is a temporary cure for loneliness.

Williams's theoretical separation of his homosexuality from his work is in conflict with his many assertions of the highly personal nature of his work and of his close relationship with his characters. It does not conform with "I draw all my characters from myself. I can't draw a character unless I know it within myself," unless one factors in an essential variable: "I draw every character out of my very multiple split personality."[5] Split personality and split vision are recurring themes in Williams's work, particularly in references to himself. They suggest not only the multiple split personalities which allow such empathetic relationships with his characters, but also the split presentation of his own homosexuality.

Part of Williams's need to deny the homosexual element in his work is an extension of his need for validation as a writer (though he seldom got it in the last twenty-five years of his life). Admitting to the homosexual dimension of his work was a professional liability:

> You still want to know why I don't write a gay play? I don't find it necessary. I could express what I wanted to express through other means. I would be narrowing my audience a great deal [if I wrote for a gay audience alone]. I wish to have a broad audience because the major thrust of my work is not sexual orientation, it's social. I'm not about to limit myself to writing about gay people.[6]

While making clear his continued, though frustrated, interest in writing for a broad audience, this statement demonstrates Williams's political naiveté: for him, homosexuality was merely a sexual issue, thus incongruent with his "social" interest. This separation is impossible for the homosexual, for whom the sexual is social, as Williams implies when he passionately asserts that "I do not deal with the didactic, ever." For him, a gay play was bound to be didactic, a notion his later work all too often bears out.[7]

The split persona is seen again in a crucial quotation from his *Memoirs*: "Of course I also existed outside of conventional society while contriving somewhat precariously to remain in contact with it. For me this was not only precarious but a matter of dark unconscious disturbance."[8] While Williams is referring to himself as a social being rather than as an artist, this statement defines the problematics of Williams's stance as homosexual artist and of the gulf between private art (poetry and fiction) and public art (drama), and the corollary gap between private homosexual and public celebrity. For most of his career, Williams was extremely protective of this split. Homosexuality was not the only element of Williams's personality which placed him outside of conventional society, but it was the subject which in the 1940s and 1950s seldom spoke its name. Williams was privately open about his sexual orientation, but publicly cautious, as he was relatively willing to treat homosexuality directly in his nondramatic writings, which would reach a limited audience (he never until his later years strove for the money and publicity of a best-selling novel), but cautious in his dramas. His caution takes two forms. One is the clever use of what he calls "obscurity or indirection" to soften and blur the homosexual element of much of his work. The other is a complex acceptance of homophobic discourse, which he both critiques and embraces.

This reliance on and occasional manipulation of the language of homophobia is the basis of Williams's treatment of the subject of homosexuality in his plays, reflecting a split he saw in his own nature. Williams wrote of his vision problems in 1940:

> My left eye was cloudy then because it was developing a cataract. But my right eye was clear. It was like the two sides of my nature. The side that was obsessively homosexual, compulsively interested in sexuality. And the side that in those days was gentle and understanding and contemplative.[9]

This double vision, which always obsessed the playwright and led to the title of his last produced play in New York, *Something Cloudy, Something Clear*, defines the split Williams conceived between his homosexual activity and his "human" side. Even in his confused later novel,

Moise and the World of Reason, in which he depicts himself as an eccentric aging playwright the narrator encounters, he fixes on a dual vision:

> He came back to the table and simultaneously two things happened of the automatic nature. He kissed me on the mouth and I started to cry. . . .
>
> "Baby, I didn't mean to do that, it was just automatic."
>
> (He thought I was crying over his Listerine kiss which I'd barely noticed.)
>
> He slumped there drinking the dago red wine as if to extinguish a fire in his belly, the rate at which he poured it down him slowing only when the bottle was half-empty. Then his one good eye focussed on me again but the luster was gone from it and its look was inward.[10]

The outward gaze becomes linked to an automatic, impersonal homosexual advance while the inward gaze signifies the writer's now uncontrollable withdrawals into memory, which form the basis of his later autobiographical work which, paradoxically, depicts his split vision and at the same time demonstrates the loss his work suffered when he blurred the public/private split which was essential to his control over memory and craft.

Williams's split vision, then, defines the internal conflict that compelled him to write of his homosexuality and, in doing so, to rely on the language of indirection and homophobic discourse. It signified a cloudy sense of his own sexual identity, but it enabled him to write clearly. On the other hand, as the sexual self became clearer, and the plays became more autobiographical, the writing became murkier.

* * *

The story "Hard Candy" (1954), characteristic of Williams's fiction in dealing with homosexuality and its evasions, embodies Williams's split vision and attendant manipulation of language. "Hard Candy" centers on the last day in the life of an elderly man, Mr. Krupper, who habitually goes to an old movie palace with a bag of hard candy and a handful of quarters, his bribes to willing young men for their sexual favors. On the day of the story, Mr. Krupper dies while performing fellatio on a handsome young vagrant. Before describing Mr. Krupper's fatal visit to the movie theater, Williams offers this peculiar rejoinder:

> In the course of this story, and very soon now, it will be necessary to make some disclosures about Mr. Krupper of a nature *too coarse* to be dealt with very directly in a work of such brevity. The grossly naturalistic details of a life, contained in the enormously wide context of that life, are softened and qualified by it, but when you attempt to set those details down in a tale, *some measure of obscurity or indirection* is called for to provide the same, or even approximate, softening effect that existence in time gives to those gross elements in the life itself. When I say that there was a *certain mystery* in the life of Mr. Krupper, *I am beginning to approach those things in the only way possible without a head-on violence that would disgust and destroy and which would only falsify the story.*
>
> To have hatred and contempt for a person . . . calls for the assumption that you know practically everything of any significance about him. If you admit that he is a *mystery*, you admit that the hostility may be unjust.[11]

Mr. Krupper's "mystery" is contained in his afternoon visits to the Joy Rio movie theater; his sexual encounters there with poor, beautiful (of course) young men are acts which would brand him in the eyes of most people as a "dirty old man" or worse. Williams's rejoinder both shows his sympathy and understanding of his audience's sensibilities and prejudices, and plays with those prejudices. The language of mystery and evasion allows him to write about the forbidden in a sympathetic, even subversive way. That mystery, however, is also clothed in harsh authorial judgment, which places the narrator in a superior position to his central character and allies him with the "average reader's" moral judgment. As Mr. Krupper approaches the Joy Rio theater, the narrator describes it as "the place where the mysteries of his nature are to be made unpleasantly manifest to us."[12] Williams is both compassionate and judgmental: the story is both grotesque and touching. The "mysteries," however natural, are "unpleasant."

This dual vision functions in a number of ways in the story. There is the split between the physical grotesqueness and disease of the subject, which implies a connection between disease/ugliness and homosexual desire, and the shadowy beauty of the object of that desire. More important, the story embodies an intense consciousness of the split between the public persona and the private actor central to Williams's treatment of homosexuality:

> When around midnight the lights of the Joy Rio were brought up for the last time that evening, the body of Mr. Krupper was discovered in his remote box of the theater with his knees on the floor and his ponderous torso wedged between two wobbly gilt chairs as if he had expired in an attitude of prayer. The notice of the old man's death was given unusual prominence for the obituary of someone who had no public character and whose private character was so peculiarly low. But evidently the private character of Mr. Krupper was to remain anonymous in the memories of those anonymous persons who had enjoyed or profited from his company in the tiny box at the Joy Rio, for the notice contained no mention of anything of such a special nature. It was composed by a spinsterly reporter who had been impressed by the sentimental values of a seventy year old retired merchant dying of thrombosis at a cowboy thriller with a split bag of hard candies in his pocket and the floor about him littered with sticky wrappers, some of which even adhered to the shoulders and sleeves of his jacket.[13]

Mr. Krupper dies in a public place while engaged in a very private act that is never in any way literally described in a story which is a model of playful circumspection. Yet the gay reader immediately recognizes the significance of Mr. Krupper's position and the act of worship it denotes, as he understands the sticky papers from the candies which are stuck to Mr. Krupper's shoulders and sleeves. Characteristically for Williams, an act of pederasty satisfies two hungers simultaneously; the sexual hunger of the older man and the real hunger of the boy he feeds. (This pederasty/hunger nexus will reach its extreme in *Suddenly Last Summer* when the hungry, naked boys Sebastian Venable sexually exploits literally eat him.) In what amounts to a sexual pun underscored by the young cousin's final line in the story—"*. . . the old man choked to death on our hard candy!*"—hard candy represents both hunger of the phallus and of the stomach.[14] But Mr. Krupper, unlike Williams, is also private, anonymous in the audience of a theater, not the public creator of theatrical and cinematic fantasies. Krupper is allowed an anonymity and mystery forbidden his creator whose late autobiographical work fixes on the unknown, still anonymous, private writer/homosexual.

The young cousin's final line speaks to the public misunderstanding of the private act. To the obituary writer, the old man's death was the sentimental extinction of a man with a sweet tooth and a love for westerns. To the child, a hated old man choked on the products of the family business. The real meaning of the death is a secret between the dead Mr. Krupper and the young men who shared his box at the Joy Rio. It is private and mysterious, reinforcing and embodying Williams's little treatise on mystery. Yet we also have the judgment of the narrator, the only reliable witness, who tells us that Krupper's "private character" was "peculiarly low." In making this harsh judgment on his own creation, the narrator both validates Krupper's story by telling it, and colludes with his "straight" reader by judging it harshly.

As the authorial judgment keeps Williams on the side of his reader, so the smokescreen of mystery, created with what Williams calls "obscurity or indirection," allows him to turn Mr. Krupper's death into something both tawdry and beautiful. While acknowledging his reader's possible scruples and prejudices, he manipulates them, luring his reader to see Mr. Krupper's life and death as at least pathetic. Still, Williams allows no space in this story for alternatives to Mr. Krupper's Joy

Rio meetings. Homosexual encounters are furtive, impersonal appeasements of hunger. The operative word is "anonymous," matching Krupper's nonexistent public character. It is interesting to note as well that Krupper's partners enjoyed or profited from their encounters with him.

The devices Williams uses in "Hard Candy" are much more typical of his plays than of his fiction. One can see a miniversion of the public/private problem in Blanche's monologue about her husband in *A Streetcar Named Desire*. Blanche tells of "coming suddenly into a room that I thought was empty—which wasn't empty, but had two people in it . . . the boy I had married and an older man who had been his friend for years." This extremely discreet picture of Blanche's discovery of her husband's private homosexuality is followed by her public reaction to it on a crowded dance floor: "I saw! I know! You disgust me . . . ," and then by his public act of suicide.[15] Once made public, Allan's homosexuality becomes unbearable for him: he cannot deal with public disapproval.

Suddenly Last Summer weaves an interesting set of variations on the theme of exposure for the homosexual artist. Sebastian Venable has always been a private artist, wishing to be "unknown outside of a small coterie." The privacy of Sebastian's art is a corollary to his sense that his art is his expression of his religious vision; for the rest of his experience, living was enough: "his life was his occupation."[16] Yet that life was to be even more private than his work: "He *dreaded, abhorred!*—false values that come from being publicly known, from fame, from personal—exploitation."[17] But Sebastian's private life became a public matter when his cousin/wife witnessed his death and devouring at the hands of adolescent boys Sebastian had sexually exploited. To protect Sebastian's privacy, his mother will have Sebastian's widow lobotomized.

Homosexuality in *Suddenly Last Summer* is linked with Sebastian's brutal, carnivorous sense of life, but it is also linked with Williams's private sexual proclivities. Sebastian connects sex with appetite:

> Cousin Sebastian said he was famished for blonds, he was fed up with the dark ones and was famished for blonds. . . . [T]hat's how he talked about people, as if they were—items on a menu—.[18]

Donald Spoto argues convincingly for a strong autobiographical element in *Suddenly Last Summer*, nowhere clearer than in this speech. While in Italy in 1948, Williams wrote Donald Windham: "[Prokosch] says that Florence is full of blue-eyed blonds that are very tender hearted and 'not at all mercenary'. We were both getting an appetite for blonds as the Roman gentry are all sort of dusky types."[19] Sebastian's unfeeling sexual exploitation is as much a dramatization of the playwright as is Sebastian's pill-popping and confused sense of private and public personae.

Cat on a Hot Tin Roof, written around the same time as "Hard Candy," is the most vivid dramatic embodiment of Williams's mixed signals regarding homosexuality and his obsession with public exposure. *Cat* takes place in the bedroom once occupied by Jack Straw and Peter Ochello, a room dominated by the large double bed the lovers shared for thirty years. The plantation the ailing Big Daddy now controls, and which is now being fought over by his potential heirs, was inherited from Straw and Ochello. In ways both financial and sexual, the legacy of these two lovers lies at the heart of the play, and the love of Jack Straw and Peter Ochello stands as a counter to the compromised heterosexual relationships we see played out. Their relationship, the reader is told in the stage directions, *"must have involved a tenderness which was uncommon,"*[20] yet the audience never hears the relationship spoken of in positive terms. Straw and Ochello do not carry the freight of negative stereotypes other Williams homosexuals carry: they are not frail like Blanche DuBois's suicidal husband; nor voracious pederasts like Sebastian Venable, the poet-martyr of *Suddenly Last Summer*; nor are they self-hating like Skipper, the other homosexual ghost in *Cat*. Yet, beyond the stage directions, there is no positive language for Straw and Ochello, who be-

---

come in the action of the play the targets for Brick's homophobic diatribes.

Straw and Ochello's heir was Big Daddy Pollitt, the cigar-smoking, virile patriarch who admits to loving only two things, his "twenty-eight thousand acres of the richest land this side of the Valley Nile!"[21] and his handsome, ex-athlete son, Brick, who has turned into a drunken recluse since the death of his best friend, Skipper. The central scene in the play is a violent confrontation between patriarch and troubled son in which Big Daddy tries to get at the truth of Brick's relationship with Skipper.

Williams's stage direction tells the reader that Big Daddy "*leaves a lot unspoken*" as he tells Brick of his young years as a hobo and of being taken in and given a job by Jack Straw and Peter Ochello.[22] The implication of the stage direction, and other hints Big Daddy gives in the scene, is that homosexual behavior is not alien to Big Daddy, who "knocked around in [his] time." Yet Brick is so terrified of being called "queer" that he cannot listen to what his father is trying to tell him:

> *Big Daddy:* . . . I bummed, I bummed this country till I was—
> *Brick:* Whose suggestion, who else's suggestion is it?
> *Big Daddy:* Slept in hobo jungles and railroad Y's and flophouses in all cities before I—
> *Brick:* Oh, you think so, too, you call me your son and a queer. Oh! Maybe that's why you put Maggie and me in this room that was Jack Straw's and Peter Ochello's, in which that pair of old sisters slept in a double bed where both of 'em died!
> *Big Daddy: Now just don't go throwing rocks at*—[23]

The exchange is a brilliant reversal of expectation: the object of suspicion will not listen to expressions of understanding and tolerance, countering them with homophobic ranting. Brick is obsessed, terrified of being called a "queer," and conscious of the irony of being expected to perform sexually in Straw and Ochello's bed. Big Daddy will allow no attacks on Straw and Ochello, but his defense is interrupted by the appearance of Reverend Tooker, "*the living embodiment of the pious, conventional lie*," an interruption that suggests that it is the pious conventional lie that forbids defense of Straw and Ochello.[24] The interruption is Williams's choice: it allows Brick's homophobic discourse to dominate the scene. In addition to "queer[s]" and "old sisters," Brick speaks of "sodomy," "dirty things," "dirty old men," "ducking [*sic*] sissies," "unnatural thing," and "*fairies*." Brick's acceptance of the pious conventional lie is heard in statements which sound like a caricature of the voice of pious respectability: "Big Daddy, you shock me, Big Daddy, you, you–*shock* me! Talkin' so—casually!—about a— thing like that." Yet his stated reason for his shock is not moral, religious, or psychological; it is public opinion: "Don't you know how people *feel* about things like that? How, how *disgusted* they are by things like that?"[25] Homosexuality to Brick is terrifying because it is inevitably public.

Brick's homophobia is part of his sexual/emotional malaise. He is painfully aware that his nonsexual, nominal marriage to Maggie is a far cry from the total relationship the bed signifies. Brick occupies a perilous middle state: he does not love his wife, with whom he claims never to have gotten any closer "than two people just get in bed which is not much closer than two cats on a—fence humping,"[26] an echo of Big Daddy's loveless sex with Big Mama and an expression of Brick's inability to combine sex and friendship or love. Yet he is horrified at the thought of a sexual dimension of his friendship with Skipper: "Why can't exceptional friendship, *real, real, deep, deep friendship* between two men be respected as something clean and decent without being thought of as *fairies*."[27]

Ironically, Maggie, Brick's frustrated wife, understands that Brick's friendship with Skipper "was one of those beautiful, ideal things they tell you about in Greek legends, it couldn't be anything else, you being you, and that's what made it so awful, because it was love that never could be carried through to anything satisfying or even talked about plainly."[28] Maggie knows that it is Brick's "ass-aching Puritanism" that puts him in such an unhappy position—that he would be better off if he had the courage to have a complete relationship with Skipper. But Skipper is dead as a result of his own internalized homophobia, and Brick has, as Big Daddy cogently puts it, "dug the grave of [his] friend and kicked him in it!—before you'd face truth with him!"[29]

The bed of Jack Straw and Peter Ochello represents an unstated ideal relationship which seems unattainable for the heterosexual marriages in Williams's play. In positing this ideal, the play is subversive for its time, yet the love of Jack Straw and Peter Ochello never seems a real possibility for homosexuals either. It is, to coin a phrase from Simon Gray's *Butley*, more a figure of speech than a matter of fact, and a rather paradoxical figure of speech at that, since the only positive words used to describe the relationship are silent hints in the stage directions. The only operative terminology for homosexuals the play allows is Brick's homophobic discourse.

Just at the moment that Big Daddy's dialogue with Brick reaches the crucial issue of Brick's relationship with Skipper, Williams offers a lengthy stage direction which echoes the rejoinder found in "Hard Candy":

> The thing they're discussing, timidly and painfully on the side of Big Daddy, fiercely, violently on Brick's side, is the inadmissible thing that Skipper died to disavow between them. The fact that if it existed it had to be disavowed to "keep face" in the world they lived in, may be at the heart of the "mendacity" that Brick drinks to kill his disgust with. It may be the root of his collapse. Or maybe it is only a single manifestation of it, not even the most important. The bird that I hope to catch in the net of this play is not the solution of one man's psychological problem. I'm trying to catch the true quality of experience in a group of people, that cloudy, flickering, evanescent—fiercely charged!—interplay of five human beings in the thundercloud of a common crisis. Some mystery should be left in the reve-

lation of character in a play, just as a great deal of mystery is always left in the revelation of character in life, even in one's own character to himself. This does not absolve the playwright of his duty to observe and probe as clearly and deeply as he *legitimately* can: but it should steer him away from "pat" conclusions, facile definitions which make a play just a play, not a snare for the truth of human experience.[30]

Williams begins this statement with a definite interpretation of Brick's panic that places responsibility on the false values of Brick's world, then hedges his bets by qualifying his interpretation, then moves the focus away from Brick to the problems of five people, and finally dismisses definite interpretations altogether in the name of "mystery." The last sentence of Williams's little treatise thickens the smokescreen: he wants to offer the truth of human experience without facile conclusions or pat definitions. Fair enough. But he seems to worry about such things only when homosexuality rears its problematic head. Of course, his printed warning is not shared by his audience, only his readers, but it allows him to proceed with a scene about homosexuality while denying that that is what he is doing. At the end of his statement, he directs that the scene between Big Daddy and Brick be "*palpable in what is left unspoken.*" His concern for the unspoken dominates this scene, and what is unspoken here and in the rest of the play is the positive force of the love of Jack Straw and Peter Ochello and the unrealized possibility it represents of a nonhomophobic discourse.

Love is not an operative term for the men in *Cat on a Hot Tin Roof*. It is a word used only by Maggie and Big Mama—the men can only wonder, "Wouldn't it be funny if it were true?"[31] Not able to accept the love of women, neither can the men accept the unspoken option of sexual male/male love. Nor can Williams convincingly offer that option. The tenderness Williams sees as the clear side of his vision here exists only in a stage direction: the cloudiness of homosexuality remains an object of terror, not of the act, but of public exposure.

* * *

While elements of homosexuality suffuse many of Williams's major plays, his later post-Stonewall works deal more directly with his attitudes toward homosexuality. He moves from indirection and poetic image to didacticism and thinly veiled autobiography; the problematics of Williams's treatment of homosexuality become clearer, if less dramatically viable.

Small Craft Warnings (1972) establishes a formula Williams will use again in *Vieux Carré* (1977): the antagonism between a homosexual and a heterosexual "stud," and the placement of a troubled homosexual encounter in the context of a chaotic set of heterosexual relationships. In *Small Craft Warnings* the homosexual character, Quentin, is immediately seen as out of place in the Pacific Coast bar in which the play is set, not because of his sexuality, but because of his appearance, which announces him as a stereotypical homosexual out of a 1940s movie: "dressed effetely in a yachting jacket, maroon linen slacks, and silk neck-scarf."[32] His face, "which seems to have been burned thin by a fever that is not of the flesh," makes him a brother to Williams's many aging male beauties, but here the wasting is an outward manifestation of the spiritual desiccation which has resulted from Quentin's sexual promiscuity:

> There's a coarseness, a deadening coarseness, in the experience of most homosexuals. The experiences are quick, and hard, and brutal, and the pattern of them is practically unchanging. Their act of love is like the jabbing of a hypodermic needle to which they're addicted but which is more and more empty of real interest and surprise. This lack of variation and surprise in their . . . "love life" . . . [*He smiles harshly*] . . . spreads into other areas of . . . sensibility.[33]

The result of this emptying is finally the loss of the "capacity for being surprised," which is the loss of imagination and, potentially, of the possibility of creation. Quentin speaks of himself here in the language of textbook homophobic "objectivity."

Quentin is given the profession of screenwriter, and the experiences he recounts are those of Williams with MGM in the early 1940s. Moreover, he now writes pornographic movies, candid depictions of sex, even as Williams's plays have become more simplemindedly and candidly focused on sexual activity. These autobiographical clues enable the reader to see Quentin's emotional diminution not merely as the inevitable result of a pattern of homosexual activity, but as a corollary of Williams's fear of the draining away of his emotional and imaginative resources that would eventually cripple his writing. He wrote Donald Windham in 1955, the year of *Cat on a Hot Tin Roof*:

> I think my work is good in exact ratio to the degree of emotional tension which is released in it. In a sense, writing of this kind (lyric?) is a losing game, for steadily life takes away from you, bit by bit, step by step, the quality of fresh involvement, new, startling reactions to experience, the emotional reservoir is only rarely replenished . . . and most of the time you are just "paying out", draining off.[34]

The spiritual waning that cripples the artist becomes here the inevitable cynicism of the aging homosexual who is so self-hating that he can have sex only with boys who are not homosexual, thus emerging as the most articulate and least interesting older member of the typical Williams gay liaison: an older homosexual hungry for the flesh of beautiful, young, heterosexual men.

Williams felt that Quentin's monologue is "much the most effective piece of writing in the play," and one does see in it an effective duality.[35] Quentin is suffering the physical and spiritual ravages of time and mortality, the great nemeses in Williams's world. Yet he also suffers for his awareness of the brutality of his sex life. The attraction of youth is the attraction of what has been lost emotionally, and the attraction to heterosexuality is to the possibility of an alternative to the "coarseness" of homosexual activity. Part of that coarseness involves the need to keep sex on a financial basis, a matter of distancing and control which Williams well understood—even his beloved Frank Merlo was on the payroll. (Williams saw the male prostitute, homo- or heterosexual, as saintly.) Leona tells Bobby, the boy Quentin has picked up, to take Quentin's payment: "He wants to pay you, it's part of his sad routine. It's like doing penance . . . penitence."[36]

Quentin's expression of the homeless place of homosexuality as one cause for his sexual/spiritual malaise is reinforced by echoes from the other characters, who present an image of homosexuality Jerry Falwell would cheerfully endorse. The exuberant, sexually active Leona, tells Quentin:

> I know the gay scene and I know the language of it and I know how full it is of sickness and sadness; it's so full of sadness and sickness, I could almost be glad that my little brother died before he had time to be infected with all that sadness and sickness in the heart of a gay boy.[37]

And Bill, the stud who lives by his cocksmanship with women, who proves himself through fag-bashing—"Y' can't insult 'em, there's no way to bring 'em down except to beat 'em and roll 'em"—at least sees homosexuals as victims of determinism: "They can't help the way they are. Who can?" And Monk, the bartender, does not want gay men in his bar, because eventually they come in droves: "First thing you know you're operating what they call a gay bar and it sounds like a bird cage, they're standing three deep at the bar and lining up at the men's room."[38]

Williams, who did not want to "deal with the didactic, ever," has written here not the gay play he swore he didn't want to write, but a virulently homophobic play. The only positive possibility for homosexual experience resides with Bobby, the young man who accompanies Quentin into the bar. Bobby, Williams's typical fantasy youth, is onmisexual, able temporarily to equate sex with love and enjoy whatever experience comes his way. Bobby has the sense of wonder

Quentin has lost, a function of youth; all he lacks is the sexual specialization he calls Quentin's "hangup."

Williams's relationship to *Small Craft Warnings* was complex. He saw it, in characteristically dualistic fashion, as "a sort of lyric appeal to my remnant of life to somehow redeem and save me—not from life's end, which can't be revealed through any court of appeals, but from a sinking into shadow and eclipse of everything that had made my life meaningful to me."[39] The play was originally titled "Confessional," which suggests a very personal relationship to the creation. And Williams, to keep the play running long enough to prove that he was still bankable, appeared as Doc through the last weeks of the show's run, though, as Donald Spoto points out, his drunken and drugged shenanigans and foolish ad libs "advertis[ed] the very condition for which he dreaded condemnation."[40] Ironically, Williams's performances in *Small Craft Warnings* were taking place at the same time as his creation of his most antic public performance, his *Memoirs*, in which the tables are turned and the public homosexual totally overshadows the private playwright.

Not ironically, but perhaps predictably, the equally confessional *Vieux Carré* is a desperate mining of memory and early fiction ("The Angel in the Alcove" [1943]) for material. As with Williams's first success, *The Glass Menagerie*, this late work is narrated by the playwright as a young man, here nameless and, alas, faceless. The time is the late thirties, when Williams finally had his first homosexual experiences, and the setting is a boarding house in the *Vieux Carré*. While the play seems to present Williams's "coming out," the liberation is, at best, conditional. *Vieux Carré* is the most vivid evidence for the consistency of Williams's attitude toward homosexuality: in the 1943 story and the 1977 play, homosexual activities are characterized as "perversions of longing" experienced by the young writer and an artist who is fatally diseased. Williams once again presents his past life and his past material in such a way as to expose himself to his audience while anticipating and affirming their homophobic reaction.

* * *

In his poem "Intimations" Williams states:

> I do not think that I ought to appear in public
> below the shoulders.
>   Below the collar bone
> I am swathed in bandages already.
> I have received no serious wound as yet
> but I am expecting several.
> A slant of light reminds me of iron lances;
> my belly shudders and my loins contract.[41]

While the poem is about mortality, it also suggests Williams's sense of separation from his own physicality and sexuality as well as his confusion of private and public selves. In "Intimations" only the mind is public: the body, of which only the belly and loins are specifically mentioned—appetite and sexuality—are private and already "swathed in bandages" to cover their disease. This is a regrettably fitting self-image for Williams the homosexual and for the homosexuality he depicted throughout his career.

From *South Atlantic Quarterly* 88, no. 1 (Winter 1989): 161-179. Copyright © 1989 by Duke University Press. All rights reserved. Used by permission of the publisher.

Notes

Thanks to my research assistant, Christopher Busiel.

1. Lee Barton, "Why Do Playwrights Hide Their Homosexuality," *New York Times*, 23 January 1972.

2. Paul Bailey, "Dead Stork," *New Statesman*, 4 July 1975, 29.

3. Edward A. Sklepowitch, "In Pursuit of the Lyric Quarry: The Image of the Homosexual in Tennessee Williams' Prose Fiction," in *Tennessee Williams: A Tribute*, ed. Jac Tharpe (Jackson, Miss., 1977), 526.

4. Dotson Rader, "The Art of Theatre: Tennessee Williams," in *Conversations with Tennessee Williams*, ed. Albert J. Devlin (Jackson, Miss., 1986), 344.

5. Dotson Rader, *Tennessee: Cry of the Heart* (Garden City, N.Y., 1985), 153, 289.

6. Donald Spoto, *The Kindness of Strangers: The Life of Tennessee Williams* (New York, 1986), 319.

7. Ibid., 355.

8. Tennessee Williams, *Memoirs* (New York, 1975), 162.

9. Spoto, *Kindness of Strangers*, 81.

10. Tennessee Williams, *Moise and the World of Reason* (New York, 1975), 45.

11. Tennessee Williams, "Hard Candy," in *Collected Stories* (New York, 1985), 337; emphasis mine.

12. Ibid., 340.

13. Ibid., 345. "Hard Candy" is one of two stories ("The Mysteries of the Joy Rio" is the other) in which aging, diseased, fat homosexual men go to the former opera house, now a faded movie theater, to die while reliving their homosexual fantasies.

14. Ibid., 346.

15. Tennessee Williams, *A Streetcar Named Desire* (New York, 1947), 109.

16. Tennessee Williams, *Suddenly Last Summer* (New York, 1958).

17. Ibid., 17.

18. Ibid., 40.

19. *Tennessee Williams' Letters to Donald Windham: 1940-1965*, ed. Donald Windham (New York, 1977), 215.

20. Tennessee Williams, *Cat on a Hot Tin Roof* (New York, 1955), 15.

21. Ibid., 88.

22. Ibid., 118.

23. Ibid., 117-18.

24. Ibid., 118.

25. Ibid., 121.

26. Ibid., 125.

27. Ibid., 122.

28. Ibid., 58.

29. Ibid., 127.

30. Ibid., 116-17.

31. Ibid., 80, 173.

32. Tennessee Williams, *Small Craft Warnings* (New York, 1972), 26.

33. Ibid., 46.

34. Windham, ed., *Letters*, 306-7.

35. Williams, *Memoirs*, 234.

36. Williams, *Small Craft Warnings*, 44.

37. Ibid., 40.

38. Ibid., 27-28, 50.

39. Ibid., 74.

40. Spoto, *Kindness of Strangers*, 334.

41. Tennessee Williams, *In the Winter of Cities* (New York, 1964), 62.

"sneakin' and spyin'" from Broadway to the Beltway:
Cold War Masculinity, Brick, and Homosexual Existentialism_____

John S. Bak

Homosexuals are not men who sleep with other men. Homosexuals are men who in fifteen years of trying cannot get a pissante anti-discrimination bill through City Council. Homosexuals are men who know nobody and who nobody knows. Who have zero clout. . . . Because *what* I am is defined entirely by *who* I am. Roy Cohn is not a homosexual. Roy Cohn is a heterosexual man . . . who fucks around with guys.

— Tony Kushner, *Angels in America*

No man's still got a *roommate* when he's over thirty years old. If they're not lovers, they're sisters.

— Mart Crowley, *The Boys in the Band*

The key to the recovery of masculinity lies . . . in the problem of identity. When a person begins to find out *who* he is, he is likely to find out rather soon what sex he is.

— Arthur Schlesinger, Jr., "The Crisis of American Masculinity"

When Walter Kerr criticized Williams in his famous 1955 review of the Broadway debut of *Cat on a Hot Tin Roof* for being "either less than clear or less than candid" in addressing Brick's homosexuality,[1] Williams responded almost immediately in an article for the *New York Herald Tribune*:

I know full well the defenses and rationalizations of beleaguered writers, a defensive species, but I still feel that I deal unsparingly with what I feel is the truth of character. I would never evade it for the sake of evasion, because I was in any way reluctant to reveal what I know of the truth.[2]

Near the end of his equally-famous rejoinder, Williams passionately defended his artistic stance, reasserting the need for Brick to remain heterosexual in the play:

> Was Brick homosexual? He probably—no, I would even say quite certainly—went no further in physical expression than clasping Skipper's hand across the space between their twin beds in hotel rooms—and yet his sexual nature was not innately "normal." [. . .] But Brick's overt sexual adjustment was, and must always remain, a heterosexual one. [*WIL* 72-73][3]

Worried perhaps that his message of artistic integrity would not reach posterity, Williams added to the published version of *Cat* the now-notorious extended stage direction, which appears immediately after Big Daddy's initial intimation of Brick's latent homosexuality:

> *The bird that I hope to catch in the net of this play is not the solution of one man's psychological problem. . . . Some mystery should be left in the revelation of character in a play, just as a great deal of mystery is always left in the revelation of character in life, even in one's own character to himself.*[4]

By not openly admitting to Brick's homosexuality in either case, and even blatantly countering it with his revised Broadway ending, is Williams guilty of dodging the crucial bullet that could have denied him critical and popular success with *Cat*, as Kerr and others have suggested?[5] Perhaps. Certainly, it was dangerous for Williams to write openly about homosexuality at a time when Congressional witch-hunts of artists were daily fare, as David Savran and Steven Bruhm have competently informed us,[6] and honest treatments of homosexuality onstage were not the stuff of Pulitzers,[7] an award Williams openly coveted. Perhaps what is equally plausible is that Williams found it more dramaturgically significant (if not also more politically subversive) to intentionally articulate the uncertainty of Brick's Cold War masculinity, the vagueness with which he, given the various contradictory rules and mores of his society, does or does not understand the limits of his male desire. For instance, the character Brick developed from the story "Three Players of a Summer Game" into the play as a psychologically castrated alcoholic whose sexual identity itself is now being challenged. Perhaps he questions his own sexual identity based on what others have told him homosexuality means. He may drink to hide these facts from everyone or to avoid contemplating them himself, either out of disgust for the world that has underwritten them, guilt in his role in choosing to sustain them with regards to Skipper, or fear that what his society and his family are intimating may in fact be true. To be sure, any—or, more precisely, all—of these suppositions are valid and, as I will argue, collectively essential to understanding the angst-ridden truth behind Brick's existence and the strength of Williams's play. For at the heart of Brick's reticence to name his relationship with Skipper is his inability to understand what homosexuality is or how it is precisely defined or even vaguely knowable—an epistemological mire for which Williams holds his Cold War society ultimately responsible.

I

Choice. Angst-ridden existence. Epistemology. The Cold War. Responsibility. Any faithful discussion of *Cat* within its contextualized Fifties must reckon with some combination of these words and with the two sources upon which they collectively converge: existentialism and Jean-Paul Sartre. While Kierkegaard's doctrine of the individual's existence with respect to his or her *a priori* essence had emerged more fully in the dialectical theories of Heidegger, Marcel, and Jaspers in the inter-war years, it was through Sartre that the American intelligentsia would mostly acquire its postwar knowledge of and taste for existential thought. Williams, at first only an admirer of Sartrean existentialism (even wanting to meet Sartre once while visiting Paris in August 1948[8]), would later count himself briefly among its many American practitioners. For in his 1950 introduction to Carson McCullers's *Re-*

flections in a Golden Eye, Williams wrote of the undeniable link between Sartre's existentialism and his Southern Gothic's "sense" or "intuition" of the "underlying dreadfulness in modern experience" (*WIL* 42), noting that while "the motor impulse of the French school is intellectual and philosophic," that of his American school "is more of an emotional and romantic nature" (*WIL* 42).[9] Intellectual or emotional, Williams's existentialism in *Cat* has undeniable Sartrean roots, inevitably refracted through the American prism of Cold War identity politics.[10]

Though maddeningly complex in its phenomenological explanation of ontology, Sartre's *Being and Nothingness* (*L'Être et le néant*, 1943) accurately captures the existential angst of a generation of men (i.e., humanity, though understood at the time in masculine terms) who, like Brick, contracted modernist nausea from having ingested the hypocrisy of sociopolitical identification consistent with their day. Accepting the premise that man is born devoid of any known or knowable essence to his life—be it a preordained (determinist) or an objectified (religious) one—Sartre posits that to avert the inevitable social typing that works to fill that void man must supply himself with his own essence (or meaning) for his existence. In defining his own individuality, he abates those fears that inevitably accompany thoughts of human meaninglessness when absorbed into the masses. Such thinking put Sartre at odds with Cartesian ontology, effectively inverting his *Cogito ergo sum* into *Sum ergo cogito*—I am; therefore I think.

Consciousness, Sartre maintains, "is not produced as a particular instance of an abstract possibility but that in rising to the center of being, it creates and supports its essence—that is, . . . its existence implies its essence."[11] Because it can never exist prior to Being (*l'être*), consciousness must produce nothingness (*le néant*) in order to define its limits (*l'être-pour-soi*), which is subsequently its immediate nihilation (*l'être-en-soi*). In other words, a person exists before he has knowledge of that existence, and once that knowledge begins forming, it defines the individual negatively through the recognition of what he is not.

However, once knowledge establishes the self within this void in opposition to the Other (*l'être-pour-autrui*), the *pour-soi* is forever encased within its own shell of defining nothingness and thus permanently detached from its immutable *en-soi*.

Yet, the thought of being is not enough to satisfy the state of being. To define the self, one simply must act. Given that each individual is born into a particular situation (and necessarily so since each *pour-soi* has this inescapable engagement with the world), he is totally responsible for the choices he makes. He cannot help but be defined by the sum of his choices, which are only rendered through his actions. Though it is not itself an essence, this power of self-determination pre-exists in him and challenges him daily with the freedom to choose how to define, and therefore give meaning to, his authentic existence (acting true to one's self and beliefs). To avoid choosing to act or to invoke anti-individualist axioms of determinism or of external paradigms (such as a philosophy, a religious faith, or a bourgeois morality) in order to justify one's action (or lack of it) constitutes *la mauvaise foi*, Sartrean bad faith: to live an inauthentic life, to escape the responsible freedom of the *pour-soi*, to accept social definition over individual epistemology.[12] Overwhelmed by the full implication of this imposing freedom and granted little means with which to access or explicate its precise nature on him, the existentialist experiences moral anguish, absurdity, alienation, and ultimately despair.

Existentialism, then, implies the concerted efforts of conscious man to assert himself in spite of all the external social forces working to identify him (be it Kierkegaard's corporate Christianity, Jaspers's *masse-Mensche* of technological conformity, de Beauvoir's collected ethics, or Sartre's *en-soi*). While the existent's essence (literally his past experiences as he lives them, which constitute the sum of his existence) is heavily formulated by the nothingness imposed upon it by the Other, it is ultimately the individual's responsibility to preserve his integrity by making honest choices with respect to those external forces. Already, in spite of the metaphysical complexities, it is relatively easy to understand the particular anxiety that permeates *Cat* and renders Brick impotent—physically, spiritually, and morally—in Sartrean terms.[13] Freely choosing abstinence, silence, and alcohol as active means to counter the gross attempts of his anxious wife, his prying father, and his pragmatic brother to package him materially as the wayward stud, the prodigal son, or the effete drunkard—all indirect epithets of his homosexuality—Brick becomes the archetypal existentialist hero. Once he recognizes his own participation in Skipper's death in like manner, Brick becomes the modern nihilist.[14] The basic question that remains is whether Brick's actions vis-à-vis his family, his best friend, and himself constitute bad faith or not.

Brick, it must first be acknowledged, is honest, even priding himself on having never lied to his father (*C* 3:111) nor to Maggie, which nothing in the play can contradict. It is, for instance, Brick who does not "want to fool" (*C* 3:35) Big Daddy into thinking that it was he, and not Maggie, who bought him his birthday present, just as it is only Brick who finally reveals to Big Daddy that he is dying (*C* 3:128-29) or responds to Skipper's confession of love for him with blatant disgust. Though unquestionably hard and selfish, each act is also honest and contrasts sharply with the sugar-coated lies (white or otherwise) that the rest of the family exchange as currency, and that Big Daddy, Brick, and undoubtedly Williams so detest. Similarly, Brick never lies to or for Maggie, supported by his ironic curtain-line in the original ending of act three and by his refusal to uphold her declaration of pregnancy to the Pollitt family (which also proves how Brick could not, in any real truth of the play, go back to her in the end, which he does in both the Broadway and film versions). His integrity toward the truth (for the moment, the Others' truths), then, helps Williams to establish Brick's authentic existence.

So, when questions of authentic existence (internal and external to the play) readily give rise to veiled accusations of a homosexual identity, both Brick and Williams are pressured to fess up. That both should respond to these charges in existential terms is equally telling of their situation with respect to the truth, not only in their all-too-real need to protect their respective privileged social stations from exclusionary homophobia but also, and more fundamentally, in their epistemological plight to negotiate what they know of the truth with what society informs them it is. Admittedly, Brick shies away from addressing the latency of his relationship with Skipper, which for many in (and outside of) the play is proof of it by omission (in Sartrean terms, committing bad faith):

Big Daddy:	Who's been lying to you, and what about?
Brick:	No one single person and no one lie. . . .
Big Daddy:	Then what, what then, for Christ's sake?
Brick:	—The whole, the whole—thing. . . . [*C* 3:107]

Yet, beyond the generality of his words and the suppositions they may entertain, we are given no single piece of conclusive evidence in the play that can isolate why Brick drinks or why he never names his disgust outside the term "mendacity."[15] Given Brick's honesty in the play and inability to articulate (let alone comprehend) complex problems, need we unconditionally read his reticence toward the provocative evidence leveled against him by Maggie, Big Daddy, and Gooper as a wholesale lie? Could it not also be that perhaps it is precisely this "evidence"—socially manufactured as it is through innuendo, hearsay, and imagination—that might be lying or at least promoting confusion in Brick since it counters his empirical knowledge of homosexuality? For in the play's final tally, it is surely only Brick who is incapable of lying, whereas all those responsible for the manufacture of his gay identity repeatedly demonstrate through their manipulation of Brick's truth that they have much to gain or lose in the balance.

Similarly, Williams's language in the "bird" stage direction explaining Brick's "mystery" also seems more to be hiding behind Sartrean existentialism than it does evoking it. Like his hero, Williams too appears to be guilty of bad faith in his intentionally obfuscated reply to questions concerning Brick's homosexuality. And yet, Williams had indirectly provided an earlier version of this stage direction in his McCullers introduction, long before the controversy surrounding Brick's "mystery" ever began raising doubts about Williams's artistic integrity. For his explanation of his Southern Gothic school's fascination with the "Sense of Dreadfulness" (one which Williams later echoes in his *Memoirs* to capture the "mystery" of his own life[16]) resembles more closely the existential angst just explored in Brick and thus makes Williams's "bird" comment sound more authentic:

> All of these things that you list as dreadful are parts of the visible, sensible phenomena of every man's experience or knowledge, but the true sense of dread is not a reaction to anything sensible or visible or even, strictly, materially, *knowable*. But rather it's a kind of spiritual intuition of something almost too incredible and shocking to talk about, which underlies the whole so-called thing. It is the uncommunicable [*sic*] something that we shall have to call *mystery* which is so inspiring of dread among these modern artists that we have been talking about. . . . [*WIL* 44-45, Williams's emphasis and ellipses][17]

In Sartrean terms, this anxiety of the incommunicable sublime, the nothingness that feeds the *pour-soi*'s epistemological encounters with the Other, results from repeated attempts to discern the self's truth from the Others' convincing lies, a necessary distinction if one is to stave off bad faith and live authentically.

Surely, if Brick were more philosophic than dogmatic, he would have reasoned something like this in response to Maggie's and Big Daddy's inquiries into the source of his alcoholism. But his inability either to articulate to others why he feels so disgusted with everyone and everything or to assimilate for himself this "experience or knowledge" results more from his lack of critical self-distancing from the truth than it does from his affected staging of it. Williams is simply resorting to the basic tenets and vocabulary of existentialism to explain Brick's dilemma.[18] However, if Brick (and Williams, by extension) has little else to specify the nature of his angst and is not shrouding it in "mystery," the burning question still remains: What did Brick know? Pure existentialist readings of the play are hampered, then, not just because they are stymied by the lack of certain knowledge but more because it is impossible for readers/audiences to penetrate Brick's mind and to know for certain what lies behind the spoken and unspoken. As such, it is difficult for them to imagine how Brick could not know if he were gay or not (thus inherently lying behind his "mendacity") or how Williams could contend truthfully that such basic knowledge of sexual identity in Brick ever posed an epistemological dilemma in the first place (thus disingenuously posturing behind his "mystery"). Their doubts, to be sure, are just.

We should remember, however, that even *Being and Nothingness* was not written in a political vacuum. Influenced to a great extent by the spread of Nazi collaborators in France and shaped by Sartre's eventual incarceration in 1941 for his role in the Resistance, the essay's self-as-activist credo flirts openly with nationalist sedition against the Occupation. Thus *Cat*'s existentialism too can—and should—be studied as a product of its own incendiary times. If we read the play precisely as an epistemological inquiry into the politics that governed Cold War identities, then what we discover is an existentially honest Brick, whose situation fails to sustain in him the nothingness he needs to determine the truth, and a dramatically honest Williams, whose locating of those external forces at work on Brick may begin with Maggie, Big Daddy, and Gooper but, and perhaps more importantly, ends with implicating everyone who makes up Brick's society, Williams's 1955 audience and reader included. As real questions of identity pass from the metaphysical to the political, as they certainly did for many a gay man in the hyper-homophobic Fifties, purely theoretical concepts like bad faith seem arbitrary at best, dangerous at worse. In Cold War terms, Williams expresses existentialism in *Cat* not in phenomenological but rather in sociopolitical terms. Despite the open secret of his own homosexuality during the Fifties with Frank Merlo, Williams clearly understood Sartre's Other in America as the powerful entities of government, commerce, and Hollywood, whose job it was precisely to manufacture appearance.

Robert J. Corber and Suzanne Clark, for example, explore the problems of sexual identity responsible not only for the resultant hypermasculinity that infused Cold War discourse, but also a nation's sexual self-destruction, captured to some extent by Arthur M. Schlesinger, Jr.'s 1958 essay "The Crisis of American Masculinity" and *Look* magazine's 1958 series on "The Decline of the American Male."[19] To counter the effects of this post-World War II challenge to American masculinity, political men consciously resorted to poignant heterosexist language or affected masculine sensibilities, both of which helped to project a strong national image abroad as much as it did stave off sexual suspicion at home. As Corber and Clark separately argue, the American male was effectively on trial to prove that he had the muster to earn the respect of a nation built on the myth of the cowboy warrior. At a time when identity was essentially what others considered it to be, regardless of the truth about where one's political or sexual sympathies lay, American men had to perform their masculinity or effectuate it by ridiculing the effeminacy in others.

Just as some men named names or draped themselves in the American flag in order to project this image and thus avert communist suspicion that inextricably accompanied the effete male, others resorted to more proactive sexual politics: privileging the "inflated manly bravado, the hard/soft dualisms, the excessive scorn for the feminine, and the language of perversion and penetration in so much political discourse of the early Cold War era" in order to separate and ostracize unAmerican (i.e., unmanly) men from the healthy, heteromasculine stock.[20] By assigning alleged communist sympathizers and their fellow travelers effeminate characteristics in contrast with their own more masculine ones, these voices of national identity—from Washington (such as George F. Kennan and J. Edgar Hoover, to say nothing of

Nixon and McCarthy) to Hollywood (including, though certainly not limited to, those men like John Wayne speaking through such popular films as *The Red Menace* [1949] and *Big Jim McLain* [1952])— effectively controlled identity politics for more than a decade. Their message was loud and clear: the only true American male was, in Clark's terms, the "hyper-male," the Cold Warrior: "reasonable, penetrating, vigorous, and healthy."[21]

Every political action generates a critical reaction, and Cold War America was not without its doves, though they were arguably more vocal in the American theatres than in the Capitol's rotunda. John Proctor, Tom Lee, Bo Decker and Virgil Blessing, Kilroy and Val Xavier on stage, and Matthew Garth (Montgomery Clift), Terry Malloy (Marlon Brando), and Jim Stark (James Dean) on screen reflected the liberal's vision of the masculine male whose softness deliberately countered Washington's hard-line gender propaganda (with these last three film stars successfully sporting the cowboy-warrior image while playing characters nonetheless thoughtful and sensitive). Choked daily with images of these two diametrically-opposed realities of proper manly thought and conduct, what was the average white American male to think or do? The question, Clark posits, "plunged American men into a confusion about identities that literature as well as mass culture struggled to address."[22]

With a political discourse delineating hard from soft, penetrating from penetrated, and a national conscience reflecting its uneasy melange, many American men like Brick who did not know with which to identify often found themselves trapped in what Richard Vowles pertinently calls "that shadowy no-man's land between hetero- and homosexuality."[23] Publicly, Brick is the archetype of heteromasculine America, with his good looks, his strong athletic build, and his fawning wife cheering him on from the sidelines as he scores the winning touchdown in the championship bowl game. Privately, he is its anathema, with his suspiciously intense relationship with his best friend Skipper, his refusal to sleep with the seductive Maggie, and his emasculating alcoholism that has resulted from one or the other, or both. Caught in the archetypal Sartrean struggle between authentic self-actualization and inauthentic bad faith, Brick freely chooses the bottle, an act which simultaneously diverts thoughts of social responsibility in Skipper's death as well as sexual responsibility toward his agitated wife. Like other existentialist heroes in the Fifties, then, Brick struggles to authenticate his existence by denying all external efforts to assert its essence; however, unlike those other heroes, the origins of Brick's epistemological disgust are fused with questions surrounding his sexual orientation, making his form of existentialism sexual in nature and inevitably entwined with the externalized forces at work on him internally as well.

II

In *The Second Sex* (*Le Deuxième sex*, 1949), Simone de Beauvoir, Sartre's significant/intellectual other, applies Sartrean existentialism to define the existence/essence dualism of modernist woman, whose own *a priori* lack of female selfhood is further compounded by the fact that feminine essence is singularly imposed upon a woman from forces outside her body. This is the essential meaning behind her now famous phrase, "One is not born, but rather becomes, a woman."[24] In the introduction, for example, she notes that her "perspective is that of existentialist ethics," almost singularly Sartre's:

> Every subject plays his part as such specifically through exploits or projects that serve as a mode of transcendence; he achieves liberty only through a continual reaching out towards other liberties. . . . Every time transcendence falls back into immanence, stagnation, there is a degradation of existence into the *"en-soi"* . . . and of liberty into constraint and contingence. This downfall represents a moral fault if the subject consents to it; if it is inflicted upon him, it spells frustration and oppression. In both cases it is an absolute evil. [*SS* 28]

Yet, because she implicates human nature in sexual terms (a woman and not a man), whereas Sartre had argued strictly in asexual terms of "being" (again, though, understood by many to be masculine), she cannot avoid the "passive" existence that Sartre had argued is "truly unthinkable" (*BN* 16).[25] By asserting "the sexual role of woman is largely passive" (*SS* 419) and still arguing for woman's independently formed essence, de Beauvoir paradoxically challenges Sartre's existentialism and remains loyal to it.

To be sure, since precisely "men compel her to assume the status of the Other," woman is forever doomed to transitiveness and thus prohibited from ever transcending to "another ego (consciousness) which is essential and sovereign" (*SS* 29)—in effect, being only the sexual equivalent of Sartre's *pour-autrui*. For this reason, de Beauvoir writes, "Woman is not a completed reality, but rather a becoming, and it is in her becoming that she should be compared with man; that is to say, her *possibilities* should be defined" (*SS* 66). Therefore, the "drama of women lies in this conflict between the fundamental aspirations of subject (ego)—who always regards the self as essential—and the compulsions of a *situation* in which she is inessential" (*SS* 29, my emphasis). As it is "civilization as a whole that produces this creature" (*SS* 295), de Beauvoir can no longer adhere strictly to pure existential thought; woman's social position vis-à-vis man simply lacks the freedom that Sartre maintains is essentially coextensive with human existence. Though she retains faith in the individual's free choice to act responsibly in establishing her essence, de Beauvoir cannot entirely exclude—as Sartre had effectively done in his metaphysics—the practical exchange of identity-forming values consistent with social constructionism. If Sartre's *pour-soi* saw the Other only as a means towards self-actualization, de Beauvoir's second sex saw the Other as self and thus could not pretend that self-actualization was an inherent privilege of humanity. The existent was a sexual being, and sexuality inevitably played a role in establishing that essence.

As Sartre had already acknowledged, "the proposition 'Sexuality is co-extensive with existence' can be understood in two very different ways; it can mean that every experience of the existent has a sexual significance, or that every sexual phenomenon has an existential import" (*SS* 70). Yet sexuality for Sartre remains ancillary to the existent's transcendence. De Beauvoir, however, cannot but privilege this sexuality since woman-as-Other's transcendence depends upon her interaction with her own Other: "The existent is a sexual, a sexual body, and in his relations with other existents who are also sexual bodies, sexuality is in consequence always involved. But if body and sexuality are concrete expressions of existence, it is with reference to this that their significance can be discovered" (*SS* 77). Be it another woman or a man, her Other is inescapably sexually signified, and for that reason the "body" becomes "not a *thing*" but "a situation" (*SS* 66), again in the Sartrean sense. By emphasizing sexuality in the construction of an existential identity, de Beauvoir fills the gap of modernist theory that held Sartre and his purely suprarational definition of human ontology at polarities with those of Freud or Adler (who had articulated that development in social terms passed strictly through biological ones). Though more self-defined than self-defining, de Beauvoir's woman still nonetheless has the power to choose between the assertion of her transcendence and her alienation as object (*SS* 82), and this is how de Beauvoir finally returns to Sartre's existentialism. Even if "in sexuality and maternity woman as subject can claim autonomy," to be "a 'true woman' she must accept herself as the Other" (*SS* 291), placing her at direct odds with her own sexuality.

Already we have moved out of the pure notion of human definition in Sartrean existentialism and into the role sexuality and society play in woman's sense of autonomous self in passive relation to man. De Beauvoir takes the next logical step by looking at how sexuality specifically contributes to that defining matrix, studying homosexuality (in women exclusively here) as a natural/cultural phenomenon that further complicates the ordering of an individual's existential situation.[26] "Sexologists and psychiatrists," she writes, "confirm the common observation that the majority of female 'homos' are in constitution quite like other women. Their sexuality is in no way determined by any anatomical 'fate'" (*SS* 424). Loyal again both to Sartrean tenets of an individual's complete freedom to choose and to her own claim that woman is essentially an agent of an existent's transcendence, de Beauvoir explains homosexuality as a choice but one motivated by external forces: "Woman's homosexuality is one attempt among others to reconcile her autonomy with the passivity of her flesh. And if nature is to be involved, one can say that all women are naturally homosexual" (*SS* 426-27). Consequently, sexuality both objectifies and subjectifies an existent, acting simultaneously as the *pour-soi* and the *pour-autrui*. As such, she concludes, we need to be wary of "the many ambiguities the psychoanalysts create by accepting the masculine-feminine categories as society currently defines them": "The truth is that man today represents the positive and the neutral—that is to say, the male and the human being—whereas woman is only the negative, the female" (*SS* 428).

If Brick in many ways incarnates the Sartrean existential hero, then Maggie certainly appears to be de Beauvoir's second sex, a being whose signifying femininity is constructed through her negative relation with her two defining Others: Brick and Mae. As Brick's wife, she is Margaret Pollitt, the sexual Other who defines him as heteromasculine patriarch but whose "passivity of [the] flesh" equally depends upon him for self-definition. In the play, for example, Maggie would cease to exist (socially and sexually speaking) were it not for Brick; he is her meal ticket (and she knows it) and her defining sexuality since she is existentially bound only to him through her desire. As Mae's sister-in-law, she is Maggie the Cat, the Other's Other equally seeking to justify her existence through opposition with Mae despite the fact that she and Mae are pursuing like identities—mistress of the plantation. To secure her place in this world, Maggie must maintain both transitive identities. To fail as Brick's wife would mean losing not only the plantation but her need for reciprocated desire as well, something she attempts without success to relocate in other men (such as Big

Daddy's "lech" [*C* 3:23] for her). To fail as Mae's rival for Big Daddy's estate would mean losing not only her title as Big Mama's heir-apparent but also her feminine essence since her sexuality would not have served her in her defining situation. To be sure, Brick and Mae are everything Maggie detests but have everything Maggie wants; and Maggie recognizes that, in the heteromasculine economy of the Pollitt family, a child is what will ultimately secure that identity on both fronts.

Fertility is, to be sure, the leitmotif of the play, running neck and neck with sterility as Reverend Tooker's Stork does with the Reaper (*C* 3:72). If, with her five "no-neck monsters" (and number six on the way), Mae is a "monster of fertility" (*C* 3:22), to whom Big Daddy says he will have her "bones pulverized for fertilizer!" (*C* 3:72), then Maggie, "jealous [she] can't have babies" (*C* 3:61), is the childless Diana/Artemis who mythically killed the boastful Niobe's six daughters, just as Maggie says she would like to do to Mae's children. So too does Williams instill fertility in men so as to underscore its inevitable sterility. The macho Big Daddy seeded the plantation left fallow by Straw and Ochello so that it "got bigger and bigger and bigger and bigger and bigger!" (*C* 3:77) until it became, like Mae herself, the most fertile in the Delta. Later, the effete Gooper carries a "pregnant-lookin' envelope" (*C* 3:204), which contains papers that he hopes will secure the fertile plantation for himself. Both expressions of male fertility prove ineffectual, however, since Big Daddy's plantation will not flourish under Brick's reign and the contents of Gooper's envelope remain unexamined.[27] Thus, when Maggie returns from Memphis where her gynecologist informed her that "there is no reason why" she and Brick "can't have a child whenever they want one" (*C* 3:62), she seizes the opportunity to assert her Othered identity by using sexuality to realize a maternal essence. Literally ovulating at the moment and informing Brick that "this is my time by the calendar to conceive" (*C* 3:164), Maggie only needs now to coax Brick into impregnating her, which he unconditionally rejects. And therein lies her sexual existentialism: as passive existent to Brick's nihilist inaction, Maggie is forever denied the means to fulfill her essence. All problems are seemingly rendered moot, however, when Maggie announces to Big Mama in front of the family the she and Brick "are going to–*have a child*" (*C* 3:158).

Though her pregnancy seemingly confirms that essence, Maggie's declaration could eventually impede her long-term efforts toward self-actualization. For while Maggie's ingenious lie successfully assuages the anxiety produced by her sexual existentialism in that it confirms her maternal femininity (defining her as Earth Mother and besting Mae's Sister Woman), assures the family of Brick's heterosexual potency, and secures her the family fortune, it effectively draws Brick out of his insular world and forces him into asserting an identity which potentially could undermine the one Maggie has conveniently established for him. In other words, because her declaration is a truth that will soon be borne out (or not, as the case might very well be), it reignites an existential crisis in Brick, but one that moves beyond earlier questions of heteronormality and now towards those of homosexuality.

III

While de Beauvoir had effectively spoken for and to the women of her generation and of those to follow, her theories of sexual existentialism generated an obvious drawback. In working out her positive/ negative binary of male and female identities, she made men existentially and sexually inclusive. Around the same time that de Beauvoir was penning her feminist manifesto, Alfred Kinsey was proving that American men did not in fact constitute such a binary (even in purely theoretical terms), and as such any universalizing maleness was effectively self-defeating. In its attempt to provide a scientific taxonomy of American male sexuality, Kinsey's popular 1948 study, *Sexual Behavior in the Human Male* (which, despite its own delusions of inclusiveness, was only about the sexual behaviors of white, American males, from young boys to old men), inadvertently supplied clinical evidence that showed what de Beauvoir had been applying solely to women could also be applied to men, namely that man-as-Other not only existed but was omnipresent and fluid.[28]

Kinsey's study may have done more to damage the psyche of Cold War heteromasculinity, however, than it did to transfigure it. For among the surprisingly eclectic sexual habits Kinsey documents that effectively reaffirmed the hegemonic control heteromasculinity had in America was one that equally served to deconstruct it: the homosexual outlet. In the study's controversial twenty-first chapter, Kinsey records how almost forty percent of the total male population he and his colleagues had interviewed admitted to having had "at least some overt homosexual experience to the point of orgasm," though only four percent identified themselves as exclusively homosexual. Accounting for "nearly 2 males out of every 5 that one may meet,"[29] the frequency of homosexual activity in America led Kinsey to conclude that "a considerable portion of the population, perhaps the major portion of the male population, has at least some homosexual experience between adolescence and old age" without ever considering itself as being homosexual.[30] By the chapter's end, Kinsey had not only portrayed heterosexual America as the problematic source of identity politics, but he had also singularly dismantled the hetero/homosexual continuum fashioned in Victorian America that had controlled those politics for more than a half-century.[31]

The question Kinsey's report quickly generated, then, was not who was homosexual but what constituted homosexuality and, by extension, heterosexuality. For by arguing against polarized sexual identities, Kinsey had effectively blurred not just the boundaries established between sociosexual communities but also the political, economic, and legal precepts that had underwritten them:

> It would encourage clearer thinking on these matters if persons were not characterized as heterosexual or homosexual, but as individuals who have had certain amounts of heterosexual experience and certain amounts of homosexual experience. Instead of using these terms as substantives which

stand for persons, or even as adjectives to describe persons, they may be better used to describe the nature of the overt sexual relations, or of the stimuli to which an individual erotically responds.[32]

Cold War heteromasculinity had been dealt a significant blow, and more than ever before in the United States men and boys grew "confused about what they should and should not do to fulfill their masculine roles."[33] Left bewildered, defensive, and paranoid over the uncertainties governing traditional definitions of sexual identification, heteromasculine American men began demanding proof of heterosexuality, as much for themselves as for those who were (given these politically-charged times) inevitably to judge them.

What any sensitive gay man like Williams in the hyper-homophobic Fifties would have learned from Kinsey's study was that his sexual habits had confirmed a psychological abnormality no more than it had constituted a social anomaly.[34] What the average heterosexual man would have learned was in many ways what Brick reveals in *Cat on a Hot Tin Roof*: that straight America had disingenuously been reared into privileging certain signs of a homosexual identity, all the while destabilizing those signs through its own acts of male-male desire writ large.[35] To be sure, Kinsey publicly assured the gay community that they were not perverted and isolated, privately persuaded some closeted homosexuals to emerge and join their body politic, openly alarmed a bigoted and conservative community of the prevalent feminizing of the American male, and thoroughly confused heterosexual society, male and female alike, as to what caused, shaped, or even defined homosexuality. Thus, if Sartre's existentialism informed certain American men like Brick that their identities were solely of their own making (with the implication being that socially-formed identities were to be combated), and de Beauvoir's sexual existentialism insisted upon the fact that certain social imperatives could not be excluded from their identity, then Kinsey's homosexual existentialism popularized the de facto ruling that one's social and sexual identities were inextricably bound, both for the existent's sense of essence as well as for his Other's sense of that essence.

In expressing mutual appetites for male exclusivity and masculinist iconology but lacking the performative heterosexuality to anchor them, Brick is a Kinsean male through and through—a sociosexual conundrum, a Cold War signifier without a signified. On the surface, he represents what a significant portion of (white) American men of his era had aspired to be; underneath, he is perhaps more like them than either would have ever wanted to acknowledge or admit. A *"prisonnier des conventions et de l'image de la virilité que lui a imposée la société américaine,"* as Georges-Michel Sarotte writes,[36] Brick was simply for Williams—always the consummate Broadway playwright who knew well the politics setting commercialism against artistic integrity and who repeatedly portrayed this Cold War identity crisis throughout the Fifties—his best literary expression of this emerging queer *hetero*sexual in America.[37]

Though he is no longer of an age of sexual awakening, Brick is certainly of an age of social definitioning based on sexual conditioning. As such, Brick is now sensitive to the social implications of his and Skipper's relationship, but he was not always aware of them, and that is where his troubles first began. When Skipper was alive, for example, Brick treated their friendship as he had when they were younger, which significantly removes from it any stigma of harbored or conscious desire, regardless of how it was externally perceived at the time. While in college, he and Skipper belonged to a fraternity and played football together; given their youth and participation in a socially-sanctioned, all-male milieu, society did not challenge them. No one—Brick and Skipper especially—would have suspected that there was an ulterior motive to their friendship other than its youthful male-bonding or camaraderie. Life was presumably simpler then for Brick because he understood homosexuality solely as having engaged in gay sex, evidenced in Brick's story about the suspected homosexuality of a fraternity brother:

> Don't you know how people feel about things like that? How, how disgusted they are by things like that? Why, at Ole Miss when it was discovered a pledge to our fraternity, Skipper's and mine, did a, attempted to do a, unnatural thing with—We not only dropped him like a hot rock!—We told him to git off the campus, and he did, he got! [C 3:119]

In Brick's eyes, one was homosexual simply by what one did, not by who one was, with that act threatening the benchmark of homosocial American society (here, the college fraternity, but in reality any all-male institution, such as the Elks, Masons, and Rotary clubs which Big Daddy significantly despises [C 3:108]) that both Brick and his patriarchal society felt the need here to protect.[38]

Yet, when the primacy of his and Skipper's communion endured long after their college days and up to the point where they began sharing hotel rooms during away matches and refused to be apart, society began having its doubts. Maggie acknowledges this, perhaps in convenient hindsight, when she tells Brick that, even while on a double-date during their college days, she and Skipper's girlfriend Gladys felt that they "were just sort of tagging along . . . to make a good public impression" (C 3:57). Brick, though, failed or refused to see how any innocent, male-male bond beyond a certain age or off the football field alone could be perceived as queer:

> Normal? No!—It was too rare to be normal, any true thing between two people is too rare to be normal. Oh, once in a while he put his hand on my shoulder or I'd put mine on his, oh, maybe even, when we were touring the country in pro-football an' shared hotel-rooms we'd reach across the space between two beds and shake hands to say goodnight, yeah, one or two times we— [C 3:121][39]

As an icon of Cold War heteromasculinity and free from the stigma of having actually committed a homosexual act, Brick rejects their external readings of his and Skipper's relationship: "Why can't exceptional friendship, *real, real, deep deep friendship!* between men be respected as something clean and decent without being thought of as— [. . .]—*Fairies* . . ." (*C* 3:120). In not acknowledging/recognizing how society's rules of normalized sociosexual behavior had changed for him or, more importantly, why, Brick is perhaps only guilty here of failing to discern that modern social mores of intimate male companionship come with an expiration date, an idea Williams clearly expounds in the stage note that follows Brick's outburst: "*In his utterance of this word, we gauge the wide and profound reach of the conventional mores he got from the world that crowned him with early laurel*" (*C* 3:120, *sic*).[40]

In *Epistemology of the Closet*, Eve Sedgwick historicizes the changes in these sociosexual conventions that, in many ways, recapitulate Kinsey's startling numbers at the time. In arguing that the modern homosexual was not a fixed, sexual identity but rather a fluid, socially-heterogeneous type that grew out of a bourgeois society's developing need to police its gender borders, Sedgwick sides with the many social constructionists who, like de Beauvoir, began isolating the increasingly powerful role of the Other in determining an individual's sexual identity. Contending that homosexuality as a social identity sprung "precisely from the inexplicitness or denial of the gaps *between* long-coexisting minoritizing and universalizing, or gender-transitive and gender-intransitive, understandings of same-sex relations,"[41] Sedgwick intimates that the homosexual was not born, *per se*, but evolved gradually through the increasingly bipartisan agendas of modern scientific, judiciary, and political discourses that were attempting to qualify and proscribe the limits of male-male desire. In other words, she writes, "constructions of modern Western gay male identity tend to be, not in the first place 'essentially gay,' but instead (or at least also) in a very intimately responsive and expressive, though always oblique, relation to incoherences implicit in modern male *hetero*sexuality."[42]

The implication behind Kinsey's figures and Sedgwick's theory is not that certain men just shied away from admitting (either to themselves or to another) that they were gay, but that a good many men categorically separated a homosexual identity from a homosexual act so as to avoid having to do so in the first place—a phenomenon that significantly altered modern epistemologies of sexuality in America. Constructed homosexual identity based uniquely on gender and sexual inversion allowed for masculinist male-male desire, whether homosocial or not, to persist free from suspicion. Even communities of gay men themselves formulated such a distinction. As George Chauncey, Jr., describes in *Gay New York*, the gay world divided itself between the fairies (a gay identity) and the queers (a gay act), with gender inversion effectuating that distinction. While the queer male—the homosexual male who maintained the gender constructs of heteromasculinity—despised the fairy for conjoining homosexuality to effeminacy, he also privately lauded him/her for giving him the closet space in which to practice his homosexual tastes among heteromasculine, middle-class culture.[43] Thus if Cold War heteromasculinity had responded to its crisis of masculinity by extracting homosexuality from sexual performativity alone and relocating it instead in an effeminate identity, then Cold War homomasculinity had effectively done the same. But with the fairy safely catalogued as the (homo)sexual Other, what then distinguished the two forms of masculinity from each other?

It is precisely this question that troubles Brick now and that has triggered his homosexual existentialism, for although he recognizes the obvious heteromasculinity in himself and Skipper, he cannot unilaterally deny their homomasculine traits and remain completely honest with himself. Caught in this metaphysical struggle to separate homosexual identity from a homosexual act, a dialectic upon which his very sexual identity hinges, Brick relies on what many heteromasculine and queer men before him had used to protect their sexual identities: homophobia, that performative tool *par excellence* to justify homosocial bonds and marginalize homosexual ones, as Gayle Rubin and Sedgwick have convincingly argued.[44] By systematically defaming all the gay men in the play, Brick enacts homophobia as unimpeachable proof of his heterosexuality. In addition to recounting his fraternity story, for instance, Brick denigrates the "dirty old men" Straw and Ochello by labeling them "ducking sissies" and "Queers" (*C* 3:118). For Brick, what separates him and Skipper from them is that he and Skipper had never slept together, with Brick still insisting on the primacy of the homosexual act over the identity because it is tangentially more viable as proof and also consistent with his existential nature.

For these reasons, when Big Daddy suggests that Brick and Skipper might have been in love, Brick immediately accuses Big Daddy of believing that he and Skipper "did, did, did!—sodomy!—together" (*C* 3:117), which was not Big Daddy's implication at all. Unlike most men of his time, precisely because he exudes heteromasculinity and unashamedly "knocked around" (*C* 3:115) in his time (he did not get to be heir to Peter Ochello and Jack Straw's plantation for nothing), Big Daddy offers Brick an alternative route to sociosexual identification, one which seamlessly integrates a homosexual act with a heteromasculine identity.[45] To claim this route, however, Brick would first have to admit that he was gay (certainly in identity more than in act) and then accept the responsibility of having rejected Skipper's confession of love for him—arguably his most flagrant act of homophobia. Instead, Brick rejects his father's attempt to define him (even if it represents the most enlightened definition in the play) and chooses freely to maintain his homophobia, which for the moment secures his heteromasculine identity and relieves him of any culpability he might be feeling concerning his friend's resultant suicide.

In retrospect, then, Brick's defining moment of heterosexual identification came when he refused to respond to Skipper's "drunken confession[al]" phone call of homosexuality (*C* 3:124)—an act which precisely parallels his ironic curtain-line to Maggie, as we will see later. In Sartrean terms, Brick simply chose to reject the Other's efforts to define him, for Skipper's admission of his own (apparent) homosexuality would implicate Brick's by default. In hanging up the telephone on Skipper and thus precipitating his suicide, Brick re-enacts his determining essence of heteronormality. Yet, Brick's guilt over Skipper's death and drinking to hide his "mendacity" with himself for "passing the buck" (*C* 3:124), as Big Daddy says, conjures up once again that Sartrean specter of bad faith. If Skipper were everything that Brick was and turned out to be queer (perhaps), what would suggest that Brick was not as well? Though Brick insists that Skipper's homosexuality was "*His* truth, not *mine!*" (*C* 3:125), there is no way for us to know if he is being honest or not. For Williams, however, such a question is finally irrelevant. Given his existential nature to know the truth of his and Skipper's relationship in light of modernist sexual epistemologies and to control his identity accordingly, it is easier for Brick to just reject Skipper's efforts, as he would later Big Daddy's. As both emerge from the nothingness of Brick's *pour-soi*, he sees them collectively as being predatorial in nature. In their mutual rejection lies Brick's truth to preserve his identity by himself.

Endemic homophobia was (and still is) undoubtedly a powerful performative tool with which to enact a hetero/homosexual distinction, but one exploited equally by gay and straight men alike to simultaneously excoriate the homosexual and secure one's heteromasculine alignment.[46] As such, it serves little in the way of truthfully informing the public sphere what Kinsey and Sedgwick said simply did not exist in the private one—the legitimacy of that binary. Brick's homophobia, then, in no way serves to prove Brick's attitude towards homosexuality, despite the fact that it has been the locus of critical readings of the play, homophobic and homophiliac alike, since 1955. While it admittedly does reflect his inner struggle to find a safe haven between homosocial and homosexual desire—not so much as to retroactively clear Skipper's name but rather to reassure himself that his desire would not have eventually extended beyond the football player's sanctioned embrace on the field but its required handshake off—Brick's homophobia is more a way for him to thwart any external effort to define him, since any social identity afforded him would be contained within his sexual desire. But if being the model of American masculinity and voicing public declarations of virulent homophobia were not singular proof of one's heterosexuality, what did Brick have to do to prove to his father, his wife, his society, and, ultimately, himself that he was not gay? Perhaps a more appropriate question should be, what did Williams have to do to prove it to his audience? The answer, Chauncey informs us, lies in proof of the performative heterosexual act.[47]

IV

While the uncertainties and inconsistencies surrounding the conventional mores of heterosexuality are undeniably at the heart of *Cat*, it is Williams's distaste for a society which first determines someone's private identity and then systematically marginalizes those who do not fit its model of normalized sociosexual behavior that mostly drives the play's sociocritical engines. Certainly, Brick had never desired Skipper sexually—at least not consciously—but his desire for Skipper socially over all other things now makes him equally susceptible to being labeled a homosexual since he can no longer balance his homosocial desire (Sedgwick) with a heterosexually performative one (Butler), which could at least legitimate that friendship.[48] Simply put, performing one's heteromasculinity required much more than being manly and hating queers, which Brick was successful at doing, with society calling for evidence of a sexual identity that homosexuality (which could equally achieve both) could not faithfully reproduce. At a time when evidence of an alternative family was perhaps what America most needed, Cold War society (both Brick's and Williams's) privileged the recapitulation of the nuclear family, the backbone of consumerist American society.[49] What else but his five "no-neck monsters" could have (albeit artificially) insulated the effete Gooper from similar suspicion?[50] For that reason, we have to return to Maggie's declaration, for in its attempt to secure her identity in light of her own sexual existentialism, it subsequently enforces an external identity upon Brick. And since Brick had systematically rejected Skipper's homosexual proposal, and Big Daddy's homosocial one, it is only natural that he should now reject Maggie's heterosexual one as well.

Because Maggie, like Big Daddy, has the consumerist need to sanction Brick and Skipper's relationship—for the finance-obsessed Maggie, to produce an heir to secure Big Daddy's estate; for the dying Big Daddy, to learn before his death that an heir will come from the only son he deems worthy of his legacy—she takes it upon herself to finally assert its heterosexual nature. The keenest of the machiavels in the play, Maggie manipulates society's unwritten handbook of male-male conduct by first psychoanalytically pouring into Skipper's mind "the dirty, false idea" that what he and Brick were "was a frustrated case of that ole pair of sisters that lived in this room" (C 3:123).[51] Of course, Maggie has no proof of Skipper's homosexuality except for the fact that he could not perform, for any number of reasons, a heterosexual act of love-making for her upon demand (he was, after all, drunk at the time, as Brick is now). Consequently, she next labels him queer and furthermore makes him believe that he is too—whether or not Skipper really is gay. Maggie wanted only to break up the friendship in question by forcing Skipper to sleep with her, believing, perhaps naively, that once she proved Skipper's suspected disloyalty or homosexuality, Brick would come running back to her, disgusted by the thought that his best friend turned out to be a cheat or a queer.

What Maggie did not expect in the bargain was the resultant challenge to Brick's sexual identity as well. For now, in adopting Maggie's method of supposition and dubious tactics in eliciting the truth (albeit her truth), Mae and Gooper can equate Brick's refusal to sleep with Maggie with his incapacity for heterosexual performance. This psychological impotence with regards to his seductive wife, coupled already with his exclusively homosocial preference for Skipper, provide this eavesdropping (and vindictively greedy) brother and sister-in-law with the opportunity to deduce Brick's homosexuality accordingly and thereby secure the plantation for themselves. Given HUAC's "guilt by association" politics toward American artists, who were communists simply because they were not publicly flag-waving patriots, Williams appears to be precisely critiquing Cold War society's role in determining someone's private identity, be it political or sexual, based solely on the absence of some positivist performative act. In his 1945 essay, "Something Wild . . . ," published in the *New York Star* a decade before *Cat* appeared on Broadway, we can already find proof of Williams's conscious efforts to denounce McCarthyism and HUAC:

> Today we are living in a world which is threatened by totalitarianism. The Fascist and the Communist states have thrown us into a panic of reaction. Reactionary opinion descends like a ton of bricks on the head of any artist who speaks out against the current of prescribed ideas. We are all under wraps of one kind or another, trembling before the specter of investigating committees and even with Buchenwald in the back of our minds when we consider whether or not we dare to say we were for Henry Wallace. Yes, it is as bad as that. [*WIL* 12-13]

When Big Daddy finally bellows his response to Mae's persistent intrusiveness into his and Brick's private conversation, Williams certainly intended it to be heard all the way from Broadway to the Beltway:

> . . . I hate eavesdroppers, I don't like any kind of sneakin' and spyin'. . . . You listen at night like a couple of rutten peekhole spies and go and give a report on what you hear to Big Mama an' she comes to me and says they say such and such and so and so about what they heard goin' on between Brick an' Maggie. . . . [*C* 3:82]

Such collectivist power is not only dangerous (it killed Skipper after all) but socially immoral and, ironically, entirely unAmerican.[52] When Big Daddy next warns Brick to keep his voice down because the "walls have ears in this place" (*C* 3:84), Williams cleverly turns his attack directly upon the viewing audience as well, where we too become government spies and eavesdroppers during this private scene between father and son; and when we leave the theatre asking ourselves, as Walter Kerr did in 1955, "Was Brick gay?" or "Why didn't Williams just come out and say that Brick was gay instead of hiding behind all this 'mystery' business?", we are aligning ourselves more with the rumor-mongering Maggies and Maes of the world than we are with the victimized Bricks and Skippers. In other words, we too are guilty of determining a man's sexual nature based solely on our reading of his social identity, and thus forever marginalizing him socially, sexually, and politically in the process.[53]

Williams only complicates matters further when he makes Brick, *à la* HUAC, refuse to confirm or deny the charges of homosexuality (as with Maggie and Big Daddy) or name names (as in the case of Skipper's alleged homosexuality) if he were not gay. Consequently, Brick is being forced existentially into either redefining his heterosexual role along personal epistemological lines of desire or accepting his society's vague definition of homosexuality with all of its transparent and plastic components. Like many existentialists, Brick chooses a third option: escape. Since Brick's recourse is through the bottle and not through suicide, as was Skipper's, alcoholism becomes the perfect cover—socially and physiosexually—to justify his impotence, and hence his refusal to confront or exclaim the truth of his sexual identity. Throughout the play, Brick only needs to wait long enough for his "click," for that moment of artificial detachment when he can free himself from his accusers or from any personal reflection he imposes on himself as a result of his homosexual existentialism.

Since any private answer Brick might be seeking about his desire is also contingent upon his accepting society's already gray rules of sexual definitioning, he cannot secure Charles May's "possible palliative" to his homosexual existentialism without first satisfying (or not) his wife's sexual demands. Therein lies the locus of his, and of *Cat*'s, problematic. While her demands that he return to their bed are successfully avoided throughout the play, parried either by his referencing the conditions of their earlier agreement to stay together or by his dependence upon the bottle, Maggie finally challenges Brick into heterosexual performativity with her public declaration that she is already carrying Brick's child. For everyone, especially Brick, this is Judith Butler's "defining moment of performativity," where Maggie's declaration "not only perform[s] an action, but confer[s] a binding power on the action performed."[54] Maggie backs Brick into a corner where he can no longer hide (or plead the Fifth) and has given him as much time to confront the truth of his sexuality as Big Daddy has in accepting his own impending death. So, when he rejects Maggie's love with his ironic "Wouldn't it be funny if that was true?" in the original ending of act three, it is not just out of the need to preserve his sense of self or to confirm or deny his homosexuality but also to reject all socially-based definitions of heterosexuality which Maggie upholds with her declaration, making his tragedy a more caustic indictment of society's omnipotence over the individual. Either way, though, Maggie wins, and Brick is forced into accepting one identity or the other on society's terms alone.

V

If existentialism describes the angst an individual suffers when faced with the choice of either accepting his place among the conforming masses or detaching himself from the artificial constraints of that external reality in order to assert or confirm his individual presence, then homosexual existentialism describes that same individual, now locked in the vacuum of gender identification and confronted with the choice of either proving his society wrong or right in its sexual labeling of him or detaching himself altogether from the socially artificial constraints which impede his process toward self-actualization. Though it in no way provides a final assessment of the individual's definitive sexual identity, homosexual existentialism does portray that individual's crisis of homosexual identity by exhibiting his struggle to negotiate his society's collective epistemologies of what heterosexuality is, or at least ought to be, with what he knows or thinks he knows it entails. As de Beauvoir writes,

> Like all human behaviour, homosexuality leads to make-believe, disequilibrium, frustration, lies, or, on the contrary, it becomes the source of rewarding experience, in accordance with its manner of expression in actual living—whether in bad faith, laziness, and falsity, or in lucidity, generosity, and freedom. [*SS* 444]

For Brick, certainly the former applies; for Williams himself, arguably the latter.

The true ending of *Cat*, then, is undeniably more powerful than its Broadway rewrite, which strength comes in part from its wry, ironic detachment of a man whose sexual identity can be nothing less than a social identity no matter how much he tries to preserve its private nature. Brick clearly understands the stakes behind Maggie's public declaration, as did Williams when he restored his ending for *Cat*'s 1975 revival and republication.[55] As such, when Williams added the extended "bird" stage direction to the play that addresses "*the inadmissible thing that Skipper died to disavow between them*" (*C* 3:114),[56] which John Clum sees as Williams "proceed[ing] with a scene about homosexuality while denying that that is what he is doing,"[57] he was not attempting to mire Brick's sexuality in half-truths or evasive rhetoric but rather to underscore the consequences—social, political, familial, and personal—of Brick's homosexual existentialism, demarcating more clearly the *Homo americanus* in him, that species of queer heterosexual males who have haunted the pages of the American canon since Charles Brockden Brown, at least.[58] When he changed genres by adapting "Three Players of a Summer Game" into *Cat*, Williams simply lost the necessary narrative thread found in the story to explain Brick's alcohol-cum-sexual dilemma in the play that his rather curious "bird" insertion now attempted to provide. What is most important for Williams here is that Brick in *Cat* remain heterosexual, for it better explains his struggle to negotiate his personal reflections on what homosexuality is, under-pinned no doubt by the stereotypes his society has supplied to him, as well as by his faith in the purity of homosocial relations.

Questions surrounding Brick's homosexuality are not, and perhaps should never be, conclusively affirmed or denied, for such certitude would surely depoliticize the play's intent of turning that suspicion back upon the audience's desire to know, implicating its own sexual epistemology as being at the core of the play's final tragic ambiguity.[59] As the narrator in "Three Players of a Summer Game" says in defense of Brick's private life, a judgmental voice that carries the weight of Williams's message in the story, "It is only the outside of one person's world that is visible to others, and all opinions are false ones, especially public opinions of individual cases."[60] In this respect, *Cat* is extremely adroit and sincere in its representation of Brick's response to homosexuality. The ambiguities are not in the play itself, Williams seems finally to be saying, but are imported by the prying audience, who, because of its own ambivalent attitudes toward male-male desire, is truthfully reflected in Brick. If we do not understand Brick, then we simply do not understand ourselves.

From *Theatre Journal* 56, no. 2 (May 2004): 225-249. Copyright © 2004 by The Johns Hopkins University Press. Reprinted with permission of The Johns Hopkins University Press.

Notes

I would like to thank Dr. André Kaenel, my wife Nathalie, and the two anonymous readers from *Theatre Journal* for greatly improving this essay with their sound advice and astute commentary.

1. Walter Kerr, "A Secret Is Half-Told in Fountains of Words," *New York Herald Tribune*, 3 April 1955, 4: 1. Concerning Brick's problem, Kerr asks, "Is he a homosexual? At one moment he is denouncing 'queers,' at another describing the way he clasps his friend's hand going to bed at night. . . . Listening, we work at the play in an earnest effort to unlock its ultimate dramatic meaning. But the key has been mislaid, or deliberately hidden."

2. Tennessee Williams, *Where I Live: Selected Essays*, ed. Christine R. Day and

Bob Woods (New York: New Directions, 1978), 71. Unless otherwise stated, all of Williams's essays noted in the article come from this edition and are hereafter cited parenthetically in the text and abbreviated *WIL*.

3. In an interview with Arthur Waters later that same summer, Williams reiterated this point:

> Brick is definitely not a homosexual. . . . Brick's self-pity and recourse to the bottle are not the result of a guilty conscience in that regard. When he speaks of "self-disgust," he is talking in the same vein as that which finds him complaining bitterly about having had to live so long with "mendacity." He feels that the collapse and premature death of his great friend Skipper, who never appears in the play, have been caused by unjust attacks against his moral character made by outsiders, including Margaret (Maggie), the wife. It is his bitterness at Skipper's tragedy that has caused Brick to turn against his wife and find solace in drink, rather than any personal involvement, although I do suggest that, at least at some time in his life, there have been unrealized abnormal tendencies. [73]

See Arthur B. Waters, "Tennessee Williams: *Ten Years Later*," *Theatre Arts* (July 1955): 72-73, 96.

4. Tennessee Williams, *The Theatre of Tennessee Williams*, 8 vols. (New York: New Directions, 1971-1992), 3:114-15. All references to *Cat on a Hot Tin Roof* noted in the article come from this edition and are hereafter cited parenthetically in the text and abbreviated *C*.

5. Brenda Murphy in "Seeking Direction," *The Cambridge Companion to Tennessee Williams*, ed. Matthew C. Roudané (Cambridge: Cambridge University Press, 1997), 189-203, notes that several critics "have condemned Williams for violating his artistic integrity by giving in to what they see as a manipulation of his artistic vision for profit" (189), which included altering the third act's ending to have Brick accept Maggie's pregnancy as proof of his heterosexuality. See also her *Tennessee Williams and Elia Kazan: A Collaboration in the Theatre* (Cambridge: Cambridge University Press, 1992), 98-108, 126-30, and Marian Price, "*Cat on a Hot Tin Roof*: The Uneasy Marriage of Success and Idealism," *Modern Drama* 38 (1995): 324-35.

6. See David Savran, *Cowboys, Communists, and Queers: The Politics of Masculinity in the Works of Arthur Miller and Tennessee Williams* (Minneapolis: University of Minnesota Press, 1992), 99-110, and 84-88, and his "'By coming into a room that I thought was empty': Mapping the Closet with Tennessee Williams," *Studies in the Literary Imagination* 24 (Fall 1991): 57-74, where he writes that *Cat* "dramatizes an almost astonishing bold rejoinder to the violently homophobic discourses and social practices that prevailed during the so-called domestic revival of the 1950s" (57). See also Steven Bruhm, "Blackmailed by Sex: Tennessee Williams and the Economics of Desire," *Modern Drama* 34.4 (Dec. 1991): 528-37, where he locates Williams as a "threat to national security" for McCarthy because, being a homosexual, "he harbors a secret which is linked to economic imbalance, and which makes his behavior transgressive" (529).

7. For a discussion of plays with homosexual characters or themes before *Cat*, see

Nicholas de Jongh, *Not in Front of the Audience: Homosexuality on Stage* (London and New York: Routledge, 1992), and Kaier Curtin, *"We Can Always Call Them Bulgarians": The Emergence of Lesbians and Gay Men on the American Stage* (Boston: Alyson, 1987).

8. Williams recalls in his *Memoirs* having met "quite a lot of artists" in Paris that summer but was "most interested in meeting Jean-Paul Sartre, whose existential philosophy appealed to [him] strongly, as did his play *Huit* [*sic*] *Clos*." He eventually did meet Sartre in Cuba in the late Fifties. See Williams's *Memoirs* (New York: Doubleday, 1975), 68-69, 149.

9. See Esther Merle Jackson, *The Broken World of Tennessee Williams* (Madison: University of Wisconsin Press, 1966), where she writes, "Williams finds, then, considerable support for his vision of humanity from Christian theology and existential philosophy, as well as from the modern arts" (74).

10. For two studies that treat existentialism in Williams, see Rita Mary Colanzi, "'A flame burning nothing': Tennessee Williams' Existential Drama," Diss., Temple University, 1990, which reads his canon in light of Sartrean tenets, and Deborah Marie Long, "The Existential Quest: Family and Form in Selected American Plays," Diss., University of Oregon, 1986, which only considers generalized existential ideas in *Cat*.

11. Jean-Paul Sartre, *Being and Nothingness*, trans. Hazel E. Barnes (New York: Washington Square Press, 1992), 15. Though not published in English until 1956, Sartre's book had been excerpted, with translations of various key passages appearing in such works as *Existential Psychoanalysis* (New York: Philosophical Library, 1953). All references to *Being and Nothingness* noted in the article come from this edition and are hereafter cited parenthetically in the text and abbreviated *BN*.

12. For a distillation of Colanzi's dissertation on Williams's specific use of Sartrean bad faith, see her article "Caged Birds: Bad Faith in Tennessee Williams's Drama," *Modern Drama* 35.3 (Sept. 1992): 451-65.

13. In addition to Deborah Marie Long, for another critic who has studied existentialism in *Cat*, see Charles E. May, in "Brick Pollitt as Homo Ludens: 'Three Players of a Summer Game' and *Cat on a Hot Tin Roof*," *Tennessee Williams: A Tribute*, ed. Jac Tharpe (Jackson: University Press of Mississippi, 1977), 277-91.

14. Jeffrey B. Loomis even calls Brick "a demoralized, existentially dread-ridden gloomster." See his "Four Characters in Search of a Company: Williams, Pirandello, and the *Cat on a Hot Tin Roof* Manuscripts," *Magical Muse: Millennial Essays on Tennessee Williams*, ed. Ralph F. Voss (Tuscaloosa: University of Alabama Press, 2002), 96.

15. All critical isotopes of Walter Kerr's initial comment have nearly unilaterally unmasked Brick's "mendacity" as a pseudonym for "homosexuality" and its sociopolitical component "homophobia." Foster Hirsch, for instance, finds *Cat* in *A Portrait of the Artist: The Plays of Tennessee Williams* (Port Washington, NY: Associated Faculty, 1979) to be a "shifty and evasive treatment of Brick's possible homosexuality," complaining that Williams "is obscuring the real subject of his drama with fevered language, and this plea for 'mystery' is a shabby ploy" (50), whereas Shackelford is sympathetic to how the play "confront[s] the taboo subject of homosexuality directly and without apology" (105). Dennis W. Allen argues in "Homosexuality and Artifice in *Cat*

on a Hot Tin Roof," *Coup de Théâtre* 5 (déc. 1985): 71-78, that the play is not even about homosexuality at all but that homosexuality appears on the surface to hide a deeper structure of "the sacralization of virility and the cultural worship of the male" (72), with homosexuality acting as a covert "artifice which conceals this latent ideal" (72). For more on this paradox, see C. W. E. Bigsby, *A Critical Introduction to Twentieth-Century American Drama*. Volume Two: *Williams, Miller, Albee* (Cambridge: Cambridge University Press, 1984), 85-87.

16. "Truth is the bird we hope to catch in 'this thing,' and it can be better approached through my life story than an account of my career. Jesus, career, it's never been that to me, it has just been 'doing my thing' with a fury to do it the best that I am able" (*Memoirs* 173).

17. The extent to which Williams fully understood French existentialism as a theory is contentious, but he certainly admired it and knew of its general principles. Williams did admit in a 1965 interview with John Gruen that "Perhaps we all understood existentialism before Sartre did." See *Conversations with Tennessee Williams*, ed. Albert Devlin (Jackson: University Press of Mississippi, 1986), 121.

18. Though maintaining that Brick's problem in the play is essentially metaphysical, Charles May cites this reference in order to show how Brick's flesh/spirit dialectic also assumes an existential nature.

19. Robert J. Corber, *Homosexuality in Cold War America: Resistance and the Crisis of Masculinity* (Durham: Duke University Press, 1997); Suzanne Clark, *Cold Warriors: Manliness on Trial in the Rhetoric of the West* (Carbondale: Southern Illinois University Press, 2000); Arthur M. Schlesinger, Jr., "The Crisis of American Masculinity," *The Politics of Hope* (Boston: Houghton-Mifflin, 1963), 237-46; and *Look*'s 1958 series in *Look, The Decline of the American Male* (New York: Random House, 1958).

20. K. A. Cuordileone, "'Politics in an Age of Anxiety': Cold War Political Culture and the Crisis in American Masculinity, 1949-1960," *The Journal of American History* 87.2 (Sept. 2000). http://www.historycooperative.org/journals/jah/87.2/cuordileone .html (28 Jun. 2001): par 16.

21. Suzanne Clark, 25.

22. Ibid., 1.

23. Richard Vowles, "Tennessee Williams: The World of His Imagery," *Tulane Drama Review* 3 (Dec. 1958): 54. Cf. Paul J. Hurley, in "Tennessee Williams: The Playwright as Social Critic," *The Critical Response to Tennessee Williams*, ed. George W. Crandell (Westport: Greenwood, 1996), 135.

24. Simone de Beauvoir, *The Second Sex*, trans. and ed. H. M. Parshley (1949; London: Vintage, 1997), 295. All references to *The Second Sex* noted in the article come from this edition and are hereafter cited parenthetically in the text and abbreviated *SS*.

25. Sartre adds, "I am passive when I undergo a modification of which I am not the origin; that is, neither the source nor the creator. Thus my being supports a mode of being of which it is not the source. Yet in order for me to support, it is still necessary that I exist, and due to this fact my existence is always situated on the other side of passivity" (*BN* 19).

26. As de Beauvoir is obliged to argue, if she is to remain loyal to existential

thought, "The truth is that there is never a single determining factor" in defining a woman's sexual identity. It is always "a matter of choice, arrived at in a complex total situation and based upon a free decision; no sexual fate governs the life of the individual woman. . . . Environmental circumstances, however, have a considerable influence on the choice" (*SS* 437).

27. Despite its ubiquity in the play (even in the Broadway version of act three Williams has Big Daddy deliver his elephant joke about the "excitin' odor of female fertility!" [*C* 3:205], which complements his earlier comment about Gooper's envelope), fertility is categorically denounced, for all the Pollitt "pregnancies" have produced undesirable "children": Mae's "no-neck monsters," all given "dawgs' names" (*C* 3:37); Big Daddy's plantation, which is "completely out of hand" (*C* 3.81); Big Mama's besotted Brick; and Maggie's lie. Only the gay couple, Straw and Ochello, is portrayed as having experienced a blissful partnership, in spite of—or because of—the sterility of their relationship. For these reasons, it is only fitting that the play should both begin and end with references to children, as they frame Brick's present sterility and bring into question his masculinity and sexuality. This anti-child rhetoric, of course, also reflects Williams's subtle attack against those who criticize homosexual relationships for their sterility.

28. In spite of its bone-dry scientific flavor, the Kinsey report sold an astounding 275,000 copies, remained for nearly seven months on the *New York Times* best-seller list, and became the topic of mainstream discussion.

29. Alfred C. Kinsey, Wardell B. Pomeroy, and Clyde E. Martin, *Sexual Behavior in the Human Male* (Philadelphia and London: W. B. Saunders, 1948), 650.

30. Ibid., 610.

31. The body of scholastic work devoted to the study of Victorian masculinity in America is exhaustive. Among the many excellent studies, see especially Mark C. Carnes and Clyde Griffen, eds., *Meanings for Manhood: Constructions of Masculinity in Victorian America* (Chicago and London: University of Chicago Press, 1990); E. Anthony Rotundo, *American Manhood: Transformations in Masculinity from the Revolution to the Modern Era* (New York: Basic Books, 1993); Peter Filene, *Him/Her/ Self: Sex Roles in Modern America*, 3rd. ed. (1975; Baltimore: Johns Hopkins University Press, 1998); and Michael Kimmel, *Manhood in America: A Cultural History* (New York: Free Press, 1996). See also Joseph Pleck, *The Myth of Masculinity* (Cambridge, MA: MIT Press, 1981); Elizabeth Pleck and Joseph Pleck, eds., *The American Man* (Englewood Cliffs: Prentice-Hall, 1980); Michael Kimmel, *Changing Men: New Directions in Research on Men and Masculinity* (Newbury Park, CA: Sage, 1987); Myron Brenton, *The American Male* (New York: Coward-McCann, 1966); Marc Fasteau, *The Male Machine* (New York: McGraw-Hill, 1974); and Joe L. Dubbert, *A Man's Place: Masculinity in Transition* (Englewood Cliffs: Prentice-Hall, 1979).

32. Alfred C. Kinsey, Wardell B. Pomeroy, and Clyde E. Martin, 617.

33. Beth Baily, *From Front Porch to Back Seat: Courtship in Twentieth-Century America* (Baltimore: Johns Hopkins University Press, 1988), 102.

34. In 1948, when Alfred Kinsey and his research team published *Sexual Behavior in the Human Male*, Tennessee Williams was already thirty-seven years old. Though Williams certainly did not need any scientific research to prove to him that he was gay,

the study no doubt would have supported Williams's natural sense of his sexual identity at a time when society and politics were growing increasingly vituperative in their
homophobic discourse. At the dawn of entering into what would be his only sustained
relationship with a partner, Williams could have drawn comfort from Kinsey's study,
whose popularity or notoriety (depending on the point of view) seemingly provided
scientific justification for a sexual practice deemed immoral, dirty, wrong, and, eventually, unAmerican. For more on Kinsey and Williams, see Michael Paller, "The
Couch and Tennessee," *The Tennessee Williams Annual Review* 3 (2000): 40-42.

35. In a letter to Donald Windham, dated 20 February 1954, Williams wrote,
"[T. S.] Eliot and Dr. Kinsey are the two nicest men that I've ever met" (*Tennessee Wil-
liams' Letters to Donald Windham, 1940-1965* [New York: Holt, Rinehart and
Winston, 1977], 290). While the letter does not prove that Williams had ever read the
Kinsey report (though I think it is safe to assume that he had, or at least portions of it), it
does show that he at least knew of Kinsey and had personally met him before drafting
Cat later that year. After citing another Williams letter—this one written in June 1954
during *Cat*'s rehearsals where he is asking Cheryl Crawford (*Cat*'s producer) to have
Kinsey recommend a good psychiatrist for him—Donald Spoto even claims in *The
Kindness of Strangers: The Life of Tennessee Williams* (New York: Ballantine, 1986)
that they had met "five years earlier" in order "to discuss the relationship between art
and neurosis" (217). If Spoto is accurate, then Williams would have met Kinsey as
early as 1949, just after the publication of *Sexual Behavior in the Human Male*.

36. Georges-Michel Sarotte, *Comme un frère, comme un amant: L'homosexualité
masculine dans le roman et le théâtre américains de Herman Melville à James
Baldwin* (Paris: Flammarion, 1976), 132: "As Williams once said, Brick's real problem is that he is a prisoner of the conventions and of *the image* of virility itself that
American society has imposed on him," my translation.

37. Corber's *Homosexuality in Cold War America* and Brenda Murphy's *Congressional Theatre: Dramatizing McCarthyism on Stage, Film, and Television* (Cambridge: Cambridge University Press, 1999) both study Brick within the context of the
homophobic Cold War. While Murphy fails to find any anti-McCarthy rhetoric in *Cat*,
arguing, in fact, the opposite when she says that Williams preferred avoiding controversy in the Fifties by writing apolitical psychodrama instead, Corber at least recognizes Williams's political agenda in how he "treated homosexuality as a subversive
form of identity that had the potential to disrupt the system of representation underpinning the Cold War consensus" and, in effect, "contributed to the dismantling of the signifying practices that naturalized the production of gender and sexual identity in
the postwar period" (3). Yet Corber, too, singularly views Brick as a closeted homosexual willing to sleep with Maggie in the end (which he does not in Williams's original
ending to the play) "not because he has undergone a moral transformation and is no
longer homosexual but because he refuses to relinquish the protection afforded by the
closet" (132).

38. Therefore, Brick's rejoinder to Maggie's accusation that his and Skipper's desire "had to be kept on ice" (*C* 3.58) ["I married you, Maggie. Why would I marry you,
Maggie, if I was—?" (*C* 3:58)], echoed later in his response to Big Daddy's overture
that their friendship was "Not, well, exactly *normal*" (*C* 3:114) ["How many others

---

thought Skipper and I were—" (*C* 3:115)], should not be read just as his incapability of uttering the word "homosexual" but also his inability to assimilate his and society's various (and at times contradictory) definitions of what homosexuality entails.

39. Citing the *Iliad*, Myles Raymond Hurd argues that, since Williams had been familiar with Greek literature from the age of twelve, the ideal relationship between Greek heroes Achilles and Patroclus is similar to "the equally ambiguous parallel relationship between Brick and Skipper" (63). See his "Cats and Catamites: Achilles, Patroclus, and Williams's *Cat on a Hot Tin Roof*," *Notes on Mississippi Writers* 23.2 (June 1991): 63-66.

40. Brick is not distinguishing his brand of masculine homosexuality from the typical fairy's effeminate one, as Chauncey has contended certain queer males had done. Such a conclusion would render Brick determinably gay and thus depoliticize Williams's polemic in *Cat* against establishing collective truths of someone's sexual identity. See Chauncey's chapter "The Forging of Queer Identities and the Emergence of Heterosexuality in Middle-Class Culture" in his *Gay New York: Gender, Urban Culture, and the Making of the Gay Male World, 1890-1949* (New York: Basic Books, 1994), 98-127.

41. Eve Kosofsky Sedgwick, *Epistemology of the Closet* (1990; London: Penguin, 1994), 47. See also David Halperin, *One Hundred Years of Homosexuality* (New York: Routledge, 1990), 10, and Jeffrey Weeks, *Sexuality and its Discontents: Meanings, Myths & Modern Sexualities* (London and New York: Routledge, 1985), 187.

42. Eve Sedgwick, *Epistemology of the Closet*, 145.

43. George Chauncey, Jr., 103.

44. See Gayle Rubin, "The Traffic in Women: Notes on the 'Political Economy' of Sex," *Toward an Anthropology of Women*, ed. Rayna R. Reiter (New York: Monthly Review, 1975), 180-83, and Eve Kosofsky Sedgwick, *Between Men: English Literature and Male Homosocial Desire* (New York: Columbia University Press, 1985), where she argues that "patriarchy structurally *requires* homophobia" (4), though the homophiliac patriarch Big Daddy seems to contradict this notion.

45. Big Daddy's distaste for his son's homophobia, as well as for men's clubs, shows an alternative view to homosociosexuality. For a reading of Big Daddy's sensitive respect for the gay scene, see Dean Shackelford, "The Truth That Must Be Told: Gay Subjectivity, Homophobia, and the Social History in *Cat on a Hot Tin Roof*," *The Tennessee Williams Annual Review* Premiere Issue (1998), 113-15.

46. As Kinsey notes, "The highest incidences of the homosexual, however, are in the group which often verbalizes its disapproval of such activity. . . . These are the males who most often condemn the homosexual, most often ridicule and express disgust for such activity, and most often punish other males for their homosexuality. And yet, this is the group which has the largest amount of overt homosexual activity" (384).

47. George Chauncey, Jr.: "Even as queer men began to define their difference from other men on the basis of their homosexuality, 'normal' men began to define their difference from queers on the basis of their renunciation of any sentiments or behavior that might be marked as homosexual. Only when they did so did 'normal men' become 'heterosexual men'" (100).

48. Judith Butler insists that performative gender cannot be voluntary and that sex-

ual identity can only be constituted based on what a person cannot choose to do, or be, through the act. Thus, gender should not be defined by some cultural privileging of a sex act, despite the fact that heterosexual society inevitably does. See her *Bodies That Matter: On the Discursive Limits of "Sex"* (New York: Routledge, 1993), 95. For the standard queer theory text that articulates how gender privileges heterosexual constructs through performativity, see her *Gender Trouble: Feminism and the Subversion of Identity* (New York: Routledge, 1990).

49. As a gay man who lived his homosexual life openly during the Fifties, Williams never dared to present any of his gay characters as being psychosexually sound. Given that Williams began seeking psychoanalytical help around the time of *Cat*'s rehearsals, as Michael Paller informs us, we might rightly assume that Williams himself could not fully rationalize his sexuality either.

50. As Filene notes in *Him/Her/Self: Sex Roles in Modern America*, "Members of the class of '44 . . . produced more children within ten years than the class of 1921 had borne within twenty-five" (178). Brick, potentially one of the those alumni, would have belied these cultural facts with Maggie, whereas his brother would have fit these numbers exactly. Thus, pregnancy during the 1950s was viewed as strong evidence of a performative act of heterosexuality.

51. Robert F. Gross, while examining the play's erotica in "The Pleasures of Brick: Eros and the Gay Spectator in *Cat on a Hot Tin Roof*," *Journal of American Drama and Theatre* 9.1 (Winter 1997): 1-25, notes that "Maggie lays down the law, and in so doing, gives male bonding a guilty conscience" (21).

52. Though directed toward anti-communist collectivism, this was also Arthur Miller's controlling argument in *The Crucible*, which appeared on Broadway two years before *Cat*. Williams's anti-McCarthyan diatribe here, then, just as in the second act of his *Red Devil Battery Sign* (1975) later, should be read as the gay complement to Miller's. Corber makes this point too, but his intention is to paint a Milleresque Williams as wanting "to critique the emergence of the national-security state" and particularly "those who had cooperated with HUAC" (133), like his director Kazan (which his why, Corber argues, Kazan really wanted Williams to change the ending), as opposed to a gay playwright trying to capture as best he could the sociopolitical unrest and uncertainty of his times. Though I agree with Corber that "Williams's oblique references to the national-security state simultaneously reveal and conceal his criticisms of those who, like Kazan, had betrayed former friends and colleagues in order to protect their career" (133), I feel Williams's scope with *Cat* was broader, extending much farther beyond that context of the Cold War consensus to encompass much of the history of sexual identification in America throughout the twentieth century.

53. Williams does not waste the opportunity in pointing this out either, for when Maggie says to Mae, who declares before everyone that it was Maggie who had bought Big Daddy his cashmere robe and not Brick, "Sister Woman! Your talents are wasted as a housewife and mother, you really ought to be with the FBI or—" (3.71), the audience too is being implicated in what amounts to its intelligence-gathering role as voyeur.

54. Judith Butler, *Bodies That Matter*, 224-25.

55. While it is true that Williams could not really have admitted to Brick's homosexuality back in 1955, given his free currency of the word *gay* throughout his post-

Stonewall canon, he certainly could have finally outed Brick if he had so desired. Few critics, gay or otherwise, would have chided Williams for long, since most would have considered that confession to be a *fait accompli* anyway. By restoring the original ending, however, for the New Directions re-release, Williams decidedly strengthened his resolve toward maintaining Brick's "mystery."

56. See *WIL*, 71, for another variation where "Skipper and Brick would rather die than live with" any acknowledgement of mutual homosexual desire.

57. John M. Clum, "'Something Cloudy, Something Clear': Homophobic Discourse in Tennessee Williams" in *Displacing Homophobia: Gay Male Perspectives in Literature and Culture*, eds. Ronald R. Butters, John M. Clum, and Michael Moon (Durham: Duke University Press, 1989), 161. On this, Mark Royden Winchell, in "Come Back to the Locker Room Ag'n, Brick Honey!," *Mississippi Quarterly* 48.4 (Fall 1995): 711-12, notes: "If Williams's treatment of homoeroticism seemed scandalous in 1955, more recent theorists have chided Williams for his reticence and evasiveness" (711). So, while it is easy to hold Williams accountable for his *seemingly* apolitical theatre during these politically-charged Cold War years, when we consider that even the Kinsey Institute for Sex Research lost most of its funding in 1954, can we honestly justify such revisionist attacks against him?

58. See, for example, Caleb Crain's *American Sympathy: Men, Friendship, and Literature in the New Nation* (New Haven: Yale University Press, 2000).

59. Steven Bruhm has argued a similar point about Williams and his relationship to the audience of *Suddenly Last Summer*, though he approaches it from an economic angle:

> By writing the dissolution of these boundaries, Williams writes a play which is much more subversive that its critics have allowed. Clearly, in this play, they who pay the money make the rules: both on political and libidinal grounds. But Williams has written a play for an audience, a *paying* audience, which has paid to hear a story about paying not to hear a story. In short, he implicates his audience in an economic complicity that allows sexual behavior while at the same time demanding that the story of that behavior be silenced. [535]

Though he is not speaking about *Cat* here, Bruhm obviously sees its application to the play, for in an earlier footnote, he writes: "It is my contention here that *Suddenly Last Summer* and *Cat on a Hot Tin Roof* are, among other things, indictments of the social structures that regulate homosexual behavior" (537).

60. Tennessee Williams, *Collected Stories* (New York: Ballantine, 1986), 324.

"Collecting Evidence":
The Natural World in Tennessee Williams'
*The Night of the Iguana*_____

Rod Phillips

The nature essay, the treatment of nature and landscape in fiction, and the role of nature in poetry, have all been the subject of recent studies, as critics turn their attention to this important—yet until now relatively unexplored—field of literary study. Not surprisingly, critical attention concerning nature has focused on the three main genres in American letters which have most often and most directly concerned themselves with the natural world: poetry, fiction, and the natural history essay. American drama, long seen as a predominantly urban genre—a product of Broadway—has gone virtually unnoticed during the recent resurgence of interest in nature writing. Such an omission is unfortunate, since there are a number of works in the world of theatre which can provide useful and valuable information about humankind's relationship to the natural world.[1] Although in this study I will limit my discussion to one play by one playwright—*The Night of the Iguana* by Tennessee Williams—I would like to suggest that there are many other plays, and many other playwrights, to consider regarding nature and American drama. An extended study of the natural world as it has been depicted in this "fourth genre" could yield some surprising rewards.

The natural world is strongly present in all of the major plays of Tennessee Williams. No matter how urban their immediate settings may be, there is always a natural or pastoral setting in which Williams' characters may take refuge. Often this refuge is a mental one—an escape through memory to a simpler, more idyllic past. Amanda Wingfield, the matriarch of *The Glass Menagerie* (1945), escapes the drudgery of her small tenement apartment by recalling the days of her youth on Blue Mountain.[2] Blanche DuBois, in *A Streetcar Named Desire* (1947), has her memories of Belle Reve plantation to soften the reality of her life in an impoverished section of New Orleans. Other Tennessee Williams plays put their characters in closer touch with the natural world, as in *Cat on a Hot Tin Roof* (1955), in which the action takes place on a plantation in the Mississippi Delta region.

But important though it may be in these earlier plays, the natural world plays a relatively small role in them—as either an idealized pastoral memory or a stylized local color setting. In Williams' 1961 production, *The Night of the Iguana*, however, the playwright relies on nature as a source of both symbol and theme to a much larger extent. More than any other work in the Williams canon, and indeed perhaps more than any work in American drama, *The Night of the Iguana* is a play which is firmly rooted in the natural world.

In his introductory remarks on the play's stage setting, Williams makes clear that the locale for this production be markedly different from the rather bleak urban landscapes which characterize *Glass Menagerie* and *Streetcar Named Desire*. In their place is the kind of natural setting that Amanda Wingfield and Blanche DuBois could only dream about: the jungle shaded veranda of the rustic Costa Verde Hotel. Translated, the name means "green coast," and Williams' description of the area supports the claim; his words describe a place almost untouched by man. In 1940, when the play's action takes place, he recalls:

> The west coast of Mexico had not yet become the Las Vegas and Miami Beach of Mexico. The Villages were still predominantly primitive Indian villages, and the still-water morning beach of Puerto Barrio and the rain forests above it were among the world's wildest and loveliest populated places. (5)

Into this paradise Williams brings his protagonist, the Reverend T. Lawrence Shannon. He is presented as a man on the verge of a breakdown: his suit "crumpled," he is "panting, sweating and wild-eyed." "His nervous state is terribly apparent," Williams writes. "He is a man who has cracked up before and is going to crack up again—perhaps repeatedly" (10). It is evident from his remarks that Reverend Shannon has come to the Costa Verde in search of rest and healing from the stresses of his job as a tour guide for a group of vacationing school teachers: "I've just been hanging on till I could get in this hammock on this veranda over the rain forest and the still water beach," he tells his old friend Maxine, the hotel's licentious owner. "That's all that can pull me through this last tour . . ." (25). Costa Verde, it seems, is Larry Shannon's Blue Mountain, his Belle Reve. But instead of relying on memory to take him back into a natural setting—as Blanche DuBois and Amanda Wingfield must—Shannon makes an actual pilgrimage to Costa Verde in order to restore himself whenever he feels "spooked."

As the play unfolds, it becomes clear just how far the Reverend Shannon has fallen to reach his current state of near collapse. The former minister of an affluent church in Pleasant Valley, Virginia, Shannon was forced to leave the pulpit following a scandal involving "fornication and heresy . . . in the same week" (58). The former charge was the result of a sexual involvement with a young member of his congregation, while the charge of heresy came about due to Shannon's final sermon in which he referred to God as a "senile delinquent." The sermon that Shannon preached that Sunday denounced all Western theologies which portray God as irrational, cruel, and vengeful. As Shannon later describes it:

> I mean he's represented like a bad-tempered childish old, old, sick, peevish man—I mean like the sort of old man in a nursing home that's putting together a jigsaw puzzle and can't put it together and gets furious and kicks over the table. Yes, I tell you they do that, all of our theologies do it—accuse God of being a cruel, senile delinquent, blaming the world and brutally punishing all he created for his own faults in construction. . . . (60)

After a stay in what he calls "a nice little private asylum," following his forced departure from his church in Pleasant Valley, Shannon entered the profession in which we now see him—a travel agency tour guide offering "Tours of God's world," as he puts it, "conducted by a minister of God with a cross and a round collar to prove it" (60). But Shannon has not simply been passing time with this job, he points out; his travels have allowed him to spend his time "collecting evidence" for what he calls "my personal idea of God" (60-61).

The "evidence" that Shannon has collected from his tours of the Mexican countryside has led him to a conception of God omnipresent in nature—a force which is not cruel, petty, or vengeful but is instead all-powerful and oblivious to man's existence. The God that Shannon sees in nature is neither nurturing nor punishing; he is raw power. "I want to go back to the church," Shannon says:

> and preach the gospel of God as Lightning and Thunder . . . and also stray dogs vivisected . . . and . . . and . . . and . . . [*He points out suddenly towards the sea.*] That's him! There he is now! [*He is pointing out at a blaze, a majestic apocalypse of gold light, shafting the sky as the sun drops into the Pacific.*] His oblivious majesty— (61)

Along with Shannon, Williams portrays a number of supporting characters, each representing a slightly different position on a broad continuum of attitudes concerning nature. At one end of the spectrum is the Fahrenkopf family—a vacationing clan of German nationals who amuse themselves by sun bathing, drinking beer, singing Nazi marching songs, and listening cheerfully to radio broadcasts of Hitler's shelling of London. Almost totally concerned with the sensual aspects of nature—food, drink, and sexuality—they are depicted almost as caricatures by Williams: "They are dressed in the minimum concession to decency and are all pink and gold like baroque cupids in various sizes—Rubenesque, splendidly physical" (15).

Critics have long seen the presence of the Fahrenkopf family as a flaw in the play, a group of minor characters useful only for the brief moments of comic relief that they provide (Falk 69). Director John Huston chose to omit them entirely from his 1964 film version of the play (Phillips 282). But strange and out of place though they may seem, the Fahrenkopfs do have their purposes in the play—and one of these, certainly, is to present a contrast to Shannon's view of the universe. As the Reverend Shannon hovers near the brink of collapse, grimly contemplating the dark powers of nature, the Fahrenkopfs bask on the beach and cavort about the hotel veranda with a gaily painted rubber horse, drinking and singing as the world around them prepares for another war.

At the other end of the spectrum are characters such as Judith Fellowes, the prudish school teacher from Shannon's tour group, who is blind to the beauty that Costa Verde offers. When Shannon sidetracks the tour and stops at the mountain-top retreat instead of a hotel in a nearby city, she charges up the hill to the Costa Verde "like a bull elephant on a rampage"[3] to insist that the tour be taken back to stay "in the heart of the city" (18-19). When Shannon attempts to convince her that the city's plaza is "hot, noisy, stinking, swarming with flies," and that there are "pariah dogs" dying in the city square, Miss Fellowes answers—apparently oblivious to the natural beauty surrounding her— "How is this place any better?" (19).

Later, as Shannon continues to try to convince her to reconsider staying at Costa Verde, he tries to point out to her that "there is such a thing as charm and beauty in some places." Again, however, Miss Fellowes refuses to look at the view outside her door, but instead focuses on the rustic conditions inside the hotel: "I've taken a look at those rooms" she tells the Reverend, "and they'd make a room at the 'Y' look like a suite at the Ritz" (28). In contrast to the Fahrenkopfs, who view the jungle landscape as an amusement park, it is for Judith Fellowes a prison—a thing to be shunned and avoided, in favor of the comforts of the city.

With the arrival of Hannah Jelkes and her terminally ill grandfather Nonno, the poet Jonathan Coffin, Williams introduces two characters who possess a much more positive (if at times overly romantic) view of nature. Our first view of them comes as Hannah arrives at the hotel veranda, after having pushed Nonno in a wheelchair uphill to their destination. In spite of their exertion, and the minor scratches and bee stings they've incurred along the way, both express an immediate appreciation for the beauty of their surroundings. Nonno comes on the scene shouting, "It's the cradle of life. Life begins in the sea" (33). Hannah's first reaction is that of a visual artist with an eye for landscape: "Well, now that we've made it, I don't regret the effort. What a view for a painter!" (33). The pair's appreciation for the natural world is made even clearer when, attempting to gain a night's lodging at the hotel, they present the hotel owner Maxine Faulk with a bouquet of wildflowers picked along their journey:

[*Nonno lifts a branch of wild orchids from his lap, ceremonially, with the instinctive gallantry of his kind.*]

Nonno [*shouting*]: Give the lady these—botanical curiosities!—you picked on the way up.

Hannah: I believe they're wild orchids, isn't that what they are?

Shannon: Laelia tibicina.[4]

The passage is a telling one; all three characters mark themselves as both lovers and students of nature. Hannah's familiarity and curiosity with the strange new region's flora quickly reveal her as an amateur naturalist. Perhaps more importantly, the Reverend's knowledge of the orchid's scientific name indicates a more than casual study of botany— as well as a reapplication of Latin, the language of theological study, towards Shannon's "personal idea of God" present in the natural world. There is an almost immediate bond of affection between Shannon and the two travelers—a kind of instant friendship, based not on sexual attraction or a shared past, but on a commonly held affection for the landscape of Costa Verde.

Clearly, the beauty of the hotel's surroundings is used by Williams in much the same fashion that Melville used his symbolic doubloon in

Moby-Dick. Nailed to the mast by Ahab, the coin symbolized something different to each of the many sailors who gazed at it. But nature serves as much more than just "doubloon" in *Night of the Iguana*; it is more than just a device to polarize and create subtle differences among the characters. It is also the source of one of the play's major themes: the invasion of the pastoral setting by the forces of modern progress and technology. Leo Marx, in his 1964 study *The Machine in the Garden*, outlined the importance of this theme beginning with the literature of American Romantic writers of the last century. It is a theme based, Marx wrote, "upon the contrast between two worlds, one identified with rural peace and simplicity, and the other with urban power and sophistication" (19).

Clearly, this conflict is at the root of much of the play's action. Shannon, fleeing first what he saw as an artificial and corrupt bastion of "urban power and sophistication"—the church—takes a job more to his liking: giving guided tours of "God's world." The remarks he makes to Hannah indicate that in his mind the forces of Christianity and the negative forces of progress are closely linked. At one point, he tells her that Mexico is "a country caught and destroyed in its flesh and corrupted in its spirit by its gold-hungry Conquistadors that bore the flag of the Inquisition along with the cross of Christ" (61).

But even the change in vocations is not enough to safely remove Shannon from the forces of civilization. Following the disastrous week on tour with women from a female Baptist college, a week in which he is again accused of "fornication" and the statutory rape of an underaged tour member, Shannon flees from his last vestige of the "civilized" world, the tour bus. Pocketing the keys, he leaves the bus at the base of the hill below the Costa Verde and begins the steep climb to the hotel. The keys become an important symbol to Shannon. They represent his last tie to the urban, mechanized society, and in many ways they also come to represent his mixed feelings about a job that he needs but also hates. He abandons the bus and all it represents, yet he clings to the keys and the small comfort of control they provide.

Likewise, Hannah and her grandfather Nonno are also refugees from a mechanized American society. When Hannah arrives on foot, pushing her ailing grandfather in a wheelchair, one of his first remarks is "I don't like being on wheels." Hannah dismisses the remark as a joke, saying, "Yes, my grandfather feels that the decline of the western world began with the invention of the wheel" (36). Later, however, we learn that this dislike for what Leo Marx would call the "cultural symbol" of the automobile is entirely justified in their case. The reason that Hannah has been raised by her elderly grandfather, we learn, is that both of her parents were killed in "the very first automobile crash on the island of Nantucket" (72).[5]

The loss of the bus keys and of the job which they signify starts Shannon on the downhill slide to his suicide attempt in the play's third act. The Reverend clings to the keys, boasting loudly and often that he has them in his pocket and that no one can leave without them. But despite his statements to the contrary, Shannon's actions seem to indicate that he would secretly like to be rid of the bus keys and all that they represent. When bus company strong-man Jake Latta arrives to take over Shannon's tour, Shannon goads him into a confrontation—even though he is outnumbered two-to-one by the driver and Latta. When Latta asks where Shannon's room is, so that he can look for the keys, Shannon volunteers the information that they're not in his room but in his pocket. Then, in a statement which guarantees the final outcome, he dangles the key in front of Latta and prods, "Here, right here, in my pocket! Want it? Try and get it, Fatso!" (89).

When the driver and Latta finally do wrestle the keys away from Shannon, with only a small struggle, the Reverend seems more relieved than angry. His tone is one of calm acceptance of events beyond his control. "O.K.," he tells Latta, "O.K., you've got the bus key. By force. I feel exonerated now of all responsibility. Take the bus and the ladies in it and go" (91). But before Shannon will allow the bus to leave him behind, he defends his motives one final time in one of the most moving speeches in the play:

God's world has been the range of my travels. I haven't stuck to the schedules of the brochures and I've always allowed the ones that were willing to see, to *see*!—the underworlds of all places, and if they had hearts to be touched, feelings to feel with, I gave them a priceless chance to feel and be touched. And none will ever forget it, none of them, ever, never! (94)

This eloquent speech on the pleasures available in "God's world" is short-lived, as Shannon's breakdown nears its epiphany. Uttering what Williams describes as "an abrupt, fierce sound," he runs down the hill, and in a final gesture which seems more animal than human, he urinates on the departing tourists' luggage. For a moment, animal instinct has replaced supposedly more rational human thought. Shannon's actions exorcising the bus from the rain forest seem insane in human terms, but entirely logical on a non-human level; the Reverend's expulsion of the machine from the garden takes the form of an animal marking its territory in the only way it knows how.

Shannon culminates the bizarre episode with an attempt at suicide by drowning which is half-hearted at best. The Reverend's "swim to China" is easily brought to an abrupt end, and he is dragged back to the hotel by Pedro and Pancho, the two young hotel employees. Williams notes in his direction that "his struggle is probably not much of a real struggle—histrionics mostly" (97). But it may be that the Reverend's feeble attempt at drowning himself serves another purpose—that of cleansing and renewal. Coming as it does immediately after the scene in which Shannon cuts forever his ties to his job at Blake tours, and then sheds the gold cross which hangs around his neck, the abortive "swim to China" may represent the death of the old, more "civilized" side of Shannon's personality, and the baptism and acceptance into the natural world of Costa Verde. As Nonno had observed earlier, and interestingly, in the present tense, "Life begins in the sea" (33).

Once he is brought back onto the hotel veranda, Shannon is bound and tied into a hammock to keep him from attempting further harm to himself. The Fahrenkopfs, always on hand for any cheap spectacle that the Mexican landscape can provide, "gather about Shannon's captive figure as if they were looking at a funny animal in a zoo" (97). The Germans taunt him about the episode with the tourists' luggage, despite Hannah's angry accusations that they are "tormenting him like an animal in a trap" (98). Shannon, too, uses animal imagery to describe his current situation of "being tied in this hammock, trussed up in it like a hog being hauled off to the slaughterhouse" (99).

It seems clear that Williams is attempting to equate Shannon's situation, tied and held captive in a hammock, to that of the captive iguana being held by Pedro and Pancho beneath the veranda. At other times, it seems that the iguana has become a more universal symbol—as it does at the moment when Shannon first shows the captive animal to Hannah: "See? The iguana? At the end of its rope? Trying to go past the end of its goddam rope? Like you! Like me! Like Grampa with his last poem" (120). The parallel situations of the iguana (captured and about to be eaten), Shannon ("spooked" to near nervous collapse and now jobless), Hannah (facing loneliness and the death of her grandfather), and Nonno (facing his own death), serve to link all three of the characters in the play's final moments. After a calming conversation with Hannah, in which she advises Shannon to "accept whatever situation you cannot improve," he takes the iguana's fate into his own hands (116). In the natural order that Shannon envisions, in which an oblivious "God of thunder and lightning" reigns, small acts of grace such as freeing the iguana must fall under man's jurisdiction. As he sets off to cut the iguana free, he tells Hannah, "We'll play God tonight like kids play house with old broken crates and boxes. All right? Now Shannon is going down there with his machete and cut the damn lizard loose so it can run back to its bushes because God won't do it and we are going to play God here" (123).

Nonno's final poem, completed in the minutes after the iguana's release, mirrors Shannon's situation. In it, the poet turns to images from nature as a source of courage as he faces his impending death. The poem describes an orange tree's stoic and fearless acceptance of death as its branches droop inevitably towards the end of its life:

> How calmly does the orange branch
> Observe the sky begin to blanch
> Without a cry, without a prayer,
> With no betrayal of despair.
>
> Sometimes while night obscures the tree
> The zenith of its life will be
> Gone past forever, and from thence
> A second history will commence.
>
> A chronicle no longer gold,
> A bargaining with mist and mold,
> And finally the broken stem
> The plummeting to earth and then
>
> An intercourse not well designed
> For beings of a golden kind
> Whose native green must arch above
> The earth's obscene corrupting love.
>
> And still the ripe fruit and the branch
> Observe the sky begin to blanch
> Without a cry, without a prayer,
> With no betrayal of despair.
>
> O Courage, could you not as well
> Select a second place to dwell,
> Not only in that golden tree
> But in the frightened heart of me? (124)

The poem speaks of a moment of crisis, a turning point which ends one life, and which gives rise to a new beginning. Although ostensibly written about the poet Nonno's own immanent death, this it seems, is also the situation that Shannon finds himself in as the play ends; the "zenith" of his life is over, but he seems now on the verge of a "second history." What form his new life will take is left uncertain by Williams. A life with Hannah has been effectively ruled out, and a return to the church seems highly unlikely. The Costa Verde's owner, Maxine, has offered Shannon a job "taking care" of the hotel's female guests, but it is an offer which he neither accepts nor rejects (124).

Williams leaves to our imagination exactly what form Shannon's "second history" will take, but the final stanzas of Nonno's poem seem to offer the Reverend a sliver of hope in the acceptance of nature's realities ("a bargaining with mist and mold"), including one's own mortality and the inevitable embrace of "the earth's obscene corrupting love." Nonno's life has come to an end in the play's final scene, and a severe mid-life crisis has effectively ended the life which Shannon has known up to this point. These seemingly grim physical realities are assuaged, however—for both Nonno and for the Reverend T. Lawrence Shannon—by the discovery of "courage" to be found in the natural world.

From *The Southern Literary Journal* 32, no. 2 (Spring 2000): 59-69. Copyright © 2000 by University of North Carolina Press. Reprinted with permission of University of North Carolina Press.

Notes

1. See, for instance, Henrik Ibsen's 1882 play *Enemy of the People*, which examines the impact of industrial pollution on a small Norwegian village. For more recent examples of plays which feature environmental themes, see Sam Shepard's *True West* and *Curse of the Starving Class*, Lanford Wilson's *Redwood Curtain*, and Tom Stoppard's *Arcadia*.

2. See, for example, Amanda's long speech in scene 6 of the play, in which she attempts to recall her youth as she waxes romantically about the beauty of Blue Mountain in the spring: "Afternoons, long, long, rides! Picnics—lovely! So lovely, that country in May—all lacy with dogwood, literally flooded with jonquils?" (72).

3. This is one of many examples of the playwright's use of animal imagery to define the play's characters. Maxine Faulk, the owner of the Costa Verde Hotel, is described in Williams' stage notes as laughing "with a single harsh, loud bark, opening her mouth like a seal expecting a fish to be thrown to it" (9). Later, Maxine sums up the characters of Pedro and Pancho, the two young hotel employees, by saying, "they're graceful as cats, and just as dependable, too" (38).

4. Williams' character Shannon is apparently well versed in the locale's plant life. Louis O. Williams' botanical reference volume, *The Orchidaceae of Mexico* (1951), lists this variety of orchid as being native to the region of Mexico in which *Iguana* is set.

5. Similarly, James Reynolds finds the issue of modern technology to be at the center of Williams' *The Glass Menagerie*. See "The Failure of Technology in *The Glass Menagerie*," *Modern Drama* 34 (1991): 522-527.

Works Cited

Costello, Donald P. "Tennessee Williams' Fugitive Kind." *Modern Drama* 15 (1972): 26-43.

Falk, Signi. *Tennessee Williams*. Boston: G. K. Hall, 1978.

Marx, Leo. *The Machine in the Garden: Technology and the Pastoral Ideal in America*. London: Oxford UP, 1964.

Phillips, Gene D. *The Films of Tennessee Williams*. Philadelphia: Art Alliance P, 1980.

Reynolds, James. "The Failure of Technology in *The Glass Menagerie*." *Modern Drama* 34 (1991): 522-527.

Williams, Louis O. *The Orchidaceae of Mexico*. Tegucigalpa, Honduras: Imprenta Calderón, 1951.

Williams, Tennessee. *The Glass Menagerie*. 1945. New York: New Directions, 1970.

_____. *The Night of the Iguana*. 1961. *Three by Tennessee*. New York: Signet, 1976.

Red Devil Battery Sign:
An Approach to a Mytho-Political Theatre_____

James Schlatter

Conventional critical wisdom has long held that the final two decades of Tennessee Williams's writing life constituted a sad, embarrassing, but perhaps ultimately unavoidable slide into artistic self-
caricature, self-pity, and drug-induced self-annihilation. Obsessively
working and re-working dramatic material, he still could not, so it is argued, write himself out of that great theatre of himself, returning like a
dog to his vomit to the same pubescent myths, the same psychic trau-
mas, the same guilt and remorse. He had said it all before, and better, a
long time ago.

An even more conventional and more petrified piece of critical wisdom holds that Williams was never really, except in the most generi-
cally leftist-humanist way, a committed political writer, a writer of explicit social commentary. As C. W. E. Bigsby writes in Volume Two of
A Critical Introduction to Twentieth-Century American Drama, "Williams was more inclined [than Arthur Miller] to see that public world as
an image of determinism that could never be defeated or transformed
by the impact of the moral will, but only resisted by the imagination, . . ."
(30). Whatever the ruling order—family, business, politics—it is domineering, repressive, and spiritually destructive, and the true artist must
define himself against it at all costs as the rebel, the fugitive, the romantic wanderer.

It is not the purpose of this essay to refute either of these long-
entrenched positions but rather, through an investigation of *The Red
Devil Battery Sign*, produced originally on Broadway in 1975, to render them irrelevant, not because these positions are so awfully wrong
or even only partially right but because they prevent us—writers, directors, actors, scholars—from getting at the plays themselves. They
forestall our attempts to chart the hard evolutionary struggles of one of
the greatest playwriting imaginations of the Twentieth Century to re-

shape itself into new forms for new times. *Red Devil* is significant here because it is, first of all, a work of political—or one might say more accurately public—imagination. It is also a play in which Williams, in his attempt speak to the American political culture of the 1970's, took key characters, themes, and theatrical motifs with which he had been creatively absorbed since the beginning of his writing life and radically refashioned them to create a fundamentally new work.

In order to effectively situate *Red Devil Battery Sign* both within Williams's own writing career and within the larger historical moment of mid-1970's America, it is necessary first to recall briefly the political and emotional temper of those times. It is undeniable that in the 1970's, sadly, Williams slipped into ever deepening states of delusional paranoia regarding friends, colleagues, those who had devoted a significant share of their lives to his career, in particular Audrey Wood. But the nation was also steeped in its own American brand of self-absorption, self-pity, and paranoia, or at least so was our head of state. There was probably no more lonely, frightened, or paranoid man in America in those times than the Quaker boy from Whittier.

The Seventies was also the era of Max Jacobson, "Dr. Feelgood," who shot up Hollywood celebrities, rock stars, politicians, and politicians' wives with amphetamine and barbiturate cocktails. If the drug of choice in 1965 was L.S.D., then in 1975 it was Seconal. If Williams was popping pills to deaden his private pain and retreat further into himself in the Seventies, so was a lot of the rest of the country. The Woman Downtown, one of the central characters of *Red Devil* (a slang term for a powerful sedative), at one point cries out in desperation: "Who in hell on earth doesn't have a confused head now?" (48). It could be an epitaph for the age.

And *Red Devil Battery Sign* was written for those times. I have chosen to call it a "mytho-political" play because the world it evokes has less in common with a specific socioeconomic milieu as created by, say, Arthur Miller or Clifford Odets, and more with the wasted landscapes of Sam Shepard, whose plays evoke a mythical America in which the primal forces of the national psyche—love, sex, death, dreams, and power—rise up and take exotic or grotesque human shape. *Red Devil* is grounded in an immediate political context. Conceived during the Watergate hearings, the play is set in Dallas just after Kennedy's assassination. But the atmosphere is less that of a particular and immediately recognizable time and place than of a Kafkaesque political present in which faceless men in grey suits wear dark glasses and tiny white ear phones, and in which anonymous powers rule by assassination and "disappearing" dissenters.

What is most revealing about *Red Devil*, however, is how Williams takes certain archetypes of character and ritualized action which had deeply engaged him virtually throughout his writing career and fundamentally refashions them to construct an image of a contemporary political world in crisis. King Del Rey and the Woman Downtown, the two central characters around whose passionate and passionately honest relationship the play is constructed, are both well-familiar figures from Williams's playwriting past. *Red Devil* is a remarkably reimagined version of a story to which Williams had been drawn as early as 1940: the Orpheus and Eurydice myth. *Battle of Angels* and its substantially rewritten version, *Orpheus Descending*, follow a vagabond singer-guitar player into a dark Southern underworld of racist hatred and carnal and capitalist rapacity to rescue his beloved. In these earlier Orpheus-Eurydice versions Williams seemed rather morbidly drawn to this myth. As Hugh Dickinson writes in *Myth on the Modern Stage*, "[I]t contains the three elements most appealing to his stubborn romanticism, the same that drew Cocteau to it: poetry, love, and death" (283). Such a potent admixture of powers must end in catastrophe, and Orpheus is destined, tragically if beautifully, to die.

But if King Del Rey also dies in *Red Devil* he doesn't go down without putting up an honorable fight to rescue the Woman Downtown, although her rescue, as will be discussed, is a deeply ironic one. And if King and the Woman are recognizable from earlier work, they speak here in a new voice, a voice that is unmistakably Williams's own but

strengthened by a new moral authority. It is a public rather than a specifically political voice, one that refuses any longer to retreat into narcissistic self-dramatization and wallow in self-pity. It is the voice of
characters who choose to stop running and to take a stand, however un-
steady, and who refuse any longer to be silent.

In the character of King Del Rey Williams attempts to bridge an
emotional chasm within himself in his attitude toward male power, an
ambivalence which forced a split in his imagination between the sexual
mystique of the romantic desperado and the fearful authority of the father as procreator and patriarch. In creating his male characters he
seems emotionally split between such figures as Val Xavier and Jabe
Torrance in *Orpheus Descending* or Chance Wayne and Boss Finley in
Sweet Bird of Youth. Ironically, when he did create male characters
such as Stanley Kowalski and Big Daddy, who exhibit both a vital
Lawrentian potency and patriarchal power, he produced some of his
most impressive and complex characters. But the balance was almost
impossible to maintain.

King Del Rey is just such a complex hybrid. He is, like Val Xavier, a
singer, the leader of a mariachi band. He is Latin—actually part Mexican, part American—and he carries himself with the relaxed sexual authority and unself-conscious ease that Williams perceived in and came
to love so much about the men of that culture. But King is also a father
and family man. His daughter, La Niña, is a kind of soul mate to him.
He does not own her, as Boss Finley owns his daughter. In fact, years
before father and daughter had sung "duetos" together with his band
when its star was on the rise. But because of King's patriarchal tendencies to idealize and control La Niña, she ran away to Chicago and fell in
love with a young man, Terrence McCabe. In the play the young couple
come home to be married and reconcile with King.

The image of a protective, doting father/daughter relationship is
positively alien to William's world. Indeed, the portrayal of a relationship between any parent and child, male or female, that is not emotionally wounded or crippled beyond healing is rare in his work. And Wil-

liams portrays several in *Red Devil*. King actually comes to serve as a surrogate father to his daughter's fiancé. In a moving scene that recalls that between Brick and Big Daddy in *Cat on a Hot Tin Roof*, King and McCabe come to understand and even respect each other, although King initially despises McCabe because the chief source of his allure for La Niña is the fact that he carries a gun. The first thing La Niña whispers to her mother when they meet again is, "Mama, he's got a pistol on him!" (66). McCabe is a doomed juvenile desperado in the making, and King has to stop him.

King convinces McCabe to hand him the gun as a pledge of McCabe's sincerity and honor in loving his daughter. McCabe then tells King that the real reason La Niña fell in love was because she saw that "[y]ou [McCabe] are in pain like—my father" (77). He also tells King that La Niña is pregnant, and because the two men meet now as fathers McCabe acknowledges to King that "I may be a stranger to you. You're not to me" (80). If a writer who lived much of his emotional life on the run could create a scene in which two characters, more significantly two men, could stand together and make their truce, then I think that we must at least consider that that writer is attempting to move out of his self-protective world of personal emotional fetishes and into a public world of social meaning and moral choice. It is especially moving to read this scene in the light of Lyle Leverich's biography, which reveals that Williams actually had a fierce love/hate relationship with his father, who broke his son's heart because he was incapable of loving unconditionally his "unmanly" son.

King Del Rey remains tragically split between his responsibility to his family and to the Woman Downtown, whom he also attempts to save, chiefly from herself. He not only loves but respects her. Indeed, he refuses to allow her to become, to be named, "the Woman Downtown," which is a derisive epithet for a woman who prowls the hotel bars in downtown Dallas in a pathetic search for nightly company. In this new incarnation of the Orpheus-Eurydice myth, Williams appears much more focused on the bond of respect and recognition that grows between King and the Woman Downtown and less on the catastrophe that fate, in his earlier work, seemed inevitably to wreak upon fugitive lovers.

The Woman Downtown has been as radically refashioned from earlier models of Williams's Southern women as has King Del Rey from earlier male characters. And like King, she is a fascinating hybrid. She radiates some of the genteel dignity and enduring spirit of Alma Winemiller or Lady Torrance but also the raw animal urges of Maggie the Cat. She is a product of the forces both of light and of darkness; she is both the all-American beauty queen and the Great Whore of Babylon.

The Woman Downtown does need desperately to be saved, but it is not her fragile soul or broken sexuality that needs protection but her voice, specifically the voice of her conscience. Raised by her rich and powerful Texas senator father to be symbolic public property, she supplied the wholesome human face of Machiavellian power politics. Kept always on the periphery of the inner circles of power, she remained a non-entity, essentially nonexistent, and so silently absorbed the dark secrets of powerful men. Horrified by the Kennedy assassination, she goes on the run with a pile of deeply incriminating papers and with the help of a kind judge, her godfather (and another benevolent father-figure in the play), she is on her way to Washington to tell what she knows. So she must be silenced.

For her temporary protection the Woman has been hidden away in a hotel room in Dallas, but that has rendered her "speechless," as she says, and forced her into a private hell of "anonymity" (3). Her silence and isolation have driven her into deepening states of paranoia, aggravated by large doses of sedatives. Terrified of losing herself and refusing to disappear, she flees from the room and into the hotel bar where she meets King. They recognize each other as soul mates in part because they both have "a cyclone" in their head and because, as a consequence, they both have had their brains operated on. Surgeons cut into King's skull to remove part of a tumor which continues to rob him of his power of speech, and, although the narrative is sketchy, it seems that the Woman had been given electric shock treatment to stop her mouth even before Kennedy was killed.

Tormented by her political stalkers and half-maddened by fear, the Woman wants to lose herself in fantasy, physical intimacy, and alcohol. (The perfume she wears is called "Night Flight.") But King does not allow her to lose herself, to forsake her will. He refuses to let her become "the Woman Downtown." He refuses her offer to escape into bed and sex and demands that she sit in a chair and tell him who she really is: "Just sit there like a lady and tell me who it is that I love and make love to" (49). And she does, and so recovers her voice. King actually gives her a new name. He calls her "la verdad. Truth" (91).

Trying to escape the city and the assassins closing in, King and the Woman are cornered by the Drummer, a punk on the make, who has joined and tried to take over King's band by becoming a crude, ersatz Mick Jagger. He is no Orpheus but a debased Dionysus, who loves his cock, his drums, and his gun. He becomes a paid thug hired by the C.I.A. to take back the property of the powers that be. In a final showdown, King shoots and kills the Drummer, with the gun he convinced his soon-to-be son-in-law to give up. It can be argued whether this is morally self-contradictory or an ironically appropriate application of power, but it is dramatically and emotionally fulfilling.

It's important to note that the Drummer himself represents a reworking of older dramatic material. He first appears in a one-act written by Williams in the late thirties called "Death is a Drummer," which was rewritten as a full-length play titled *Me, Vashya!* The Drummer, whose given name is Sir Vashya Zontine, is an unscrupulous arms dealer and sexual carnivore who beats the drums of war. His mentally and physically abused wife shoots him dead with one of his own guns after she is rescued from him by a young pacifist poet. In looking at the Drummer character one can see the influence on Williams of the highly politicized theatre culture of the 1930's, in which the plays of Clifford Odets, the Group Theatre, and the W.P.A. Living Newspapers played an integral role.

Red Devil Battery Sign ends with a bizarre and disturbingly ambiguous tableau. Having killed the Drummer, King himself dies. It's unclear, but it appears that his brain, which had been deteriorating through the course of the play, just finally gives out, silencing him for good. The Woman neither goes on to Washington nor falls back into the clutches of the men in grey suits. Instead, she is taken up by a roaming pack of wild children, a terrorist street gang whose turf is the "Wasteland," as Williams calls it, on the outskirts of Dallas. Here again one sees Williams reshaping older, more psychologically symbolic material into contemporary political forms. The pack of violent youths recalls the swarm of street urchins who hunt down and devour Sebastian Venable in *Suddenly Last Summer.* It also echoes the filthy orphaned children who hound Big Daddy and Big Mama during their trip through Europe, one of whose sexual overtures so sickens Big Daddy. Since the horrific "wilding" attack in Central Park in 1987 and the advent of gangbanger warfare and drive-by shootings in America's inner cities, *Red Devil Battery Sign* seems even more a play for the 1990's than for the 1970's.

The image that closes the play is apocalyptic. The Woman Downtown has joined this pack of young predators, whose leader is called "Wolf." He names her the "[m]other of all" (93), and she becomes the she-wolf nurturer of this primal brood. The Woman, returning to the lifeless body of King, lets out an "awesome" animal cry that seems full both of grief and rage. Rejoining the pack, she takes the hand of her brother, Wolf, and turns silently to face the audience as white electrical explosions detonate in the distance.

It may be argued whether the play earns the grotesque power of this final apocalyptic image. Clearly, Williams intends the action of *Red Devil* to move inexorably from the plane of realism toward a deepening condition of collective dementia and expressionistic nightmare. One may also question whether the radical refashioning of so much old material amounts to a truly reconstituted and coherent theatrical vision or just a many-headed monster of scattered ideas, images, and sensational affects. But it is possible to approach the play not as a unified dramaturgical whole but rather as a complex network of motifs woven around the central action of the play, the ritual of the Orpheus/Eurydice quest and also, more important, around the play's central idea, which is that of the political worth of a free, independent, public voice.

And a discussion of voice inevitably brings us back to the real Tennessee Williams, the Williams we seem to know so—or too—well. But here in *Red Devil Battery Sign* we find, I would argue, a new Williams. The voice is still unmistakably his, but here it no longer sounds only the lonely lyric of the nightingale or the soft song of an impassive Orpheus. It is grounded in a wounded or psychically damaged heroism, but it can still reach the world in a desperate cry of moral defiance or a fury's mad howl. We are in a new, if no less forbidding world as well. The hot, dark jungle of primal desires and drives gives way to a devastated wasteland, an alien plane of utter emotional sterility and efficient, *1984*-style brutality.

As I stated at the outset of this essay, the real damage done by uncontested critical opinion is that it keeps Tennessee Williams's plays from us, specifically by keeping them from the stage. *Red Devil* is a fractured, phantasmagoric, postmodern opera, complete with mariachi band chorus. Only directors, actors, designers, and dramaturgs, working together, can really make even a provisional—let alone any final—judgment about this difficult and complex work. It is hoped, perhaps foolishly, that this present essay may help to begin to turn the critical tide that threatens to carry Tennessee Williams's later work still further from us.

From *Tennessee Williams Annual Review* 1 (1998): 93-101. Copyright © 1998 by the Historic New Orleans Collection. Reprinted with permission of the Historic New Orleans Collection.

Selected Bibliography

Bigsby, C. W. E. *A Critical Introduction to Twentieth-Century American Drama*, Volume Two. Cambridge, New York: Cambridge University Press, 1984.

Dickinson, Hugh. *Myth on the Modern Stage*. Chapter 10: "Tennessee Williams: Orpheus as Savior." Urbana, Chicago, London: University of Illinois Press, 1969.

Leverich, Lyle. *Tom: The Unknown Tennessee Williams*. New York: Crown Publishers, Inc., 1995.

Williams, Tennessee. *The Red Devil Battery Sign*, A New Directions Book. New York: New Directions Publishing Corporation, 1988.

Tennessee Williams' *Out Cry* in *The Two-Character Play*_____

Nicholas O. Pagan

In keeping with a widespread tendency in the study of American drama, when scholars have shown an interest in Tennessee Williams' late plays they have tended to see them as pandering to the American theatergoer's penchant for "realism." Unfortunately, though, the striking realism of, say, *The Glass Menagerie* or *A Streetcar Named Desire* has lost some of its force; and so for some it becomes almost painful to watch this cranky Southern playwright attempting, they believe in vain, to reapply or reinvent the realism which was largely responsible for his earlier huge successes.

The two plays which I will examine here, *Out Cry* and *The Two-Character Play*, have been especially prone to treatment in terms of "psychological realism." In "The Circle Closed: A Psychological Reading of *The Glass Menagerie* and *The Two-Character Play*," for example, R. B. Parker brings the plays together in terms of the theme of brother-sister incest which he connects to Williams' own "near-incestuous" relationship with his sister, Rose (523). In her examination of *Out Cry*, Judith Thompson also emphasizes incest; but, unlike Parker, she sees the incest in mythic terms, finding counterparts for Felice and Clare in Orestes and Electra. Thompson also suggests that the two characters are trying to escape "the tragic repetition of the Past," and the play ends with the characters' acceptance of the Past and hence their "embrace of reality rather than violent destruction by it" (*Tennessee Williams' Plays: Memory, Myth, and Symbol* 192-93).

There has been some recognition by other critics like Adler and Bigsby of the way that these plays draw attention to theatricality, but usually theatricality is invoked to help us to understand Williams' characters.[1] Here I will argue that the way that these plays draw attention to their own theatricality needs to be looked at more closely; for if there is a reality to be faced in *Out Cry* and *The Two-Character Play*, this reality is inexorably intertwined with the reality of drama itself. These plays may be described as quintessentially "metadramatic" because they investigate, analyze, and comment on their own nature as plays. They are not worthy of attention because they focus on a particular playwright's attempt to come to terms with his own "near-incestuous relationship" with his sister or because they depict the simplistic idea that we must accept our pasts or because of their portrayal of character. They are worthy of attention because they give us one of the finest and most sustained meditations in all twentieth century drama on the difficulties facing *all* playwrights. These difficulties include problems of beginning and ending, and above all, the need for playwrights to eventually let go of their plays and allow them an independent existence.

I

With its play-within-a-play structure, *Out Cry* is one of Williams' most obviously "metadramatic" works. The outer play performed by an actor and an actress abandoned by their company in "the state theater of a state unknown" surrounds an inner play performed by the same actor and actress playing a brother and sister living in their Southern home where they too have been abandoned, in this case by their parents—the father killed the mother because she wanted to send him to the state asylum; he then shot himself. The inner play, entitled *The Two-Character Play*, gave its title to the play as a whole when it was first performed in London in 1967; but it was revised for production in Chicago in 1971 and again in New York in 1973, with the title *Out Cry*. Revised yet again, it reappeared in New York in 1975 and again in San Francisco in 1976, with the old title restored, *The Two-Character Play*.[2]

The play-within-a-play structure is immediately apparent to readers of the play, for the Synopsis of Scenes specifies that the setting for the play is "in an unspecified locality," "before and after the performance" which takes place on "a nice afternoon in a deep Southern town called New Bethesda" (OC 6, TP ix). Thus, in principle, the inner and outer plays have two different sets. For the opening of *Out Cry*, Felice is to appear on a platform "on which a fragmentary set has been assembled" (OC 7). Described in more detail in *The Two-Character Play*, the set includes "pieces of scenery which contain the incomplete interior of a living room in Southern summer," and "about the stage enclosing this incomplete interior are scattered unassembled pieces of scenery for other plays than the play-within-a-play which will be 'performed.'" "Perhaps," the stage direction continues, "this exterior set is the more important of the two" (TP 1). Surely, however, because the interior set is incomplete, it cannot be completely enclosed; and so we may find ourselves wondering where the interior set ends and where the exterior set begins, and vice versa. This problem of separating inner and outer set will later be carried over to the problem of separating inner and outer play.

The action of *Out Cry* begins with Felice's attempt to move a large statue: "Is someone, anyone, back here to help me move this—please, I can't alone!" he exclaims, and he reflects, "Where did it begin, where, when? This feeling of confusion began when—I can't think where" (OC 7). In a few minutes Clare will indicate that the performance is about to start; and she and her brother, retaining their outer play names, Clare and Felice, will begin to perform *The Two-Character Play*. Even when the play-within-a-play seems to get under way, however, the characters will frequently comment from the perspective of the outer play. Thus, when Clare seems to falter because of the telegram, Felice tells her that she need not worry because "there isn't a telegram in *The Two-Character* Play" (OC 28). The slippage between the two plays is also indicated when a character points out that a line used by the other is not in the script (OC 30); when one accuses the other of jumping a page (OC 39); and when the characters squabble over lines, saying, for example, "That's my line, not yours" (OC 38). When Clare announces that she is going upstairs for her brother's jacket and tie, Felice notices that "the set's incomplete," but Clare then indicates to Felice that he should pretend that she has gone upstairs and that he is alone in the parlor (OC 49, TP 41). She then gets him to pretend to put on the invisible jacket and tie (OC 50, TP 41-2). This pretending or role-playing is of course a feature of all dramas, but in specifically drawing attention to role-playing, individual plays can be seen as foregrounding their own natures as dramas.

Another way in which *Out Cry* and *The Two-Character Play* foreground metadrama is by the direct address to the audience. Thus, after stepping out through a window, Felice becomes a kind of stage manager, explaining to the audience what the production had intended in terms of blocking and what is actually happening on stage now:

> The audience is supposed to imagine that the front of the house, where I am standing now, is shielded by sunflowers, too, but that was impractical as it would cut off the view. I stand here—move not a step further. Impossible without her. No, I can't leave her alone. I feel so exposed, so cold. And behind me I feel the house. It seems to be breathing a faint, warm breath on my back. I feel it the way you feel a loved person standing close behind you. (OC 55, TP 46)

This monologue comes from a place, as it were, between the inner and outer plays: the house and imagined sunflowers may remind us of the play about a brother and sister living in the Old South; the exposure, the cold, may remind us of the play about a brother and sister performing in an empty theater in a frozen northern town. Felice seems to be neither fully inside nor outside the house, just as he is neither fully inside nor outside the inner play. We realize that this confusion of inside and outside has been on the characters' minds for some time. Often they tend to emphasize the words "in" and "out." Earlier, Clare asked her brother, "Didn't you say that you went *out* today?" "Yes, you saw me come *in*," replied Felice, "When you see somebody come *in* you know he's been *out*" (my emphasis, OC 28). This "out," of course, plays off the title, *Out Cry*, and also foreshadows later emphasis on the word "out," for toward the end of the play Clare will shout, "Out, out, out! Human Out Cry!" (OC 66-7, TP 56). We are continually faced with the task of understanding this all-pervasive cry.

Re-entering the house that he was unable to leave, Felice continues to play the stage manager, announcing that "there is a pause, a silence, our eyes avoiding each other's" (OC 46, TP 55); and he begins to direct himself, commenting on actions before they are carried out, saying things like, "—And now I touch her hand lightly, which is a signal that I am about to speak a new line in *The Two-Character Play*. . . . And then I pick up the property of the play which she's always hated and dreaded, so much that she refuses to remember that it exists in the play" (OC 58, TP 48). "Now," continues Felice, "I turn to my sister who has the face of an angel and say to her: 'Look! Do you see?'" (OC 59, TP 50). This "Look! Do you see?" may be seen as a further challenge to the audience to comprehend.

The inner play seems to end as Clare, striking a note on the piano, reminisces about how long a road she and her brother "have traveled together." "[T]oo long now for separation," she says, "Yes, all the way back to sunflowers and soap bubbles, and there's no turning back on the road even if the road's backward, and backward" (OC 59-60, TP 50). Suddenly, however, after Clare seems to have recognized the end of the inner play, she sees that Felice is still involved in the performance of that play. She orders him to "come out of the play!" but Felice complains about being "lost in the play" (TP 50). As they continue to talk, however, they both seem to be in some doubt as to whether the play is really over: "This still seems like a performance of *The Two-Character Play*," says Clare (OC 62, TP 53), and she wonders if it is possible that *The Two-Character Play* ever had an ending (OC 63, TP 53). The only way to find out whether there is an ending or not is for the two characters to re-enter the inner play, and so after realizing that they are trapped in the theater and that the theater is a kind of prison (OC 68, TP 57), they decide to re-enter the inner play (OC 69, TP 59). In the theater, instead of watching Pirandello's *Six Characters in Search of an Author*, the audience is now watching *Two Characters in Search of a Play's Ending*.

The problem of the beginning has led logically to the problem of the ending. The question of beginnings and endings is a question of limits, the line in this case between performance and non-performance. Thus, just as we may expect the performance as a whole to end, Felice announces that "The performance commences" (OC 70). Then, as Felice looks out of the window at the enormous sunflower, Clare considers picking up the revolver, but does not do so. Instead, she moves to her brother, touches his hand, and says, "Magic is a habit." Felice completes Clare's thought by saying, "Magic is the habit of our existence" (OC 72). Even this last line may be taken to refer to theater, at least if we concur with Antonin Artaud when he suggests in *The Theater and Its Double* that theater identifies itself with the forces of ancient magic (86).

Magic has been a thread running through Williams' plays at least since *Battle of Angels*, Williams' first full-length play to be given a professional production. *Battle of Angels* begins and ends with a "wizard-like figure" who sells tokens and charms to "the superstitious." Referred to as the Conjure Man, he may be regarded as a surrogate playwright. In the theater a playwright cannot speak directly to the audience, for his or her words must be mediated by the actors and actresses on stage. In a sense, then, the playwright is forced into silence. Similarly the Conjure Man cannot speak; for although he mutters sounds, his words are never audible to an audience. At the end of the play, the Conjure Man unfolds Val's snakeskin jacket and "goes to the back wall and hangs it above his head in the shaft of sunlight. . . ." The fact that "he seems to make a slight obeisance before it" (BA 238) may be regarded as an acknowledgment of the power of magic which suffuses not only the Conjure Man but also the play and the writing of plays.

"Yes, I have tricks in my pocket," says Tom Wingfield at the beginning of *Menagerie*, "I have things up my sleeve. But I am the opposite of a stage magician . . ." (GM 22), but later he will talk to Laura about

---

Malvolio, the Magician's "wonderful tricks." He becomes linked to the magician by the magic scarf that the magician gives him and that he in turn gives to Laura. As the possessor of the magic scarf, she, in turn is touched by the thread of magic established in the first line. This magic thread then finds its way into *Streetcar*. As magician, Blanche transforms the Kowalski apartment. Stanley exclaims, "You come in here and sprinkle the place with powder and spray perfume and cover the light bulb with a paper lantern, and lo and behold the place has turned into Egypt and you are the Queen of the Nile" (SND 127-28). Blanche has retreated into her theatrical world where she becomes a kind of manager of magic. Earlier, she had confessed to Mitch, "I don't want realism. I want magic. . . . Yes, yes, magic! I try to give that to people" (SND 117).

When the characters in *Out Cry* find themselves caught in an "empty vault" which is "full of echoes and echoes and echoes" (OC 66), we may be reminded that Williams' plays themselves are full of "echoes," in other words, allusions to other plays. Thus, Felice's speech concerning his dilemma about leaving his sister is strikingly reminiscent of another playwright's speech, Tom Wingfield's, at the close of *Menagerie*: "Then all at once my sister touches my shoulder. I turn around and look into her eyes. Oh Laura, I intended to leave you behind me, but I am more faithful than I intended to be" (GM 115). This inability of the characters to separate is linked to the problem of ending. An ending entails closure.

The collapsing of boundaries, then, involves not only the boundary between inner and outer play or between *Out Cry* and *The Two-Character Play* but also between other Williams plays or, if you will, between early and late Williams. Williams himself has contributed to the tendency to divide the plays up historically. In *Memoirs*, for example, he mentions his later, "less traditional style of writing" (xvii). Elsewhere when discussing one of his screenplays, he commented, "About the style of (*All Gaul is Divided*). It belongs to that period of my writing that critics refer to as 'the early Williams.' It was a time of youthful spontaneity and of true freshness" (*Stopped Rocking and Other Screenplays* 3). Once we begin to perceive the connecting threads between the various plays, however, we may feel a great sense of continuity rather than rupture between the so-called early and late plays. The inevitable reference to other plays is, in fact, hinted at in the beginning of *The Two-Character Play* by the indication that the outer set contains "scattered unassembled pieces of scenery for other plays" (TP 1).

In Williams' particular case, we could also argue that the plays are linked by a plethora of delicate objects representing the fragility of the theatrical performance and the vulnerability of the playwright. There may be a connection in this respect between the glass unicorn of *Menagerie*, the paper lantern of *Streetcar*, and the soap bubble of *Out Cry* and *The Two-Character Play*. After inviting us to observe with "Look! Do you see?" Felice blows imaginary soap bubbles and gets us to picture one in particular: "sometimes the soap bubble bursts before it rises, but this time please imagine you see it rising through gold light above the gold sunflower heads" (OC 59, TP 49). Clare says she can see it, and she observes that "it's lovely and you made it . . . and it still hasn't broken" (OC 59, TP 50).

Williams admitted that *The Two-Character Play* "was conceived and written when [he] was almost completely phased out and was rewritten several times following [his] release from a psychiatric hospital" (*Conversations with Tennessee Williams* 193). Having some idea of what happened to Williams in the sixties, which Williams had a predilection for referring to as his "stoned age," it is all too easy to see his late plays as the creation of a broken man and to therefore condemn them in the way so many critics have done. Rex Reed, for example, claimed that the play should have stayed in Tennessee Williams' trunk. "A lot of doors opened and closed," said Reed, "but nobody ever went anywhere." He found the play "pretentious, static, and all but incomprehensible" ("Tennessee Williams' *Out Cry*: A Colossal Bore" 5). Another reviewer, Herbert Kretzemer, wrote, "It would need a psychoanalyst—and preferably Tennessee Williams's own—to offer a rational interpretation for the enigmas that litter the stage like pieces of an elaborate jigsaw" (in Catherine M. Arnott, *Tennessee Williams on File* 55).

People have often been hard on "artists" who in later years do not seem to live up to their former greatness. I believe, however, that in the case of *Out Cry* and *The Two-Character Play*, when we see the threads of Williams' earlier work in these plays and see how the plays question the idea of boundaries—boundaries between reality and play, boundaries between plays—it becomes clear that Williams' bubble/theater has not been shattered.

II

Finally, let us turn to the extent to which *Out Cry* may be read as Williams' own outcry. It is easy to see parallels between Williams' personal experience of confinement in the late sixties and his characters' experience trapped in the empty theater/Southern house. Indeed, Williams himself has encouraged biographical readings. Asked about *Out Cry*, in one interview he claimed, "I had to cry out and I did. . . . It's a history of what I went through in the Sixties transmuted into the predicament of a brother and sister" (*Conversations* 239). Elsewhere, he suggested, "In my writings I always reveal myself; my plays actually deal only with me" (*Conversations* 297). When we realize, however, that the plays are part of a network where it is difficult to separate inside from outside or one play from another, we may also realize that an author cannot be confined or trapped in his own play.

The inability of the plays to end may be a reflection of Williams' own inability to stop working on them. Never satisfied with *Out Cry*, Williams could never consider it complete. He could not let it go. Thus for the 1976 San Francisco production, he worked very closely with both the director and cast. Lyle Taylor tells us that on one occasion "because of an indefinable sense of anticlimax toward the end of the play . . . to the actors anguished dismay Williams sat with them in a dressing room and proceeded to X out whole speeches" ("*The Two-Character Play*: A Producer's View" 23). This process of dramatic composition or decomposition is given embodiment in the play itself. Felice, "a playwright as well as a player" (TP 2), as the author of the inner play, claims that Clare should only make cuts when he indicates that she should do so. Clare, however, decides to make her own cuts and indicates them by playing a "C" sharp on the piano (TP 16-17). Control is passing from playwright to player. Felice later refuses to obey Clare's signal to cut, exclaiming, "I will not cut into texture!" (TP 19). Felice is crying out here against the playwright's loss of control of his work. The play comments here not just on Felice's plight or Williams' plight, but the plight of all playwrights who must in a sense part with their plays and suffer the inevitable anguish of dispossession. Williams' constant rewriting is a relentless attempt to delay this moment of dispossession. Part of the struggle is the struggle for an ending which is at the same time just what the playwright wants to avoid, precisely what he most resists, because with the ending comes the loss of control, the handing over of what he thought and still thinks is his to actors, directors, and audience.

Mark, an artist, in another of Williams so-called late plays, *In the Bar of a Tokyo Hotel*, provides an appropriate analogy for this situation when he talks about the artist's desire to complete his work, to "[p]ut the words back in the box and nail down the lid. *Fini*" (DC 50). He goes on to suggest that "there is an edge, a limit to [a] circle of light." "The circle is narrow. And protective." He says, "We have to stay inside. It's our existence and our protection. The protection of our existence. It's our home if we have one" (DC 51).

Inside the circle playwrights may be seen as working on their plays; but when they present them to someone else, the plays move out of the circle and into the threatening darkness, the space of the audience. *The Two-Character Play* and *Out Cry* may be seen as dramatizing this process. Thus, Tennessee Williams' outcry in these plays is not just one playwright's outcry, but all playwrights' outcry. Williams dramatizes the mourning inherent in the inexorable separation between playwright and play. Instead of dismissing *Out Cry* and *The Two-Character Play*, then, as simply the works of an older declining artist, we can appreciate them for exploring the nature of drama and the playwright's tantalizing relation to his or her work.

Notes

1. See C. W. E. Bigsby's *A Critical Introduction to Twentieth-Century American Drama*, Volume 2, and Thomas P. Adler's "The Dialogue of Incompletion: Language in Tennessee Williams' Later Plays."

2. For Williams' plays, I have used the following abbreviations: *Out Cry*, OC; *The Two-Character Play*, TP; *Battle of Angels*, BA; *Dragon Country* (which includes *In the Bar of a Tokyo Hotel*), DC; *The Glass Menagerie*, GM; *A Streetcar Named Desire*, SND.

Works Cited

Adler, Thomas P. "The Dialogue of Incompletion: Language in Tennessee Williams' Later Plays." In *Tennessee Williams: A Collection of Critical Essays*. Ed. Stephen S. Stanton. Englewood Cliffs: Prentice Hall, 1977.

Arnott, Catherine M. *Tennessee Williams on File*. London: Methuen, 1985.

Artaud, Antonin. *The Theater and Its Double*. Trans. Mary Caroline Richards. New York: Grove Press, 1958.

Bigsby, C. W. E. *A Critical Introduction to Twentieth-Century American Drama*, Volume 2, *Tennessee Williams, Arthur Miller, Edward Albee*. New York: Cambridge University Press, 1982.

Devlin, Albert J., ed. *Conversations with Tennessee Williams*. Jackson: Univ. Press of Mississippi, 1986.

Parker, R. B. "The Circle Closed: A Psychological Reading of *The Glass Menagerie* and *The Two-Character Play.*" *Modern Drama* 28:4 (Dec. 1985) 517-34.

Reed, Rex. "Tennessee Williams's *Out Cry*: A Colossal Bore," *Sunday News*, 11 March 1973, p. 5, in *Dictionary of Literary Biography, Documentary Series: An Illustrated Chronicle*. Volume 4. *Tennessee Williams*, eds. Margaret A. Van Antwerp and Sally Jones (Detroit: Gale Research Company, 1984) 287-89.

Taylor, Lyle. "*The Two-Character Play*: A Producer's View." *The Tennessee Williams Review* (Fall 1979) 20-23.

Thompson, Judith J. *Tennessee Williams' Plays: Memory, Myth, and Symbol.* New York: Peter Lang, 1987.

Williams, Tennessee. *Dragon Country.* New York: New Directions, 1970.

_____. *The Glass Menagerie.* New York: New Directions. 1945.

_____. *Memoirs.* New York: Doubleday, 1975.

_____. *Orpheus Descending with Battle of Angels.* New York: New Directions, 1958.

_____. *Out Cry.* New York: New Directions, 1969.

_____. *Stopped Rocking and Other Screenplays.* New York: New Directions, 1984.

_____. *A Streetcar Named Desire.* New York: Signet, 1947.

_____. *The Two-Character Play.* New York: New Directions, 1969.

Peeping Tom:
Voyeurism, Taboo, and Truth in the World of Tennessee Williams's Short Fiction _____

George W. Crandell

To enter the fictional world of Tennessee Williams is to come in through the keyhole, to gaze, unobserved, at the intimate actions of characters often engaged in behaviors normally considered to be religiously, socially, or morally taboo. To read the stories of Tennessee Williams is thus to become a kind of voyeur, surreptitiously watching—and deriving pleasure from watching—at the same time incurring no obligation to become engaged with the subject, either physically (an impossibility) or emotionally. With our implied consent, Williams places us in the role of the spectator and the voyeur, safely distant in time and place, and equally distant emotionally from the characters whose lives we observe in secret.

By providing entrée into this imaginary world, Williams satisfies a fundamental curiosity, the reader's basic desire to know, to see—with the possibility of understanding—how other people live, how the world appears through different eyes. Commenting on the voyeuristic nature of the experience of reading fiction, William Gass suggests that fiction provides access to what is otherwise inaccessible to us, the consciousness of another human being, for example, or the private and thus intimate acts of ordinary domestic life (83-84). What readers desire, Gass contends, is "the penetration of privacy. We want to see under the skirt. . . . For the voyeur, fiction is what's called *going all the way*" (84-85).

Gass reminds us, however, that what we witness between the covers of a fictional book is really a "manufactured privacy," an artificial creation that makes real life more interesting than it actually is, "because the real world plainly bores us" (85). For the reader whose ordinary life experience does not include sacrilege, poverty, homelessness, sadism, masochism, homosexuality, attempted rape, mass murder, or cannibalism, the stories of Tennessee Williams provide for the voyeuristic reader a virtual spectacle.

Shocking as this list of taboo topics may seem, Williams actually treats these subjects more circumspectly than this summary listing suggests, and the medium of fiction plays a role in muting the startling effect. As Gass remarks, the fictional work is not like a billboard or a movie: "The privacy which a book makes public is . . . made public very privately" (85). Initially, to avoid giving offense to uninitiated and unsuspecting readers, Williams took precautions to insure that his potentially shocking work was distributed privately rather than displayed publicly. When, for example, his first collection of short stories was published in 1949, Williams insisted that copies of the book be distributed with the following special message to booksellers from the author and the publisher:

> Tennessee Williams' stories—ONE ARM—have been published in a limited edition. May we request that you handle their sale by personal solicitation and subscription rather than by general display. We are particularly anxious that the book should not be displayed in windows or on open tables. While this request may be unusual, you will oblige both author and publisher by fulfilling it. (Crandell 75)

Even as many as twenty years before the publication of this first volume, the imagined spectator and witness to violations of taboo, specifically religious taboo, is present in Williams's fiction. In an early story called "The Vengeance of Nitocris,"[1] for example, we observe the sacrilege of a young Egyptian pharaoh who purposely allows the altar fires honoring the god Osiris to go out and to remain extinguished for a period of five days, when "[e]ven for one moment to allow darkness upon the altars of the god was considered by the priests to be a great offence against him" (1). The pharaoh, angered by Osiris for destroying a bridge across the Nile that took the Egyptian ruler five years to construct, compounds his offense by driving the priests from Osiris's temple, personally blowing out the candles lighting the holy chambers, and violently defiling "the hallowed altars with the carcasses of beasts" (2). According to the narrator's account, the pharaoh had even "burned the carrion of a hyena" on the altar, the beast "most abhorrent" to Osiris (2). Osiris is avenged, however,when the "haughty" pharaoh confronts an angry mob that gathers at the base of the palace steps demanding that he re-light the fires (3). Brandishing his sword, the pharaoh defiantly refuses, but when he puts his weight upon a crumbling stone at the top of the steps, he loses his balance and "in a series of wild somersaults" tumbles to his death, an event interpreted by one of the priests as "[a] sign from the god!" (3).

The pharaoh's violations of religious taboos are but a prelude, however, to the narrator's primary focus of interest and thus the object of the readers' sustained view: the vengeful machinations of the pharaoh's sister, the empress Nitocris, who gives the story its title. Chosen by the priests to succeed her brother, Nitocris exacts her socially and morally reprehensible revenge in methodical but elaborate fashion. She begins by erecting a palatial temple, especially designed and constructed to suit her vengeful purposes. Upon its completion, she hosts a banquet there, inviting as her unsuspecting guests all of the people whom she holds personally responsible for her brother's death. At the height of the celebration, Nitocris slips away, her absence unnoticed by her guests. Safely removed from the temple, the empress and her conspirators unleash a flood of water from the Nile River into the temple, trapping her intended victims in an underground chamber from which there is no escape:

> With the ferocity of a lion springing into the arena of a Roman amphitheater to devour the gladiators set there for its delectation, the black water plunged in. Furiously it surged over the floor of the room, sweeping tables before it and sending its victims, now face to face with their harrowing doom, into a hysteria of terror. (10)

As part of the narrative description of this scene, Williams includes a statement that articulates the stance he imagines for his readers: "And what a scene of chaotic and hideous horror might a spectator have beheld!" (11). The point of view that Williams envisions aims to satisfy the reader's desire to be present in order to see and the simultaneous wish to be absent, in this case, to be safely removed from the site (but not the sight) of destruction. In this respect, the imagined spectator's point of view in Williams's story corresponds to what Joel Rudinow describes as the "paradoxical basis" of the voyeur's position: the simultaneous wish "to be and not to be in the presence of the object of interest" (176).

In "The Vengeance of Nitocris" Williams employs religious taboo as a pretext to his more detailed representation of the artful design of revenge. In subsequent work he exploits more frequently the humorous and critical potential inherent in social and moral wrongdoing. In some of these later stories, the voyeur figures prominently as a character whose point of view affords Williams the opportunity to examine with impunity behaviors considered by cultural standards of normality to be taboo.

In the fictional world of Tennessee Williams, the voyeur assumes a variety of forms. In a study of the voyeur's gaze in Hollywood films, Norman K. Denzin classifies as many as a dozen kinds of voyeurs, at least three of which—the detective (or investigator), the sexual pervert (or erotic gazer), and the reporter—appear repeatedly in Williams's fiction (1). In a pair of stories, "The Dark Room" and "The Yellow Bird," for example, the investigator is a woman whose shocked reactions to moral turpitude provide the basis for comedy.

The investigator in "The Dark Room" is a female social worker, Miss Morgan, sent to look into the lives of a poor Italian family seeking some kind of relief from the state. Gradually Miss Morgan learns that the family's sixteen-year-old daughter, Tina, has closeted herself in a dark room for nearly six months, refusing to come out (except to go to the bathroom), piqued because her once steady boyfriend has left her to marry another woman. In an interview with Tina's mother, Miss Morgan quickly learns that Tina suffers from "pains in her stomach," but the investigator fails to detect this evidence as a sign of Tina's apparent pregnancy (94). Not until Miss Morgan learns that Tina spends most of her time in the nude, at the same time continuing to entertain her married former boyfriend, does she finally conclude: "I see! I *see!*" (97).

Similar to Miss Morgan, the voyeur in "The Yellow Bird" also sees the evidence of aberrant and immoral behavior but fails to draw the conclusion obvious to readers. The investigator in this story is a married woman sent to New Orleans by Mr. and Mrs. Increase Tutweiller to spy on their profligate daughter, Alma. While chatting with the young Miss Tutweiller, the unnamed married woman notices (by peering into an open armoire) that Alma's white summer dresses are covered with grass stains. Confronted with this sight, the emissary innocently asks: "You go on picnics?" to which Alma replies, "Yes, but not church ones" (226-27). Obviously intending to embarrass the prudish spy, Alma succeeds in bringing the conversation to an abrupt close. As Williams writes, "[t]he woman tried to think of something more to ask but she was not gifted with an agile mind" (227). In each of these stories, as in the comic films that Denzin describes, "[c]omedy unravels the voyeuristic eye, showing that such persons miss what is obvious to others, while they spend their time looking at things that either don't matter, or do matter, but in ways that the voyeur does not understand" (Denzin 65). As the prim and proper representatives of the social norm, Williams's detectives respond with indignity to the sight or suggestion of inappropriate behavior. At the same time, their comically illiberal responses point up the relative sobriety of the narrative voice, the voice of a consciousness seemingly undismayed by the observation of what is usually considered to be taboo.

While, on the one hand, Williams's detectives (who serve officially or unofficially in the employ of others) seemingly derive no pleasure from their observations, Williams's erotic voyeurs, on the other hand, gratify themselves by watching. In "Big Black: A Mississippi Idyll," for example, the voyeur is a black laborer, who, chancing to observe a young white girl bathing in a river, cannot repress his sexual longing: "Watching her from his bushy covert, his breath came thick and so loud that he feared she might hear it. . . . Big Black devoured her with his eyes, clenched his fists, stiffened in every muscle, felt sick with desire of her" (32). Big Black, who later in the story assaults the young girl, is an unusual figure in Williams's fiction, where violent voyeurs are the exception rather than the rule. More frequently, Williams's erotic voyeurs remain distant from the objects of their interest, fearful of both contact and intimacy. Typically these erotic voyeurs experience a sense of loneliness or alienation that prompts them to seek intimacy with others, but fear prevents them from obtaining what they desire. Instead, voyeurism becomes for them a substitute for intimacy, a "perverted" behavior which in turn, makes impossible the kind of reciprocal relationship they desperately desire.

At least since the time of Sigmund Freud, voyeurism has been considered a sexual perversion,[2] but even before that time, an action punishable by blindness. According to legend, when Lady Godiva, wife of the Earl of Mercia, made her famous ride through the streets of Coventry (clad in nothing more than a garment of her long, flowing hair), the tailor who peeked, the original "Peeping Tom," was "struck blind" for his offense (Hawkes 3). Coincidentally, Tennessee Williams's given name, in abbreviated form, Tom, is the same as that of the unfortunate tailor. It is not by chance, however, that the erotic voyeur in Williams's autobiographical story "The Resemblance Between a Violin Case and a Coffin" is also called Tom.

The self-confessed voyeur in this story is a pre-pubescent boy who experiences a sense of alienation and loss when his sister experiences her first menstrual period and thus enters into adulthood, leaving behind her brother and childhood companion as if she has "gone on a journey" and yet "remained in sight" (270). The first-person narrator repeatedly describes their severed relationship in terms of desertion and estrangement, but what he feels most painfully is the loss of intimacy that he once shared with his sister: "for now that she had abandoned me, mysteriously and willfully withdrawn her enchanting intimacy, I felt too resentful even to acknowledge secretly, to myself, how much had been lost through what she had taken away" (272).

The figurative "departure" of the sister and the consequent loss of intimacy is the traumatic event that precipitates Tom's voyeuristic behavior. As the narrator confesses, "I watched her from a distance and under a shadow" (273). Even more importantly, the act of voyeurism becomes for the narrator a habitual way of seeing, the retrospective act of storytelling, "looking back" on events from the past, a re-envisioning of the voyeuristic scene (273). As Rudinow insightfully points out, although voyeurism stems from "the wish to be in two places at once, both in and out of the presence of the object of interest," voyeurism is really "concerned not with location but with intimacy, i.e., mutual presence" (177). Unable to achieve or maintain a satisfactorily intimate relationship with a desired other, "[t]he voyeur attempts to quench the thirst for intimacy through the substituent of the voyeuristic spectacle" (Rudinow 178).

As a consequence of his separation from his sister and the resulting loss of intimacy, Tom not only engages in voyeuristic activity but also experiences feelings of uncertainty about his own relationships with others, as well as doubts and confusion about his own sexual identity. Apart from his sister, Tom is forced, for the first time, to define the boundaries of his self, to define himself in relationship to others. Although initially the focus of Tom's gaze is upon his sister, he soon finds himself attracted to her frequent companion, Richard Miles. When Tom and his sister on one occasion chance to meet Richard, Tom is overwhelmed by conflicting desires. On the one hand, he is physically attracted to Richard, fantasizing that his fair skin would be "desirable to touch" (276). On the other hand, Tom is fearful of contact, mindful that homoerotic desire is, for those like Tom who "associate the sensual with the impure," a moral taboo (277). When Richard, for example, extends his hand in greeting, the confused Tom panics. As Tom recalls the experience: "Instead of taking the hand I ducked away from him. I made a mumbling sound that could have had very little resemblance to speech . . . and fled into a drugstore" (276).

To place himself more at ease, Tom adopts the position of the voyeur, locating himself at a safe distance from the objects of his interest, at the same time harboring a desire to be close to them. Tom is thus similar to the voyeur described by Rudinow who "stands in a paradoxical relation to intimacy: craving and dreading it at once" (178). Substituting the voyeur's experience for the possibility of a close relationship with his sister or Richard Miles, Tom conceals himself behind his bedroom door, preferring to watch the pair from a distance as they practice together in preparation for a musical recital. "[W]ith a fantastic stealth," Tom guiltily confesses, "as if a sound would betray a disgusting action, I would open the door two inches, an aperture just enough to enclose the piano corner as by the lateral boundaries of a stage" (277). Tom's voyeuristic behavior, however, precludes the possibility of a reciprocal relationship forming with either his sister or Richard Miles. As Rudinow explains, the voyeuristic relationship is characterized by its "asymmetry" (176). The voyeur insists that "something or someone should be open to his inspection and contemplation; *but no reciprocal revelation or openness is conceded,* for the voyeur requires at the same time to remain hidden" (Rudinow 176). In the context of Williams's story, to crave intimacy seems only normal, just as to dread it, considering the prevailing cultural prohibitions against both incest and homosexuality, also seems normal. To crave it and dread it at the same time, however, is to be caught in the paradoxical place of the erotic voyeur.

As in "The Resemblance Between a Violin Case and a Coffin," the erotic voyeur in "The Night of the Iguana" is a person in need of "sympathetic companionship," a lonely individual searching for intimacy but who sabotages the possibility of a close relationship by observing others voyeuristically (230). While vacationing near Acapulco at the Costa Verda Hotel, Edith Jelkes, a spinster who has given up art instruction for "a life of refined vagrancy," is suddenly captivated by a pair of writers lodged in the same hotel (229). To be near them, Edith positions herself each morning close to the place where the writers work. Later she times her own trips to the beach to coincide with theirs, as Williams writes, "for the purpose of espionage" (232). Similar to Williams's other female voyeurs, Miss Jelkes is shocked by the writers' socially taboo behavior. She observes the two men holding hands, for example, and witnesses the younger man disrobing on the beach. Her comically prudish response is to ask the Patrona of the hotel to persuade the young writer to "keep the dorsal side of his nudity toward the beach" (234).

At the same time craving and dreading an intimate relationship with a man, Edith spies on the writers, substituting the voyeuristic act for the possibility of "mutual presence" (Rudinow 177). In the process, although Edith attempts to conceal her spying, she nevertheless reveals herself and her intentions. As a result, instead of becoming the writers' intimate companion, she becomes a source of irritation to them and the target of their rebuke. When Miss Jelkes moves from one room to another room adjacent to one of them, putting her "within close range of their nightly conversations" (239), the men respond by making cruel remarks about her, knowing that she is probably eavesdropping. Indeed, she is, and, as Williams adds: "[i]f she could have risen from bed and peered through one of the cracks without betraying herself she might have done so" (241). The deliberate cruelty of the writers is finally enough to flush the wounded voyeur from the relative safety of her ineptly concealed position. In the encounter with the two men that follows, after Edith rushes to the door of their room, the younger writer accuses Edith of "spying" and bruskly departs (242). The older writer, however, invites her inside. Still desiring intimacy, Edith wonders if this man, in whom she recognizes a kindred spirit, might be the one with whom she establishes a close relationship: "She felt herself upon the verge of saying incommunicable things to this man whose singularity was so like her own in many essential respects" (243). Misled by desire, however, Edith fails to anticipate the writer's unexpectedly violent response. The older writer suddenly "thrust his knees between hers" in a rape attempt, but the "demon of her virginity . . . fought off the assailant more furiously than he attacked her" (244). Although Edith is surprised by a "wing-like throbbing against her belly, and then a scalding wetness," she escapes the attack seemingly unharmed, even grateful for the briefly violent but seemingly intimate experience (244). Reflecting on the events of the evening, she concludes that "the strangling rope of her loneliness" has at last "been severed by what had happened" (245). Although Edith feels changed as a result of the encounter, the possibility of a lasting relationship based upon intimacy has been thwarted by her voyeuristic activity.

Unlike the erotic voyeurs who are stimulated by a desire for intimacy, Williams's reporters are motivated primarily by curiosity, a desire to understand the mysteries of life and to report (narrate) the truth. The subjects of their voyeuristic interest are people whose lives are tainted with the taboo. In "Hard Candy," for instance, the protagonist, Mr. Krupper, is a "shameful and despicable" old man, who seeks his sexual satisfaction from chance acquaintances in the upper balconies of a movie theater called the Joy Rio (345). Although more respectable than Mr. Krupper, Brick Pollitt in "Three Players of a Summer Game" has similarly tarnished his reputation by engaging in taboo behavior, succumbing to the temptations of both alcohol and adultery.

Curious about the lives of disreputable people, the typical reporter in Williams's fictional world is an anonymous first-person narrator, a curious onlooker who, distant in time and place from the people and events described in his story, "soften[s]" and arranges the "grossly naturalistic details" of a person's life into a satisfying and significant whole ("Hard Candy" 337). The reporter in "Three Players of a Summer Game," for instance, is another pre-pubescent boy whose voyeuristic interest is the alcoholic Brick Pollitt and the widowed mother with whom Brick engages in an adulterous affair. The young narrator watches with "unabated interest" as the history of their taboo relationship unfolds (318). Similar to the narrator in "Hard Candy," the young voyeur violates the principles of "literal history" to expose the "hidden truth" revealed by the events that he observes (305). As the narrator reports: "It would be absurd to pretend that this is altogether the way it was, and yet it may be closer than a literal history could be to the hidden truth of it" (304-05). As in *The Glass Menagerie*, memory functions for this narrator as the prism through which the story is refracted. "Whenever," for example, the narrator chances to see "a flagpole on an expanse of green lawn," he begins to recall the story of Brick Pollitt and so puts together the "baffling bits and pieces that make his legend" (304).

About this narrator, and about Williams's reporters in general, we often discover little, except that they express a sensitivity toward their subjects that is generally uncharacteristic of objective news reporting. Unlike journalists whose reputations are staked upon factual accuracy, Williams's voyeuristic reporters are bound by fidelity to "the artist's method," a technique described in "The Resemblance Between a Violin Case and a Coffin" as "not explaining but putting the blocks together in some other way that seems more significant" to the artist (274). This alternative method of reporting involves, for example, mitigating the harshness of ordinary life. As the narrator in "Hard Candy" explains: "when you attempt to set those details down in a tale, some measure of obscurity or indirection is called for to provide the same, or even approximate, softening effect that existence in time gives to those gross elements in the life itself" (337).

Despite obvious differences, each of Williams's voyeurs—the detective, the erotic gazer, and the reporter—is engaged in a kind of search for truth. Williams's detectives are often disturbed by the discovery of truth, especially by the uncovering of behaviors normally considered to be taboo. As comic figures in Williams's fiction, the investigators unwittingly call into question the very social and moral norms that they themselves represent. Ironically, then, they function as social critics, serving to make the unacceptable acceptable by exposing it to public view.

Williams's erotic voyeurs search for the kind of intimate truth that can only be shared between two people in private. Unfortunately, for these characters, the "voyeuristic spectacle" becomes a substitute for the intimacy that they both desire and fear simultaneously (Rudinow 178). By their actions, the erotic voyeurs testify to the difficulty of forming reciprocal relationships and to the impossibility of establishing intimacy or "mutual presence" so long as the truth of one's presence must be concealed (Rudinow 177).

The voyeuristic reporter is also concerned with exposing the truth, not only to inform but also to facilitate understanding. Williams's reporters question whether the mere factual representation of events is adequate to present the truth of life in all its complexity. Instead, they adopt "the method of the artist," selecting and arranging their objects according to a sense of design superior to the strictly chronological order of events (Williams, "Resemblance" 274). Casting doubt on the value and truthfulness of photographic realism, Williams's reporters echo the author's sentiments in his "Production Notes" to *The Glass Menagerie*: "Everyone should know nowadays the unimportance of the photographic in art: that truth, life, or reality is an organic thing which the poetic imagination can represent or suggest, in essence, only through transformation, through changing into other forms than those which were merely present in appearance" (131).

All of Williams's voyeurs engage in exposing to view subject matter normally considered to be taboo. By treating these topics with sensitivity, however, Williams makes more acceptable that which is taboo, at the same time lending respectability to those who violate religious, moral, and social norms. As critics of culturally defined standards of behavior, Williams's voyeurs thus challenge readers to reconsider the nature of truth, even what it is possible to know, as well as what should or should be not considered taboo.

From *The Southern Quarterly* 38, no. 1 (Fall 1999): 28-35. Copyright © 1999 by University of Southern Mississippi. Reprinted with permission of *The Southern Quarterly*.

Notes

1. "The Vengeance of Nitocris" was first published in *Weird Tales* 12.2 (Aug. 1928): 253-60, 288.

2. Freud writes in "Three Essays on the Theory of Sexuality" that "pleasure in looking [scopophilia] becomes a perversion (a) if it is restricted exclusively to the genitals, or (b) if it is connected with the overriding of disgust (as in the case of *voyeurs* or people who look on at excretory functions), or (c) if, instead of being *preparatory* to the normal sexual aim, it supplants it" (157).

Works Cited

Crandell, George W. *Tennessee Williams: A Descriptive Bibliography*. Pittsburgh: U of Pittsburgh P, 1995.

Denzin, Norman K. *The Cinematic Society: The Voyeur's Gaze*. London: Sage, 1995.

Freud, Sigmund. "The Sexual Aberrations." *Three Essays on The Theory of Sexuality*. 1905. *The Standard Edition of the Complete Psychological Works of Sigmund Freud*. Trans. and ed. James Strachey et al. Vol. 7. London: Hogarth P, 1953. 135-172.

Gass, William. *On Being Blue: A Philosophical Inquiry*. Boston: Godine, 1975.

Hawkes, Henry William. *A Brief History of The Earl of Mercia, Lady Godiva, and Peeping Tom of Coventry, From the earliest Period to the present Day*. Coventry: Charles A. N. Rollason, 1836.

Rudinow, Joel. "Representation, Voyeurism, and the Vacant Point of View." *Philosophy and Literature* 3 (1979): 173-86. Subsequent references are cited parenthetically within the text.

Williams, Tennessee. "Big Black: A Mississippi Idyll." *Collected Stories*. 26-31.

_____. *Collected Stories*. New York: New Directions, 1985.

_____. "The Dark Room." *Collected Stories*. 93-98.

_____. *The Glass Menagerie. The Theatre of Tennessee Williams*. Vol. 1. New York: New Directions, 1971. 123-238.

_____. "Hard Candy." *Collected Stories*. 335-46.

_____. "The Night of the Iguana." *Collected Stories*. 229-245.

_____. "The Resemblance Between a Violin Case and a Coffin." *Collected Stories*. 270-82.

_____. "Three Players of a Summer Game." *Collected Stories*. 303-25.

_____. "The Vengeance of Nitocris." *Collected Stories*. 1-12.

_____. "The Yellow Bird." *Collected Stories*. 221-28.

"The Transmutation of Experience":[1]
The Aesthetics and Themes of
Tennessee Williams's Nonfiction_____

D. Dean Shackelford

Readers have often used the nonfiction essays of Tennessee Williams to interpret his plays, fiction, and poetry, and to assess his work as a whole. Although there have been frequent references to Tennessee Williams's personal essays, prefaces to his own plays, and reviews of others' creative work, little if any critical attention has been given to what these nonfiction pieces contribute to our understanding of Williams the individual, the artist, the intellectual, and the critic. Williams the personal essayist, social critic, and literary theorist does, however, deserve serious scholarly attention.

Close examination of the many short pieces[2] Williams wrote for periodicals and as introductions and prefaces to the creative work of his own and his friends and colleagues reveals not only an effective and worthy prose style but also a perceptive sense of the world after World War II and the creative potential and practice of fellow artists. In "Critic Says 'Evasion,' Writer Says 'Mystery,'" which originally appeared in the *New York Herald Tribune* of 17 April 1955, in response to Walter Kerr's critique of *Cat on a Hot Tin Roof*, and is reprinted in *Where I Live*, Williams also anticipates contemporary theories of the reader and the multiplicity of meanings in a text by suggesting that the "truth about human character in a play, as in life, varies with the variance of experience and viewpoint of those that view it" (70). While he is referring to criticisms that he is being ambiguous about Brick's sexual identity, this passage is only one example of how his nonfiction works illustrate his sophisticated style as well as anticipate and open the possibility for contemporary poststructuralist approaches to reading literature.

Williams's nonfiction includes personal essays and reflections, prefaces to his own works, and reviews and criticism of the creative work of others, mostly friends. These subgenres are by no means mutually exclusive, for Williams's prose is often loosely structured, organic, and informal, and he combines these three categories oftentimes in one essay or review. Therefore, for purposes of discussion, the present study of Williams's nonfiction will address the primary themes evident in the personal essays and some theoretical components of his commentaries about his own and others' work. Before examining significant themes in and examples of the nonfiction, one should, however, be familiar with pertinent biographical details related to these ignored works.

According to Lyle Leverich's *Tom: The Unknown Tennessee Williams*, after twelve-year-old Tom was asked to read a commentary on Tennyson's "Lady of Shalott" in front of class and he received a positive response, he decided to become a writer (64); moreover, his first publication, "Isolated," was an essay. It appeared in the student newspaper, *The Junior Life*, in November 1924, while he was a student at Blewett Junior High School. He was first published professionally in *Smart Set* and *Weird Tales*, a pulp magazine, in 1928 (Leverich 82). During his high school years he won several literary contests, but only when he entered college in St. Louis at Washington University did he begin the serious study of literature and the Western critical heritage.

After graduating from University City High School in St. Louis in June 1929, Williams enrolled as an undergraduate journalism major at the University of Missouri in Columbia. At that time he studied the poetry and biography of Percy Bysshe Shelley and became a member of the Missouri Chapter of the College Poetry Society (Leverich 125). His critical and biographical reading, and his journalism classes, likely helped him develop stylistic clarity and precision in prose. After a stint at the St. Louis International Shoe Company, he enrolled at Washington University, beginning in September 1935. There he studied literature more formally and began to develop a critical sensibility which can be observed through studying his own prefaces and other literary criticism.

During these college years, he read many canonical writers as well as contemporary playwrights. He examined the plays of Eugene O'Neill for a course in which he wrote a critical essay entitled "Some Representative Plays of O'Neill and a Discussion of His Art," whose style the professor labeled "a bit too truculent" (Leverich 183). He also studied English literature under Dr. Otto Heller, a well-known scholar of Henrik Ibsen, and wrote a term paper entitled "Birth of an Art (Anton Chekhov and the New Theatre) by T. L. Williams" (Leverich 217). However, he ended his career at Washington University partly because he did not enjoy his classes under Heller: "Although Tom's notebooks attest to the fact that he was well read . . . he became increasingly annoyed by the professor's intellectual posturings" (Leverich 183).

His reaction to Heller was the beginning of a long animosity with the critical and, to some extent, academic world which, in his estimation, failed to understand his artistry and appreciate his plays, especially his most experimental and late ones. He would become a college graduate only after attending the Writers' Workshop at the University of Iowa and experiencing what Leverich calls "a drama department that espoused his philosophy of a theatre in action" (226).

These shaping influences enabled Williams to develop as a prose stylist and critic of his own and others' works. When he began to establish himself as a playwright, he had already written prose for his public school and college classes, and had been actively involved in reading, assessing, and writing poetry and prose. His personal essays and literary criticism demonstrate not only his knowledge of classical and modern literature, including drama, but also his distrust of "intellectual posturings." Since the biographical context for examining Williams as a prose writer has been established, a closer look at some representative illustrations of the style and subject matter of Williams's nonfiction will be undertaken at this point.

Several recurring themes are evident in his personal essays. These include endurance and struggle; the problem of the artist in American society; the struggle over class, materialism, and the American dream; and the devaluation of the individual. Within these contexts, a number of essays contain a social critique of McCarthyism itself or the tendency toward such an extreme in American society.

To Williams endurance and struggle build stronger character. In one of his best essays, "On a Streetcar Named Success," a piece which originally appeared in the *New York Times* on 30 November 1947, just before the premiere of *A Streetcar Named Desire*, he reflects this own experience as a successful new writer first receiving supportive critical attention. While discussing his past experience, he implies that the hard work may have been more beneficial than the actual reality of success: "The sort of life which I had had previous to this popular success was one that required endurance, a life of clawing and scratching along a sheer surface and holding on tight with raw fingers to every inch of rock higher than the one caught hold of before, but it was a good life because it was the sort of life for which the human organism is created" (*Where I Live* 16). Success is "a catastrophe" because to Williams a life without struggle ceases to be a life with meaning, as this passage suggests: "But once you fully apprehend the vacuity of a life without struggle you are equipped with the basic means of salvation" (21). This essay shows that not only does Williams see endurance as the triumph of humanity, a theme which he repeats in his plays time and again, but he also sees himself in his characters.

Part of the problem with success for the artist in American society, according to Williams, is a curious ambivalence toward his place in a culture which has marginalized him. In another significant personal essay, "A Writer's Quest for Parnassus," he addresses this ambivalence. Drawing upon assumptions about the ideal locale for the American expatriate, he points out that for him, both personally and artistically, Rome inspires much more creative writing and personal freedom than America or Paris, the site of the "Lost Generation" after World War I. Throughout the essay Williams suggests that Rome is the ideal place for the writer. He states of the Romans: "Their history has made them wiser than Americans. It has also made them more tolerant, more patient, and considerably more human as well as a great deal sadder"

(34). Referring to the mythical Parnassus in his title, Williams also admonishes America for her lack of appreciation for sensitivity and romance—implying the harshness of everyday life in this country which is so antithetical to the pursuit of art.

Art thus becomes secondary to pursuit of the American dream, a material quest for success which often destroys the human (and the artist's) spirit. In the pre-*Streetcar* essay referred to earlier, Williams also refers to the Cinderella story as "our favorite national myth" ("On a Streetcar" 15), implicitly criticizing capitalism and its potential for exploitation: "Nobody should have to clean up anybody else's mess in this world. It is terribly bad for both parties, but probably worse for the one receiving the service" ("On a Streetcar" 20). The only endeavor worth pursuing is done so at the price of struggle, suggesting that capitalism becomes problematic as an end in itself—especially when one feels too comfortable.

At the heart of these social critiques is an implicit attack on McCarthyism and its devaluation of the individual. Significantly, Williams identifies the social roots of McCarthyism, a distrust of difference and people of other cultures and beliefs: "If these comments make me seem the opposite of a chauvinist, it is because of my honest feeling, after three years of foreign travel, that human brotherhood that stops at borders is not only delusive and foolish but enormously evil" ("A Writer's Quest" 34). His critical attitude concerning political McCarthyism is most fully revealed in another section of "A Writer's Quest": "British and American writers are more inclined to travel than others. I think the British travel to get out of the rain, but the American artist travels for a more particular reason, and for one that I hesitate to mention lest I be summoned before some investigating committee in Congress" (29). In this passage and elsewhere, Williams implicitly criticizes American society as being cold and intolerant of the individual, an attitude he surreptitiously explores through Brick's mysterious past in *Cat on a Hot Tin Roof*, produced originally in 1955 during the McCarthy era, as David Savran's book *Communists, Cowboys, and Queers* points out.[3]

In general the central themes of his personal essays are developed through a clarity of voice and vision. His essays clearly exemplify a style which is leisurely and inviting for the audience, as Alec Baldwin's readings from Williams's prose at the 1997 Tennessee Williams Literary Festival clearly demonstrated.[4] His prose style is almost always characterized as terse, witty, concrete, poetic, intelligent, and precise while, like his plays, simultaneously lyrical, even rhapsodic.

For example, in his essay entitled "Tennessee Williams: The Wolf and I," Williams narrates the entertaining but painful story of his bad experience with Wolf, his new dog. After being bitten in a hotel room, Williams is treated by an inept physician. Characterized by self-mockery, what some people today might label a "camp sensibility,"[5] this essay is anecdotal and more entertainment than serious artistry, but it shows that even during a difficult period in Williams's personal life, he was able to laugh at himself. His prose style is exemplified well through the essay's use of wit, as this passage reveals: "The doctor looked at my ankles and said, 'Oh, the Wolf has bitten you to the bone of each ankle,' which was an astute and accurate observation" (5). Later on, he describes the process of being taken to the hospital by two men in white jackets: "I had never been on a stretcher before nor had I ever before gone downstairs in the freight elevator of a large hotel. The novelty of both experiences did nothing to reassure me . . ." (5). As a whole, the essay "Wolf and I" reflects the kind of self-mockery, campiness, and humor often associated with Williams's plays. In addition; the style reflects the same tendency toward clarity, terseness, and metaphor seen elsewhere.

Another characteristic feature of Williams's nonfiction is the use of frequent references and allusions to the works of the people whom he most admired. His primary dramatic forbear, he often liked to say, was Anton Chekhov. In addition, Williams deeply admired the poetry and drama of Federico García Lorca, a fellow homosexual. His fellow southern writers, William Faulkner, Carson McCullers, Donald Windham, and Truman Capote, and his other friends and associates, including Paul and Jane Bowles, and Clark Mills (whom he had known in St.

Louis while enrolled at Washington University), are also frequently referred to in Williams's nonfiction and letters—often directly by name (Leverich 155). As these examples suggest, perhaps the most characteristic feature evident in his nonfiction works is personal reflection on his own and others' work. In fact, the difficulty of examining Williams's nonfiction is that, like much contemporary literature, it resists neat categorization and thus anticipates the blurring of genre and form so often discussed in connection with postmodernism.

Rather than look at the prefaces to and commentaries about his own work in separate categories, therefore, the best way to approach these critical and theoretical works is through examining the concepts upon which Williams draws and those from which he departs. A significant purpose of the present examination of Williams's nonfiction is to establish how he anticipates many contemporary debates about the nature of literature, theory, and interpretation. Thus, an exploration of individual essays is less instructive than a look at some literary and theoretical constructs with which Williams is working in his nonfiction and his criticism.

A student of western literature and the Eurocentric dramatic heritage, Williams, in his critical works, drew upon two primary theories of art. The first, derived largely from Aristotle's conception of tragedy but generally practiced in the history of western literature from the ancients to the twentieth century, was representation, a concept which contemporary literary theorists have begun to problematize more and more. Conventional readings of Aristotle place emphasis on mimesis, or art as a mirror or imitation of life because in *The Poetics* Aristotle describes tragedy in this manner.

> Tragedy, then, is an imitation of an action that is serious, complete, and of a
> certain magnitude; in language embellished with each kind of artistic orna-
> ment, the several kinds being found in separate parts of the play; in the
> form of action, not narrative; through pity and fear affecting the proper pur-
> gation of these emotions. (36)

In "The Timeless World of a Play," Williams reiterates Aristotle's notion of drama as a mirror or reflection of reality: "So successfully have we disguised from ourselves the intensity of our own feelings, the sensibility of our own hearts, that plays in the tragic tradition have begun to seem untrue" (263). Implicitly, then, he is agreeing with Aristotle's view that art is a mirror of reality. Similarly, when describing his commitment to the still problematic play *Orpheus Descending*, Williams states, in "The Past, the Present, and the Perhaps," that "beneath that now familiar surface it is a play about unanswered questions that haunt the hearts of people and the difference between continuing to ask them, a difference represented by the four major protagonists of the play . . ." (220). Williams clearly shows that he is after representation and, at the same time, suggests, like Aristotle, that tragedy can only imitate or mirror life—not literally convey it (note the phrase "familiar surface"). To get at the truths through which his dramas penetrate, one, therefore, has to look beneath the surface. Looking at Williams's prefaces to his works suggests that he accepts Aristotelian conceptions of tragedy and representation but is aware of the problems brought about by a purely mimetic theory of art.

A second, conventional approach to art which is evident in Williams's nonfiction is romantic and expressivistic. When discussing *Cat on a Hot Tin Roof* in "Person—to—Person," he admits, "Of course it is a pity that so much of all creative work is so closely related to the personality of the one who does it" (3). This comment reflects not only the Aristotelian conception of mimesis but also echoes the Platonic notion of the world beyond the real to the imagined or idealized. To expand upon this view, Williams uses the term "organic" more than any other in his nonfiction to describe his conception of art and the artist.

In his essays on the controversial *Camino Real* particularly, Williams embraces the organic theory of art and heavily criticizes audiences for their response to the play. Deconstructing Aristotelian notions of mimesis, Williams, in the foreword to *Camino Real*, calls it "the construction of another world, a separate existence" and claims "it is nothing more nor less than my conception of the time and world that I live in . . ." (419). This organic theory—that is, the idea that art is an outgrowth of the poetic imagination—places Williams in the tradition of the literary criticism of Coleridge in *Biographia Literaria*. Coleridge suggests that the poet of imagination is able to use the tradition to create his own aesthetic experience, distinguishing between the imagination and the fancy. "Fancy" implies a kind of artistic control and "mechanical" mastering of the techniques of art.[6]

When describing a book of poetry written by his friend Oliver Evans, Williams also refers to the organic theory of art. His foreword to *Young Man with a Screwdriver*, for example, emphasizes their friendship and places his work within "the oldest and purest tradition" of writing spontaneous, immediate poetry (2)—again, organic and romantic theory. He also praises Evans's "latitude and variety both in subject and quality" (2) and refers to him as "singer" (3)—all romantic images of the artist.

Other reviews reflect this conventional approach to textuality as well. When introducing the poetry collection of Gilbert Maxwell, entitled *Go Looking: Poems 1933-1953*, Williams compares his situation in assessing his friend's work with that of Eugene O'Neill in trying to write a foreword to Hart Crane's first book. Though such effusiveness is characteristic of Williams's tendency toward romantic emotionalism, Maxwell is far from being Hart Crane, and I am sure Williams, who admired and identified with Crane more than any other poet, knew this was hyperbole as well. Maxwell is, however, a lyric poet who would appeal to a playwright who sees personal lyricism as his most characteristic element.

The critical tension between art as a representation of external reality—society—and art as a reflection of the subjectivity of the writer in western literature and criticism is evident not only in Williams's nonfiction but also through contemporary gay approaches to Williams's works. Furthermore, his essays anticipate current debate over the role of authorship and work. With regard to the death of author arguments of contemporary theorists such as Michel Foucault and Roland Barthes,[7] Williams would be both in agreement and disagreement for varying reasons.

He could never envision art without the presence of the artist— making him clearly a neoromantic, humanistic, and poetic artist despite his frequently naturalistic, brutally realistic portrayals of violence and sexuality. Yet his attitudes are not always consistent even about the autobiographical dimensions of his works. As anyone who has read the numerous interviews regarding the role of homosexuality in his plays can recall, he often denies and underestimates the role of his own gay subjectivity in his creative work.[8] Perhaps the best way to see Williams's ambivalence about his gay subjectivity is to suggest that, like Foucault, he tries to decenter the text and erase, at least in print, the idea that his works are about homosexuality—rejecting essentialist notions about textuality, the construction of the self, and the author's presence.

Such a practice also enables Williams to effect his organic theory of writing as well as to practice now recognized truisms of contemporary literary criticism: the inseparability of the text from the reader and the subjectivity at the heart of all interpretation. When he writes about Brick in *Cat on a Hot Tin Roof*, probably his gayest play before he came out in an interview on television with David Frost in 1970, he strongly resists reductionist readings of his alcoholic character—a notion which perhaps indicates his desire for multiple interpretations of the play and anticipates deconstructionist approaches to literature arguing for the multiplicity of meaning. In describing Brick's character, for example, he says, in what amounts to a short essay and analysis in the printed version of the play: "Some mystery should be left in the revelation of character in a play, just as a great deal of mystery is always left in the revelation of character in life, even in one's own character to himself. This does not absolve the playwright of his duty to observe and probe as clearly and deeply as he legitimately can . . ." (115). The resistance to one reading of Brick's character anticipates deconstructionist arguments against essentialism. While Williams would be probably uncomfortable with the increasing complexity in debate surrounding textuality, he would, at the same time presumably, be open to many possible readings of Brick's character.

Thus, like many contemporary literary theorists, Williams problematizes subjectivity as a critical construct and opens up the possibility for Lacanian and other poststructuralist readings of literature. For example, in "If the Writing Is Honest," in which he reviews Inge's play *The Dark at the Top of the Stairs*, he distinguishes between representation theory—that is, art as a reflection of truth—and romantic conceptions of the artist. Sounding Platonic, Williams suggests that writing "isn't so much . . . [the artist's] mirror as it is the distillation, the essence, of what is strongest and purest in his nature, whether that be gentleness or anger, serenity or torment, light or dark" (100). Such words also bring to mind Jungian mythical criticism and Lacan's references to the mirror stage of a child's development.

Even some of the language in the essay opens up the text to Lacanian readings, as the following anecdote referring to the shadow and light would seem to suggest:

> After I had gone back to Chicago to finish out the break-in run of *Menagerie*, Bill came up one weekend to see the play. I didn't know until then that Bill wanted to be a playwright. After the show, we walked back to my hotel . . . and on the way he suddenly confided to me, with characteristic simplicity and directness, that being a successful playwright was what he most wanted in the world for himself. This confession struck me, at the time, as being just a politeness, an effort to dispel the unreasonable gloom that had come over me at a time when I should have been most elated, an ominous letdown of spirit that followed me like my shadow wherever I went. . . . I think that Bill Inge had already made up his mind to invoke this same shadow and to suffuse it with light: and that, of course, is exactly what he has done. (103-04)

Williams uses a mythical approach to textuality as well as opens up the possibility for psychoanalytic explorations of art. Furthermore, Inge's shadow could be interpreted as an image of the self and an exploration of the problematized subject, which Lacan sees as a construction of language and art.[9] Williams's slippery subjective voice and Inge as a construction of this voice open up further possibilities for poststructuralist readings.

Moreover, Williams anticipates current literary debates concerning privileging one form or genre of literature over another. In other words, he is already raising questions about conventional formalism and canonicity. This is particularly evident when one examines his reviews of the novels of Carson McCullers, a personal friend. *Reflections in a Golden Eye*, certainly not the best of Carson McCullers's novels, was the subject for one of Williams's most effective works of nonfiction, the introduction to the novel's first edition of 1950.

The essay implicitly attacks traditional critics for their lack of appreciation for McCullers's second novel. Once categorized as a member of the southern gothic school, McCullers, he argues, is unable to move beyond this limited and essentialist notion of her fiction. Pointing out the tenderness of *The Heart Is a Lonely Hunter* as a buttress against criticism for her use of the grotesque in *Reflections*, Williams believed the harsh assessment of the latter novel resulted in critical attitudes that McCullers had not lived up to the potential shown in her first novel and reflected a darker vision. Calling McCullers the "greatest living writer" (136) in his essay "Biography of Carson McCullers," Williams praises *Clock without Hands*—McCullers's biggest critical disaster (and, to my mind, too imitative of Faulkner). Such comments suggest Williams is aware of the tendency to canonize—thus privilege—her first novel and read the remainder of her work as lesser fictions. The essay also raises questions about representation in McCullers's works and criticizes non-southerners for their misreadings of southern literature in a manner reminiscent of Flannery O'Connor in *Mystery and Manners*.

Another poststructuralist dimension to Williams's literary criticism is a tendency to accept certain assumptions of formalism and modernism and to reject others. In the same essay, he argues that McCullers's second novel demonstrates a mastery of design—a term reminiscent of formalism—and succeeds more perfectly in establishing its own reality, in creating a world of its own, a quality which he considers characteristic of a great artist (46-47)—commentary which again reflects his awareness of formalism and his application of the assumptions of his organic theory. On the other hand, he states that *The Member of the Wedding* is a better novel, saying that it combined the heartbreaking tenderness of the first with the sculptural quality of the second (47). Although privileging one McCullers novel over another, this commentary implies that art is an organic whole while at the same time deconstructs the problem of form in the second novel by suggesting that content may be separate from form in incongruous ways. He goes further: "*Reflections in a Golden Eye* is one of the purest and most powerful of those works which are conceived in that Sense of the Awful which is the desperate black root of all significant modern art" (46).

Williams would also be comfortable with the assumptions of Cultural Studies[10] and New Historicism concerning the relation of art to time and place. In a review of Paul Bowles's novel *The Sheltering Sky*, Williams acknowledges that he lives in a different world than writers of the past and places Bowles within the context of post-World War II existentialism. Describing Bowles in almost postmodern terms which suggest the breakdown of conventional literary form, William, using a poetic style characteristic of all his nonfiction and his plays as well, states concerning *The Sheltering Sky*:

> There is a curiously double level to this novel. The surface is enthralling as narrative. It is impressive as writing. But above that surface is the aura I spoke of, intangible and powerful, bringing to mind one of those clouds that you have seen in summer close to the horizon and dark in color and now and then silently pulsing with interior flashes of fire. ("Allegory" 7)

Using impressionistic language, Williams assesses the allegorical dimensions of Bowles's vision and the dangerous moral nihilism into which humanity is going at present (38). Williams's reading of Bowles connects with traditional historicism while opening up the possibility for examining tensions within popular culture and American society after World War II in a way similar to Foucault's arguments against the human subject as apart from the construction of time and place.

In "The Human Psyche—Alone," a review of another work by Paul Bowles, Williams repeats his earlier reference to the existentialist dimensions of Bowles's fiction. Here he addresses the same questions which he does in the prefaces to his own plays and nonfiction: human alienation, the artist in society, and hardness of perception (39), the latter phrase of which I take to mean Bowles's portrayal of the realities of life as he sees them (compare Williams's brutality and violence in his own plays). Bowles is described as predominantly a philosophical writer concerned with human alienation in *The Delicate Prey and Other Stories*. At the same time Williams emphasizes personal lyricism and critiques literature celebrating American culture in a positive way and denying the darkness within the human psyche. This review also includes Lacanian elements problematizing the subject, as this passage reveals: "Nowhere in any writing that I can think of has the separateness of the one human psyche been depicted more vividly and shockingly" (37).

By pointing out Bowles's deconstruction of the self, Williams anticipates Jacques Derrida's notion of the multiplicity of meaning and the destruction of binaries as well.[11] Like Julia Kristeva's arguments in "Semiotics: A Critical Science and/or a Critique of Science," Williams recognizes Bowles's complex interrogation of the self as a signifying agent and the fiction writer's approach to the fragmented human condition. His subjective response to Bowles reflects both his friendship and his perhaps unconscious awareness that meaning is at least partly constructed by the self and society. He sees in Bowles a shift in western literature and anticipates contemporary theoretical approaches such as reader-response theory and deconstructionism—providing for a multiplicity of meanings for Bowles's novel by pointing out its ambiguities and emphasizing the novel's irresolutions of the modern dilemma.

Throughout all his literary criticism, Williams blurs the social and critical constructions of author and subject, self and other, and art and life. His awareness that these binaries are almost inseparable from one another shows his affiliation with postmodern debates concerning the object and the subject and contemporary literary explorations of the "funhouse"—the artist's withdrawal into a world of imagination. In other essays Williams also anticipates postmodern questions about the role of art and social construction, leading to further debates about feminism, queer theory, and cultural studies in his critical and creative work.

In a piece entitled "Let Me Hang It All Out," Tennessee Williams describes his attempts at writing personal and critical essays as awkward adventures in the field of nonfictional prose. Despite such self-criticism, Williams the playwright is an effective, entertaining, and often perceptive prose writer. As a personal essayist, he moves from the personal to the critical to the social in one fell swoop. As a theorist of drama and critic of his own work, he is particularly significant. He understands his place in the western dramatic and literary traditions, and he recognizes the value of and importance of literature and nonfiction prose to American society and culture. When Williams reviews the fiction, poetry, and drama of fellow writers, he praises the work, saving severe criticism for the mean-spirited critics who, in his estimation, had failed to appreciate his experimental late plays and the works of his friends. Much of what is reflected in Williams nonfiction is a sensitive soul who understands the inseparability of art and the artist, subject and object, self and other—and an individual who will not be deliberately cruel (at least in print) toward his close friends and colleagues. As such a brief survey of his prose work suggests, there is much more to be said concerning this unexplored territory in Williams studies.

Notes

1. The title of this essay comes from Williams's "A Summer of Discovery," which was originally published in the *New York Herald Tribune* and reprinted in *Where I Live: Selected Essays*. There he describes the process of writing as "the most necessary impulse or drive toward . . . [the writer's] work, which is the transmutation of experience into some significant piece of creation . . ." (140).

2. Williams wrote many prefaces and introductions to his own works as well as reviews and introductions to the works of others. George W. Crandell's *Tennessee Williams: A Descriptive Bibliography* references more than fifty such pieces. The majority have been reprinted in *Where I Live*.

3. This play has frequently been read as a commentary on McCarthyism. Brick's fear of the possible repercussions about his relationship with Skipper is sometimes read as a reflection of the playwright's fear of disclosure, a point which Savran mentions. Philip C. Kolin's new book, *Tennessee Williams: A Guide to Research and Performance*, cites other readings of the play, including Clum's "'Something Cloudy, Something Clear,'" Dukore's "The Cat Has Nine Lives," and Shackelford's "The Truth That Must Be Told: Gay Subjectivity, Homophobia, and Social History in *Cat on a Hot Tin Roof.*"

4. At the 1997 Tennessee Williams/New Orleans Literary Festival in March 1997, Baldwin was the invited celebrity speaker. During one segment of the festival, he read selected essays by Williams and commented on the personal immediacy and comical dimensions within them.

5. While the term camp is subjective and contextual, I am using it to suggest the gay sense of self-mockery and "double consciousness" (a term borrowed from W. E. B. DuBois) of comic irony evident through a detached view of self through one's own and others' eyes simultaneously. David Bergman's *Camp Grounds: Style and Homosexuality* and Judith Butler's *Gender Trouble* are two important resources on the complexity of camp in the gay sensibility.

6. In *Biographia Literaria* Coleridge identifies the primary imagination as "the living power and prime agent of all human perception" and fancy, or the secondary imagination, "as an echo of the former . . . differing only in degree, and in the mode of its operation" (387).

7. Foucault problematizes the constructs of authorship and work in "What Is an Author?," saying, "The author is . . . the ideological figure by which one marks the manner in which we fear the proliferation of meaning" (353). Following Foucault's logic, Barthes argues for the "death of the Author" and the "birth of the reader" (226) as a result.

8. In numerous interviews reprinted in Albert Devlin's *Conversations with Ten-*

nessee Williams and elsewhere, he tries to deny that homosexuality is a central issue in his works.

9. See, for example, Lacan's essay "Desire and the Interpretation of Desire in *Hamlet*" and "The Mirror Stage as Formative of the Function of the I as Revealed in Psychoanalytic Experience."

10. For a good introduction and definition of the broad category "Cultural Studies," see "Notes towards a Definition of Cultural Studies" by Robert Con Davis and Ronald Schleifer.

11. This can be seen of course in many works by Jacques Derrida, including *Of Grammatology* and *Writing and Difference*. A good resource would be Peggy Kamuf's *A Derrida Reader.*

Works Cited

Aristotle. *Poetics. Dramatic Theory and Criticism: Greeks to Grotowski*. Ed. Bernard F. Dukore. New York: Holt, 1974. 31-55.

Barthes, Roland. "The Death of the Author." *Falling into Theory: Conflicting Views of Reading Literature*. Ed. David H. Richter. New York: Bedford Books, 1994. 222-26.

Bergman, David, ed. *Camp Grounds: Style and Homosexuality*. Amherst: U of Massachusetts P, 1993.

Butler, Judith. *Gender Trouble: Feminism and the Subversion of Identity*. New York: Routledge, 1990.

Clum, John M. "'Something Cloudy, Something Clear': Homophobic Discourse in Tennessee Williams." *South Atlantic Quarterly* 88 (1989): 161-79.

Coleridge, Samuel Taylor. "From *Biographia Literaria*." *The Norton Anthology of English Literature*. Vol. 1. Ed. M. H. Abrams. New York: Norton, 1993. 378-95.

Crandell, George W. *Tennessee Williams: A Descriptive Bibliography*. Pittsburgh: U of Pittsburgh P, 1995.

Davis, Robert Con, and Ronald Schleifer. "Notes towards a Definition of Cultural Studies." *Contemporary Literary Criticism: Literary and Cultural Studies*. Eds. Robert Con Davis and Ronald Schleifer. White Plains, NY: Longman, 1994. 668-80.

Derrida, Jacques. *Of Grammatology*. Trans. Gayatri Chakravorty Spivak. Baltimore: Johns Hopkins UP, 1976.

_____. *Writing and Difference*. Trans. Alan Bass. Chicago: U of Chicago P, 1978.

Devlin, Albert J., ed. *Conversations with Tennessee Williams*. Jackson: UP of Mississippi, 1986.

Dukore, Bernard F. "The Cat Has Nine Lives." *Tulane Drama Review* 8.1 (1963): 95-100.

Foucault, Michel. "What Is an Author?" Davis and Schleifer. 365-76.

Kolin, Philip C., ed. *Tennessee Williams: A Guide to Research and Performance*. Westport, CT: Greenwood, 1998.

Kristeva, Julia. "Semiotics: A Critical Science and/or a Critique of Science." Davis and Schleifer. 274-82.

Lacan, Jacques. "Desire and the Interpretation of Desire in *Hamlet*." *The Seminar, Book VII: The Ethics of Psychoanalysis, 1959-1960*. Trans. Dennis Porter. New York: Norton, 1992.

_____. "The Mirror Stage as Formative of the Function of the I as Revealed in Psychoanalytic Experience." Davis and Schleifer. 383-86.

Leverich, Lyle. *Tom: The Unknown Tennessee Williams*. New York: Crown, 1995.

Murphy, Brenda. *Tennessee Williams and Elia Kazan: A Collaboration in the Theatre*. Cambridge: Cambridge UP, 1992.

O'Connor, Flannery. *Mystery and Manners: Occasional Prose*. Ed. Sally Fitzgerald. New York: Farrar, 1969.

Savran, David. *Communists, Cowboys, and Queers: The Politics of Masculinity in the Work of Arthur Miller and Tennessee Williams*. Minneapolis: U of Minnesota P, 1992.

Shackelford, Dean. "The Truth That Must Be Told: Gay Subjectivity, Homophobia, and Social History in *Cat on a Hot Tin Roof*." *Tennessee Williams Annual Review* 1 (1998): 103-18.

Williams, Tennessee. "An Allegory of Man and His Sahara." *New York Times Book Review* 4 Dec. 1949: Sec. 7.

_____. "Biography of Carson McCullers." *Where I Live*. 133-36.

_____. *Cat on a Hot Tin Roof. The Theatre of Tennessee Williams*. Vol. 2. 9-215.

_____. "Critic Says 'Evasion,' Writer Says 'Mystery.'" *Where I Live*. 70-74.

_____. Foreword/Afterword. *Camino Real. The Theatre of Tennessee Williams*. Vol. 2. New York: New Directions, 1990. 419-424.

_____. Foreword. *Young Man with a Screwdriver*. By Oliver Evans. U of Nebraska P, 1950. 1-3.

_____. "The Human Psyche—Alone." *Where I Live*. 35-39.

_____. "If the Writing Is Honest." *Where I Live*. 100-04.

_____. Introduction. *Reflections in a Golden Eye*. By Carson McCullers. *Where I Live*. 40-48.

_____. "Let Me Hang It All Out." *New York Times* 4 Mar. 1973: Sec. 2.

_____. "On a Streetcar Named Success." *Where I Live*. 15-22.

_____. "The Past, the Present, and the Perhaps." *The Theatre of Tennessee Williams*. Vol. 3. 219-24.

_____. "Person—to—Person." *Where I Live*: 75-80.

_____. "Some Words Before." *Go Looking: Poems 1933-1953*. By Gilbert Maxwell. Boston: Bruce Humphries, 1954. 5-6.

_____. "A Summer of Discovery." *Where I Live*. 137-47.

_____. "Tennessee Williams: The Wolf and I . . . ." *New York Times* 20 Feb. 1966: Sec. 2.

_____. *The Theatre of Tennessee Williams*. New York: New Directions, 1990.

_____. "The Timeless World of a Play." *The Theatre of Tennessee Williams*. Vol. 2. 259-64.

_____. "The Timeless World of a Play." *Where I Live*. 49-54.

_____. *Where I Live: Selected Essays*. Eds. Christine R. Day and Bob Woods. New York: New Directions, 1979.

_____. "A Writer's Quest for a Parnassus." *Where I Live*. 28-34.

RESOURCES

1911	On March 26, Thomas Lanier Williams is born in Columbus, Mississippi, to Cornelius Coffin and Edwina Dakin Williams. His sister Rose was born in 1909.
1911-1918	While his father is a traveling salesman, Williams lives with his grandparents, sister, and mother; they move several times before settling in Clarksdale, Mississippi. Williams falls sick for a year with diphtheria and Bright's disease.
1918	Edwina, Rose, and Tom move to St. Louis, Missouri, to be with Cornelius.
1919	Brother Walter Dakin Williams is born.
1927	Williams wins a prize for his essay "Can a Good Wife Be a Good Sport?," which is published in *Smart Set* magazine.
1928	Williams's short story "The Vengeance of Nitocris" is published in *Weird Tales*. He tours Europe with his grandfather.
1929	Williams enrolls at the University of Missouri at Columbia.
1932	Williams withdraws from the university and begins working at the International Shoe Company; he writes stories and plays at night.
1935	Williams experiences a physical and emotional breakdown and then recuperates at his grandparents' home in Memphis. His one-act play *Cairo! Shanghai! Bombay!* is performed by the Memphis Garden Players, an amateur theater group.
1936	Williams enters Washington University, St. Louis. His one-act play *27 Wagons Full of Cotton* is published in *Manuscript*.
1937	Williams's first full-length plays, *Fugitive Kind* and *Candles to the Sun*, are produced by the amateur group the Mummers in St. Louis. Williams transfers to the University of Iowa, where several of his short plays are produced. His sister is institutionalized for schizophrenia.

1938	Williams graduates from the University of Iowa with a bachelor of arts degree.
1939	Williams lives briefly in several different places, including the French Quarter in New Orleans. He sends four one-act plays to a contest organized by the Group Theatre in New York and travels to Mexico, then California, then New York. He meets Audrey Wood, who becomes his agent. He publishes the short story "The Field of Blue Children" in *Story* under the name Tennessee Williams. He is awarded a Rockefeller Foundation grant of one thousand dollars.
1940	Williams enrolls in The New School in New York for a playwriting seminar. He travels to Provincetown, Massachusetts, where he has his first major love affair. His play *Battle of Angels* opens in Boston.
1941-1942	Williams lives in various locations, including Key West, New Orleans, and Georgia.
1943	Williams's sister, Rose, undergoes a prefrontal lobotomy. Williams signs a six-month contract to be a scriptwriter for Metro-Goldwyn-Mayer (MGM) in Hollywood. *You Touched Me!* opens in Cleveland.
1944	Williams's grandmother dies. Williams is awarded one thousand dollars by the National Institute of Arts and Letters. *The Glass Menagerie* opens in Chicago.
1945	*The Glass Menagerie* opens on Broadway and wins the New York Drama Critics' Circle Award. Williams starts writing *A Streetcar Named Desire*, and *27 Wagons Full of Cotton, and Other One-Act Plays* is published.
1946	Williams begins a relationship with Pancho Rodriguez y Gonzalez. He meets the writer Carson McCullers.
1947	*Summer and Smoke* opens in Dallas, Texas. *A Streetcar Named Desire* opens in New York and goes on to win the New York Drama Critics' Circle Award, the Donaldson Award, and the Pulitzer Prize for drama.

1948	A collection of Williams's short fiction, *One Arm, and Other Stories*, is published, as is *American Blues: Five Short Plays*. *Summer and Smoke* opens in New York. Williams begins what will be a fourteen-year relationship with Frank Merlo.
1950	Williams's novel *The Roman Spring of Mrs. Stone* is published. The film version of *The Glass Menagerie* is released. *The Rose Tattoo* opens in Chicago.
1951	*The Rose Tattoo* opens in New York and wins a Tony Award for best play. The film version of *A Streetcar Named Desire* is released and wins the New York Film Critics Circle Award.
1952	An Off-Broadway production of *Summer and Smoke* opens in New York. Williams is elected to the National Institute of Arts and Letters.
1953	*Camino Real* opens in New York.
1954	*Hard Candy: A Book of Stories* is published.
1955	Williams's grandfather dies. *Cat on a Hot Tin Roof* opens in New York; it runs for 694 performances and wins the Pulitzer Prize and the New York Drama Critics' Circle Award. The film version of *The Rose Tattoo* is released.
1956	*Baby Doll,* a film for which Williams wrote the screenplay, opens in New York. His collection of poems *In the Winter of Cities* is published.
1957	*Orpheus Descending* opens in New York. Williams's father dies. Williams starts psychoanalysis with Dr. Lawrence Kubie.
1958	*Garden District* (a double bill of the two one-act plays *Suddenly Last Summer* and *Something Unspoken*) opens Off-Broadway. The film version of *Cat on a Hot Tin Roof* is released.
1959	*Sweet Bird of Youth* opens in New York. Williams travels to Cuba, where he meets Ernest Hemingway and Fidel Castro. The film version of *Suddenly Last Summer* is released.

1960	*Period of Adjustment* opens in New York. The film *The Fugitive Kind* (based on *Orpheus Descending*) is released.
1961	*The Night of the Iguana* opens in New York, and Williams wins his fourth New York Drama Critics' Circle Award.
1962	The film version of *Sweet Bird of Youth* is released.
1963	*The Milk Train Doesn't Stop Here Anymore* opens in New York. Frank Merlo dies of cancer.
1964	The film version of *The Night of the Iguana* is released.
1966	*Slapstick Tragedy* opens in New York.
1967	*The Knightly Quest: A Novella and Four Short Stories* is published.
1968	*Kingdom of Earth* (also known as *The Seven Descents of Myrtle*) opens in New York. *Boom!*, the film version of *The Milk Train Doesn't Stop Here Anymore*, is released.
1969	Williams receives the National Institute of Arts and Letters Gold Medal. *In the Bar of a Tokyo Hotel* opens Off-Broadway in New York. Williams spends three months in Barnes Hospital, St. Louis, for drug withdrawal.
1970	*Dragon Country* is published.
1971	*Out Cry*, a revised version of *The Two-Character Play*, opens in Chicago. Williams replaces Audrey Wood, his literary agent for thirty-two years, with Bill Barnes.
1972	*Small Craft Warnings* opens Off-Broadway.
1973	*Out Cry* (a third revision of *The Two-Character Play*) premieres in New York. Williams is awarded the first Centennial Medal of the Cathedral of St. John the Divine. He gives what later becomes known as his famous *Playboy* magazine interview.
1974	*Eight Mortal Ladies Possessed: A Book of Stories* is published.

1975	Williams receives the National Arts Club's Medal of Honor for Literature. *The Red Devil Battery Sign* opens in Boston. Williams's *Memoirs* and his novel *Moise and the World of Reason* are published.
1977	*Vieux Carré* opens in New York.
1978	*Creve Coeur* opens in New York. *Where I Live: Selected Essays* is published.
1979	*A Lovely Sunday for Creve Coeur,* a revised version of *Creve Coeur,* opens in New York. Williams is honored at the Kennedy Center by President Carter.
1980	Williams's mother dies. He is appointed Distinguished Writer in Residence at the University of British Columbia, Vancouver. *Clothes for a Summer Hotel* opens in New York.
1981	*A House Not Meant to Stand* opens in Chicago. *Something Cloudy, Something Clear* opens in New York. Williams and playwright Harold Pinter are both presented the Common Wealth Award of Distinguished Service for the dramatic arts.
1982	Williams receives an honorary degree from Harvard University.
1983	On February 24, Williams dies at the Hotel Elysée in New York City.

Works by Tennessee Williams_____

Plays and Librettos (date shown is that of first production)
Cairo! Shanghai! Bombay!, 1935 (with Bernice Dorothy Shapiro)
Headlines, 1936
The Magic Tower, 1936
Candles to the Sun, 1937
Fugitive Kind, 1937
Spring Song, 1938
Spring Storm, 1938
Battle of Angels, 1940
The Long Goodbye, 1940
You Touched Me!, 1943 (with Donald Windham)
The Glass Menagerie, 1944
27 Wagons Full of Cotton, and Other One-Act Plays, 1945
Moony's Kid Don't Cry, 1946
This Property Is Condemned, 1946
The Last of My Solid Gold Watches, 1947
Portrait of a Madonna, 1947
Stairs to the Roof, 1947
A Streetcar Named Desire, 1947
Summer and Smoke, 1947
American Blues: Five Short Plays, 1948
The Rose Tattoo, 1950
Camino Real, 1953
Cat on a Hot Tin Roof, 1955
Lord Byron's Love Letter, 1955 (libretto)
The Case of the Crushed Petunias, 1957
Orpheus Descending, 1957 (revision of *Battle of Angels*)
Something Unspoken, 1958
Suddenly Last Summer, 1958
Talk to Me Like the Rain and Let Me Listen, 1958
I Rise in Flame, Cried the Phoenix, 1959
Period of Adjustment, 1959
Sweet Bird of Youth, 1959
The Night of the Iguana, 1961
The Milk Train Doesn't Stop Here Anymore, 1963
Eccentricities of a Nightingale, 1964 (revision of *Summer and Smoke*)
Slapstick Tragedy: "The Mutilated" and "The Gnädiges Fräulein," 1966
The Two-Character Play, 1967

The Seven Descents of Myrtle, 1968 (also performed as *Kingdom of Earth*, 1975)
Dragon Country, 1969
In the Bar of a Tokyo Hotel, 1969
Confessional, 1971
I Can't Imagine Tomorrow, 1971
Out Cry, 1971 (revision of *The Two-Character Play*)
The Theatre of Tennessee Williams, 1971-1981 (7 vols.)
Small Craft Warnings, 1972 (revision of *Confessional*)
The Red Devil Battery Sign, 1975
This Is (An Entertainment), 1976
Vieux Carré, 1977
Creve Coeur, 1978 (also performed as *A Lovely Sunday for Creve Coeur*, 1979)
Tiger Tail, 1978
Clothes for a Summer Hotel, 1980
Some Problems for the Moose Lodge, 1980 (also performed as *A House Not Meant to Stand*, 1981)
Will Mr. Merriwether Return from Memphis?, 1980
Something Cloudy, Something Clear, 1981
Not About Nightingales, 1998 (written 1939)

Screenplays
The Glass Menagerie, 1950 (with Peter Berneis)
A Streetcar Named Desire, 1951 (with Oscar Saul)
The Rose Tattoo, 1955 (with Hal Kanter)
Baby Doll, 1956
Suddenly Last Summer, 1959 (with Gore Vidal)
The Fugitive Kind, 1960 (with Meade Roberts)
Stopped Rocking, and Other Screenplays, 1984

Fiction
One Arm, and Other Stories, 1948
The Roman Spring of Mrs. Stone (novel), 1950
Hard Candy: A Book of Stories, 1954
Three Players of a Summer Game, and Other Stories, 1960
The Knightly Quest: A Novella and Four Short Stories, 1966
Eight Mortal Ladies Possessed: A Book of Stories, 1974
Moise and the World of Reason (novel), 1975
It Happened the Day the Sun Rose, and Other Stories, 1982
Collected Stories, 1985

Poetry

In the Winter of Cities, 1956
Androgyne, Mon Amour, 1967
The Collected Poems of Tennessee Williams, 2002

Nonfiction

Memoirs, 1975
Letters to Donald Windham, 1940-1965, 1977
Where I Live: Selected Essays, 1978
Five O'Clock Angel: Letters of Tennessee Williams to Maria St. Just, 1948-1982, 1990
The Selected Letters of Tennessee Williams, 2000, 2004 (2 vols.; Albert J. Devlin and Nancy M. Tischler, editors)
Notebooks, 2006 (Margaret Bradham Thornton, editor)

Bibliography

Bloom, Harold, ed. *Tennessee Williams*. New York: Chelsea House, 1987.

Boxill, Roger. *Tennessee Williams*. 1987. London: Macmillan, 1996.

Bray, Robert. "The Burden of the Past in the Plays of Tennessee Williams." *The Many Forms of Drama*. Ed. Karelisa V. Hartigan. Lanham, MD: University Press of America, 1985.

Clum, John M. "From *Summer and Smoke* to *Eccentricities of a Nightingale*: The Evolution of the Queer Alma." *Modern Drama* 39.1 (1996): 31-50.

Crandell, George W. *Tennessee Williams: A Descriptive Bibliography*. Pittsburgh: University of Pittsburgh Press, 1995.

_____, ed. *The Critical Response to Tennessee Williams*. Westport, CT: Greenwood Press, 1996.

Falk, Signi. *Tennessee Williams*. 2d ed. Boston: Twayne, 1978.

Fleche, Anne. *Mimetic Disillusion: Eugene O'Neill, Tennessee Williams, and U.S. Dramatic Realism*. Tuscaloosa: University of Alabama Press, 1997.

Griffin, Alice. *Understanding Tennessee Williams*. Columbia: University of South Carolina Press, 1995.

Gross, Robert F. "Consuming Hart: Sublimity and Gay Poetics in *Suddenly Last Summer*." *Theatre Journal* 47.2 (1995): 229-52.

_____, ed. *Tennessee Williams: A Casebook*. New York: Routledge, 2002.

Hale, Allean. "*Not About Nightingales*: Tennessee Williams as Social Activist." *Modern Drama* 48.3 (1995): 346-62.

Hayman, Ronald. *Tennessee Williams: Everyone Else Is an Audience*. New Haven, CT: Yale University Press, 1993.

Hirsch, Foster. *A Portrait of the Artist: The Plays of Tennessee Williams*. Port Washington, NY: Kennikat Press, 1979.

Holditch, Kenneth, and Richard Freeman Leavitt. *Tennessee Williams and the South*. Jackson: University Press of Mississippi, 2002.

Jackson, Esther Merle. *The Broken World of Tennessee Williams*. Madison: University of Wisconsin Press, 1965.

Johnston, Monica Carolyn. *Tennessee Williams and American Realism*. Berkeley: University of California Press, 1987.

Kolin, Philip C. *Williams: "A Streetcar Named Desire."* New York: Cambridge University Press, 2000.

_____, ed. *Confronting Tennessee Williams's "A Streetcar Named Desire": Essays in Critical Pluralism*. Westport, CT: Greenwood Press, 1993.

_____. *Tennessee Williams: A Guide to Research and Performance*. Westport, CT: Greenwood Press, 1998.

_____. *The Tennessee Williams Encyclopedia*. Westport, CT: Greenwood Press, 2004.

_____. *The Undiscovered Country: The Later Plays of Tennessee Williams*. New York: Peter Lang, 2002.

Leavitt, Richard F. *The World of Tennessee Williams*. London: W. H. Allen, 1978.

Leff, Leonard J. "And Transfer to Cemetery: The *Streetcars Named Desire*." *Film Quarterly* 55.3 (2002): 29-37.

Leverich, Lyle. *Tom: The Unknown Tennessee Williams*. New York: Crown, 1995.

Londré, Felicia Hardison. *Tennessee Williams*. New York: Frederick Ungar, 1979.

McCann, John S. *The Critical Reputation of Tennessee Williams: A Reference Guide*. Boston: G. K. Hall, 1983.

Martin, Robert A., ed. *Critical Essays on Tennessee Williams*. New York: G. K. Hall, 1997.

Murphy, Brenda. *Tennessee Williams and Elia Kazan: A Collaboration in the Theatre*. New York: Cambridge University Press, 1992.

Nelson, Benjamin. "Tennessee Williams and Cold War Politics." *Staging a Cultural Paradigm: The Political and the Personal in American Drama*. Ed. Barbara Ozieblo and Miriam López Rodriguez. New York: Peter Lang, 2002.

_____. *Tennessee Williams: The Man and His Work*. New York: Obolensky, 1961.

Pagan, Nicholas O. *Rethinking Literary Biography: A Postmodern Approach to Tennessee Williams*. Madison, NJ: Fairleigh Dickinson University Press, 1993.

Paller, Michael. *Gentlemen Callers: Tennessee Williams, Homosexuality, and Mid-Twentieth-Century Broadway Drama*. New York: Palgrave Macmillan, 2005.

Parker, R. B. "The Circle Closed: A Psychological Reading of *The Glass Menagerie*." *Modern Drama* 28.4 (1985): 517-34.

Prossner, William. *The Late Plays of Tennessee Williams*. Lanham, MD: Scarecrow Press, 2008.

Roudané, Matthew C., ed. *The Cambridge Companion to Tennessee Williams*. New York: Cambridge University Press, 1997.

Rouse, Sarah A. *Tennessee Williams*. Jackson: Mississippi Library Commission, 1976.

Saddik, Annette J. "The (Un)Represented Fragmentation of the Body in Tennessee Williams's 'Desire and the Black Masseur' and *Suddenly Last Summer*." *Modern Drama* 41.3 (Fall 1998): 347-54.

Schlueter, June. *Dramatic Closure: Reading the End*. Madison, NJ: Fairleigh Dickinson University Press, 1995.

Smith-Howard, Alycia, and Greta Heintzelman. *Critical Companion to Tennessee Williams*. New York: Facts On File, 2005.

Spoto, Donald. *The Kindness of Strangers: The Life of Tennessee Williams*. Reprint. New York: DaCapo Press, 1998.

Stanton, Stephen S., ed. *Tennessee Williams: A Collection of Critical Essays*. Englewood Cliffs, NJ: Prentice-Hall, 1977.

Tharpe, Jac, ed. *Tennessee Williams: A Tribute*. Jackson: University Press of Mississippi, 1977.

Thompson, Judith J. *Tennessee Williams' Plays: Memory, Myth, and Symbol*. New York: Peter Lang, 1989.

Tischler, Nancy M. *Student Companion to Tennessee Williams*. Westport, CT: Greenwood Press, 2000.

Vannatta, Dennis P. *Tennessee Williams: A Study of the Short Fiction*. Boston: Twayne, 1988.

Voss, Ralph F., ed. *Magical Muse: Millennial Essays on Tennessee Williams*. Tuscaloosa: University of Alabama Press, 2002.

Williams, Dakin, and Shepherd Mead. *Tennessee Williams: An Intimate Biography*. New York: Arbor House, 1983.

Williams, Tennessee. *The Collected Poems of Tennessee Williams*. Ed. Nicholas Moschovakis and David Roessel. New York: New Directions, 2002.

_____. *Collected Stories*. New York: New Directions, 1985.

_____. *Conversations with Tennessee Williams*. Ed. Albert J. Devlin. Jackson: University Press of Mississippi, 1986.

_____. *Five O'Clock Angel: Letters of Tennessee Williams to Maria St. Just, 1948-1982*. New York: Alfred A. Knopf, 1990.

_____. *Letters to Donald Windham, 1940-1965*. Ed. Donald Windham. New York: Holt, Rinehart and Winston, 1977.

_____. *Notebooks*. Ed. Margaret Bradham Thornton. New Haven, CT: Yale University Press, 2006.

_____. *The Selected Letters of Tennessee Williams*. 2 vols. Ed. Albert J. Devlin and Nancy M. Tischler. New York: New Directions, 2000-2004.

_____. *Tennessee Williams: Plays*. 2 vols. Ed. Mel Gussow and Kenneth Holditch. New York: Library of America, 2000.

_____. *Where I Live: Selected Essays*. Ed. Christine R. Day and Bob Woods. New York: New Directions, 1978.

Woodhouse, Reed. *Unlimited Embrace: A Canon of Gay Fiction, 1945-1995*. Amherst: University of Massachusetts Press, 1998.

CRITICAL
INSIGHTS

Brenda Murphy is Board of Trustees Distinguished Professor of English at the University of Connecticut. Her scholarly work, spanning more than thirty years, reflects her interest in placing American drama, theater, and performance in the broader context of American literature and culture. She has written numerous articles about American playwrights and other writers, but her most significant work is in the ten books she has authored on the American theater. Among Murphy's books are *The Provincetown Players and the Culture of Modernity* (2005), *O'Neill: Long Day's Journey into Night* (2001), *Congressional Theatre: Dramatizing McCarthyism on Stage, Film, and Television* (1999), *Miller: Death of a Salesman* (1995), *Tennessee Williams and Elia Kazan: A Collaboration in the Theatre* (1992), *American Realism and American Drama, 1880-1940* (1987), and, as editor, *Twentieth Century American Drama: Critical Concepts in Literary and Cultural Studies* (2006) and the *Cambridge Companion to American Women Playwrights* (1999). She has been recognized as breaking new ground through her synthesis of the study of the play as literary text and the play as performance in her books on Tennessee Williams, Arthur Miller, and Eugene O'Neill. *Congressional Theatre*, her study of the theater's response to the House Committee on Un-American Activities in the 1950s, was honored by the American Society for Theatre Research in 1999 for outstanding research in theater history and cognate studies.

Professor Murphy has been active in a number of international professional organizations throughout her career. She serves on the editorial boards of several journals and book series and on the boards of several societies that promote the study of American playwrights, and she has served as President of the American Theatre and Drama Society and The Eugene O'Neill Society. Her research has been supported by grants from the National Endowment for the Humanities, the American Council for Learned Societies, the National Humanities Center, and other sources.

About *The Paris Review*

The Paris Review is America's preeminent literary quarterly, dedicated to discovering and publishing the best new voices in fiction, nonfiction, and poetry. The magazine was founded in Paris in 1953 by the young American writers Peter Matthiessen and Doc Humes, and edited there and in New York for its first fifty years by George Plimpton. Over the decades, the *Review* has introduced readers to the earliest writings of Jack Kerouac, Philip Roth, T. C. Boyle, V. S. Naipaul, Ha Jin, Ann Patchett, Jay McInerney, Mona Simpson, and Edward P. Jones, and published numerous now classic works, including Roth's *Goodbye, Columbus*, Donald Barthelme's *Alice*, Jim Carroll's

Basketball Diaries, and selections from Samuel Beckett's *Molloy* (his first publication in English). The first chapter of Jeffrey Eugenides's *The Virgin Suicides* appeared in the *Review*'s pages, as well as stories by Rick Moody, David Foster Wallace, Denis Johnson, Jim Crace, Lorrie Moore, and Jeanette Winterson.

The *Paris Review*'s renowned Writers at Work series of interviews, whose early installments include legendary conversations with E. M. Forster, William Faulkner, and Ernest Hemingway, is one of the landmarks of world literature. The interviews received a George Polk Award and were nominated for a Pulitzer Prize. Among the more than three hundred interviewees are Robert Frost, Marianne Moore, W. H. Auden, Elizabeth Bishop, Susan Sontag, and Toni Morrison. Recent issues feature conversations with Salman Rushdie, Joan Didion, Norman Mailer, Kazuo Ishiguro, Marilynne Robinson, Umberto Eco, Annie Proulx, and Gay Talese. In November 2009, Picador published the final volume of a four-volume series of anthologies of *Paris Review* interviews. *The New York Times* called the Writers at Work series "the most remarkable and extensive interviewing project we possess."

The Paris Review is edited by Philip Gourevitch, who was named to the post in 2005, following the death of George Plimpton two years earlier. A new editorial team has published fiction by André Aciman, Colum McCann, Damon Galgut, Mohsin Hamid, Uzodinma Iweala, Gish Jen, Stephen King, James Lasdun, Padgett Powell, Richard Price, and Sam Shepard. Poetry editors Charles Simic, Meghan O'Rourke, and Dan Chiasson have selected works by John Ashbery, Kay Ryan, Billy Collins, Tomaž Šalamun, Mary Jo Bang, Sharon Olds, Charles Wright, and Mary Karr. Writing published in the magazine has been anthologized in *Best American Short Stories* (2006, 2007, and 2008), *Best American Poetry, Best Creative Non-Fiction*, the Pushcart Prize anthology, and *O. Henry Prize Stories*.

The magazine presents two annual awards. The Hadada Award for lifelong contribution to literature has recently been given to Joan Didion, Norman Mailer, Peter Matthiessen, and, in 2009, John Ashbery. The Plimpton Prize for Fiction, awarded to a debut or emerging writer brought to national attention in the pages of *The Paris Review*, was presented in 2007 to Benjamin Percy, to Jesse Ball in 2008, and to Alistair Morgan in 2009.

The Paris Review was a finalist for the 2008 and 2009 National Magazine Awards in fiction, and it won the 2007 National Magazine Award in photojournalism. The *Los Angeles Times* recently called *The Paris Review* "an American treasure with true international reach."

Since 1999 *The Paris Review* has been published by The Paris Review Foundation, Inc., a not-for-profit 501(c)(3) organization.

The Paris Review is available in digital form to libraries worldwide in selected academic databases exclusively from EBSCO Publishing. Libraries can contact EBSCO at 1-800-653-2726 for details. For more information on *The Paris Review* or to subscribe, please visit: www.theparisreview.org.

Contributors

Brenda Murphy is Board of Trustees Distinguished Professor of English at the University of Connecticut. She has written a number of articles about Tennessee Williams as well as the book *Tennessee Williams and Elia Kazan: A Collaboration in the Theatre* (1992). Her books on American drama include *The Provincetown Players and the Culture of Modernity* (2005), *O'Neill: Long Day's Journey into Night* (2001), *Miller: Death of a Salesman* (1995), the casebook *Understanding Death of a Salesman* (1999), *Congressional Theatre: Dramatizing McCarthyism on Stage, Film, and Television* (1999), *American Realism and American Drama, 1880-1940* (1987), and, as editor, the *Cambridge Companion to American Women Playwrights* (1999) and several collections of essays.

Susan Rusinko was Professor and Head of the English Department at Bloomsbury University in Pennsylvania.

Sasha Weiss is a writer living in Brooklyn. She is on the editorial staff of the *New York Review of Books*.

Jennifer Banach is a writer and independent scholar from Connecticut. She has served as the Contributing Editor of *Bloom's Guides: Heart of Darkness* (2009) and *Bloom's Guides: The Glass Menagerie* (2007) and is the author of *Bloom's How to Write About Tennessee Williams* (2009) and *Understanding Norman Mailer* (2010). She has also composed teaching guides to international literature for Random House's Academic Resources division and has contributed to numerous literary reference books for academic publishers such as Facts On File, Inc., and Oxford University Press on topics ranging from Romanticism to contemporary literature. Her work has appeared in academic and popular venues alike; her fiction and nonfiction have appeared under the *Esquire* banner. She is a member of the Association of Literary Scholars and Critics.

Susan C. W. Abbotson is Professor of Modern and Contemporary Drama at Rhode Island College and author of *Critical Companion to Arthur Miller* (2007), *Masterpieces of Twentieth-Century American Drama* (2005), *Thematic Guide to Modern Drama* (2003), and *Student Companion to Arthur Miller* (2000) as well as *Understanding Death of a Salesman* (1999) (coauthored with Brenda Murphy). She has also published articles on Tom Stoppard, August Wilson, and Sam Shepard. She is currently the Performance Editor for the *Arthur Miller Journal*.

Henry I. Schvey has been Professor of Drama and Comparative Literature at Washington University in St. Louis since 1987. Prior to that time, he taught at Leiden University in the Netherlands, where he also founded the Leiden English Speaking Theatre. A playwright and director in addition to a scholar, he has written extensively on American and modern European drama. His forthcoming works include a memoir, *The Poison Tree*, and a new play about Tennessee Williams, *Tennessee Kissed Me!*

Kenneth Elliott has directed many Off-Broadway plays and musicals, including the original productions of Charles Busch's *Vampire Lesbians of Sodom* and *Psycho Beach Party*. He has also directed at regional theaters across the United States and in London's West End. His work has appeared in such publications as *Theatre Journal* and *Text and Presentation*. He is currently Assistant Professor of Theater at Rutgers University, Camden.

Nancy M. Tischler is Professor Emerita of English and the Humanities at the Pennsylvania State University. Her books include *Thematic Guide to Biblical Literature* (2007), *All Things in the Bible* (2006), *Men and Women of the Bible* (2002), and *Student Companion to Tennessee Williams* (2000). She has served as editor at large for *Christianity Today* and as a member of the editorial board for the *Tennessee Williams Annual Review*.

Thomas P. Adler is Professor of English and Associate Dean of Liberal Arts at Purdue University, where he has been teaching for more than thirty-five years. He has published many articles, contributions, and works, among them *American Drama, 1940-1960: A Critical History* (1994) and a monograph titled *"A Streetcar Named Desire": The Moth and the Lantern* (1990).

Jacqueline O'Connor is Associate Professor of English at Boise State University. Her work has appeared in *The Southern Quarterly, Theatre Journal, Studies in American Humor*, and *The Tennessee Williams Annual Review*. She is the author of *Dramatizing Dementia: Madness in the Plays of Tennessee Williams* (1997).

Lori Leathers Single was a doctoral student in English at Georgia State University when her essay "Flying the Jolly Roger" was first published in the *Tennessee Williams Annual Review* in 1999. Her essay "Reading Against the Grain: The Reception for Kenneth Branagh's *Frankenstein*," which appeared in the journal *Studies in American Culture*, won the Ray Browne award in 1998.

George Hovis is Assistant Professor of English at the State University of New York College at Oneonta. He is the author of *Vale of Humility: Plain Folk in Contemporary North Carolina Fiction*, and his short stories and literary essays have appeared in *Mississippi Quarterly* and *Carolina Quarterly*, among other journals.

Philip C. Kolin has published several books on American playwrights and specifically Tennessee Williams, his most recent being *The Influence of Tennessee Williams: Essays on Fifteen American Playwrights*, released in 2008. He is also the editor of *The Tennessee Williams Encyclopedia* (2004), which remains the most up-to-date work on Williams. He was the first to receive the honor of being Charles W. Moorman Alumni Distinguished Professor in the Humanities, and in 2006 he won the Innovation Award in Applied Research. He is currently teaching as Professor of English at the University of Southern Mississippi.

John M. Clum is Professor of English and Professor of the Practice of Theatre at Duke University (North Carolina). He is the author of several books, including *He's All Man: Learning Masculinity, Gayness, and Love from American Movies* (2002), *Some-*

thing for the Boys: Musical Theater and Gay Culture (2000), and Still Acting Gay: Male Homosexuality in Modern Drama (2000). He has also written original essays on Tennessee Williams, Sam Shepard, and Larry Kramer, and has had seven of his plays published. He has edited two major anthologies of contemporary drama and directed more than sixty theatrical productions, and he has won two Duke's Distinguished Teaching Awards.

John S. Bak is *Maître de Conférences* (Associate Professor) of English at the Université Nancy 2—C.T.U. He is the author of *Homo Americanus: Ernest Hemingway, Tennessee Williams, and Queer Masculinities* (2010) and *Post/modern Dracula: From Victorian Themes to Postmodern Praxis* (2007) and has published work in *American Drama, Tennessee Williams Literary Journal*, and *Journal of American Drama and Theatre*. He is the editor of the Williams collection *New Selected Essays: Where I Live* (2009).

Rod Phillips is Assistant Professor of Writing at Michigan State University's James Madison College. He is the author of *Forest Beatniks and Urban Thoreaus* (2000) and many articles that have been published in professional journals. He also writes poetry and was the winner of the 1997 Midwest Poetry Prize.

James Schlatter currently teaches drama and theater courses at the University of Pennsylvania, directs programs and productions, and authors conference papers and articles on famous American plays and playwrights. In addition to serving as Director of the Theatre Arts Program from 2004 to 2007, he received the 2007-2008 award for Distinguished Teaching by Affiliated Faculty.

Nicholas O. Pagan serves as Professor in the Department of English Literature and Humanities at Eastern Mediterranean University in Turkey. His published books include *Ethics and Subjectivity in Literary and Cultural Studies* (2002), *Literary Studies: Beginning and Ends* (2001), and *Rethinking Literary Biography: A Postmodern Approach to Tennessee Williams* (1993). In addition to giving more than eighteen presentations, he has created many original essays, book chapters, and reviews as well as a one-act play.

George W. Crandell is Professor and Acting Associate Dean of the Graduate School at Auburn University in Alabama. His research interests include American realism and naturalism, the short story, and Tennessee Williams. He is editor of *The Critical Response to Tennessee Williams* (1996) and author of *Tennessee Williams: A Descriptive Bibliography* (1995) and *Ogden Nash: A Descriptive Bibliography* (1990).

D. Dean Shackelford contributed monographs and articles to several literary journals and reference works and gave more than fifteen presentations at literature conferences across the nation. He taught as Associate Professor of English at Southeast Missouri State University until his death in 2003.

Acknowledgments_____

"Tennessee Williams" by Susan Rusinko. From *Magill's Survey of American Literature*. Rev. ed. Copyright © 2007 by Salem Press, Inc. Reprinted with permission of Salem Press.

"The *Paris Review* Perspective" by Sasha Weiss. Copyright © 2011 by Sasha Weiss. Special appreciation goes to Christopher Cox, Nathaniel Rich, and David Wallace-Wells, editors at *The Paris Review*.

"A Gallery of Witches" by Nancy M. Tischler. From *Tennessee Williams: A Tribute* (1977), pp. 494-509. Copyright © 1977 by University Press of Mississippi. Reprinted with permission of University Press of Mississippi.

"Culture, Power, and the (En)gendering of Community: Tennessee Williams and Politics" by Thomas P. Adler. From *Mississippi Quarterly* 48, no. 4 (1995): 649-665. Copyright © 1995 by Mississippi State University Press. Reprinted with permission of Mississippi State University Press.

"Deranged Artists: Creativity and Madness" by Jacqueline O'Connor. From *Dramatizing Dementia: Madness in the Plays of Tennessee Williams* (1997), pp. 81-89. Copyright © 1997 by the Board of Regents of the University of Wisconsin System. Reprinted with permission of The University of Wisconsin Press.

"Flying the Jolly Roger: Images of Escape and Selfhood in Tennessee Williams's *The Glass Menagerie*" by Lori Leathers Single. From *Tennessee Williams Annual Review* 2 (1999): 69-85. Copyright © 1999 by the Historic New Orleans Collection. Reprinted with permission of the Historic New Orleans Collection.

"'Fifty Percent Illusion': The Mask of the Southern Belle in Tennessee Williams's *A Streetcar Named Desire*, *The Glass Menagerie*, and 'Portrait of a Madonna'" by George Hovis. From the *Tennessee Williams Literary Journal* 5, no. 1 (2003): 11-22. Copyright © 2003 by the *Tennessee Williams Literary Journal*. Reprinted with permission of the *Tennessee Williams Literary Journal*.

"Williams in Ebony: Black and Multi-racial Productions of *A Streetcar Named Desire*" by Philip C. Kolin. From *Black American Literature Forum* 25, no. 1 (1991): 147-181. Copyright © 1991 by *African American Review*. Reprinted with permission of *African American Review*.

"'Something Cloudy, Something Clear': Homophobic Discourse in Tennessee Williams" by John M. Clum. From *South Atlantic Quarterly* 88, no. 1 (Winter 1989): 161-179. Copyright © 1989 by Duke University Press. All rights reserved. Used by permission of the publisher.

"'sneakin' and spyin'" from Broadway to the Beltway: Cold War Masculinity, Brick, and Homosexual Existentialism" by John S. Bak. From *Theatre Journal* 56, no. 2 (May 2004): 225-249. Copyright © 2004 by The Johns Hopkins University Press. Reprinted with permission of The Johns Hopkins University Press.

_____

"'Collecting Evidence': The Natural World in Tennessee Williams' *The Night of the Iguana*" by Rod Phillips. From *The Southern Literary Journal* 32, no. 2 (Spring 2000): 59-69. Copyright © 2000 by University of North Carolina Press. Reprinted with permission of University of North Carolina Press.

"*Red Devil Battery Sign*: An Approach to a Mytho-Political Theatre" by James Schlatter. From *Tennessee Williams Annual Review* 1 (1998): 93-101. Copyright © 1998 by the Historic New Orleans Collection. Reprinted with permission of the Historic New Orleans Collection.

"Tennessee Williams' *Out Cry* in *The Two-Character Play*" by Nicholas O. Pagan. From *Notes on Mississippi Writers* 24, no. 2 (1992): 67-79. Copyright © 1992 by University of Southern Mississippi. Reprinted with permission of the English Department at the University of Southern Mississippi.

"Peeping Tom: Voyeurism, Taboo, and Truth in the World of Tennessee Williams's Short Fiction" by George W. Crandell. From *The Southern Quarterly* 38, no. 1 (Fall 1999): 28-35. Copyright © 1999 by University of Southern Mississippi. Reprinted with permission of *The Southern Quarterly*.

"'The Transmutation of Experience': The Aesthetics and Themes of Tennessee Williams's Nonfiction" by D. Dean Shackelford. From *The Southern Quarterly* 38, no. 1 (Fall 1999): 104-116. Copyright © 1999 by University of Southern Mississippi. Reprinted with permission of *The Southern Quarterly*.

Southern belles, 21, 89, 102, 106, 114, 171, 176, 182, 193, 209, 216
Spoto, Donald, 124, 235, 243, 282
Spring Storm (Williams), 5, 24
Stairs to the Roof (Williams), 42
Stairways, 42, 100, 311
Stanley Kowalski. *See* Kowalski, Stanley
Stein, Roger B., 154
Stella Kowalski. *See* Kowalski, Stella
Stewart, Carolyn Hill, 195
Stewart, Edna, 196
Stewart, Nick, 196
Streetcar Named Desire, A (Williams), 52, 99, 106, 121, 133, 176, 180, 185, 234, 286, 315; ballet version, 205; black and multiracial productions, 190, 195, 201, 207, 212, 218; critical reception, 3, 26; expressionism in, 63, 72; film version, 76; music, 43, 191; working titles, 78
Strindberg, August, 60, 75, 105, 113
Styan, J. L., 154
Suddenly Last Summer (Williams), 5, 27, 47, 53, 108, 233, 285, 306
Suicide, 128, 181, 234, 269, 274, 293
Sullivan, Ed, 124
Summer and Smoke (Williams), 26, 50, 99, 106
Sweet Bird of Youth (Williams), 27, 46, 103, 126, 190, 302
Sylvester, Harold, 210

T. Lawrence Shannon. *See* Shannon, T. Lawrence
Tandy, Jessica, 193, 217
Tasker, Barbara, 210
Taylor, Jackie, 215
Taylor, Lyle, 317
Three Guineas (Woolf), 118
"Three Players of a Summer Game" (Williams), 64, 110, 248, 276, 330

Tiger Tail (Williams), 29
"Timeless World of a Play, The" (Williams), 341
Tischler, Nancy M., 38, 49, 55, 154
Tom Wingfield. *See* Wingfield, Tom
Treadwell, Sophie, 61
Two-Character Play, The (Williams), 6, 28, 55, 146, 309, 316

Valgemae, Mardi, 78
Venable, Sebastian (*Suddenly Last Summer*), 5, 48, 109, 233
"Vengeance of Nitocris, The" (Williams), 23, 322
Vieux Carré (Williams), 29, 240, 243
Von Blon, Katherine, 198
Vowles, Richard, 256
Voyeurism, 284, 321, 327, 331

Water imagery, 74, 111, 163, 323, 326
Weales, Gerald, 38
Where I Live (Williams), 60, 334
Wilder, Thornton, 61
Wilhelmi, Nancy O., 180
Willett, John, 148
Williams, Cornelius Coffin (father), 8
Williams, Edwina Dakin (mother), 8, 16, 104
Williams, Rose (sister), 6, 8, 16, 21, 55, 131, 136, 149, 309
Williams, Tennessee; awards and honors, 9, 22, 28; on *Camino Real*, 60, 341; on *Cat on a Hot Tin Roof*, 86, 278, 343; childhood, 8; education, 9, 335; on *The Glass Menagerie*, 149, 156; on homosexuality, 227, 278, 343; on *The Knightly Quest*, 39; on *Out Cry*, 317; on politics, 119, 273, 338; revision of works, 30, 44; and sister Rose, 6, 55; on theater, 29, 121; on

themes of his work, 38, 44, 54; on
writing, 32, 61, 337, 344, 349;
writing career, 9, 22, 58, 335
Wills, Garry, 134
Winchell, Walter, 124
Wingfield, Amanda (*The Glass
Menagerie*), 21, 89, 99, 104, 138,
157, 161, 165, 176, 286, 297
Wingfield, Laura (*The Glass
Menagerie*), 63, 136, 143, 157, 162,
179
Wingfield, Tom (*The Glass Menagerie*),
38, 45, 122, 136, 144, 157, 166, 315

Witt, Mary Ann Frese, 150
Woman Downtown (*The Red Devil
Battery Sign*), 54, 130, 133, 300, 306
Wood, Audrey, 10, 25, 38, 81, 140, 190,
197, 300
Woolf, Virginia, 118
Wright, Richard, 177
"Writer's Quest for Parnassus, A"
(Williams), 337

"Yellow Bird, The" (Williams), 325

Zuccaro, Marianne, 215